A TRANSATLANTIC COMMUNITY OF LAW

As a medium for communication between the EU and the USA, law has the ability to provide unique insights into the state of contemporary transatlantic relations. *A Transatlantic Community of Law* offers legal perspectives on the emerging institutional characteristics of transatlantic relations and contemporary rule-making in both trade and security. Making use of rule of law analysis, which has hitherto not been conducted in transatlantic relations scholarship, it draws together EU law, governance and rule-making scholarship and offers new ways of thinking about the use of law and contemporary transatlantic institutions.

ELAINE FAHEY is a senior postdoctoral researcher at the Amsterdam Centre for European Law and Governance (ACELG), University of Amsterdam, the Netherlands.

DEIRDRE CURTIN is Professor of European Law and founding director of the Amsterdam Centre for European Law and Governance (ACELG), University of Amsterdam, the Netherlands.

A TRANSATLANTIC COMMUNITY OF LAW

Legal Perspectives on the Relationship between the EU and US Legal Orders

Edited By

ELAINE FAHEY AND DEIRDRE CURTIN

CAMBRIDGE
UNIVERSITY PRESS

CAMBRIDGE
UNIVERSITY PRESS

University Printing House, Cambridge CB2 8BS, United Kingdom

Cambridge University Press is part of the University of Cambridge.

It furthers the University's mission by disseminating knowledge in the pursuit of education, learning and research at the highest international levels of excellence.

www.cambridge.org
Information on this title: www.cambridge.org/9781107060517

First published 2014

Printed in the United Kingdom by Clays, St Ives plc

A catalogue record for this publication is available from the British Library

Library of Congress Cataloguing in Publication data
A transatlantic community of law : legal perspectives on the relationship between the EU and US legal orders / edited by Elaine Fahey, Deirdre Curtin.
pages cm
Includes bibliographical references and index.
ISBN 978-1-107-06051-7 (hardback)
1. Law–United States. 2. Law–European Union countries. I. Fahey, Elaine, editor of compilation. II. Curtin, Deirdre, editor of compilation.
K561.T729 2014
349.24–dc23
2014011194

ISBN 978-1-107-06051-7 Hardback

CONTENTS

List of contributors *page* vii
Foreword by Koen Lenaerts ix
Prologue by Mark Pollack xii
Acknowledgements xviii

1 Introduction and overview 1
ELAINE FAHEY AND DEIRDRE CURTIN

PART I **Institutionalisation and transatlantic relations from a legal perspective** 7

2 The US Supreme Court and the Court of Justice of the European Union: emergence, nature and impact of transatlantic judicial communication 9
ELAINE MAK

3 The European Parliament and EU–US relations: revamping institutional cooperation? 35
DAVOR JANČIĆ

4 Transatlantic adjudication techniques: the Commerce Clause and the EU's internal market harmonisation clause in perspective 69
JOSÉ A. GUTIERREZ-FONS

5 A 'bottom-up' perspective on EU–US relations: the role of sub-national authorities 102
JOSEPHINE A. W. VAN ZEBEN

PART II **Rule-making between the EU and USA** 129

6 Towards a transatlantic community of law? The use of law between the EU and US legal orders: questions of legal form and characterisation 131
ELAINE FAHEY

7 Transatlantic regulatory cooperation in trade: objectives, challenges and instruments for economic governance 158

TAMARA TAKÁCS

8 Addressing transatlantic regulatory barriers: can the USA and the EU create an effective equivalency instrument? 186

JAMES MATHIS

9 A postnational marketplace: negotiating the Transatlantic Trade and Investment Partnership (TTIP) 210

MARIJA BARTL AND ELAINE FAHEY

PART III **Security and transatlantic relations** 235

10 Transatlantic relations and security: reflections from a politician, practitioner and litigator 237

SOPHIE IN'T VELD

11 Obstacles to transatlantic security cooperation in the 'War on Terror' 246

WYN REES

12 Transatlantic counterterrorism cooperation agreements on the transfer of personal data: a test for democratic accountability in the EU 256

JUAN SANTOS VARA

13 Transatlantic counterterrorism cooperation and European values: the elusive quest for coherence 289

VALSAMIS MITSILEGAS

Index 316

CONTRIBUTORS

MARIJA BARTL, Senior Postdoctoral Researcher, Amsterdam Centre for the Study of European Contract Law (CSECL), University of Amsterdam

DEIRDRE CURTIN, Professor of European Law, Amsterdam Centre for European Law and Governance (ACELG), University of Amsterdam

ELAINE FAHEY, Senior Postdoctoral Researcher, Amsterdam Centre for European Law and Governance (ACELG), University of Amsterdam

JOSÉ A. GUTIERREZ-FONS, Legal Secretary at the Cabinet of the Vice-President of the European Court of Justice

SOPHIE IN' T VELD, Member of the European Parliament

DAVOR JANČIĆ, British Academy Newton Fellow, Department of Law, London School of Economics and Political Science

JUDGE KOEN LENAERTS, Vice-President of the European Court of Justice

ELAINE MAK, Professor of Empirical Study of Public Law, in particular of Rule-of-Law Institutions, Erasmus School of Law, Erasmus University Rotterdam

JAMES MATHIS, Associate Professor, Amsterdam Centre for International Law (ACIL), University of Amsterdam

VALSAMIS MITSILEGAS, Professor of European Criminal Law and Head of the Department of Law, Queen Mary University of London

MARK POLLACK, Professor of Political Science and Law and Jean Monnet Chair at Temple University, Philadelphia

WYN REES, Professor of International Security, School of Politics and International Relations, University of Nottingham

JUAN SANTOS VARA, Associate Professor of Public International and European Law, University of Salamanca, Spain

TAMARA TAKÁCS, Senior Researcher and Academic Programme Coordinator of CLEER (Centre for the Law of EU External Relations) at the T.M.C. Asser Institute

JOSEPHINE A. W. VAN ZEBEN, Visiting Postdoctoral Researcher at the Vincent and Elinor Ostrom Workshop in Political Theory and Policy Analysis, Indiana University, Bloomington; Harvard LL.M. (2014)

FOREWORD

Transatlantic cooperation and the European integration project share a common origin and, possibly, a common destiny. That is because European integration cannot be correctly understood without exploring its transatlantic dimension. Indeed, the United States has always been a supporter of a strong union among European states. In the aftermath of the Second World War, the US government was convinced that economic integration would prevent European states from entering into a war. A 'new Europe' composed of liberal democracies was thus seen as a remedy against Europe's fragmentation and the expansion of the soviet threat. At the same time, a strong Europe would facilitate cooperation on both sides of the Atlantic, by improving trade relations and by defending common interests in the wider world. As President Kennedy famously said, the USA does not regard 'a strong and united Europe as a rival but as a partner'. Thus, he encouraged further integration so that, in the near future, a transatlantic partnership of equals could be established.[1] At the end of the Cold War transatlantic relations also played a key role in erasing the East–West frontier that had divided the Continent into two camps for half a century. Both the USA and the EU firmly believed that supporting the accession of Eastern European states to the Union would bring stability to the region and prosperity to the peoples of Europe. Continuing the process of creating an ever-closer union was, once more, seen as the best way of pursuing those objectives.

Logically, transatlantic relations have evolved ever since EU–US diplomatic relations began in 1953, when the first US observers were sent to the European Coal and Steel Community. The reason is twofold. First, transatlantic relations have had to cope with the new challenges brought about by changing times. Currently, new emerging economies, international terrorism, failed states, and the proliferation of weapons of mass destruction may influence the agenda of transatlantic relations. In this regard,

[1] Speech by John F. Kennedy (Philadelphia, 4 July 1962).

the 1995 New Transatlantic Agenda (the NTA), which is still today the most significant transatlantic policy document, sets out a comprehensive framework within which EU–US relations may develop. The rationale underpinning the NTA was to ensure continuity in transatlantic relations, while allowing room for change. In particular, that framework seeks to establish regular meetings at presidential, ministerial, and staff levels, to coordinate efforts when facing similar challenges, to establish parliamentary links, to foster economic relations on both sides of the Atlantic, and to build ties between EU and US representatives of civil society. Second, the evolution of transatlantic relations also mirrors the constitutional changes brought about by the reforming treaties. Notably, through the establishment of a common foreign and security policy, European states may, in principle, speak with one voice to their US counterparts. In the same way, as the EU is now empowered to adopt measures in the area of freedom, security, and justice, the USA may turn to the EU when joining efforts in the fight against international terrorism. It follows that transatlantic relations raise interesting and complex issues that this book, edited by Prof. Curtin and Dr Fahey, seeks to explore. It is divided into three parts. Part I focuses on the institutional aspects of transatlantic relations. It examines, for example, the role that the European Parliament has played in EU–US relations, as well as the contribution of sub-national entities to the development of those relations. This section also shows that the political branches of government do not enjoy a monopoly over EU–US relations, but that courts may also engage in a transatlantic dialogue. Thus, European courts have referred to the case law of the US Supreme Court when deciding similar cases. In the same way, the latter court has, albeit rather exceptionally, drawn inspiration from the case law of the former courts, notably the European Court of Human Rights, when deciding important constitutional questions such as the right to privacy.[2] Also, it is worth noting that the US Supreme Court and the European Court of Justice (the ECJ) hold meetings on a biannual basis where the exchange of ideas and experiences is common practice. This section also contains a very interesting comparative study on the way in which the US Supreme Court and the ECJ have interpreted the constitutional provision that respectively empowers Congress and the EU legislator to pass legislation regulating interstate trade. Part II looks at the substance of EU–US relations, that is, at the way in which transatlantic rule-making is carried out. 'Law', broadly understood, is explored not only as a means of building

[2] *Lawrence* v. *Texas*, 539 U.S. 558 (2003).

bridges between the two sides of the Atlantic, but also as source of conflict between the EU and the USA. Of course, in a bilateral context, whether law is a friend or a foe of transatlantic integration would often depend on the degree of convergence (proximity) between those two legal orders. Regulatory convergence may not only result from an international agreement, but may also take place informally: legal solutions adopted on one side of the Atlantic may serve as a source of inspiration on the other side. Thus, the cross-fertilization of legal orders and the mutual borrowing of ideas are part and parcel of transatlantic rule-making. Conversely, where divergences arise, compromise and negotiations must take place. That is why, in my view, the conclusion of the Transatlantic Trade and Investment Partnership will open a new era of EU–US relations. In addition, transatlantic regulatory conflicts are an important element of EU–US relations, which this section examines. Notably, it looks at trade disputes that have arisen in a multilateral context such as the World Trade Organization. Finally, Part III focuses on transatlantic security. This aspect of EU–US relations has, needless to say, been of paramount importance in the aftermath of 9/11. Accordingly, this book looks at the way in which the EU has sought to strike the right balance between cooperating with the USA in the fight against international terrorism and complying with its own internal values, in particular with respect to fundamental rights. In this regard, bilateral agreements, such as the EU–US Agreements on the Transfer of Passenger Name Records and the EU–US Agreements on the Terrorist Finance Tracking Programme, are thus examined in light of that balance. At the same time, this section also explores whether transatlantic security may be difficult to reconcile with transparency and democratic accountability. In a clear and entertaining style, this book contains a thorough and critical overview of the legal aspects of transatlantic relations. It thus provides the reader with all the necessary elements to fully understand the nature, objectives, and dynamics underpinning the interactions between those two legal orders. On all accounts, it is a great pleasure to welcome this book. Students, scholars, and practitioners on both sides of the Atlantic will all benefit greatly from it.

Prof Dr Koen Lenaerts
Vice-President of the Court of Justice of the European Union

PROLOGUE

MARK POLLACK

Aaron Sorkin's television series *The West Wing* presents a fictionalized United States' White House, one in which political actors are driven by noble motives, and reasoned deliberation and persuasion at least occasionally prevail over bare-knuckled political bargaining. While reading this book on transatlantic relations, I was reminded of a particular episode in which the president's Democratic speechwriter Sam Seaborn, memorably and handsomely played by Rob Lowe, engages in a long and vigorous debate with a Republican colleague over a memo about an arcane piece of legislation. After hours of back-and-forth argument and mutual exasperation, Seaborn finally hands his policy memo to the president's chief of staff. The chief of staff looks it over, and notes that Seaborn has abandoned his original argument in favor of the one advocated by the Republican. "You got turned around?" he asks. "Yeah," Seaborn replies, simply.[1]

In teaching international relations theory, I screen that scene to students as an example of Habermas' ideal of deliberative democracy and the power of the better argument, while at the same time suggesting that genuine deliberation is a hothouse flower, which thrives only under specific, and rare, conditions. Even in academia, where in principle minds are most open and the search for truth is most imperative, it is rare for scholars to be truly "turned around" on any important issue, particularly one about which they have opined in print.

Yet this book has largely "turned me around" about the legal quality of the contemporary relationship between the United States and the European Union. In the introduction to this book, Elaine Fahey and Deidre Curtin note that the received wisdom about the transatlantic relationship is that it is "institutionally light." In 2005, in my Annual Lecture in the *Journal of Common Market Studies*, I contributed to this received wisdom, suggesting that the 1995 New Transatlantic Agenda (NTA) represented an experiment in "deep integration in the absence of deep institutionalization." The

[1] A. Sorkin, *The West Wing*, Season 2, Episode 6, "The Lame Duck Congress".

transatlantic economic relationship of the 1990s and 2000s, I argued, had abandoned the earlier, "shallow integration" focusing on tariffs and quotas, in favor of a deeper effort to remove, or at least manage, the growing raft of "behind-the-border," non-tariff barriers to trade and investment. However, unlike in Europe, the USA and the EU "would attempt such deep integration in the absence of binding institutions, regulatory harmonization, or across-the-board mutual recognition, relying primarily on formal or informal co-operation between regulators."[2] The NTA's periodic Washington–Brussels summits, the informal dialogues among regulators, and the well-intentioned encouragement of transatlantic civil-society dialogue were all promising, but they constituted at best informal, soft-law efforts to address issues that, within each polity, had required hard-law commitments to achieve. The significance of the NTA, and its at-best-partial record of success, I concluded, lay in its "combination of substantive ambition and legal-institutional modesty."[3]

At a superficial level, this statement about formal transatlantic institutions remains as accurate today as it was a decade ago. To be sure, the EU and the USA have now committed to negotiating a formal Transatlantic Trade and Investment Partnership (TTIP), which if successful will lay down a raft of hard-law commitments across a wide range of issue areas from tariffs to investment to sanitary and phytosanitary issues such as the regulation of genetically modified foods, and potentially a legal forum for the settlement of future disputes.[4] Such an agreement would indeed represent "deep institutionalization," and a major step forward in transatlantic relations; yet at the time of writing this prologue it remains an aspiration, with many difficult and politicized differences to be bridged before a legalized, hard-law partnership can be achieved. In the meantime, the transatlantic partnership lacks all or most of the overt legal trappings of the EU, including a constitutional architecture allowing for the making of legally binding rules and for the interpretation and enforcement of those rules by an independent Court of Justice.

What has "turned me around" on the role of law in the transatlantic partnership, therefore, is not the as-yet-unrealized promise of a future TTIP, but rather the demonstration, by the editors and the other contributors to this book, that, beneath the surface of its "institutionally light"

[2] M. Pollack, "The New Transatlantic Agenda at Ten: Reflections in an Experiment in International Governance" (2005) 43 *Journal of Common Market Studies* 899, 902.

[3] *Ibid.*, 916.

[4] Bartl and Fahey, this volume.

formal architecture, the transatlantic partnership is becoming increasingly "legalized," which is to say that US–EU relations are increasingly channeled into legal processes, and that these legal processes have arguably "hardened," at least selectively, over time.

In a landmark study published over a decade ago, a group of legal and political science scholars defined "legalization" as a process that occurs along three dimensions: obligation, or the legal bindingness of international agreements; precision, or the clarity and detail of legal rules; and delegation to third parties of the authority to interpret and apply those rules.[5] Along these three dimensions, they argued, legalization could vary from "soft" to "hard," and each of these presented advantages and disadvantages to their members. Soft law, characterized by low levels of legal commitment, precision, and delegation, has the advantages of being relatively easy to negotiate and flexible in the face of uncertain and changing circumstances, yet it may fail to generate clear rules and credible commitments necessary to sustain cooperation among states. Hard law, by contrast, has multiple advantages, including the establishment of clear rules, monitoring, dispute settlement, and credible commitments, but at the potential cost of high *ex ante* negotiation costs and greater *ex post* rigidity.[6] The point of this analysis is not to suggest that either soft or hard law is always preferable, but that states might rationally choose hard or soft law as a function of their cooperation challenges.

In the years immediately following the end of the Cold War, the USA and the EU generally opted for a soft-law approach to their bilateral relations, preferring low-cost negotiations *ex ante* and flexibility *ex post* to the more rigid and legally binding commitments of hard law. Over time, as the authors in this volume demonstrate, the two sides have demonstrated a greater willingness to move towards hard-law agreements and processes, although not uniformly or across-the-board. The founders of the legalization approach, writing about international relations more broadly, made the argument that international politics was becoming increasingly "legalized," but they also argued that the "move to law is hardly uniform," varying across issue-areas, forums, and over time.[7] The chapters in the volume trace a similar theme-and-variation in the transatlantic

[5] J. Goldstein, M. Kahler, R. O. Keohane, and A.-M. Slaughter, "Introduction: Legalization and World Politics" (2000) 54 *International Organization* 385.

[6] K. W. Abbott and D. Snidal, "Hard and Soft Law in International Governance" (2000) 53 *International Organization* 421.

[7] *Ibid.*, 386.

relationship, which is shown to be moving towards greater legalization over time, but in complex and different ways across different issue-areas.

Fahey and Curtin organize their exploration of transatlantic legalization in terms of a tripartite distinction among (1) the institutional features of the relationship, (2) trade and economic rule-making, and (3) security issues. Taken together, these chapters provide a panoramic view of transatlantic cooperation across the full array of issue-areas, including both the traditional "bread-and-butter" issues of trade, competition policy, and regulatory cooperation, as well as the internal and external security issues that have come to occupy an equally important place in the relationship since the attacks of September 11, 2001.

Looking across all of these issue-areas, we can see a common set of developments at three distinct levels of analysis: (1) the bilateral, Washington–Brussels level, where security agreements have become increasingly hardened, with economics promising to follow; (2) the multilateral level in which the USA and EU channel at least some of their disputes and their cooperative efforts through broader legal venues; and (3) the transnational, transgovernmental, or "interstitial" level, at which US and EU actors have increasingly begun to participate in the processes of making, interpreting, and enforcing each other's *domestic* laws.

The bilateral US–EU relationship was institutionalized primarily during the early post-Cold War years of the 1990s, focusing on substantive, mostly economic cooperation between Washington and Brussels, channeled primarily through mostly voluntaristic soft-law processes of dialogue and regulatory cooperation, which scored low across all three criteria of obligation, precision, and delegation, and later by soft-law nonbinding agreements and memoranda of understanding. As predicted by the legalization framework, the advantages of these soft-law agreements included their relative ease of negotiation and their flexibility, while their disadvantages included the lack of credible commitments or effective implementation.[8]

In the months and years immediately following September 11, US and EU officials pursued a similar approach to internal security and antiterrorism initiatives, pursued through close regulatory cooperation rather than through legally binding, hard-law treaties. With the passage of time, however, the nature of these agreements became a concern particularly to EU officials, who worried about the protection of the rights of European

[8] M. A. Pollack and G. Shaffer (eds.), *Transatlantic Governance in the Global Economy* (Lanham, MD: Rowman & Littlefield Press, 2001).

citizens in the absence of clear, legally binding, and enforceable standards. The result was the conclusion of legally binding agreements regarding the sharing of airline passenger information (the so-called Passenger Name Record, or PNR agreements) as well as banking information (the SWIFT agreements), through which European authorities (represented in this volume by Sophie in't Veld) insisted upon the protection of the data privacy rights of European citizens. However, these moves also illustrated the *costs* of legalization, which have increased the difficulty and complexity of intergovernmental cooperation, as witnessed by the European Court of Justice's decision to annul an initial PNR agreement, and the subsequent vote by the European Parliament to reject the US–EU SWIFT agreement, later renegotiated by the two sides.[9] While the security realm has arguably led the process of bilateral legalization, the proposed TTIP raises similar issues, and the initial difficulties that have cropped up in the early stages of negotiations already hint at the costs and challenges of a move to hard law in the economic sector.[10]

In short, the bilateral Washington–Brussels relationship is changing, and hardening, across various issue-areas, in ways that promise to yield both greater legal certainty and enforceability, but also higher *ex ante* negotiation costs and *ex post* litigation. As the authors in this book demonstrate, however, the legal quality of the relationship does not reside solely in the nature of Washington–Brussels agreements. To some extent, US and EU cooperation and conflict are nested in a wider set of multilateral legal agreements and forums. This is most obvious in the trade realm, where transatlantic disputes have often been channeled through the World Trade Organization dispute settlement process.[11] More recently, in the environmental realm, the bitter dispute over the extension of the EU's emissions trading scheme to US and other airlines has been referred to the International Civil Aviation Organization, which has been tasked with negotiating multilateral rules on such issues.[12]

[9] See the chapters by in't Veld and Rees in this volume.

[10] Bartl and Fahey, this volume.

[11] E. U. Petersmann and M. A. Pollack (eds.), *Transatlantic Economic Disputes: The EU, the US, and the WTO* (New York: Oxford University Press, November 2003). It is striking, however, that in recent years the USA and the EU have entered a more "pacific" period of transatlantic trade relations, with a dramatic decrease in US–EU disputes before the WTO; see A. Young, "Pacific Transatlantic Trade Relations," paper presented at the Temple University workshop on "Transatlantic Relations under Obama," May 18 2012.

[12] See e.g. Reuters, "U.N. Aviation Body Agrees on Emissions Deal," October 4 2013, www.reuters.com/article/2013/10/04/us-aviation-climate-idUSBRE99302A20131004, accessed on October 27 2013.

Perhaps the most striking, yet least noticed, aspect of the legalization of transatlantic relations, however, is the increasing interpenetration of the US and EU legal systems, such that European authorities and citizens become active players in the making, interpretation, and implementation of US law, and vice versa. This transnational or transgovernmental interpenetration of the US and EU legal orders arguably represents a quiet revolution in the relations between them, and nowhere has it been captured more vividly and more thoroughly than by the contributors in this volume. The USA and the EU are not, of course, merging into a single legal space, nor do the authors claim that they are doing so, but the two legal orders are increasingly proximate and porous, and they show us vivid images of US officials and citizens weighing in as participants before EU lawmakers and courts, and vice versa.[13] This is arguably a new type of legalization, and the systematic exploration of it constitutes the greatest contribution of this volume, and one that is likely to turn around many readers regarding the legal nature of transatlantic relations in the twenty-first century.

[13] See e.g. Fahey, this volume, and Mak, this volume.

ACKNOWLEDGEMENTS

The editors are grateful to Judge Lenaerts for agreeing to write the foreword, as someone who has been involved for some time in comparative transatlantic understandings of legal method, doctrine, and theory. The editors wish to thank the following people who agreed to read drafts of chapters and give comments, including Samo Bardutzky, Christina Eckes, Martijn Hesselink, Machiko Kantetake, Chantal Mak, Thomas Vandamme, Maria Weimer, Jonathan Zeitlin, and the external referees. Also a special thanks go to the staff of Sophie in't Veld, in particular Thomas Van Der Valk, for their help. Thanks to Tamara Takács for participating in the volume during and after giving birth! Anna Nagelbach provided tremendous assistance to us.

Thanks to Elizabeth Spicer for all of her help, advice, and encouragement, and also to Rebecca Roberts. Thanks also to Finola O'Sullivan, Elizabeth Spicer once again, and the Board of Cambridge University Press for their willingness to develop this volume.

1

Introduction and overview

ELAINE FAHEY AND DEIRDRE CURTIN

I

The volume title *A Transatlantic Community of Law* is designed to provoke an immediate question – what *is* a Transatlantic Community and *why* formulate it as a Community of Law? Can law be said to have a normative relationship with the integration of an 'Atlantic Area'? Is there a strict territorial understanding of legal interactions? Is law objectively understood to be part of the formulation of transatlantic relations, in a dynamic sense or simply 'functionally'? Is there a strict territorial understanding of legal interactions? Can law only play a meaningful role in distinct forums and areas? Can we readily deploy the term 'Community',[1] given the overarching tendency in global geopolitics as well as global legal theories of integration to explore only unions, associations, partnerships and regionalised territorial spaces, and little else below – or between – this?

The reason that the title of this volume might provoke such questions is most likely because there is much disagreement in scholarship about the main scientific characteristics of the relationships between the European Union (EU) and the United States (USA). However, non-legal scholarship on transatlantic relations is generally unambiguous about the extent to which bilateral transatlantic relations are 'institutionally light'. This specific thesis is one that this volume aims to explore, and to some extent contradict and question. It is suggested in a number of chapters that there are various formal and informal institutional dimensions to transatlantic relations that suggest that they are at least quasi-institutional – or beyond this, veer towards 'institutionalisation', both normatively and descriptively. More generally, institutionalisation gives greater depth to the idea of the 'Community' behind this book. Transatlantic 'rule-making' – that is the development of rules by the EU and USA together – is

[1] In our formulation as such, we draw inspiration loosely from B. Anderson, *Imagined Communities* (London: Verso Books, 1991) and R. Dworkin, *Law's Empire* (Cambridge, MA: Harvard University Press, 1986).

conventionally conceived as having a modest legal component. Yet as a case study, its rule-making and its substantive legal dynamics have both inspired and informed leading theorisations of governance, for example networks,[2] global governance and the democratisation of international trade.[3] As the subject and object it remains a stimulating and worthwhile enterprise to be subjected to provocative and questioning reflections.

This volume resulted from a workshop held early in 2013 in Amsterdam, and the publication includes some additional contributions expanding the momentum of the initial event. The volume is formally structured around the legal dimensions of the interactions between the EU and the US legal orders in three domains: (1) legal perspectives on emerging institutional characteristics of transatlantic relations; (2) legal perspectives on contemporary transatlantic rule-making, largely but not exclusively centred upon trade; and (3) legal perspectives on contemporary rule-making in security. It has attempted to draw together novel perspectives of EU law, governance and rule-making scholarship on the use of law and institutions involved in contemporary transatlantic relations. The volume includes many legal scholars working in the field of European law generally, in various sub-fields, with a specific focus in their work on forms of interactions, including processes, instruments and communications, as well as formal and informal relationships – in varying degrees – between the EU and US legal orders. The editors have not sought to 'reinvent the wheel' and provide a comprehensive policy-based field-by-field assessment of transatlantic relations. While not detracting from the merits of such scholarship, such a publication would inevitably have a rather modest legal component or would perhaps focus substantively upon the uses of international law. This volume has not sought to provide a complete historical overview of transatlantic relations and instead has sought to depict the nature of specific dynamic contemporary interactions through law between the two legal orders. As a result, leading new socio-legal and empirical research on interactions between the EU and US legal orders is captured. Insights from judicial and political practices are also covered

[2] A. M. Slaughter, *A New World Order* (Princeton University Press, 2005).

[3] E. U. Petersmann, 'Dispute Prevention and Dispute Settlement in the EU–US Transatlantic Partnership' in M. Pollack and G. Shaffer (eds.), *Transatlantic Governance in the Global Economy* (Lanham, MD: Rowman & Littlefield, 2001); K. Nicolaidis and G. Shaffer, 'Transnational Mutual Recognition Regimes: Governance Without Global Government' (2005) 68 *Law & Contemporary Problems* 263; R. Howse, 'Transatlantic Regulatory Cooperation and the Problem of Democracy' in G. Bermann, P. Lindseth and M. Herdegen (eds.), *Transatlantic Regulatory Cooperation* (Oxford University Press, 2000).

in the volume. Given the approach of the volume to its subject, the editors nonetheless felt that experts from the more traditional but non-legal transatlantic relations scholarship also had to be involved. Their contributions add a rich variety and depth to its focus overall. They identify new and established themes and perspectives and sometimes (but not always) endeavour to understand legal perspectives on the same developments.

II

Part I highlights questions of institutionalisation. Many of the contributions in the first part can be considered, we think, as innovative and novel scholarship on the themes they traverse. They might be said to be not necessarily well represented in existing literature and provide a striking range of empirical, socio-legal and theoretical ideas, drawing at times from the *Trias Politica* (or not), on the institutionalised nature of transatlantic relations or phenomena of relevance to considering its institutionalisation. Parts II and III attempt to capture two specific policy-based themes: transatlantic trade and transatlantic security. Does security place an Atlantic-sized 'schism' between the two legal orders or does it simply show its impossibility in a particular period? Does trade offer the prospect of a deeper institutionalisation of transatlantic relations? What should that entail? They undoubtedly play a very significant role in any analysis of contemporary transatlantic relations. But their selection and the cross-cutting concentration of the scholarship in these sections are deliberate. There is an effort here to include governance, legitimacy and accountability issues in the policy-themed sections, so as to provide and provoke a richer depiction of these types of interactions between the two legal orders.

In the middle of the writing and later the editing process of this volume, the EU–US surveillance affair involving the National Security Agenda, PRISM and Snowden was unfolding – and continues to do so – and the European Parliament began an inquiry on many aspects of transatlantic security covered in this volume, issuing a notable resolution on 24 October 2013. Also, negotiations on a Transatlantic Trade and Investment Partnership were suspended seemingly temporarily due to the US government shutdown, in respect of the funding of the US federal government. These events provided a vivid context in which to complete a project such as this – a context of high politics, much hope and despair, and a constant exposure of the boundaries of the use of law and governance. The editors hope that this volume demonstrates the virtues of the European law perspectives. This voice shows how law plays a tangible presence in contemporary transatlantic relations, which may provide useful insights to other disciplines concerning the state of transatlantic relations.

III

In Part I, Jančić depicts parliamentary diplomacy as an international politico-legal phenomenon and explores how the European Parliament performs less visible diplomatic activities in EU–US relations that contribute to an informal constitutionalisation of its powers. He explores the Transatlantic Legislators Dialogue (TLD) as part of an examination of parliamentary politico-legal diplomacy as a research agenda.

Gutierrez-Fons conducts a comparative study of transatlantic adjudication techniques, examining how the Supreme Court of the United States of America has applied the principle of enumerated powers in the context of the Commerce Clause, and how the ECJ has interpreted the EU's internal market harmonisation clause, Article 114 of the Treaty on the Functioning of the European Union (TFEU). He considers high-profile contemporary case law, including the Roberts Court adjudication of the so-called ObamaCare Law[4] and the analysis of the European Court of Justice on the EU Roaming Regulation.[5] He argues that they should both take into account the values of federalism and proposes that the right balance between different levels of governance can only be struck if courts go beyond the borderline federalism paradigm.

Based upon socio-legal research and also targeting the 'in-between' theme of this volume more carefully, Mak probes the actual nature of transatlantic judicial communication and its impact on judicial decision-making in the US Supreme Court and the ECJ qua judicial dialogue. She explores how no systematic approach exists regarding judicial communication between the US Supreme Court and the ECJ, and yet develops a most insightful account of the significance of these communications for our understanding of 'in-between' interactions between legal orders.

Van Zeben considers the current and potential role of sub-central entities in external affairs in the form of sub-national authorities (SNAs) as a future research agenda, thereby looking beyond conventional

[4] *NFIB* v. *Sebelius*, 132 S.Ct. 2566 (2012).

[5] OJ [2007] L 171/32. Regulation No. 544/2009, OJ [2009] L 167/12, amending Regulation No. 717/2007 so as to extend the imposition of maximum wholesale and retail prices to SMS and data roaming: Case C-58/08 *Vodafone and Others* [2010] ECR I-4999.

typologies of actors in transatlantic relations.[6] She explores the lack of any formal infrastructures for entities under EU law and policy in EU–US relations. She considers the risks of engaging sub-federal and sub-state entities in international relations and the possible impact of local civil society upon EU–US relations.

In Part II, Fahey, building upon the themes of Part I on institutionalisation, considers a series of recent interactions and rule-making exercises between the EU and US legal orders, suggesting institutionalisation or proximity between the legal orders of the EU and USA. She considers the concept of an Atlantic Community of Law, and also tentatively some questions of its legitimacy, and argues that the examination of the 'non-bilateral' 'non-multilateral' context of transatlantic relations via law may reveal more about conceptions of institutionalisation in transatlantic relations and the conduct of two major global governance actors.

Mathis considers the type of technical instrument required to address non-tariff barriers to trade in goods and services in a transatlantic regional trade agreement, one that could be both intensive and effective. He examines in detail the agreements both the EU and USA have recently negotiated with Korea and focuses upon the idea that the transatlantic standard could be adopted more universally.[7]

Takács offers a review and assessment of transatlantic regulatory initiatives and policy instruments in trade as well as their defined objectives since the New Transatlantic Agenda in 1995 and their structural frameworks. She suggests that regulatory cooperation must build upon achievements such as the understanding on Regulatory Principles and Best Practices as well as the Regulatory Cooperation Best Cooperative Practices. She suggests that the limitations of sector-specific regulatory convergence show that legal harmonisation is less realistic. However, she notes, with the advent of the Transatlantic Trade and Investment Partnership (TTIP), there is real political commitment to address the issues. Bartl and Fahey consider who has set the normative agenda in the negotiation of the TTIP, reflecting upon both the actors and processes thereof. They focus on the questions of participation in crafting the TTIP, the role of knowledge in justifying this enterprise, the objectives of the TTIP and the institutions that should underpin it. Bartl and Fahey argue

[6] Pollack and Shaffer (eds.), *Transatlantic Governance.*

[7] Free Trade Agreement between the European Union and its Member States, of the one part, and the Republic of Korea, of the other part (EU Korea agreement) OJ L 127/6, 14 May 2011.

that parliamentary legitimation, including approval and information rights, is inadequate in light of the institutionalisation process that forms the goal of the TTIP.

The themes of Part III are opened by contributions from both political practice and politics from in't Veld and Rees, followed thereafter by academic contributions from the perspective of European Law. In't Veld provides highly critical but also candid and insightful reflections derived from her many capacities in contemporary transatlantic relations, primarily as a Member of the European Parliament. In particular, she gives a vivid account of the wide-ranging sets of litigation taken to procure EU transparency and openness in transatlantic relations, initially before the General Court. Her individual instigation of high-profile litigation made her an obvious invitee to participate in the workshop on which this publication was based, a contribution that is now readable as a critical account, which we think is of much public interest. It is one that may eventually be of much historical value.

Rees explores from the perspective of politics and international security the reordering of the transatlantic relationship in counterterrorism. He focuses upon four specific foreign policy tensions between the EU and USA, and provides a clear yet forceful overview of the failings and also more generally the nature of the phenomenon of Homeland Security that has emerged in recent times.

Penultimately, Santos Vara charts the use by the European Parliament of its powers in transatlantic personal data agreements and considers how it has used its accountability powers in recent times. He considers how the National Security Agency (NSA) surveillance affair will compare as an exercise in accountability. He argues that the European Parliament is now significantly part of the process, but concerns itself more with negotiations and concluding agreements rather than attempting to radically alter the substantive core content. Finally, Mitsilegas considers the idea of coherence in the promotion of EU values globally as a means to move beyond narrow understandings of 'consistency' between EU external and internal action in security. He offers a typology of counterterrorism cooperation agreements and examines the mechanism put forward to ensure coherence, including coherence via oversight, coherence via regular monitoring, coherence through the presumption of adequacy and coherence through reciprocity.

PART I

Institutionalisation and transatlantic relations from a legal perspective

2

The US Supreme Court and the Court of Justice of the European Union

Emergence, nature and impact of transatlantic judicial communication

ELAINE MAK

1 Introduction

Do the judges of the Court of Justice of the European Union (ECJ) and the US Supreme Court communicate with each other and, if so, what does this communication consist of? This question has become pertinent in the globalised legal context, where legal systems and actors within these legal systems are increasingly interconnected.[1] These interconnections have brought an increasing number of cases with international or foreign aspects to the courts on both sides of the Atlantic Ocean. Moreover, systemic changes, such as the development of the legal order of the European Union (EU) and the increase in the number of international legal instruments, have obliged the courts to develop expertise concerning the application of legal sources elaborated outside of their national legal systems. At the same time, meetings in transnational judicial networks and the

The research for this chapter was supported by a postdoctoral VENI grant from the Netherlands Organisation for Scientific Research (NWO). I would like to thank the organisers and participants of the Workshop on Transatlantic Relations, as well as the anonymous reviewers, for their comments on the paper that formed the basis for this chapter. Any mistakes remain my own.

[1] Mark Tushnet has defined globalisation in the legal sphere as the 'convergence among national constitutional systems in their structures and in their protection of fundamental human rights'; M. Tushnet, 'The Inevitable Globalisation of Constitutional Law' in S. Muller and S. Richards (eds.), *Highest Courts and Globalisation* (Hague Academic Press, 2010), p. 130. Patrick Glenn has defined globalisation in the legal sphere in a more general sense as the 'trend toward world domination of specific regimes'; H. P. Glenn, *Legal Traditions of the World: Sustainable Diversity in Law*, 3rd edn (Oxford University Press, 2007), p. 49.

availability of foreign legal sources, for example through internet databases, have made it easier and natural for judges to take an interest in developments outside of their national borders.[2]

Starting from these observations, this chapter explores the relations between the highest courts in the USA and in Europe, and the impact of these relations on judicial decision-making in the US and European legal orders. What kind of contacts exist between the US Supreme Court and the ECJ, and how do these contacts influence judicial decision-making in the US and EU legal orders? This central research question can be divided in several sub-questions: what examples of transatlantic communication can be identified in the relations between the US Supreme Court and the ECJ? What motives do the two courts have for engaging in this communication? Does the communication between the courts constitute a real 'dialogue', involving an aspect of deliberation? To what extent does this communication have an influence on the decision-making of the courts?

Based on a socio-legal research approach, this chapter will probe the actual nature of transatlantic judicial communication and its impact on judicial decision-making in the US Supreme Court and the ECJ. This comparative and empirical study of judicial practices is representative of a relatively new field of research, in which concepts, theories and methods from different disciplines are combined to obtain a better understanding of judicial decision-making in a changing legal, political and societal context.[3] Publicly available information about the practices of courts and individual judges is a first relevant source of information for the analysis in this chapter. In this regard, the publications of judges of the US Supreme Court and the ECJ as well as available academic studies provide insight into the views of individual judges on judicial interpretation and concerning the influence of individual judges on decision-making in

[2] Concerning this development, see inter alia A.-M. Slaughter, 'A Global Community of Courts' (2003) 44 *Harvard International Law Journal* 191; B. Markesinis and J. Fedtke, *Judicial Recourse to Foreign Law* (Abingdon: Routledge-Cavendish, 2006); Muller and Richards, *Highest Courts and Globalisation*; A. Hol and others, 'Special Issue on Highest Courts and Transnational Interaction' (2012) 8(2) *Utrecht Law Review*.

[3] See further inter alia B. Flanagan and S. Ahern, 'Judicial Decision-Making and Transnational Law: A Survey of Common Law Supreme Court Judges' (2011) 60 *International and Comparative Law Quarterly* 1; T. Nowak and others, *National Judges as European Union Judges. Knowledge, Experience and Attitudes of Lower Court Judges in Germany and the Netherlands* (The Hague: Eleven International Publishing, 2012); U. Jaremba, *National Judges as EU Law Judges: The Polish Civil Law System* (Leiden: Brill, 2014).

their courts.[4] However, to answer these research questions also requires the study of information that is not publicly available. Therefore, the analysis in this chapter draws on data collected in the course of a research project regarding the development of the decision-making of the highest national courts in five Western legal systems (the United States, Canada, the United Kingdom, France and the Netherlands) in the globalised legal context.[5] This research was based on interviews with highest court judges, combined with an analysis of their case law and public speeches. The interviews included: two judges of the US Supreme Court; two judges and two retired judges of the Supreme Court of Canada; seven judges of the UK Supreme Court and one retired Law Lord; four judges with experience in one or more of the French highest courts, the Cour de cassation (Court of Cassation), the Conseil d'État (Council of State) and the Conseil constitutionnel (Constitutional Council); thirteen judges and five Advocates-General of the Dutch Hoge Raad (Supreme Court of the Netherlands) as well as two members of the Afdeling bestuursrechtspraak Raad van State (Administrative Jurisdiction Division of the Council of State).[6] The research project for which these interviews were conducted did not include the ECJ. However, information about the involvement of the ECJ in judicial exchanges emerged from the interviews with the national judges in the UK, France and the Netherlands. Additional information on the ECJ was found in academic publications addressing European judicial networks, EU–US relations and the functioning of the European Court more generally.[7]

[4] Concerning the US Supreme Court, see inter alia A. Scalia, *A Matter of Interpretation: Federal Courts and the Law*, ed. A. Gutmann (Princeton University Press, 1997); S. Breyer, *Making Our Democracy Work: A Judge's View* (New York: Alfred A. Knopf, 2010). Concerning the ECJ, see inter alia A. M. Donner, 'Inleiding' (1980) 42 *Rechtsgeleerd Magazijn Themis* 354. The influence of Judge Donner on the outcome of the ECJ case of *Van Gend en Loos* has been discussed by F. Bruinsma, 'Kamervoorzitters en hun jurisprudentie' (2010) 60 *Ars Aequi* 652, and M. Claes, 'Nawoord bij "Kamervoorzitters en hun jurisprudentie"' (2010) 60 *Ars Aequi* 655. Concerning the role of lawyers in the development of the EU legal order more generally, see A. Vauchez and B. De Witte (eds.), *Lawyering Europe: European Law as a Transnational Social Field* (Oxford: Hart Publishing, 2013).

[5] E. Mak, *Judicial Decision-Making in a Globalised World: A Comparative Analysis of the Changing Practices of Western Highest Courts* (Oxford: Hart Publishing, 2013). See Chapters 1 and 3 for an explanation of the research methodology.

[6] As the Supreme Court of Canada falls outside the scope of the current inquiry, the results of the Canadian interviews will not be included in the analysis in this chapter.

[7] I. Solanke, '"Stop the ECJ"? An Empirical Analysis of Activism at the Court' (2011) 17 *European Law Journal* 764; M. Claes and M. de Visser, 'Are You Networked Yet? On Dialogues in European Judicial Networks' (2012) 8(2) *Utrecht Law Review* 100;

The structure of the chapter is as follows. Firstly, the emergence of transatlantic judicial communication is analysed, addressing the institutional setting of this communication and the causes of its emergence (Section 2). Secondly, we will examine the nature of transatlantic judicial communication, including an overview of the exchanges of judges in this context and an analysis of the dialogical character of these exchanges (Section 3). Thirdly, we will analyse the impact of the transatlantic judicial communication on judicial decision-making. This analysis will address the approaches of the US Supreme Court and the ECJ with regard to two main aspects of judicial functioning in the globalised legal context: (1) the use of inspiration from comparative law in judicial decision-making; and (2) the development of a methodology for the use of comparative legal sources in judicial deliberations and reasoning (Section 4). Some concluding remarks will be made concerning the insights that the analysis provides for future transatlantic judicial communication (Section 5).

2 Emergence of transatlantic judicial communication

Before studying the nature and impact of judicial communication in EU–US relations, a clearer view is required, firstly, of the courts that play a role in these relations (2.1). Secondly, we will investigate what reasons underlie the emergence of transatlantic judicial communication (2.2).

2.1 Institutional setting of transatlantic judicial communication

How do the US Supreme Court and the ECJ stand in relation to each other, and what role do the highest national courts in EU Member States play in transatlantic judicial communication? First of all, judicial communication between courts in different jurisdictions seems to be most relevant for the highest courts in legal orders, which have the final authority to decide legal questions in their jurisdictions. More often than first-instance courts and courts of appeal, the highest courts have to deal with difficult cases in which no precedents are available. Also, the highest courts are often better equipped to conduct comparative research or have the means to

E. Fahey, 'On the Use of Law in Transatlantic Relations: Legal Dialogues between the EU and US', *European Law Journal* (forthcoming) and see also in this volume E. Fahey, Chapter 6.

commission external research.[8] When considering the transatlantic legal context, the following possible lines of communication between highest courts can be identified.[9]

As a federal supreme court with limited jurisdiction, the US Supreme Court's position in the US legal order is comparable to some extent to the position of the ECJ as the court with final authority to decide on the interpretation of legal rules in the multi-level legal order of the European Union. Both courts have developed case law concerning the nature and scope of their authority in the multi-level legal system in which they are functioning, addressing their authority vis-à-vis the courts at state level and vis-à-vis international courts and tribunals.[10] However, the dynamics between the US Supreme Court and other courts in the US legal system differ significantly from the dynamics between the ECJ and courts in EU Member States. The US Supreme Court's jurisdiction is limited in the sense that the supreme courts of the states of the USA are the final courts for cases concerning state law and the Supreme Court is the appellate judge only in federal cases.[11] Although the Court's judgments in some cases give rise to controversy, the authority of these judgments is generally accepted by the other courts in the US system as well as by the national society.[12] By contrast, the ECJ's authority remains a topic of debate.[13] The scope of the

[8] Mak, *Judicial Decision-Making in a Globalised World*, in particular Chapters 4 and 5. See also Muller and Richards, *Highest Courts and Globalisation*.

[9] Because of the focus of this chapter on EU–US relations, the European Court of Human Rights (ECtHR) will not be included in the analysis. Concerning the ECtHR and its place in the European legal context, see inter alia K. Dzehtsiarou and others (eds.), *Human Rights Law in Europe: The Influence, Overlaps and Contradictions of the EU and the ECHR* (Abingdon: Routledge, 2014); G. Martinico and O. Pollicino (eds.), *The National Judicial Treatment of the ECHR and EU Laws: A Comparative Constitutional Perspective* (Groningen: Europa Law Publishing, 2010).

[10] Concerning the US Supreme Court, see D. L. Sloss, M. D. Ramsey and W. S. Dodge (eds.), *International Law in the US Supreme Court: Continuity and Change* (Cambridge University Press, 2012). Concerning the ECJ, see M. Claes, *The National Courts' Mandate in the European Constitution* (Oxford: Hart Publishing, 2006); R. A. Wessel and S. Blockmans (eds.), *Between Autonomy and Dependence: The EU Legal Order under the Influence of International Organisations* (The Hague: TMC Asser Press, 2012). From a comparative perspective, see for example R. S. Avi-Yonah, J. Hines and M. Lang, *Comparative Fiscal Federalism: Comparing the European Court of Justice and the US Supreme Court's Tax Jurisprudence* (Alphen aan den Rijn: Kluwer Law International, 2007).

[11] Article 3(2) of the US Constitution.

[12] See Breyer, *Making Our Democracy Work*, p. 1.

[13] Concerning the ECJ's status and role in the European legal order, see inter alia A.-M. Slaughter, A. Stone Sweet and J. H. H. Weiler (eds.), *The European Court and National Courts: Doctrine and Jurisprudence: Legal Change in its Social Context* (Oxford: Hart

Court's jurisdiction is limited and it centres on the handing down of preliminary rulings on the interpretation of EU law at the request of national courts in EU Member States.[14] National courts have sometimes shown resistance with regard to the implementation of the ECJ's case law.[15] This resistance highlights the tension between national sovereignty and the supremacy of supranational law and, in this regard, the perception of the ECJ's case law as based on an activist approach aimed at the promotion of the European integration.[16]

When considering the US Supreme Court's role as the highest court in a national legal system, its position can be considered to bear resemblance to the position of the highest national courts in EU Member States. Highest national courts apply legal rules in individual cases, taking into account the particularities of the case and of the national legal and societal context.[17] In the transatlantic context, lines of communication between highest national courts might exist: (1) directly between the US Supreme Court and highest courts in EU Member States, and (2) indirectly through the intermediary role of the ECJ, participating in exchanges with the US Supreme Court and with the highest courts in EU Member States.

This overview of the highest courts in the transatlantic context suggests that judicial communication might involve the US Supreme Court, the ECJ and supreme courts and constitutional courts in EU Member States. These lines of communication combine horizontal and vertical aspects.[18] The exchange between highest national courts, holding the same status in

Publishing, 1998); H.-W. Micklitz and B. De Witte (eds.), *The European Court of Justice and the Autonomy of the Member States* (Cambridge: Intersentia, 2012).

14 Article 267 of the Treaty on the Functioning of the European Union.

15 See inter alia M. de S.-O.-l'E. Lasser, *Judicial Transformations: The Rights Revolution in the Courts of Europe* (Oxford University Press, 2009); B. Davies, *Resisting the European Court of Justice: West Germany's Confrontation with European Law 1949–1979* (Cambridge University Press, 2012); W. Kaiser, B. Leucht and M. Rasmussen (eds.), *The History of the European Union: Origins of a Supra- and Transnational Polity 1950–1972* (London: Routledge, 2008).

16 See H. Rasmussen, *On Law and Policy in the European Court of Justice: A Comparative Study in Judicial Policymaking* (Dordrecht: Martinus Nijhoff Publishers, 1986). See further Section 2.2.

17 In this respect, see for example R. Rogowski and T. Gawron (eds.), *Constitutional Courts in Comparison: The US Supreme Court and the German Federal Constitutional Court* (Oxford/New York: Berghahn Books, 2002); Flanagan and Ahern, 'Judicial Decision-Making and Transnational Law'. A study that combines analysis of the US Supreme Court with the ECJ and a national court, the French Cour de cassation, is M. de S.-O.-l'E. Lasser, *Judicial Deliberations: A Comparative Analysis of Judicial Transparency and Legitimacy* (Oxford University Press, 2004).

18 A.-M. Slaughter, 'A Typology of Transjudicial Communication' (1994) 29 *University of Richmond Law Review* 99, at 103–12.

the transnational context, is horizontal in nature. The exchange between highest national courts and a supranational court can be vertical, such as the hierarchical relation between the ECJ and the highest courts in EU Member States. This exchange can also be mixed horizontal–vertical, for instance if the US Supreme Court takes notice of common legal principles of EU Member States distilled by the ECJ in its case law.[19] Our analysis will primarily address the communication between the US Supreme Court and the ECJ, while also drawing on the available data concerning exchanges between the US Supreme Court and highest national courts in a selection of EU Member States, namely the UK, France and the Netherlands.[20]

2.2 Background: developing laws and judicial 'best practices' in the transnational legal context

Possible reasons for the emergence of transatlantic judicial communication might be related to the increased internationalisation of law. In the globalised legal context, highest courts need to reconsider their position with regard to foreign legal orders. This reflection has, firstly, an institutional and, secondly, a substantive legal aspect.

Firstly, the internationalisation of law affects the formal hierarchy between legal systems. Insight into the approaches of courts in other jurisdictions can provide a court with useful ideas for strengthening its position, internally in the legal order of which it is the highest court and externally vis-à-vis international legal regimes.[21] In Europe, the ECJ has had to define its position vis-à-vis the courts in the EU Member States and vis-à-vis the international legal order. The ECJ considers that no other court than the ECJ itself has the final authority to interpret and apply EU law,[22] and that the EU legal order and the international legal order are separate and distinguishable.[23] Within the EU context, this view has

[19] *Ibid.*

[20] This selection corresponds with the jurisdictions that could be addressed in the framework of the research project from which data are used in this chapter. See the introduction above.

[21] E. Benvenisti and G. W. Downs, 'Going Global to Preserve Domestic Accountability: The New Role of National Courts' in Muller and Richards, *Highest Courts and Globalisation*, pp. 163ff.

[22] Case 26–62 *Van Gend en Loos* v. *Netherlands Inland Revenue Administration* [1963] ECR 00003; Case 6–64 *Costa* v. *ENEL* [1964] ECR 1141.

[23] See inter alia Case C-402/05 P *Kadi and Al Barakaat International Foundation* v. *Council and Commission* [2008] ECR I-06351.

led to frictions with highest national courts, in particular the German Bundesverfassungsgericht. Famous examples are the *Solange* judgments, in which the German Constitutional Court refused to accept the ECJ's interpretation of the hierarchy between EU law and national constitutional law regarding fundamental rights protection,[24] and the German Court's judgment concerning the constitutionality of the Treaty of Lisbon.[25] With regard to the international legal order, the further expansion and constitutionalisation of international law entails an increasing overlap with areas of EU law and a proliferation of international courts and tribunals. This development makes the ECJ's claim to final authority to interpret the law in the EU legal order increasingly difficult to defend.[26]

As regards the US Supreme Court, similar questions have arisen. The internationalisation of law is causing a shift in the type of sources considered in judicial decision-making. Statutes in the USA need to be interpreted in light of binding international treaty law, which has become domestic law through its implementation in the US legal system. Therefore, international law is directly relevant for the deciding of cases. Indeed, the Supreme Court has a long-standing practice of interpreting acts of Congress in conformity with international law.[27] Still, legal questions can arise, concerning for example the self-executing nature of ratified treaty provisions[28] or the authority of judgments of an international court in the US legal system.[29] In this context of increased interaction between legal orders and between courts in these legal orders, transatlantic judicial communication might provide the ECJ and the US Supreme Court with a platform to discuss and learn from each other's experiences and benefit from this exchange in further shaping their own positions.

Secondly, and also related to the interaction between legal orders, the increased substantive overlap between legal rules has enhanced the relevance of comparative legal studies. In this regard, it is significant

[24] BVerfG 29 May 1974, *Solange I* [1974] 2 CMLR 540, 37 BVerfGE 271; BVerfG 22 October 1986, *Solange II* [1987] 3 CMLR 225, [1986] 73 BVerfGE 339.

[25] BVerfG 30 June 2009 [2009] 2 BvE 2/08. See N. Lavranos, 'The ECJ's Relationship with Other International Courts and Tribunals', available at: ssrn.com/abstract=1672727, accessed 25 October 2013.

[26] Lavranos, 'The ECJ's Relationship with Other International Courts and Tribunals', 2–3.

[27] *Ibid.*, 350.

[28] Restatement (Third) of the Foreign Relations Law of the United States, s 111(4). See J. D. van der Vyver, *Implementation of International Law in the United States* (Frankfurt am Main: Peter Lang, 2010), pp. 34–5.

[29] For example in *Medellin* v. *Texas*, 552 US 491 (2008), concerning the status of a judgment of the International Court of Justice. See also Section 3.2.

to note how the discussions about the role of public international law and comparative law have become intertwined, both in the USA and in Europe. In a public lecture, Justice Stephen Breyer enumerated several ways in which international and foreign law have had an impact on his professional life, for example by way of the awareness of relevant sources for reflection in domestic cases or in the form of exchanges with foreign judges on institutional issues.[30] He then made the following general observation:

> For one thing, my description blurs the differences between what my law professors used to call comparative law and public international law. That refusal to distinguish (at least for present purposes) may simply reflect reality. The commercial law of various States, for example, has become close to a single, unified body of law, in part through the work of uniform state law commissioners, in part through a pattern of similar judicial responses to similar problems, in part because of the work of intermediate judicial institutions such as federal bankruptcy courts, in part because the interstate nature of commercial contracts means that judges in different states apply each other's law. Formally speaking, state law is state law. But practically speaking, much of that law is national, if not international in scope. Analogous developments internationally, including the development of regional or specialised international legal bodies, also tend to produce cross-country results that resemble each other more and more, exhibiting common, if not universal, principles in various legal areas.[31]

In general, the trend of internationalisation of law seems to have mitigated the effects of the traditional dualist approach towards international law in the USA.[32] Some US judges admit to paying attention to international treaty law, in particular in the field of human rights law, even if the studied international treaties do not have domestic effect.[33] This acknowledgement of the harmonisation of laws across state borders, including the impact of international legal rules at the local level, bears resemblances to the process of legal integration in the context of the EU. Indeed, the intellectual perspective of judges also plays a role with regard to the status accorded to international and comparative legal sources in judicial decision-making in European jurisdictions. The influence of judicial

[30] S. Breyer, 'The Supreme Court and the New International Law' (American Society of International Law, Washington DC, 4 April 2003).

[31] *Ibid.*

[32] M. A. Waters, 'Creeping Monism: The Judicial Trend toward Interpretive Incorporation of Human Rights Treaties' (2007) 107 *Columbia Law Review* 628. See also V. C. Jackson, *Constitutional Engagement in a Transnational Era* (Oxford University Press, 2009).

[33] See also Waters, 'Creeping Monism', 633.

approaches, in combination with national legal culture, can be seen in the development of the engagement of national judges with EU law. Concerning binding international and supranational law, Dutch judges seem to be more open to accepting the influence of these sources, in particular the European Convention on Human Rights (ECHR) and EU law, than their counterparts in the UK.[34] The approach of the French judges has evolved from a position of resistance to a position of engagement with these legal sources.[35] The formal authority of legal sources is not a decisive factor in this respect.

When analysing the ECJ, it is important to realise that this diversity between national judges is present within the European Court, which is composed of judges from all EU Member States.[36] The representation of different national legal cultures within the Court requires that the judges of the ECJ reflect on their individual approaches to the interaction between EU law and the laws of the Member States and that they establish a shared approach concerning the role of the ECJ itself in the further development of EU law. In this sense, the broadening of judges' views within the context of the ECJ can be seen as a precursor to the current development of increased openness of national judges to international and comparative legal influences.[37]

These observations complete our analysis of the institutional setting and background of transatlantic judicial communication. Next we will analyse what forms the judicial communication between the courts on both sides of the Atlantic has taken in practice.

3 Nature of transatlantic judicial communication

The transatlantic exchange of information between the US Supreme Court and the ECJ, like transnational judicial communication more generally, takes two specific forms. On the one hand, judges learn about the views and experiences of their foreign peers through visits, conferences and personal contacts. On the other hand, judges obtain information through the study of foreign legal materials, including legislation and the

[34] E. Mak, 'Why Do Dutch and UK Judges Cite Foreign Law?' (2011) 70 *Cambridge Law Journal* 420, at 432–5.

[35] See Claes, *The National Courts' Mandate*, pp. 224–31.

[36] A new panel with advisory competences on judicial appointments was introduced by the Treaty of Lisbon. See Article 255 of the Treaty on the Functioning of the European Union.

[37] See further M. Bobek, *Comparative Reasoning in European Supreme Courts* (Oxford University Press, 2013); G. Martinico and O. Pollicino, *The Interaction between Europe's*

case law of foreign courts. Publicly available sources and the interviews with judges clarify which activities have been developed in this respect in the framework of EU–US relations. We will address both the form of the exchange and examples of discussed subjects. We will then consider whether this transatlantic exchange can be called a 'dialogue', that is, whether the judges truly engage in a discussion with each other about specific topics or merely use the exchange with foreign colleagues as a source of potentially interesting information.[38]

3.1 Visits, conferences and personal contacts

The obtained research data yielded examples of bilateral exchanges between the US Supreme Court and the ECJ. Furthermore, examples were found of multilateral exchanges involving the US Supreme Court, the ECJ and highest court judges from EU Member States.

3.1.1 Bilateral exchanges between the US Supreme Court and the ECJ

Let us first consider the bilateral exchanges between the US Supreme Court and the ECJ. These exchanges enable judges to share experiences with the application of the law in a multi-level legal system. Publicly available information, that is information disseminated by the ECJ itself, reveals that US Supreme Court Justices have visited the ECJ on a number of occasions.[39] A press release of the ECJ reports a visit in July 2003 by the Supreme Court Justices O'Connor, Ginsburg and Breyer. The exchange between the American and European judges concerned a discussion about 'topical European issues' and the recent case law of the US Supreme Court.[40] This press release emphasised that the visit 'occurred in the context of the constant and close relations enjoyed by the Court

Legal Systems: Judicial Dialogue and the Creation of Supranational Laws (Cheltenham: Edward Elgar Publishing, 2012).

[38] About the concept of '(judicial) dialogue', see in more detail Claes and de Visser, 'Are You Networked Yet?', 103; L. B. Tremblay, 'The Legitimacy of Judicial Review: The Limits of Dialogue between Courts and Legislatures' (2005) 3 *International Journal of Constitutional Law* 617; A. Torres Pérez, *Conflicts of Rights in the European Union: A Theory of Supranational Adjudication* (Oxford University Press, 2009), pp. 95ff. See further Section 3.3.

[39] The US Supreme Court's website (www.supremecourt.gov, accessed 25 October 2013) does not contain any press releases on judicial visits by foreign delegations.

[40] Press Release No. 57/03, 'Visit to the Court of Justice of the European Communities by a Delegation from the United States Supreme Court' (7 July 2003).

of Justice and the Supreme Court of the United States'.[41] A later press release mentions a visit by Chief Justice Roberts and Associate Justices Ginsburg and Breyer in February 2010. During this visit, the American judges participated in 'working sessions' on procedural and substantive themes – namely: 'Relations with Other Judicial Bodies', 'Methodology and interpretation', 'Impact of the Treaty of Lisbon', and the organisation and working methods of the ECJ. They also attended a hearing before the Grand Chamber.[42] The press release about this visit indicated that the visit was 'part of the frequent and close contacts which the Court of Justice has maintained with the Supreme Court of the United States since 1998'.[43]

Another press release issued by the ECJ mentioned that a visit of judges of the ECJ to the United States had taken place in 2000 and that US Supreme Court Justices had visited the ECJ in 1998 and 2003.[44] This press release was issued on the occasion of a visit of judges of the ECJ to the United States in February 2007. The delegation, which consisted of the President of the Court, Vassilios Skouris, seven judges and two Advocates-General, attended a hearing before the US Supreme Court and discussed with Justices of the Supreme Court 'various subjects of mutual interest'.[45] The judges of the ECJ further met with several judges of federal and state courts in the United States.

This information clarifies that visits between the ECJ and US Supreme Court occur with a certain frequency. Furthermore, the ECJ finds it important to draw public attention to its contacts with the US Supreme Court. Yet the significance of these visits remains unclear. Critics have argued that judicial visits are aimed at the 'wining and dining' of judges rather than at the establishment of substantive and relevant communication.[46] The views of judges on this matter will be analysed in more detail below. First we will consider the multilateral exchanges in which the ECJ and the US Supreme Court participate.

[41] *Ibid.*

[42] Press Release No. 9/10, 'Visit to the Court of Justice of a Delegation from the Supreme Court of the United States of America and Professors from an American University, SMU Dedman School of Law' (10 February 2010).

[43] *Ibid.*

[44] Press Release No. 18/07, 'Visit of a Delegation of the Court of Justice of the European Communities to the United States of America' (27 February 2007).

[45] *Ibid.*

[46] See Rasmussen, *On Law and Policy in the European Court of Justice.*

3.1.2 Multilateral exchanges involving highest national courts

Transatlantic communication also occurs through multilateral exchanges between the US Supreme Court, the ECJ and highest national courts in Europe. In the EU legal context, an important network is the Network of the Presidents of the Supreme Judicial Courts of the EU (NPSJC).[47] The President of the ECJ is invited to participate in the activities of this network, such as general assemblies and colloquiums.[48] The NPSJC has a reunion every two years. In respect of the matters discussed in this network, the interviews clarified that topics have mostly concerned organisational issues, such as the administration of the highest courts and the duration of proceedings. At the inaugural conference in 2004, the participating judges discussed representation and assistance in highest court proceedings.[49] In July 2007 a conference of the network was organised in Paris with the US Supreme Court on the following three themes: (1) judicial administration, in particular the selection of appeals to the Supreme Court; (2) education of judges; and (3) subsidiarity and federalism. The participating judges were, among others, US Chief Justice Roberts, US Associate Justice Bader Ginsburg, US Associate Justice Breyer, the then-Lord Chief Justice of England and Wales Lord Phillips, and the then-President of the Dutch Hoge Raad Willibrord Davids.[50] The programme published on the NPSJC's website does not specify whether judges of the ECJ also participated in this meeting. More generally, no information is provided concerning the outcome of the organised reunions. Therefore, as with the bilateral visits between the ECJ and the US Supreme Court, it remains unclear to what extent the participation of judges in multilateral exchanges has an impact on the views and approaches of these judges or on the decision-making of their courts.[51] Before analysing this further, we will consider another form of judicial communication: the judicial study of foreign legal materials.

3.2 *Judicial study of foreign legal materials*

The research on and discussion about international and comparative legal materials appear to have become institutionalised to some degree in

[47] www.network-presidents.eu, accessed 25 October 2013.

[48] Claes and de Visser, 'Are You Networked Yet?', 113.

[49] www.network-presidents.eu, accessed 25 October 2013.

[50] *Ibid.*

[51] Similar criticism regarding the poor reporting of the ECJ on its participation in judicial networks has been voiced by Claes and de Visser, 'Are You Networked Yet?', 113.

the US Supreme Court and the ECJ. Our research yielded the following examples.

3.2.1 Experiences in the US Supreme Court

The judges in the US Supreme Court, similarly to their peers in other Anglo-Saxon highest courts, feel that counsel should bring forward all legal materials that are relevant for deciding the case, including foreign judgments and academic resources concerning foreign law. This view fits the originally British adversarial system for court proceedings, in which the parties present their case and all relevant arguments to the court.[52] In a public lecture given in 2003, US Justice Stephen Breyer emphasised the importance of the contribution of lawyers to comparative legal research. He observed:

> Neither I nor my law clerks can easily find relevant comparative material on our own. The lawyers must do the basic work, finding, analysing, and referring us to, that material. I know there is a chicken and egg problem. The lawyers will do so only if they believe the courts are receptive. By now, however, it should be clear that the chicken has broken out of the egg. The demand is there.[53]

Nevertheless, judges still conduct research by themselves as well or request their judicial assistants to do research. In the US Supreme Court, judges sometimes carry out extra research of international and comparative legal materials by themselves. Each Supreme Court judge is assisted by law clerks, hired for one judicial year. Anecdotal evidence suggests that law clerks might have knowledge of EU law.[54]

Information on EU law or the laws of European countries reaches the US Supreme Court mostly through other channels, in particular through *amicus curiae* briefs filed in individual cases. An example mentioned during the interviews concerned an *amicus* brief filed by the EU in a case concerning the transmitting of documents between companies in different countries.[55] *Amicus* briefs were also submitted by the EU in several

[52] Lord Woolf, *Access to Justice: Interim Report to the Lord Chancellor on the Civil Justice System in England and Wales* (London: Lord Chancellor's Department, 1995).

[53] Breyer, 'The Supreme Court and the New International Law'.

[54] An example is Daniel Halberstam, who has a US background and clerked for US Supreme Court Justice Souter and also worked at the ECJ. See www.law.umich.edu, accessed 25 October 2013.

[55] *Intel Corp.* v. *Advanced Micro Devices Inc.*, 542 US 241 (2004).

death penalty cases[56] and in a case concerning the presumption against extraterritoriality with regard to claims under the Alien Tort Statute.[57] As another example, a brief prepared by several European countries (the UK, Ireland and the Netherlands) was submitted in an antitrust case concerning a cartel in the Netherlands. The US Supreme Court in this case had to decide whether a suit should be brought in the USA or in Europe.[58] However, questions have been raised concerning the EU's motives and competence to intervene in this way.[59] Moreover, the impact on the US Supreme Court's judgments is not clearly visible, apart from general references of the Justices to 'international opinion' or the views of the 'world community'.[60]

Interestingly, the examples mentioned by the judges interviewed mostly concerned research on questions of international law rather than research on EU law or comparative legal research on foreign national legal systems. One judge interviewed mentioned, for example, personal research on international law in the case of *Medellin* v. *Texas*.[61] The difference might be explained by the necessity to study international legal sources in specific cases brought before the US Supreme Court as opposed to the voluntary use of comparative law.[62]

Finally, although the use of comparative legal materials is not always easily apparent in the published judgments of the US Supreme Court, the research conducted for this chapter clarifies that comparative law is studied and discussed, and if it is not persuasive, at least it has a guiding role in the deciding of some cases. Judges of the US Supreme Court who are in favour of the citation of comparative law seem to prefer using a vague standard for assessing the usefulness of reference

[56] Fahey, 'On the Use of Law in Transatlantic Relations', 7–9, mentioning *McCarver* v. *North Carolina*, 533 US 975 (2001); *Atkins* v. *Virginia*, 536 US 304 (2002); *Roper* v. *Simmons*, 534 US 551 (2005); *Medellin* v. *Texas*, 552 US 491 (2008).

[57] *Kiobel* v. *Royal Dutch Petroleum Co.*, 133 US 1659 (2013).

[58] *F. Hoffman-LaRoche Ltd* v. *Empagran SA*, 542 US 155 (2004). See also W. van Reenen, 'The Submission of Amicus Curiae Briefs to United States Courts' in N. Blokker and others, *Essays in Honour of Johan G. Lammers* (Leiden: Nijhoff, 2006).

[59] Fahey, 'On the Use of Law in Transatlantic Relations', 8, citing M. Cremona, 'Values in EU Foreign Policy' in M. Evans and P. Koutrakos (eds.), *Beyond the Established Legal Orders: Policy Interconnections between the EU and the Rest of the World* (Oxford: Hart Publishing, 2011).

[60] Fahey, 'On the Use of Law in Transatlantic Relations', footnote 37, referring to Justice Steven's opinion in *Atkins* v. *Virginia*, 317, n. 21.

[61] *Medellin* v. *Texas*, 552 US 491 (2008). Interestingly, this is a case where the EU made submissions; see above, n. 56.

[62] See above, Section 2.2.

to foreign law in specific cases. Two judges interviewed indicated that comparative law can be taken into account when it seems appropriate to do so. According to one judge interviewed, references to foreign law might be used in the reasoning of judgments if this helps to clarify the argument. The judge mentioned the example of cases concerning questions of federalism and observed that resemblances exist between the use of the principles of subsidiarity and proportionality in the USA and the EU.[63] Given these resemblances, the judge observed that it might be helpful if the US Supreme Court points out when it uses these principles in judicial interpretation. Comparative legal sources might also help in convincing others to accept the judicial argument. However, the judge was not sure about the validity of this second statement. Hence, it seems that this judge's aim in citing foreign law is related to a desire to be clear rather than a desire to be persuasive through comparative legal arguments.

3.2.2 Experiences in the ECJ

Although similarities with other courts can be identified, in particular with the French Cour de cassation, the organisation of the ECJ is considered not to have an equivalent in other legal systems.[64] The Court is composed of judges representing all EU Member States. The judges of the ECJ receive relevant information from the Advocate-General, who acts as an advisor to the Court on how to decide a case referred for a preliminary ruling.[65] Comparative materials can form part of the Advocate-General's opinion. In addition to the information provided in this way, the judges receive information through the research conducted by their assistants (*réferendaires*). Like the judges of the US Supreme Court, the judges can conduct their own research to find out about foreign legal materials that might help in deciding a specific case. Taking into account the experiences in highest national courts, it can be expected that some judges of the ECJ are more inclined than others to carry out extra research.

[63] See also below, Section 4.2.

[64] Solanke, '"Stop the ECJ"?', 765 and 767ff.; K. Borgsmidt, 'The Advocate General at the European Court of Justice: A Comparative Study' (1988) 13 *European Law Review* 106.

[65] Although agreement exists that the ECJ follows the Advocate General's opinion in the majority of cases, no precise numbers are available; see S. Robertson, 'How Often Does the ECJ Follow Advocates General? Or Should That Be CJEU?', available at: www.out-law.com/page-11458, accessed 25 October 2013. See further N. Burrows and R. Greaves, *The Advocate General and EC Law* (Oxford University Press, 2007).

References to the US Supreme Court are very rare and so far have occurred only in opinions of Advocates-General.[66] This low frequency of citations to comparative legal sources fits the Continental European (French) style of judicial reasoning. For reasons of tradition and the requirement of a unanimous decision, judgments in civil law systems tend to be relatively short. For this reason, the citation of foreign law would be exceptional. Indeed, some judges in the highest courts of France and the Netherlands interviewed felt that the reasoning of a judgment might be weakened because of possible criticism of the highest court's use of foreign law, for example with regard to the scope and relevance of the legal comparison with other jurisdictions. The citation of foreign legal materials is more easily accepted in Anglo-Saxon courts, which stand in the tradition of law development through case law and which permit individual judges to issue their own opinions on cases.[67] The ECJ can be considered to be closer to the Continental European tradition in this regard.[68]

3.3 A '*dialogue*'?

Do the transatlantic exchanges between judges constitute a 'dialogue', that is, do the judges engage in deliberations on the topics of common interest to them as opposed to mere conversation about these topics?[69] Claes and de Visser have argued that transnational dialogue between judges can take place more easily in the informal exchanges between judges than in the context of formal judicial procedures.[70] In the EU context, the preliminary reference procedure and the case law of the ECJ and the national courts in EU Member States constitute a 'series of monologues'

[66] Fahey, 'On the Use of Law in Transatlantic Relations', footnote 18, mentioning four results in a five-year period up to 27 June 2012.

[67] But see below, Section 4.1.

[68] See also Lasser, *Judicial Deliberations*, p. 103.

[69] Tremblay, 'The Legitimacy of Judicial Review'.

[70] See further D. S. Law and W.-C. Chang, 'The Limits of Global Judicial Dialogue' (2011) 86 *Washington Law Review* 523, who present empirical evidence demonstrating that the engagement of the US Supreme Court and the Constitutional Court of Taiwan with comparative constitutional law depends less on judicial interaction than on institutional factors concerning the organisation of the courts as well as legal education and training. A promising conceptual framework for the further analysis of patterns in the relationships between courts in the transnational legal context, considering communication in judicial networks as well as communication through the study of foreign law, has been developed by O. Frishman, 'Transnational Judicial Dialogue as an Organisational Field' (2013) 19 *European Law Journal* 739.

rather than a true 'dialogue'.[71] By contrast, the exchanges between judges through judicial visits, conferences and personal contacts 'allow for a free exchange of ideas and arguments on a more equal footing and even give room for deliberation on common issues'.[72] Our study of the exchanges between the US and European judges corroborates this conclusion. Indeed, examples of the use of EU legal sources in the deliberations of the US Supreme Court and, vice versa, examples of the use of US legal sources in the deliberations of the ECJ are very limited. Visits, conferences and personal contacts seem to have created a more constructive form of communication between the two courts.

Some further nuances emerge from the considerations of the judges interviewed concerning the usefulness of transnational exchanges in the form of judicial visits, conferences and personal contacts, or in the form of the study of comparative law. Many of the judges interviewed were optimistic. A British judge considered that judicial exchanges broaden the outlook and viewpoint of an individual judge. This judge considered this to be 'healthy', as legal systems show a parallel political movement to closer union. Another judge observed that transnational exchanges make one realise that judges in other jurisdictions are sometimes facing the same problems. Yet another British judge remarked that some academic conferences had been thought-provoking. A French judge observed that participation in judicial networks provides judges with a possibility to better understand internal solutions chosen in the national legal system. Moreover, this experience nourishes the awareness that the state of positive law is subject to change. These exchanges with their colleagues from other legal systems helps judges to look at their own national law with some distance and from a different perspective. Finally, a judge of the US Supreme Court compared judicial exchanges to the exchange between academics, who also sometimes contact each other to find out about the foreign law in a specific field. This judge considered that a phone call to a foreign colleague might help one to better understand an issue that has arisen in one's own legal system. This judge considered transnational judicial exchanges to be a good way of learning about foreign law.

However, some judges expressed hesitations. For example, a British judge felt that exchanges with foreign judges can be quite boring,

[71] Claes and de Visser, 'Are You Networked Yet?', 106.
[72] *Ibid.*

because – according to this judge – the differences between the substantive laws in different countries generally are too large for a fruitful exchange of legal ideas to take place! Judges in other Western highest courts also felt that international exchanges often were too open-ended to be of any use.

Concerning the consultation of foreign law for comparative purposes in concrete cases, the judges in Western highest courts interviewed indicated that several motives play a role, on their own or in combination. The use of foreign legal sources is considered useful, firstly, when the case to be decided holds particular public importance. Secondly, foreign legal materials are considered helpful when judges want to obtain better knowledge or a yardstick for the judgment of the case at hand. Thirdly, judges measure themselves against other courts and want to meet the same quality standards as their 'peers' in other jurisdictions. Finally, the research of foreign legal materials allows judges to spot trends regarding the evolution of the law in other legal systems and to determine their own positions regarding these trends. Judges in all of the examined courts felt that the guiding influence of foreign legal materials does not push them to follow the solution found in another legal system.

In order to better appreciate such optimistic and yet also critical remarks, we will next analyse to what extent transatlantic judicial communication between the US Supreme Court and the ECJ can have an influence on the actual decision-making of these two courts.

4 Assessment of transatlantic influences on judicial decision-making

The above analysis clarifies that judicial exchanges between US and European judges take place with a certain frequency. As yet, no *systematic* approach has been developed with regard to this transatlantic communication. However, the increased contact between judges and the occasional references to each other's case law raise the question: what influence can transatlantic judicial communication have on the decision-making of the US Supreme Court and the ECJ? We will first analyse the possible impact of transatlantic communication on the use of comparative legal sources by the two courts. Secondly, we will analyse the impact of EU–US judicial communication on judicial methodology in light of changing standards for the process of judicial discovery and the style of reasoning of judgments.

4.1 Taking inspiration from transatlantic law and practices

When judging domestic cases, the US Supreme Court and the ECJ occasionally refer to each other's case law as comparative legal sources.[73] In the transatlantic judicial exchange, the experiences of judges in foreign jurisdictions provide a point of departure for judges to reflect on the process of judicial decision-making in their own courts. However, the legitimacy of this exercise has been questioned, in particular in the United States. In the following we will analyse this debate and its relevance for transatlantic judicial communication.

4.1.1 A controversial topic, or is it?

In the USA, the use of comparative law in constitutional cases has led to heated debate. Critics usually focus on the absence of authority of comparative law to bring about constitutional change in the US legal system.[74] However, proponents usually do not claim that comparative law should give the decisive arguments for constitutional change. Instead, those in favour of the use of comparative legal sources emphasise the lessons that can be learnt regarding the meaning of specific concepts. A judge of the US Supreme Court interviewed observed that the justification of looking to foreign law or international opinion in constitutional cases is of an indirect nature. This judge emphasised that constitutional provisions in other countries are not binding on the US Supreme Court. Nonetheless, this judge considered that the fact that people can read about the law of foreign countries makes it relevant for use in legal cases.

It can be observed that the differences between critics and proponents, including US Supreme Court Justices, do not seem to be as big as is often suggested. The opponents of the citation of comparative legal sources might express an interest in learning about foreign law as such, while supporters of the use of comparative law downplay the role played by cited foreign legal sources as arguments in the decisions in concrete cases. Indeed, the courts in the USA for a long time have considered the 'inspirational' function of comparative law to be non-problematic. Research has shown that the citation of comparative law constitutes a long-standing practice

[73] See above, Section 3.2.

[74] The arguments in favour of and against the use of comparative law in judicial decision-making emerge clearly from N. Dorsen, 'The Relevance of Foreign Legal Materials in US Constitutional Cases: A Conversation between Justice Antonin Scalia and Justice Stephen Breyer' (2005) 3 *International Journal of Constitutional Law* 519.

of the US courts.[75] The judges interviewed, too, did not have difficulties in finding examples of cases in which reference was made to comparative legal sources by the US Supreme Court. Jurisdictions often looked at by US judges include the UK, because of the historical connection with the USA, and European countries, because of the human rights regimes that have developed there.

Concerning the ECJ, the views of the judges in the highest national courts in Europe examined are instructive. Among these judges, the use of foreign law in judicial decision-making is not a matter of much discussion. However, the judges interviewed generally considered that the usefulness of non-binding comparative sources for judicial decision-making should not be overrated.[76] Judicial statistics seem to corroborate this view, as citations of comparative sources occur in relatively few cases.[77]

In light of this generally limited normative impact of comparative law on judicial decisions, the transatlantic communication between the US Supreme Court and the ECJ does not need to be problematic. At the same time, expectations concerning the possible normative influence of the EU on the US legal order or of the USA on the EU legal order through judicial forums should not be too high.[78] Nevertheless, transatlantic communication could have a broader impact than judicial deliberations as such. The judicial practices of their transatlantic counterparts provide the US Supreme Court and the ECJ with a yardstick for a general reflection on their own practices.

4.1.2 An opportunity for transatlantic reflection

The different tone of the debates in the USA and in Europe concerning the use of foreign law creates an opportunity for judges to reflect on their own approach in light of experiences elsewhere. Why has the debate in the USA developed in the way that it has? US Supreme Court Justice Breyer

[75] S. G. Calabresi and S. Dotson Zimdahl, 'The Supreme Court and Foreign Sources of Law: Two Hundred Years of Practice and the Juvenile Death Penalty Decision' (2005) 47 *William and Mary Law Review* 743; D. A. Farber, 'The Supreme Court, the Law of Nations, and Citations of Foreign Law: The Lessons of History' (2006) UC Berkeley Public Law Research Paper No. 954359, available at: ssrn.com/abstract=954359, accessed October 2013.

[76] See above, Section 3.3.

[77] Concerning the highest national courts in European countries, see M. Gelter and M. M. Siems, 'Language, Legal Origins, and Culture before the Courts: Cross-Citations between Supreme Courts in Europe' (2013) 21 *Supreme Court Economic Review*, available at: ssrn.com/abstract=1719183, accessed 25 October 2013.

[78] Differently Fahey, 'On the Use of Law in Transatlantic Relations', 9.

has suggested in a public lecture that political interests related to the judicial recourse to foreign law lie at the heart of the controversy in the US debate.[79] He has further pointed out that the use of foreign law took place in cases that were already controversial because of their subject matter, for example cases regarding homosexual relationships[80] or the death penalty.[81] Therefore, critics of the use of foreign law might be subject to what psychologists call 'displacement': if you cannot blame A (here: the US courts), blame B (here: the foreign courts cited).[82] Legal scholars in the USA have identified other reasons that can account for the controversy, including the influence on public opinion of Supreme Court Justice Scalia's resistance to the use of comparative law,[83] the growth of xenophobia in the United States after the invasion of Iraq in 2003,[84] and the divide between judicial and academic cultures, on the one hand, and public opinion, on the other hand.[85]

Why has the same controversy not arisen elsewhere, for example in Europe? A judge of the US Supreme Court interviewed suggested several reasons. Firstly, people in Europe have lived closer together for a long time than people in the USA. This argument suggests that cross-cultural influences are more natural in the interaction between people in Europe than in the USA. Secondly, national courts in Europe do not have the same visibility as the US Supreme Court. This argument reflects the idea that courts that are more visible in the public debate, such as the US Supreme Court, will be criticised more often for their decisions and their functioning.[86] Another US Supreme Court Justice interviewed advanced an

[79] S. Breyer, 'The Court and Foreign Law' (Rostov Lecture on International Affairs, Johns Hopkins University, Paul H. Nitze School of Advanced International Studies, 31 March 2010).

[80] *Bowers* v. *Hardwick*, 478 US 186 (1986); *Lawrence* v. *Texas*, 539 US 558 (2003).

[81] *Atkins* v. *Virginia*, 536 US 304 (2002); *Roper* v. *Simmons*, 543 US 551 (2005).

[82] Breyer, 'The Court and Foreign Law'.

[83] Jackson, *Constitutional Engagement in a Transnational Era*.

[84] M. Rosenfeld, 'Principle or Ideology? A Comparativist Perspective on the US Controversy over Supreme Court Citations to Foreign Authorities' (2008), Cardozo Legal Studies Research Paper No. 213, available at: ssrn.com/abstract=1081854, accessed 25 October 2013.

[85] See S. G. Calabresi, '"A Shining City on a Hill": American Exceptionalism and the Supreme Court's Practice of Relying on Foreign Law' (2006) 86 *Boston University Law Review* 1335, at 1336–7.

[86] Criticism of the 'other European court', the ECtHR, focusing on its supposedly non-democratic character, corroborates this idea. See inter alia B. Çah, A. Koch and N. Bruch, *The Legitimacy of the European Court of Human Rights: The View from the Ground* (Strasbourg, 2 May 2011), available at: ecthrproject.files.wordpress.com/2011/04/ecthr-legitimacyreport.pdf, accessed 25 October 2013.

argument based on the history of judicial review in the USA and in the world. This judge explained that the US Supreme Court was one of the first courts in which constitutional review was developed. When other countries established constitutional courts, many looked to the USA for inspiration. Only when these courts had developed their own case law did it become practice for US judges to consider the judgments of these constitutional courts elsewhere in the world. The judge reasoned that people in the USA 'had or have to get used to this'.

In light of these considerations, we can observe the following with regard to the ECJ. Differently from the US Supreme Court, the ECJ is functioning in a system in which legal integration in a pluralistic cultural context is the point of departure. This creates a good starting point for the use of comparative law in the ECJ's decision-making. However, some arguments can be raised against this development. First of all, the ECJ has the same visibility in society as the US Supreme Court. Moreover, its judicial approach remains closely watched by national courts and governments in EU Member States. The ECJ is therefore vulnerable to criticism. Furthermore, practical constraints might be an obstacle to the study of comparative legal sources. After all, the ECJ already has to consider the national laws and constitutional traditions of the EU Member States. This could reduce the incentive for engaging in comparative legal studies concerning other jurisdictions. Keeping these constraints in mind, some observations can be made regarding a methodology for the use of comparative law by judges in EU–US relations.

4.2. Developing a methodology for the use of comparative law in transatlantic relations

Transatlantic judicial communication might have an effect on the process of judicial discovery and on the reasoning of judgments in the US Supreme Court and in the ECJ. However, the particularities of the US and EU legal orders and of the two courts delimit the possibilities for the construction of a real judicial 'dialogue'.[87] It emerged from the interviews that highest courts select partners for exchange on the basis of legal tradition, language and the prestige of foreign courts. When translating these results to EU–US judicial relations, we can make the following observations.

[87] See also above, Section 3.3.

Firstly, the differences between Anglo-Saxon courts, based on the common law tradition, and courts with a Continental European (French) heritage, based on the civil law tradition, create obstacles for exchange on certain matters.[88] This divide between the Anglo-Saxon and Continental European traditions also sets apart the US Supreme Court and the ECJ. However, the two courts have a common ground for discussion based on their position as highest court in a multi-level system with a large territorial scope and based on their politicised role in the US and EU legal orders respectively. Concerning comparability, a judge of the US Supreme Court outlined the possible clarifications on questions of federalism that can be obtained from a study of the role of the principles of subsidiarity and proportionality in the EU legal context. This judge considered that the ideas of Hamilton and other 'founding fathers' of the United States Constitution can be captured in the principle of subsidiarity. Concerning the principle of proportionality, the judge was of the opinion that this is used by the US Supreme Court in the same way as in the EU.[89]

The possibilities for useful judicial exchanges also depend on practical aspects. Several judges interviewed observed that participation in judicial exchanges is time-consuming. Furthermore, a problem with networks is that the delegates of the participating courts change frequently. Moreover, some judges are very active in judicial exchanges and in the public debate while others are not. In sum, even though most of the described examples of judicial exchanges seem to have a specific purpose, and could therefore be considered to form part of a real 'dialogue', no systematic approach exists.

Finally, language poses a significant obstacle in transnational judicial exchanges. The interviews revealed that judges who are multilingual engage more easily in judicial exchanges with foreign colleagues than judges who know only one language. These aspects also influence the judicial communication between the US Supreme Court and the ECJ. The aspects of time and changing participants are controlled to some extent in EU–US relations through the establishment of a structure of regular visits between the courts.[90] Concerning language, the judges of the US Supreme Court are not required to work with foreign languages. A judge interviewed confirmed that language plays a role in the selection of

[88] Concerning the common law and civil law traditions, see Glenn, *Legal Traditions of the World*, Chapter 5 and 7. See also Mak, *Judicial Decision-Making in a Globalised World*, Chapters 2 and 4.

[89] See also above, Section 3.2.

[90] See above, Section 3.1.

systems for comparison by the US judges. This judge read French, but not German.[91] However, this judge observed that a lot of information is currently available in English. Indeed, the judgments of the ECJ are available in English, and they are easily accessible through the Court's website.[92] The judges of the ECJ, by contrast, are used to working with foreign languages. The Court uses French as its internal working language. Since all official languages of the EU may be used as the language of procedure in cases, the Court employs a large staff of lawyer-linguists to provide translations of documents.[93] As a result of English also being one of the 'global' languages, many of the judges of the ECJ are able to participate in exchanges with the US Supreme Court.

5 Conclusion

Transatlantic judicial exchanges, in which organisational as well as substantive issues are discussed, can provide judges in Western legal systems with information on how to define their position in the globalised legal context. In this regard, transatlantic judicial communication could provide the US Supreme Court and the ECJ with a platform for discussing substantive topics of common interest, and to reflect on the similarities and differences influenced by national legal culture and the legal education, professional experience and personal background of judges in these courts. This exchange might stimulate reflection about the increased intertwinement of laws, in particular in the context of processes of legal harmonisation above the level of states. The exchange might also create more awareness among judges about the opportunities and pitfalls of the recourse to foreign law, and the appropriate methodology for the use of international and comparative sources in judicial deliberations and judgments. This kind of communication can form a basis for building 'best practices' of judicial decision-making across jurisdictions.

However, the research in this chapter reveals that no systematic approach currently exists with regard to the judicial communication

[91] Since German is the third official working language of the EU, language could form an obstacle for US judges when engaging in comparative legal research.

[92] See curia.europa.eu, accessed 25 October 2013.

[93] K. McAuliffe, 'Languages and Institutional Dynamics of the Court of Justice of the European Communities: Lawyer-Linguists and the Production of a Multilingual Jurisprudence' in M. Gueldry (ed.), *How Globalizing Professions Deal with National Languages: Studies in Cultural Conflict and Cooperation* (Lewiston, Queenstown, Lampeter: The Edwin Mellen Press, 2010), pp. 239ff.

between the US Supreme Court and the ECJ. Moreover, some obstacles for a fruitful judicial dialogue exist in the form of: (1) the differences between court organisation in the Anglo-Saxon model, in which the US Supreme Court functions, and in the Continental European (French) model, which formed the basis for the organisation of the ECJ; (2) practical constraints, such as language and access to foreign sources; and (3) the societal and political acceptance of the courts' practices in the US and EU legal orders. However, awareness of these possibilities and constraints is the first step on the way to an improvement in transatlantic judicial communication. If these aspects are addressed in the further development of judicial relations across the Atlantic, a more constructive, deliberative dialogue can be established.

3

The European Parliament and EU–US relations

Revamping institutional cooperation?

DAVOR JANČIĆ

1 Introduction: the European Parliament's frailty in foreign affairs and the transatlantic opportunity

Parliamentary affairs in the European Union have gradually become one of the most topical institutional matters in political and scholarly debates. Thanks to the incessant and ubiquitously felt need to democratise EU decisions in both internal and external affairs, policy-makers and academics alike have industriously sought ways to upgrade the status of EU democracy. Representative, and more specifically parliamentary democracy has ultimately prevailed as the key instrument for achieving this.[1] This chapter adopts an EU-centric perspective and observes the transatlantic relations between the EU and the USA as a possible channel for the European Parliament informally to fortify its powers. It therefore brings the transatlantic partnership within the auspices of the internal constitutional and institutional mechanics of the Union and makes it part of the European Parliament's ongoing endeavour to be recognised as an equal EU decision-maker that is capable of safeguarding the interests of EU citizens effectively.

To be sure, pundits claim that the Treaty of Lisbon is the 'Treaty of Parliaments'. This is so because both the European Parliament and the national parliaments of the Member States have gained powers in the EU's

Research for this chapter has been funded by the British Academy through its postdoctoral Newton International Fellowship scheme. The author wishes to thank the editors, the anonymous reviewers and participants at the 2013 Amsterdam Workshop on 'Transatlantic Relations: The Nature of Rule-Making' for their valuable and constructive comments.

[1] As Article 10(1) of the Treaty on the European Union (TEU) confirms, 'the functioning of the Union shall be founded on representative democracy'.

processes of policy- and decision-making.[2] The European Parliament, the Union's only directly elected institution, has been argued to have become 'an equal counterpart to the Council and the Commission' and 'the centre of democratic control in the EU, structurally resembling the US Congress'.[3] For Dann, this justifies describing the Union's composite system of democratic legitimacy as a semi-parliamentary democracy.[4]

Yet while the internal powers of the European Parliament have substantially increased, its prerogatives in foreign affairs remain meagre.[5] In matters of the Common Foreign and Security Policy (CFSP) and the Common Security and Defence Policy (CSDP), the European Parliament is merely consulted on the main aspects and the basic choices of these policies, and informed of their evolution. Its formal involvement is exhausted in receiving information, holding progress debates twice a year, putting questions to the Council, making recommendations to the Council and the High Representative, and having its views duly taken into account.[6] Even though frequent contacts, hearings and consultations between Members of the European Parliament (MEPs) and the EU's High Representative, Commissioner for External Relations and the Council Presidency contribute to a more substantial parliamentary control over EU foreign affairs,[7] the democratic deficit in this area has been widely rehearsed.[8] For example, Eeckhout finds parliamentary involvement in CFSP matters wanting, which is 'unacceptable in a polity governed by the rule of law', where policy-making is 'excessively dominated by the

[2] K. Lenaerts and N. Cambien, 'Democratic Legitimacy of the EU after the Treaty of Lisbon' in J. Wouters *et al.* (eds.), *European Constitutionalism beyond Lisbon* (Antwerp: Intersentia, 2009), p. 207.

[3] P. Dann, 'The Political Institutions' in A. von Bogdandy and J. Bast (eds.), *Principles of European Constitutional Law* (Oxford: Hart Publishing, 2010), pp. 250–1.

[4] *Ibid.*, p. 271.

[5] S. Becker-Alon, *The Communitarian Dimension of the European Union's Common Foreign and Security Policy* (Baden-Baden: Nomos Verlagsgesellschaft, 2010), p. 263; M. Comelli, 'The Democratic Accountability of the CSDP and the Role of the European Parliament' in E. Greco *et al.* (eds.), *EU Crisis Management: Institutions and Capabilities in the Making* (Rome: Istituto Affari Internazionali, 2010), p. 85.

[6] Article 36 TEU.

[7] U. Diedrichs, 'The European Parliament in CFSP: More than a Marginal Player?' (2004) 39 *International Spectator* 35–45, at 35–6.

[8] See for instance: E. Barbé, 'The Evolution of CFSP Institutions: Where Does Democratic Accountability Stand?' (2004) 39 *International Spectator* 47–60; H. Born and H. Hänggi (eds.), *The 'Double Democratic Deficit': Parliamentary Accountability and the Use of Force under International Auspices* (Aldershot: Ashgate Publishing, 2004); D. Peters *et al.*, 'Parliaments and European Security Policy: Mapping the Parliamentary Field' (2010) 14

executive'.[9] In a similar vein, Curtin and Dekker assess the European Parliament's power in CFSP as 'relatively marginal'.[10]

As regards international agreements concluded by the EU, the European Parliament possesses the right of consent but not that of initiative. In addition to four enumerated categories of agreements,[11] the consent prerogative applies to another important and sweeping category: agreements that cover fields in which an internal EU legal act may only be adopted with the consent of the European Parliament, whether in accordance with the ordinary legislative procedure or a special one. However, the European Parliament's consent is only requisite once the agreement has already been signed, which precludes MEPs from influencing the contents of the initial version of the agreement before signature as well as from amending individual provisions thereof after signature. The agreement can only be accepted or rejected *in toto*. What is worse, an international agreement that the EU has signed can even be provisionally applied without the European Parliament having a say in it. As regards international agreements in all other fields, the European Parliament is merely consulted.[12] Thus, the so-called 'parallelism paradigm', construed in 1971 by the Court of Justice in its *AETR* judgment, which advocated that the system of internal Community measures may not be separated from that of external relations, remains unfulfilled even after the Treaty of Lisbon.[13]

Comparing the European Parliament to the US Congress, Thym argues that while this take-it-or-leave-it approach impedes any meaningful

European Integration Online Papers 1–25; W. Wagner, 'The Democratic Deficit in the EU's Security and Defence Policy – Why Bother?', RECON Online Working Paper No. 2007/10 (University of Oslo, ARENA Centre for European Studies, 2007).

9 P. Eeckhout, 'The EU's Common Foreign and Security Policy after Lisbon: From Pillar Talk to Constitutionalism' in A. Biondi *et al.* (eds.), *EU Law after Lisbon* (Oxford University Press, 2012), p. 290.

10 D. Curtin and I. Dekker, 'The European Union from Maastricht to Lisbon: Institutional and Legal Unity out of the Shadows' in P. Craig and G. de Búrca (eds.), *The Evolution of EU Law* (Oxford University Press, 2011), p. 172.

11 According to Article 218(6)(a) of the Treaty on the Functioning of the European Union (TFEU), these four categories of agreements are: (1) association agreements; (2) agreement on Union accession to the European Convention for the Protection of Human Rights and Fundamental Freedoms; (3) agreements establishing a specific institutional framework by organising cooperation procedures; and (4) agreements with important budgetary implications for the Union.

12 Article 218(6)(b) TFEU.

13 D. Thym, 'Parliamentary Involvement in European International Relations' in M. Cremona and B. De Witte (eds.), *EU Foreign Relations Law* (Oxford: Hart Publishing, 2008), pp. 203 and 230.

democratic debate, the consent requirement is potentially more effective than in domestic parliamentary systems because of the European Parliament's political autonomy from the Commission and the Council, which are the key actors when it comes to EU international agreements. He also usefully emphasises that while the US Congress possesses a constitutional right to amend individual provisions, multilateral bargaining tends to be successful only when Congress voluntarily decides not to utilise its amendment right.[14]

Regardless of the type of international agreement, the European Parliament must be immediately and fully informed at all stages of the procedure of conclusion of international agreements.[15] This is a significant requirement, because it enables MEPs to react promptly and try to impress their views on the EU negotiators prior to the conclusion of the agreement. However, the examples of the EU–US SWIFT Agreements and the multilateral Anti-Counterfeiting Trade Agreement (ACTA) show how apt executive EU institutions and agencies are in withholding information from the European Parliament.[16] Whether at the negotiation or implementation stages, the Council, the Commission and Europol resorted to various techniques to deny the European Parliament access to information that was necessary adequately to scrutinise the negotiation process. As Curtin demonstrates, these techniques included reliance on internal Council rules that classify the information sought by MEPs in such a way that access is precluded despite the provisions of the Treaties, as well invocation of the American classifying rules that require reciprocity in order to shield the information in question from public disclosure.[17]

Yet case-by-case activism by individual MEPs has led to litigations against EU institutions and certain gains in transparency of negotiations of EU international agreements. For example, on the very last day of 2009 MEP Sophie in't Veld of the Alliance of Liberals and Democrats for Europe brought an action against the Council of Ministers requesting access to an opinion of the Council's Legal Service on the legal basis for adopting a

[14] *Ibid.*, pp. 210–11. [15] Article 218(10) TFEU.

[16] M. Geist, 'The Trouble with the Anti-Counterfeiting Trade Agreement (ACTA)' (2010) 30 *The SAIS Review of International Affairs* 137–47, at 144–5. See also a brief reflection thereon in: V. Kreilinger, 'A Veto of the European Parliament Against ACTA Would Be a Way for MEPs to Reassert Themselves Against Member States', *LSE European Politics and Policy (EUROPP)*, available at: http://blogs.lse.ac.uk/europpblog/2012/04/16/acta-european-parliament-veto/.

[17] D. Curtin, 'Official Secrets and the Negotiation of International Agreements: Is the EU Executive Unbound?' (2013) 50 *Common Market Law Review* 423–57, at 449 and 453–4.

Council decision to authorise the opening of negotiations on the SWIFT Agreements.[18] In July 2010 she sought to annul the Commission's decision not to be granted full access to a range of documents related to the draft ACTA.[19] On both occasions she was partially successful.

On the whole, therefore, one may rightly speak of a parliamentary deficit in supranational decision-making in EU external relations.[20] As Eeckhout submits, the European Parliament's role in the conclusion of EU international agreements raises 'significant issues of legitimacy and democracy',[21] whereas in the field of CFSP, except for budgetary powers, MEPs enjoy no rights of genuine participation.[22] In any event, the European Parliament is at an institutional disadvantage compared to the Commission and the Council and, given that an increasing number of policies concern transnational matters, the question of democratic oversight of such policies becomes tangible. In a situation where interdependence between states is ever more pronounced and where dynamic political circumstances hamper democratic accountability, such a development needs to be addressed.

Nevertheless, despite interinstitutional rivalry and informal powerwresting,[23] MEPs proactively participate in the formulation of EU foreign policy. The European Parliament thereby seeks to build a distinct institutional identity in international affairs and to assert its competence both within the Union and worldwide.[24] As Bickerton argues, the

[18] Case T-529/09, *Sophie in't Veld* v. *Council of the European Union*, Judgment of the General Court (Fifth Chamber) of 4 May 2012. See further : H. Flavier, 'Accès aux documents et démocratisation de l'action extérieure de l'Union européenne' (2012) 2 *Revue des affaires européennes* 417–25. See also: *EUobserver*, 'Commission Pushes for Document Secrecy Despite Court Judgment' (8 May 2012), available at: http://euobserver.com/justice/116181, accessed 2 October 2013.

[19] Case T-301/10, *Sophie in't Veld* v. *European Commission*, Judgment of the General Court (Second Chamber) of 19 March 2013. See her personal reflection on transatlantic relations and security in Chapter 10 in this volume.

[20] D. Thym, 'Foreign Affairs' in Bogdandy and Bast (eds.), *Principles of European Constitutional Law*, p. 323.

[21] P. Eeckhout, *EU External Relations Law* (Oxford University Press, 2011), p. 194.

[22] P. Eeckhout, *Does Europe's Constitution Stop at the Water's Edge? Law and Policy in the EU's External Relations* (Groningen: Europa Law Publishing, 2005), p. 19.

[23] See for example: B. Crum, 'Parliamentarisation of the CFSP through Informal Institution-Making? The Fifth European Parliament and the EU High Representative' (2006) 13 *Journal of European Public Policy* 383–401; A. Maurer *et al.*, 'Interinstitutional Agremeents in the CFSP: Parliamentarisation through the Back Door?' (2005) 10 *European Foreign Affairs Review* 175–95.

[24] See the chapter by O. Costa and C. Dri, 'How Does the European Parliament Contribute to the Construction of EU's Interregional Dialogue' in F. Söderbaum *et al.* (eds.),

European Parliament's pursuit of a greater role in foreign affairs is driven by a desire to expand its influence within the EU policy-making process.[25] Concretely, he holds that:

> MEPs view foreign policy as a field where the EP can forge for itself a role that distinguishes it from both the Council and the Commission ... this is one of the ways in which the EP *understands* its own role and is one where it feels it has good chances of expanding its powers.[26]

In general, therefore, the limited formal powers of the European Parliament do not prevent its Members from using them 'imaginatively, providing a constant stream of resolutions and reports on all kinds of foreign policy questions'.[27] Similarly, it has been reported that the European Parliament's Committee for Foreign Affairs (AFET) 'contributes actively to the policy debate with various own-initiative reports on key aspects of European foreign policy'.[28] When it comes to EU international agreements in justice and home affairs matters, the European Parliament has displayed a 'constant interest in influencing the course of action in this field by adopting regular resolutions and recommendations emphasising the lack of democratic accountability of the JHA external dimension'.[29] This situation is especially valid in EU–US relations. It is precisely the international agreements in this area – such as the PNR (Passenger Name Record) and SWIFT agreements – that have in the recent years been the subject of much debate between the EU and the USA.[30] The negotiations on a PNR agreement have been appraised both as a transatlantic irritant and as an instance

Intersecting Interregionalism: Globalisation, New Regionalism, Multilateralism and the EU (London: Springer, 2013). See also: S. Santander, *Le régionalisme sud-américain, l'Union européenne et les Etats-Unis* (Brussels: Editions de l'Université de Bruxelles, 2008), p. 172.

[25] C. J. Bickerton, 'Functionality in EU Foreign Policy: Towards a New Research Agenda?' (2010) 32 *Journal of European Integration* 213–27, at 217.

[26] *Ibid.*, 220 (emphasis in original).

[27] G. de Baere, *Constitutional Principles of EU External Relations* (Oxford University Press, 2008), p. 166.

[28] D. Thym, 'Beyond Parliament's Reach? The Role of the European Parliament in the CFSP' (2006) 11 *European Foreign Affairs Review* 109–27, at 127.

[29] S. Wolff *et al.*, 'The External Dimension of Justice and Home Affairs: A Different Security Agenda for the EU?' (2009) 31 *Journal of European Integration* 9–24, at 14. See a more general appraisal of the parliamentary empowerment in this area in: E. de Capitani, 'The Evolving Role of the European Parliament in the AFSJ' in J. Monar (ed.), *The Institutional Dimension of the European Union's Area of Freedom, Security and Justice* (Brussels: P.I.E. Peter Lang, 2010), pp. 113–44.

[30] See more on this in Chapter 12 by Juan Santos Vara in this volume.

of the European Parliament's power struggle and identity-building.[31] For Cremona, the outcome of the transatlantic negotiations on the SWIFT Agreements is very positive for the European Parliament, because 'although the crafting of a compromise is in the hands of Commission and Council, the European Parliament will have the last word'.[32] Conversely, Fahey warns that, despite the consent power, the European Parliament's position has been weakened by the substantive result of the two agreements, because the governance mechanisms put in place are shrouded in secrecy and, as such, inhibit parliamentary oversight and accountability.[33] This necessity to intervene in defence of EU legislation and of the legitimate interests protected thereby makes the transatlantic partnership a potentially fertile soil for the European Parliament's 'muscle-flexing'.

It is plausible, therefore, that in order to enhance its lower profile in foreign affairs, the European Parliament generally engages on the international plane in a variety of multilateral and bilateral interparliamentary forums. These activities are often loosely termed 'parliamentary diplomacy' for their mimicking of intergovernmental negotiations. The pivotal international 'diplomatic' activity of the European Parliament concerns the development of relations with its American counterpart, the US Congress. There is barely any scholarly insight into the European Parliament's transatlantic actorship as an alternative avenue for the democratisation of EU external affairs and for an informal assertion or even expansion of its competences. Concomitantly, the European Parliament is actively involved in intra-EU parliamentary 'diplomacy' with the national parliaments of the Member States,[34] which arguably might also

[31] P. Pawlak, 'Transatlantic Homeland Security Cooperation: The Promise of New Modes of Governance in Global Affairs' (2010) 8 *Journal of Transatlantic Studies* 139–57, at 146.

[32] M. Cremona, 'Justice and Home Affairs in a Globalised World: Ambitions and Reality in the Tale of the EU–US SWIFT Agreement', *Working Paper No. 04/2011* (Austrian Academy of Social Sciences, Institute for European Integration Research, 2011), p. 27.

[33] E. Fahey, 'Law and Governance as Checks and Balances in Transatlantic Security: Rights, Redress and Remedies in EU–US Passenger Name Records and the Terrorist Finance Tracking Program' (2013) 32 *Yearbook of European Law* 368–88, at 371.

[34] Some authors refer to this as international networking. See: T. Raunio, 'From the Margins of European Integration to the Guardians of the Treaties? The Role of National Parliaments in the EU' in S. Kröger and D. Friedrich (eds.), *The Challenge of Democratic Representation in the European Union* (Basingstoke: Palgrave Macmillan, 2012), p. 180. Yet it is arguable whether this is a precise appellation for this type of interparliamentary contact, because activities internal to the EU are labelled 'international', whereas 'international' should better be applied to activities directed to the world outside the Union's borders.

contribute to the enhancement of the European Parliament's position in EU foreign affairs by equipping MEPs with additional support from domestic parliamentarians where their views converge.

Against this background, this chapter carries out a fourfold analysis. First, we conduct a theoretical conceptualisation of the international activities of the European Parliament that fall under the politico-legal phenomenon of 'parliamentary diplomacy', because the bulk of transatlantic interparliamentary collaboration substantively falls under this category. We adumbrate the origins of this phenomenon, define its modern meaning and sketch the legal basis for the international activity of the European Parliament. Second, we inquire about the legal and institutional framework for the European Parliament's cooperation with the Congress of the United States, as the EU's key strategic partner. Not only do we examine the way transatlantic interparliamentary relations were formalised, we also analyse the prerogatives and outreach of the Transatlantic Legislators' Dialogue as the main format for transatlantic parliamentarism. Third, we inquire whether forums for the European Parliament's collaboration with national parliaments, such as the Interparliamentary Conference for CFSP and CSDP and, much less so, COSAC as the Conference of European Affairs Committees can add any value in shaping EU parliamentary input in Euro-American relations. These intra-EU interparliamentary forums are assessed in order to paint a broader picture of the scope of the European Parliament's actorship towards the United States. Fourth, we analyse the incentives and disincentives for the 'diplomatic' activities of the European Parliament in general and towards the United States in particular. Based on this, we conclude with several observations on the possible consequences of the European Parliament's 'diplomatic' action across the Atlantic for its standing within the Union's constitutional order. It is submitted in this chapter that the political practice of transatlantic parliamentarism contributes to an informal, incremental shaping of the European Parliament's legal competences in foreign affairs. This argument views MEPs' external actions as part of the EU's living constitution, whereby the meaning, content and exercise of foreign affairs powers evolve over time closer or farther away from their written fundament.[35]

[35] See the juridico-constitutional perspective on various aspects of the EU's living constitution in: D. Curtin, *Executive Power of the European Union: Law, Practices, and the Living Constitution* (Oxford University Press, 2009). See the political science approach to this in: S. Gustavsson, 'The Living Constitution of the EU' in B. Kochler-Koch and F. Larat (eds.), *Efficient and Democratic Goverance in the European Union*, CONNEX Report Series Vol. 9 (University of Mannheim, Centre for European Social Research, 2008), pp. 325–38. See

2 Parliamentary diplomacy as an international politico-legal phenomenon

2.1 Origin and notion of parliamentary diplomacy

Coined in the mid 1950s by Dean Rusk, the US Secretary of State to Presidents John F. Kennedy and Lyndon B. Johnson, the phrase 'parliamentary diplomacy' was originally used to refer to international multilateral diplomatic negotiations proper. The adjective 'parliamentary' was used to denote the use of procedures that were redolent of those typically used in parliamentary chambers, such as those governing the process of debate and adoption of formal conclusions.[36] Parliamentary diplomacy sprung into use in the context of the United Nations.[37] The phrase is rooted in the then novel conference diplomacy method of intergovernmental negotiation. In that period, parliamentary diplomacy therefore related to interstate relations and not to relations between parliaments.[38] What mattered more was the 'diplomacy' element and not the 'parliamentary' one. Even so, Dag Hammarskjöld – a Swedish diplomat, the second UN Secretary-General and a posthumous Nobel Peace Prize winner – emphasised in 1958 that this phenomenon was partially aimed at introducing democratic procedures in the field of international politics.[39]

an American perspective in: B. Ackerman, 'The Living Constitution' (2007) 120 *Harvard Law Review* 1,738–812.

[36] D. Rusk, 'Parliamentary Diplomacy – Debate vs. Negotiation' (1955) 26 *World Affairs Interpreter* 121–2. See also: C. W. Freeman Jr, *The Diplomat's Dictionary* (Washington, DC: National Defense University Press, 1994), pp. 104–5.

[37] P. C. Jessup, 'Parliamentary Diplomacy: An Examination of the Legal Quality of the Rules of Procedure of Organs of the United Nations' (1956) 89 *Recueil des Cours de l'Académie de Droit International de La Haye* 181–320, at 185. Essentially, parliamentary diplomacy in this context was described as a 'new process which involves nations with widely differing goals in activity formally organised as a continuing system of regulated debate. The United Nations provides the only forum in which admittedly hostile nations repeatedly meet in debate over the widest imaginable range of topics. This debate is ostensibly meant to produce statements of joint intent in a form that is appropriate for a public vote.' N. Rosenbaum, 'Cyprus and the United Nations: An Appreciation of Parliamentary Diplomacy' (1967) 33 *Canadian Journal of Economics and Political Science* 218–31, at 218. See also the description of the UN as 'a world centre for diplomatic communication, both as an agency of parliamentary diplomacy and as "the world's greatest switchboard for bilateral diplomacy"'. R. E. Riggs, 'The United Nations as an Influence on United States Policy' (1967) 11 *International Studies Quarterly* 91–109, at 100.

[38] See further in: K. W. Thompson, 'The New Diplomacy and the Quest for Peace' (1965) 19 *International Organization* 394–409.

[39] S. D. Bailey, 'Parliamentary Diplomacy' (1962) 16 *Parliamentary Affairs* 308–14, at 310.

A more contemporary meaning of parliamentary diplomacy relates to a significant growth in the number of international or transnational parliamentary bodies and a generally increased parliamentary input in global affairs. As explained by Stavridis, these developments were catalysed chiefly by four processes: (a) the democratisation of politics; (b) the domestication of foreign policy; (c) the European integration process; and (d) a rapid technological advancement.[40] The blurring of the traditional divide between domestic and foreign policy-making was particularly propelled by the post-Second World War integration process in Western Europe, which now encompasses almost the entire European continent. With the Internet becoming not only the most important means of communication but also a fundamental right of citizens,[41] democracy and parliamentary affairs have acquired a device for borderless deliberation and collaboration. Certainly, these considerations neither neglect nor deny the thesis of a widespread parliamentary decline and the notorious assumption that foreign policy and parliamentary process do not make good bedfellows due to the necessity of urgent and secret decision-making.[42]

Conceptually, parliamentary diplomacy has a rather broad catchment area and includes a variety of international activities by various parliamentary actors (individual parliamentarians, political parties and parliaments as a whole) at various levels (intrastate, interstate, intraregional, interregional and international).[43] This aspect of parliamentary work has unjustifiably been neglected by many scholars dealing with EU democracy. As Thym argues:

> The European Parliament has always played a genuine role in foreign policy independently of its information, consultation and control rights … Its impact on the real world is reinforced … by the projection of a tentative 'parliamentary diplomacy' in its own right through the public debate

[40] S. Stavridis, '"Parliamentary Diplomacy": Some Preliminary Findings', *Jean Monnet Working Papers in Comparative and International Politics No. 48* (University of Catania, 2002).

[41] See more in this respect: D. Jančić, 'The European Political Order and Internet Piracy: Accidental or Paradigmatic Constitution-Shaping?' (2010) 6 *European Constitutional Law Review* 430–61.

[42] See for instance: D. Chryssochoou *et al.*, 'European Democracy, Parliamentary Decline and the "Democratic Deficit" of the European Union' (1998) 4 *Journal of Legislative Studies* 109–29; D. Pélassy, 'Le déclin du parlement en Europe' in C. Flinterman *et al.* (eds.), *The Evolving Role of Parliaments in Europe* (Antwerp/Apeldoorn: Maklu Uitgevers, 1994), pp. 55–71.

[43] D. Fiott, 'On the Value of Parliamentary Diplomacy', (2011) 4 *Madariaga Paper 7*, 2.

of important foreign policy developments and periodic contact with representatives of third countries and international organisations.[44]

One of the key components of parliamentary diplomacy, however, is the participation of parliamentarians in transnational parliamentary bodies. These bodies can be both of a bilateral nature and of a multilateral nature. Perhaps the most notable example of a bilateral international parliamentary body is the Transatlantic Legislators' Dialogue, analysed in greater detail below. Multilateral international parliamentary bodies mainly take the form of assemblies. These assemblies may belong to an already established international organisation or they may exist as independent institutions. The assemblies of international organisations have been described by Walker as instances of 'transnational parliamentarianism'.[45] Examples thereof include Parlasur, which is the Parliament of Mercosur (Mercado Común del Sur, that is the Southern Common Market), the Parliamentary Assembly of the Council of Europe[46] and the Pan-African Parliament of the African Union.[47] Examples of independently existing international parliamentary assemblies include Parlatino (Latin American Parliament) and EuroLat (Euro-Latin American Parliamentary Assembly). Yet parliamentary diplomacy also includes more or less formalised visits by parliamentary delegations to parliaments and other national or international institutions, missions of parliamentarians abroad, involvement in the monitoring of elections in third countries, conflict prevention, crisis management, mediation and so on.[48]

Parliamentary diplomacy is thus a multifaceted concept and its outreach is virtually boundless. Yet rather than giving birth to a wholly new constitutional function, parliamentary diplomacy is best defined as a collection of parliamentary activities catalysing, facilitating and strengthening the existing constitutional functions of parliaments through dialogues between peers on countless open policy questions across continents and levels of governance. Frans Weisglas, a former Speaker of the

44 Thym, 'Parliamentary Involvement in European International Relations', p. 225.

45 N. Walker, 'Postnational Constitutionalism and Postnational Public Law: A Tale of Two Neologisms' (2012) 3 *Transnational Legal Theory* 61–85, at 80.

46 There is an explicit provision in the European Parliament's Rules of Procedure (Rule 199) stating that its bodies, particularly the committeess, shall cooperate with their counterparts in the Council of Europe Parliamentary Assembly in fields of mutual interest in order to improve the efficiency of their work and avoid duplication of effort.

47 The Pan-African Parliament should not be confused with the Assembly of the Union, which is the supreme organ of the African Union composed of Heads of State and governments. See Article 6(1)–(2) of the Constitutive Act of the African Union.

48 Stavridis, "Parliamentary Diplomacy".

Dutch Lower House (Tweede Kamer), has argued that these international activities of parliamentarians primarily facilitate the democratic scrutiny of national governments in the respective parliaments.[49]

The democratic element of parliamentary diplomacy is of particular importance, especially within the EU context, because the international action of European parliamentarians could bolster their position in interinstitutional horse-trading with the Commission and the Council. Equally, 'closer diplomatic strategising' between the European External Action Service and the EU's High Representative with MEPs may add democratic legitimacy to EU foreign affairs.[50] The European Parliament's diplomacy carries weight thanks to its institutional and electoral legitimacy, which enables it to conduct external affairs as a foreign policy actor in its own right.[51] It is precisely independent action outside the framework of traditional intergovernmental diplomacy and free of government constraints and political party discipline that lends parliamentary diplomacy strength and credence.[52] In EU–US relations in particular, prior discussion and analysis of contentious matters of mutual concern might result in information and knowledge that MEPs could utilise to corroborate their stance and increase their clout regarding both the EU's international agreements with the USA and secondary EU law that significantly impacts the USA.

2.2 Legal basis for the European Parliament's international 'diplomatic' action

The EU treaties do not provide a specific legal basis for the international 'diplomatic' activity of the European Parliament. Nonetheless, the legal basis indirectly lies in Article 21 of the EU Treaty via the general principles of the international action of the EU as a whole. The provisions laid down in this Article state inter alia that the Union's international action shall be guided by the principles that have inspired its own creation and development, and that the Union seeks to advance these principles in the wider world. Further, it is explicitly prescribed that the EU shall seek to develop relations and build partnerships with third countries and

[49] F. W. Weisglas and G. de Boer, 'Parliamentary Diplomacy' (2007) 2 *Hague Journal of Diplomacy* 93–9, at 94.

[50] Fiott, 'On the Value of Parliamentary Diplomacy', 6.

[51] Thym, 'Parliamentary Involvement in European International Relations', pp. 226 and 232.

[52] Fiott, 'On the Value of Parliamentary Diplomacy', 4.

international, regional or global organisations that share these principles. The list of general principles and objectives of EU external action is extensive and ranges from protecting the Union's own security and integrity to preserving international peace and development to strengthening global governance.[53]

The objective of the European Parliament's action as an autonomous 'diplomatic' player on the global scene is both to foster the democratic element of EU international relations and to promote values on which the EU is based. These values are laid down in the EU founding treaties and primarily include human dignity, freedom, democracy, equality, respect for human rights and the rule of law.[54] To these ends, the European Parliament has formed numerous delegations. Their members are elected by the European Parliament on a proposal from the Conference of Presidents soon after the re-election of Parliament for the duration of the parliamentary term.[55] Delegations should ensure a fair representation of the Member States and political views.[56] A total of forty European Parliament delegations are classified into four categories: delegations to parliamentary assemblies; delegations to joint parliamentary committees; delegations to parliamentary cooperation committees; and delegations for relations with third countries and external entities.[57] The last category includes the Delegation for Relations with the United States. The Delegation currently has fifty-three members and is chaired by Christian Ehler, a German member of the European People's Party.

[53] Article 21(2) TEU reads: 'The Union shall define and pursue common policies and actions, and shall work for a high degree of cooperation in all fields of international relations, in order to: (a) safeguard its values, fundamental interests, security, independence and integrity; (b) consolidate and support democracy, the rule of law, human rights and the principles of international law; (c) preserve peace, prevent conflicts and strengthen international security, in accordance with the purposes and principles of the United Nations Charter, with the principles of the Helsinki Final Act and with the aims of the Charter of Paris, including those relating to external borders; (d) foster the sustainable economic, social and environmental development of developing countries, with the primary aim of eradicating poverty; (e) encourage the integration of all countries into the world economy, including through the progressive abolition of restrictions on international trade; (f) help develop international measures to preserve and improve the quality of the environment and the sustainable management of global natural resources, in order to ensure sustainable development; (g) assist populations, countries and regions confronting natural or man-made disasters; and (h) promote an international system based on stronger multilateral cooperation and good global governance.'

[54] Article 2 TEU.

[55] Rule 198(1) of the Rules of Procedure of the European Parliament.

[56] Rule 198(2) of the Rules of Procedure of the European Parliament.

[57] See: www.europarl.europa.eu/delegations/en/home.html, accessed 30 August 2013.

For lack of an explicit legal basis in the treaties or in an international agreement, EU–US relations in the parliamentary sphere can optimally be typified as indices of parliamentary diplomacy. As we demonstrate under the following headings, transatlantic interparliamentary cooperation is institutionally and procedurally structured, which permits the adoption of mutually agreed conclusions.

3 The European Parliament and the US Congress: a budding relationship or reluctant dialogue?

3.1 Transatlantic parliamentarism formalised

While the EU and the USA have maintained diplomatic relations since 1953, these were only formalised in November 1990 with the adoption of the Transatlantic Declaration on EC–US Relations.[58] This document set outs the goals, principles and institutional framework pertaining to transatlantic cooperation and identifies transnational areas that pose both common and global threats, such as terrorism, production and trafficking of narcotics, international crime, environment deterioration, and the proliferation of nuclear, biological and chemical weapons. It ought to be underlined that joint Euro-American aspirations greatly exceed bilateralism. As the Declaration mandates, the EU and the USA also share responsibility to 'face transnational challenges affecting the well-being of all mankind' not least through democracy and human rights promotion worldwide, safeguarding of peace and international security, and support of the achievement of a sound world economy based on market principles.

The central principle on which EU–US cooperation is based is that of mutual information and consultation on important political and economic matters of common interest so as to bring their positions as close as possible, also in international bodies. According to the Transatlantic Declaration, 'regular and intensive' consultations are to be achieved through several channels: (a) biannual consultations between the

[58] See more in: H. G. Krenzler and W. Kaiser, 'The Transatlantic Declaration: A New Basis for Relations between EC and US' (1991) 42 *Außenpolitik: German Foreign Affairs Review* 363–72. On the various aspects of the development of transatlantic cooperation see: M. Pollack and G. Shaffer (eds.), *Transatlantic Governance in the Global Economy* (Lanham, MD: Rowman & Littlefield, 2001); M. Pollack *et al.*, *The Political Economy of the Transatlantic Partnership*, EUI Report (Florence: Robert Schuman Centre for Advanced Studies, 2003), available at: www.eui.eu/Documents/RSCAS/e-texts/200306HMTMvFReport.pdf, accessed 7 February 2014.

Presidents of the European Council and the Commission on the one hand, and the US President on the other (EU–US summits); (b) biannual consultations between the foreign affairs ministers of the Member States and the Commission, on the one hand, and the US Secretary of State, on the other; (c) ad hoc consultations between the foreign affairs minister of the EU Member State holding the Presidency and the US Secretary of State; (d) biannual consultations between the Commission and the US Government at the Cabinet level; and (e) briefings by the EU Presidency to US representatives on CFSP at the ministerial level. Importantly, the Declaration mentions transatlantic interparliamentary relations insofar as it welcomes 'the actions taken by the European Parliament and the Congress of the United States in order to improve their dialogue and thereby bring closer together the peoples on both sides of the Atlantic'.[59] The EU and US officials are therefore cognisant of the necessity to improve the democratic aspect of their polities' partnership.[60]

These intergovernmental arrangements were further solidified and complemented on 3 December 1995, when the second biannual EU–US summit adopted the New Transatlantic Agenda (NTA).[61] This document places strong emphasis on the upgrade of security cooperation and tackling global challenges. Besides this, the Agenda also underlines the wish of both sides to further develop mutual trade and investment relations by building a New Transatlantic Marketplace so as to facilitate the flow of goods, services and capital across the Atlantic. Following up on the aforesaid Declaration, the Agenda attached 'great importance to enhanced parliamentary links' and called for discussions with parliamentary leaders on establishing consultative mechanisms. Unlike the Declaration, the Agenda contained a comprehensive Joint EU–US Action Plan in order to implement the action devised.[62] However, this Action Plan did not specify how transatlantic parliamentary links were to be boosted. Soon afterwards, however, it was agreed to establish a transnational EU–US interparliamentary body called the Transatlantic Legislators' Dialogue, which we analyse in the next section.

[59] Transatlantic Declaration of 1990, last sentence.

[60] See more in Chapter 9 by Marija Bartl and Elaine Fahey in this volume.

[61] See commentaries in: H. G. Krenzler and A. Schomaker, 'A New Transatlantic Agenda' (1996) 1 *European Foreign Affairs Review* 9–28; J. van Oudenaren, 'The New Transatlantic Agenda' (1996) 51 *Internationale Politik* 49–52; A. L. Gardner, *A New Era in US-EU Relations? The Clinton Administration and the New Transatlantic Agenda* (Aldershot: Avebury, 1997).

[62] See the Action Plan reproduced in: *Foreign Policy Bulletin* 7 (1996) 109–16.

Three years after the NTA, the Transatlantic Economic Partnership (TEP) was established following the EU–US Summit of 18 May 1998 in order to intensify and broaden both bilateral and multilateral cooperation in trade and investment. The Action Plan that was drafted to give life to this Partnership inter alia stated that the EU and the USA give 'active and full support to the current efforts of the European Parliament and the US Congress to increase their cooperation on TEP-related issues and to contribute to the TEP process'. Following the terrorist attacks of 11 September 2001, parliamentary participation in the prevention of international terrorism became increasingly significant in an otherwise heightened need for transatlantic cooperation in tackling urgent transnational challenges that directly impinge on the quality of life of the citizens.[63] The necessity to protect not only the citizens' lives but also their privacy and personal data led to much advocacy by the European Parliament in favour of safeguarding these values, which continued in the decade that followed.[64]

The culmination of transatlantic cooperation in the economic field is the start on 8–12 July 2013 of negotiations on an EU–US international agreement aimed at creating a free trade area between the two polities, commonly referred to as the Transatlantic Trade and Investment Partnership (TTIP).[65] The role of the European Parliament was stressed months before this, when the European Commissioner for Trade, Karel de Gucht, in a speech to the Committee for International Trade in February 2013, emphasised the importance of this institution and assured MEPs that the negotiation parameters that they had issued the year before

[63] See further in: D. Dubois, 'The Attacks of 11 September: EU–US Cooperation Against Terrorism in the Field of Justice and Home Affairs' (2002) 7 *European Foreign Affairs Review* 317–35; W. Rees, 'EU–US Cooperation on Counter-Terrorism and the Internationalisation of Law Enforcement' in M. Cremona *et al.* (eds.), *The External Dimension of the European Union's Area of Freedom, Security and Justice* (Brussels: P.I.E. Peter Lang, 2011), pp. 389–408.

[64] See, for instance, its participation in the conclusion of the EU–US PNR Agremeents and its consequences in: Fahey, 'Law and Governance as Checks and Balances in Transatlantic Security'; V. Papakonstantinou and P. de Hert, 'The PNR Agreement and Transatlantic Anti-Terrorism Cooperation: No Firm Human Rights Framework on Either Side of the Atlantic' (2009) 46 *Common Market Law Review* 885–919; M. Nino, 'The Protection of Personal Data in the Fight Against Terrorism: New Perspectives of PNR European Union Instruments in the Light of the Treaty of Lisbon' (2010) 6 *Utrecht Law Review* 62–85.

[65] See an analysis thereof in: G. Felbermayr *et al.*, 'Transatlantic Trade and Investment Partnership (TTIP): Who Benefits from a Free Trade Deal?', *Bertelsmann Stiftung* (2013); G. Felbermayr and M. Larch, 'The Transatlantic Trade and Investment Partnership (TTIP): Potentials, Problems and Perspectives' (2012) 14 *CESifo Forum* 49–60. See also Chapter 9 by Marija Bartl and Elaine Fahey in this volume.

found their way into the final report of the High-Level Working Group.[66] Yet again, the European Parliament very vocally expressed its views on TTIP early on in the negotiation process. While strongly supporting the essence of this agreement, MEPs called for the exclusion of cultural and audiovisual services from it.[67] The European Parliament also confirmed its commitment to taking a 'proactive role in collaborating with its US counterparts when introducing new regulations'.[68] Several weeks later, reacting to the revelations of unauthorised surveillance and online espionage of EU citizens and institutions by the US National Security Agency through its PRISM program, the European Parliament took a bold stance by threatening that such activities might jeopardise the establishment of TTIP and lead to the suspension of the PNR and SWIFT Agreements.[69]

These considerations testify to an intensified parliamentary implication in international negotiations between the EU and the USA. This is a trend that is likely to grow, especially given the impetus, albeit not full-blown powers, that the Treaty of Lisbon injected to democratic participation in EU external relations.

3.2 *Transatlantic Legislators' Dialogue and European Parliament links with other forums for transatlantic cooperation*

The Transatlantic Declaration and the New Transatlantic Agenda both acknowledge the long tradition of biannual EU–US interparliamentary meetings, which were set out in 1972 when a delegation of the US Congress first visited the European Parliament. It was on 15–16 January 1999, on the occasion of the fiftieth interparliamentary meeting, that the EU and US delegations decided to set up a Transatlantic Legislators' Dialogue in order to implement the call made four years before to enhance transatlantic

[66] Speech by Karel de Gucht of 21 February 2013, 'Transatlantic Trade and Investment Partnership: Opening Free Trade Negotiations with the United States', doc. no. SPEECH/13/147, p. 2, available at: http://trade.ec.europa.eu/doclib/docs/2013/february/tradoc_150581.pdf, accessed 4 October 2013.

[67] European Parliament, Resolution of 23 May 2013 on EU Trade and Investment Negotiations with the United States of America, doc. no. P7_TA(2013)0227, point 11.

[68] *Ibid.*, point 23.

[69] European Parliament, Resolution of 4 July 2013 on the US National Security Agency Surveillance Programme, Surveillance Bodies in Various Member States and Their Impact on EU Citizens' Privacy, doc. no. P7_TA(2013)0322, recital K and point 4. European Parliament Resolution of 23 October 2013 on the Suspension of the TFTP Agreement as a Result of US National Security Agency Surveillance (2013/2831(RSP)).

parliamentary ties. The Transatlantic Legislators' Dialogue was designed so as to add a 'new level of democratic oversight to the expanding transatlantic relationship',[70] develop harmonised approaches to issues of common interest and prevent disputes in sensitive areas. This could 'facilitate agreement in the larger international context', for instance in the fields of energy and climate change.[71]

To all these ends, the Transatlantic Legislators' Dialogue gathers together the EU and US parliamentary delegations and while, as we have seen, the European Parliament has a large number of delegations, the US Delegation is only one of three such delegations, the other two covering relations with Canada and Mexico. The US Congressional Delegation is typically composed of Members of the House of Representatives, so Senators usually do not take part in it.[72] The chairpersons of the two delegations are co-chairs of the Dialogue. Within the European Parliament a Steering Committee has been created with the purpose of 'strengthening parliamentary supervision in the areas covered by the New Transatlantic Agenda and promoting timely consultation of parliamentary committees'.[73] The Steering Committee assures a wide representation of European Parliament committees and is co-chaired by the chairmen of the Delegation for Relations with the US and of the Committee on Foreign Affairs.[74] Further, the EU and US parliamentary delegations ought to appoint committee liaison persons among their members to keep abreast of legislative developments at the committee level and facilitate early intervention in order to avoid disputes. In 2011 the two delegations agreed

[70] Transatlantic Legislators' Dialogue, Joint Statement of the 50th Interparliamentary Meeting, Strasbourg, 15–16 January 1999.

[71] Transatlantic Legislators' Dialogue, Joint Statement of the 68th Interparliamentary Meeting, Madrid, 3–6 June 2010.

[72] See: www.europarl.europa.eu/intcoop/tld/what_is/history_en.htm, accessed 30 August 2013.

[73] European Parliament, Terms of Reference and Composition of the Transatlantic Legislators' Dialogue Steering Committee, Conference of Presidents Decisions of 16 September 1999, 2 May 2000, 18 May 2000 and 6 July 2000.

[74] The other members of the Steering Committee are the members of the Bureau of the US Delegation, the Chairman of the European Parliament's Conference of Committee Chairmen and the chairmen of the following European Parliament committees: the Committee on Foreign Affairs; the Committee on Industry, External Trade, Research and Energy; the Committee on Agriculture and Rural Development; the Committee on Civil Liberties, Justice and Home Affairs; the Committee on International Trade; the Committee on Economic and Monetary Affairs; the Committee on the Environment, Public Health and Food Safety; the Committee on the Internal Market and Consumer Protection; the Committee on Transport and Tourism; and the Committee on Culture and Education.

that working groups should be established within the Dialogue on both sides of the Atlantic to carry out preparatory work on two focus areas: financial markets and stability, and transport security. Other focus areas include agriculture and food safety as well as cybersecurity.[75]

The work of the Dialogue is organised chiefly through biannual personal meetings between the two parliamentary delegations, on which occasions they are received at the highest levels of both EU and US executive institutions. These biannual full delegation meetings are complemented by continuous consultations by means of videoconferences, workshops on themes of common interest and direct committee-to-committee exchanges of views.[76] Notably, the two delegations should each maintain contact twice a year with members of the Senior-Level Group, which is a body that prepares EU–US summits. This is an important channel for MEPs and Congress members to bring matters of special interest to the attention of the executive officials who attend these intergovernmental summits and thus attempt to have a degree of influence on the summitry process.

Yet the Transatlantic Legislators' Dialogue is not the only institutionalised forum for EU–US cooperation. The other dialogues between the EU and the USA are: the Transatlantic Economic Council (TAEC), the Transatlantic Business Council (TABC), the Transatlantic Labour Dialogue,[77] the Transatlantic Consumer Dialogue,[78] the EU–US Financial Markets Regulatory Dialogue,[79] the EU–US Development

[75] Transatlantic Legislators' Dialogue, Joint Statement of the 71st Interparliamentary Meeting, Jacksonville, 2–4 December 2011 and of the 72nd Interparliamentary Meeting, Copenhagen/Strasbourg 9–11 June 2012. On the divergences between EU and US regulation in this area see: M. Pollack and G. Shaffer, 'The Challenge of Reconciling Regulatory Differences: Food Safety and GMOs in the Transatlantic Relationship' in Pollack and Shaffer (eds.), *Transatlantic Governance in the Global Economy*, pp. 153–78.

[76] See: www.europarl.europa.eu/intcoop/tld/default_en.htm, accessed 4 October 2013.

[77] Established in 2001. See more in: J. Knauss and D. Trubek, 'The Transatlantic Labour Dialogue: Minimal Action in a Weak Structure' in Pollack and Shaffer (eds.), *Transatlantic Governance in the Global Economy*, pp. 235–54.

[78] Established in 1998. See: www.tacd.org, accessed 7 October 2013.

[79] Established in 2012. See more in: H.-J. Hellwig, 'The Transatlantic Financial Markets Regulatory Dialogue' in K. J. Hopt *et al.* (eds.), *Corporate Governance in Context: Corporations, States, and Markets in Europe, Japan, and the US* (Oxford University Press, 2005), pp. 363–79. This author underlines that although EU–US cooperation in this field is conducted between the respective executive branches, the European Parliament and the US House of Representatives are 'internally included' in this dialogue through their respective committees (p. 374).

Dialogue,[80] the EU–US Education Policy Forum,[81] the EU–US Energy Council,[82] the EU–US Task Force on Biotechnology Research,[83] the EU–US Insurance Regulatory Dialogue,[84] and a range of unofficial dialogues that are not government-sponsored, such as the Transatlantic Policy Network, the Transatlantic Dialogue on Sustainable Development, the Transatlantic Dialogue of Aviation and Climate Change, and the Transatlantic Donors Dialogue.[85] Of all of these more or less structured frameworks for policy collaboration, EU–US dialogues in the areas of business and biotechnological research are the most wide-ranging and most successful, whereas the dialogue between American and European legislators is expanding its scope but, as we will see, still has limited policy influence. We show below how the Transatlantic Legislators' Dialogue liaises with other EU–US dialogues, such as TAEC and TABC.

The Transatlantic Legislators' Dialogue is linked with the Transatlantic Economic Council, which was established by the EU–US Summit of 30 April 2007 to oversee, support and accelerate the accomplishment of common economic goals of the EU and the USA in a variety of sectors.[86] This Council gathers members of the European Commission and the US Cabinet who are in charge of a given policy area. The Council is also assisted by a Group of Advisers, which is composed of co-chairs of the three main transatlantic dialogues: the Transatlantic Business Dialogue,

[80] Relaunched in 2009. See more in: A. Gaus and W. Hoxtell, 'The EU–US Development Dialogue: Past, Present and Future', *Working Paper* (Berlin: Global Public Policy Institute, 2013), available at: www.gppi.net/fileadmin/media/pub/2013/gaus-hoxtell_2013_TCSD-working-paper_backgrounder.pdf, accessed 7 October 2013.

[81] Established in 2009. See more in: U. Kriebernegg, *The Transatlantic Dialogue on Higher Education: An Analysis of Cultural Narratives* (Berlin: Logos Verlag, 2011).

[82] Established in 2009. See the EU–US Summit document on its creation: http://eeas.europa.eu/us/sum11_09/docs/energy_en.pdf, accessed 7 October 2013.

[83] Established in 1990. See: http://ec.europa.eu/research/biotechnology/eu-us-task-force/index_en.cfm, accessed 7 October 2013.

[84] Established in 2012. See its five-year programme in: 'EU–US Dialogue Project: The Way Forward: Objectives and Initiatives for the Future', available at: https://eiopa.europa.eu/fileadmin/tx_dam/files/publications/protocols/EU_US_Dialogue_Project_The_Way_Forward_December_2012.pdf, accessed 7 October 2013.

[85] See more on the unofficial dialogues in: F. Bignami and S. Charnovitz, 'Transatlantic Civil Society Dialogues' in Pollack and Shaffer (eds.), *Transatlantic Governance in the Global Economy*, pp. 274–5.

[86] EU–US Summit, 'Framework for Advancing Transatlantic Economic Integration between the United States of America and the European Union', Part IV. Available at: http://ec.europa.eu/enterprise/policies/international/files/tec_framework_en.pdf, accessed 30 August 2013.

the Transatlantic Consumers' Dialogue and the Transatlantic Legislators' Dialogue. In this way the European Parliament can have a say, albeit minor, in the shaping of the regulatory landscape that governs EU–US economic relations.

Another channel whereby MEPs seek to assert their views in transatlantic relations is that of informal visits by European Parliament delegations to the Transatlantic Business Council, which is a business association of some seventy multinational companies that are headquartered both on American and European soil.[87] This Council, which is chiefly composed of CEOs of these companies, was established on 1 January 2013 by a merger between the Transatlantic Business Dialogue and the European-American Business Council. Since the establishment of TABC, European Parliament personnel have rather actively sought to liaise with its members at different levels.[88] Several examples illustrate this. For instance, in March 2013 MEP Malcolm Harbour, Chair of the European Parliament's Committee on the Internal Market and Consumer Protection, met TABC representatives in Brussels at the margins of the Data Protection Forum to discuss this thorny policy area in transatlantic relations. In April 2013 a ten-strong European Parliament delegation led by MEP Vital Moreira, Chair of the European Parliament's International Trade Committee and Standing Rapporteur for the USA, held a meeting in Washington DC with TABC members to discuss the TTIP and related regulatory issues. A few months later, in July 2013, a high-level delegation of the European Parliament's Economic and Monetary Affairs Committee – composed of fifteen MEPs, advisors, coordinators, administrators and liaison officers – visited TABC in order to exchange views on the inclusion of financial services in the TTIP, which was broadly endorsed by both sides. About a fortnight later, a cross-committee delegation of ten European Parliament staff, who are experts in fields such as intellectual property, telecommunications, aviation and energy efficiency, met with TABC members to analyse the TTIP process and, significantly, ways in which the US Congress could be lobbied.

These examples unveil the informal channels in which European Parliament members and staff seek to gather information about transatlantic policy-making other than through EU institutions with which they

[87] See more in: M. G. Cowles, 'The Transatlantic Business Dialogue: Transforming the New Transatlantic Dialogue' in Pollack and Shaffer (eds.), *Transatlantic Governance in the Global Economy*, pp. 213–34. See another view on this in Chapter 9 by Marija Bartl and Elaine Fahey in this volume.

[88] See: http://transatlanticbusiness.org/past-events/, accessed 30 August 2013.

have a 'constitutional' nexus. They thereby also express the European Parliament's stance on contentious issues so as to gain insight into where the EU and the US positions conflict and whether these could be reconciled through *ex ante* deliberations. Another way for MEPs to 'access' members of the US Congress and Administration is through its Liaison Office.

3.3 *European Parliament Liaison Office*

To provide further support to transatlantic interparliamentarism, on 29 April 2010 Jerzy Buzek, the then President of the European Parliament, officially opened this institution's first ever overseas representation – the Liaison Office in Washington DC. Apart from its Head, the Office comprises EU staffers and policy experts. The principal role of this Office is to maintain regular contact with American lawmakers and legislative staffers on issues requiring political cooperation so as to secure an independent voice for MEPs in the US Congress. In fact, in trying to gain international recognition of the European Parliament's stature, the Liaison Office arguably seeks to send the message that 'in many respects – separation of powers, oversight of the executive – the European Parliament is more akin to the US Congress than it is to a parliament of a European state'.[89]

Other functions of the Liaison Office are to: (a) promote joint legislative planning and a joint legislative early warning system; (b) identify issues of mutual interest, monitor US legislative activity and relay information about it between the two sides; (c) assist visits by MEPs; and (d) reinforce cooperation with the EU Delegation in Washington DC so as to aid information exchange and transatlantic policy-making.[90]

The current President of the European Parliament, Martin Schulz, described the added value of this Office in the following words: 'This exercise has already proved to be a success, with more intensive contacts at all levels, a broader understanding of how things work and improved two-way information flow.'[91] Given that adequate and timely information

[89] G. Martin, 'European Parliament Inaugurates Its Own Liaison Office in Washington', *European Affairs* (2010), available at: www.europeaninstitute.org/April-May-2010/european-parliament-inaugurates-its-own-liaison-office-in-washington.html, accessed 15 March 2012.

[90] See: www.europarl.europa.eu/us/en/Resources.html, accessed 4 October 2013.

[91] See: www.europarl.europa.eu/us/en/parliamentary_dialogue/greetings2.html, accessed 4 October 2013.

is crucial to effective decision-making, this Office has the potential significantly to facilitate the EU–US interparliamentary dialogue.

3.4 *Transatlanticism in the parliamentary field: reaping the benefits*

3.4.1 Incentivising transnational parliamentarism in general

The challenge of involving democratically elected representatives in diplomatic negotiations and legislative dialogues between states and international and regional organisations is a global one, because this type of activity remains insufficiently attractive for them in terms of benefits of engaging in it. However, the involvement of parliaments in dialogues that cross the competence boundaries of their own legal systems is highly relevant for a wide range of stakeholders, ranging from citizens to policy-makers.

As an important forum for the creation of EU-wide public opinion, the European Parliament, when acting within international and inter-regional parliamentary frameworks, could substantially contribute to an increased awareness among the citizenry of the level of the democratic legitimation of EU foreign affairs and improve their sense of ownership of the policies thus enacted and applied to them. The voters, as well as civil society organisations, would thus have an opportunity to reflect on, and potentially alter, the widespread perception of the EU democratic deficit.[92] Concomitantly, the interests of citizens and business organisations could be better represented by governments, EU institutions, and organs of international and regional organisations as well as lobby and pressure groups if they received feedback on the manner in which the European Parliament perceives and treats their positions. The lack of participation of MEPs in the aforesaid processes precludes this.

The policy-making relevance stems from the fact that parliaments worldwide, including national parliaments of the EU Member States, such as the Dutch Staten Generaal,[93] and parliaments of other regional organisations, such as the nascent Parliament of the Union of South American Nations,[94]

[92] On the role of civil society and representation in transnational governance see: J. A. Scholte, 'Civil Society and Democratically Accountable Global Governance' (2004) 39 *Government and Opposition* 211–33; P. Nanz and J. Steffek, 'Global Governance, Participation and the Public Sphere' (2004) 39 *Government and Opposition* 314–35; J. Mendes, 'Participation and the Role of Law after Lisbon: A Legal View on Article 11 TEU' (2011) 48 *Common Market Law Review* 1,849–78.

[93] Weisglas and Boer, 'Parliamentary Diplomacy', 93–9.

[94] See more in: J. Bennett, 'The Union of South American Nations: The New(est) Regionalism in Latin America' (2008) 32 *Suffolk Transnational Law Review* 103–33.

could gain valuable insight into the practical functioning of parliamentary diplomacy and the consequences of their actions from the institutional, legal and political points of view.[95] Their members and staff could utilise this knowledge to consider the advantages and disadvantages of engaging in parliamentary diplomacy, which would enable them to streamline their participation in international parliamentary forums and enhance their internal organisation. This could be achieved by establishing new working methods or by sharpening the existing ones. A better use of parliamentary resources – such as time, money and expertise – could lead to a more focused specialisation of parliamentarians, legislative staffers and permanent clerks of parliamentary committees and delegations, and a more efficient scrutiny of the external dimension of EU policies.

Some of the more concrete potential benefits of the international engagement of the European Parliament have been correctly identified in the literature. It has been argued that harmonised parliamentary approaches to matters of common interest could:

- facilitate the acceptance of the European Parliament's requests in international affairs;[96]
- stimulate public debate on contemporary global issues and prevent lethargy and non-responsiveness of governmental actors;[97]
- fortify the legitimacy, credibility and smooth application of EU legislation by securing the cooperation of authorities external to the Union;[98]
- nurture the creation of shared norms and values;[99] and
- avoid the sense of tutelage in relations between the EU and its key strategic partners, such as the USA.[100]

In any event, a more substantial parliamentary input into transnational policy-making processes in general is desirable to attenuate the legitimacy and accountability problems that arise not only within the context of the

[95] The empirical spread of the diplomatic action of parliaments is gaining normative attention. See: Walker, 'Postnational Constitutionalism and Postnational Public Law', 80.

[96] S. Di Paola, 'International Treaty Making in the EU: What Role for the European Parliament?' (2003) 38 *International Spectator* 75–90, at 80.

[97] Z. Šabič, 'Democracy Across Borders: Parliamentarians and International Public Spheres' (2008) 15 *Javnost – The Public* 75–88, at 80.

[98] D. Acosta, *Latin American Reactions to the Adoption of the Returns Directive* (Centre for European Policy Studies, 2009).

[99] Šabič, 'Democracy Across Borders', 77.

[100] Y. Devuyst, 'European Community Integration and the United States: Toward a New Transatlantic Relationship?' (1990) 14 *Journal of European Integration* 5–29, at 22.

EU and transatlantic relations,[101] but also worldwide,[102] since many contemporary problems transcend European borders and require concerted action of authorities at various levels.[103]

3.4.2 Incentivising EU–US parliamentarism

The importance of forging closer ties between the European Parliament and the US Congress is palpable with regard to both international agreements and secondary EU law. With several examples, we demonstrate in turn below the implications of EU–US interparliamentary cooperation with regard to these two types of legal acts.

As far as international agreements are concerned, in some policy fields such as civil liberties, the stance of the European Parliament may diverge from those of the Commission, the Council and, certainly, the US Congress. This was especially the case with EU–US negotiations on the PNR and SWIFT Agreements, where the EU citizens' privacy and data protection rights in matters of passenger name records (PNR) and financial transactions (SWIFT) were at stake. It has, for instance, been submitted that the European Parliament was the only institution that genuinely insisted upon ensuring the PNR Agreement's compliance with the EU's Data Protection Directive.[104] Even so, and despite the fact that the European Parliament had the power to veto the 2012 version of the PNR Agreement, it did not do so, due to political pressures. In this case, what eroded the European Parliament's opposition was the necessity for the EU to possess a common legal framework for transferring air passengers' data, but also the fear that a veto would jeopardise the EU's participation in the US Visa Waiver Program and perhaps even lead the USA to exclude EU Member States from the Program.[105] In the SWIFT

[101] M. Egan, 'Mutual Recognition and Standard Setting: Public and Private Strategies for Governing Markets' in Pollack and Shaffer (eds.), *Transatlantic Governance in the Global Economy*, p. 203.

[102] See the view that transnational constitutionalism, especially in its pluralist form, needs 'conceptually independent principles' such as democracy and rule of law in: T. Isiksel, 'Global Legal Pluralism as Fact and Norm' (2013) 2 *Global Constitutionalism* 160–95, at 172.

[103] See more on the legitimacy of global governance in: M. Zürn, 'Global Governance and Legitimacy Problems' (2004) 39 *Government and Opposition* 260–87.

[104] I. Tukdi, 'Transatlantic Turbulence: The Passenger Name Record Conflict' (2008) 45 *Houston Law Review* 587–620, at 620.

[105] Y. Suda, 'Transatlantic Politics of Data Transfer: Extraterritoriality, Counter-Extraterritoriality and Counter-Terrorism' (2013) 51 *Journal of Common Market Studies* 772–88, at 779.

saga,[106] the European Parliament did veto the first Agreement and did so specifically to test the strength of the then-newly acquired power of consent.[107] This move contributed to exerting some amendments of the SWIFT Agreement towards maintaining higher data protection standards.[108] In Monar's view, this rejection of the SWIFT Agreement is proof that the Treaty of Lisbon has effected a significant change in the internal balance of power between EU institutions, inasmuch as the European Parliament 'has come of age and has to be taken seriously' also by international interlocutors.[109] Along the same lines, Cremona concludes that there has been a 'substantial shift' regarding treaty-making by the EU because, thanks to the existence of the consent requirement, the European Parliament 'will in practice need to be involved by the Commission and the Council at earlier stages'.[110] Yet as some authors argue, this does not automatically result in a more powerful European Parliament.[111] Both the PNR and SWIFT episodes have been viewed as instances of the EU's and the European Parliament's norm reception rather than those of norm making.[112]

As far as secondary EU law is concerned, it should be highlighted that much of the legislation and policy-making in this area has transatlantic impact.[113] In fact, the EU and the USA are the two most integrated and interconnected regions in the world, employing up to 15 million workers

[106] See more on the background of the saga in: C. Shea, 'A Need for SWIFT Change: The Struggle Between the European Union's Desire for Privacy in International Financial Transactions and the United States' Need for Security from Terrorists as Evidenced by the SWIFT Scandal' (2008) 8 *Journal of High Technology Law* 143–68; G. G. Fuster *et al.*, 'SWIFT and the Vulnerability of Transatlantic Data Transfers' (2008) 22 *International Review of Law, Computers and Technology* 191–202.

[107] M. de Goede, 'The SWIFT Affair and the Global Politics of European Security' (2012) 50 *Journal of Common Market Studies* 214–30, at 218.

[108] Suda, 'Transatlantic Politics of Data Transfer', 783.

[109] J. Monar, 'The Rejection of the EU–US SWIFT Interim Agreement by the European Parliament: A Historic Vote and its Implications' (2010) 15 *European Foreign Affairs Review* 143–51, at 145 and 150.

[110] Cremona, 'Justice and Home Affairs in a Globalised World', p. 25.

[111] See further in Chapter 6 by Elaine Fahey and Chapter 12 by Juan Santos Vara in this volume.

[112] See to this effect: J. Argomaniz, 'When the EU is the "Norm-Taker": The Passenger Name Records Agreement and the EU's Internalisation of US Border Security Norms' (2009) 31 *Journal of European Integration* 119–36; A. R. Servent and A. MacKenzie, 'The European Parliament as a "Norm Taker"? EU–US Relations after the SWIFT Agreement' (2012) 17 *European Foreign Affairs Review* 71–86.

[113] See: J. Scott, 'From Brussels with Love: The Transatlantic Travels of European Law and the Chemistry of Regulatory Attraction' (2009) 57 *American Journal of Comparative Law* 897–942.

and accounting for some 54 per cent of world gross domestic product, 28 per cent of global exports and 33 per cent of global imports.[114] A good example of interdependence between the EU and US legislative processes can be found in the field of environment protection and concerns the EU's Emissions Trading Scheme, which employs a system of trading in carbon emission allowances in order to reduce the amount of greenhouse gas emitted not least by aircraft flying in and out of the EU.[115] Due to increased costs for American airline companies, this Scheme was debated in a hearing in the US House of Representatives on 27 July 2011, under a title that labelled it 'a violation of international law',[116] and in the US Senate on 6 June 2012.[117] The European Commission's Director-General for Climate Change submitted written testimony for the Senate's hearing assuring American lawmakers that the contested piece of EU legislation would not be suspended, not least because it enjoyed massive support by the European Parliament.[118] The Emissions Trading Scheme was finally repudiated by the US Congress and, after US President Barack Obama put his signature on the bill on 27 November 2012, the so-called European Union Emissions Trading Scheme Prohibition Act was enacted. This Act obliges the US Secretary of Transportation to prohibit US civil aircraft operators from participating in the Scheme whenever the Secretary determines that the prohibition is in the public interest of the USA, but only after holding a public hearing.[119] This Act also contains an obligation for the Transportation Secretary to reassess the need for a prohibition if the EU amends the Scheme, if a relevant international agreement is concluded or

[114] K. Archick and V. Morelli, *The US Congress and the European Parliament: Evolving Transatlantic Legislative Cooperation*, Report for Congress No. R41552 (Washington, DC: Congressional Research Service, 2011), p. 1.

[115] Directive 2003/87/EC of the European Parliament and of the Council of 13 October 2003 Establishing a Scheme for Greenhouse Gas Emission Allowance Trading Within the Community and Amending Council Directive 96/61/EC. This Directive was amended in 2004, 2008 and 2009.

[116] US House of Representatives, Committee on Transportation and Infrastructure, Subcommittee on Aviation, Hearing of 27 July 2011, available at: www.gpo.gov/fdsys/pkg/CHRG-112hhrg67582/pdf/CHRG-112hhrg67582.pdf, accessed 8 October 2013.

[117] US Senate, Committee on Commerce, Science and Transportation, Hearing of 6 June 2012, available at: www.commerce.senate.gov/public/index.cfm?p=Hearings&ContentRecord_id=3cfc8134-0ee8-4296-b0de-93d28b9f086c&ContentType_id=14f995b9-dfa5-407a-9d35-56cc7152a7ed&Group_id=b06c39af-e033-4cba-9221-de-668ca1978a, accessed 8 October 2013.

[118] Written testimony by Jos Delbeke to the US Senate hearing on the EU's Emissions Trading Scheme, p. 10, available at: http://ec.europa.eu/clima/news/docs/testimony_senate_hearing.pdf, accessed 8 October 2013.

[119] Section 2(a)–(b) thereof.

if a statute is enacted in the USA that addresses aircraft emissions.[120] Even before this enactment, the dispute over the Scheme was brought before the Court of Justice, which upheld the Scheme while making no mention of parliamentary pronouncements on this matter.[121] Therefore, the existence of parliamentary avenues for *ex ante* policy discussion evidently did not bear fruit.

These exemplary considerations on EU–US parliamentary involvement in the making of international agreements and secondary EU law reveal gaps in transatlantic parliamentarism. To narrow these gaps, the European Parliament has advocated the transformation of the current interparliamentary exchange between the EU and the USA into a de facto Transatlantic Assembly and that a legislative early warning system should be established between the European Parliament and the US Congress.[122] This potentially beneficial mechanism of early monitoring of legislative approaches could be of particular importance for avoiding regulatory discrepancies between the EU and the USA such as those described above. For instance, the Transatlantic Economic Partnership Action Plan envisages the establishment of an arrangement to provide for 'early exchanges of views on any policy proposals that either side believes capable of having an adverse impact on business conditions for service provides'. Along those lines, this Action Plan further calls for the creation of a steering group, whose task inter alia is to provide a horizontal forum for bilateral consultation and 'early warning on any matter of trade and investment relevance, with a view to preventing conflicts and resolving trade frictions'. The awareness of advantages of early involvement is therefore present, and effort should be made to reap the benefits it may produce.

[120] Section 2(c)(2) thereof.

[121] Case C-366/10 *Air Transport Association of America and others* v. *Secretary of State for Energy and Climate Change*, Judgment of the Court (Grand Chamber) of 21 December 2011. See analyses of this case in: E. Denza, 'International Aviation and the EU Carbon Trading Scheme: Comment on the Air Transport Association of America Case' (2012) 37 *European Law Review* 314–26; B. Mayer, 'Case Note C-366/10' (2012) 49 *Common Market Law Review* 1,113–40; E. Fahey, 'The EU Emissions Trading Scheme and the Court of Justice: The "High Politics of Indirectly Promoting Global Standards"' (2012) 13 *German Law Journal* 1,247–67; S. Bogojevic, 'Legalising Environmental Leadership: A Comment on the CJEU's Ruling in C-366/10 on the Inclusion of Aviation in the EU Emissions Trading Scheme' (2012) 24 *Journal of Environmental Law* 345–56; G. de Baere and C. Ryngaert, 'The ECJ's Judgment in Air Transport Association of America and the International Legal Context of the EU's Climate Change Policy' (2013) 18 *European Foreign Affairs Review* 389–410.

[122] European Parliament, Resolution of 25 April 2007 on Transatlantic Relations, doc. no. P6_TA(2007)0155, paras. 35 and 37.

There is, nonetheless, very little evidence of immediate fruits of direct consultation between MEPs and US Congress members on matters such as those outlined above. Indeed, as Pollack observes, the Transatlantic Legislators' Dialogue, along with other EU–US dialogues, is the least successful component of the New Transatlantic Agenda.[123] This is because some of the most bitter regulatory disputes since 2000 originated in initiatives of the US Congress and the European Parliament. The two legislatures frequently adopted legislation with little or no consideration of the implications for the other side, and it did not help that EU and US parliamentarians in charge of the dossiers were most of the time absent from the interparliamentary debate.

However, even where the respective positions of the two legislatures are not in harmony, interparliamentary contact could equip MEPs and Congress members with useful information that could help them to refine and defend their views better. For instance, the problems that the US Congress encountered in the SWIFT affair were fairly similar to those experienced by the European Parliament, since a good number of congressmen were not only ill-informed about the US government's dealings with SWIFT but also questioned the legality of the Terrorist Finance Tracking Program.[124] These facts could have been utilised to prompt the respective executive branches to be more forthcoming in heeding parliamentary preferences. Furthermore, while the goals of their respective governments may be different, EU and US parliamentarians may profit from explaining each other's positions and justifying their standpoints so as to create a sense of respect and understanding for differing approaches to shared problems. This could all help to prevent transatlantic disputes from arising later on.[125] Parliamentary exchanges across the Atlantic could also increase the level of political accountability of the executive actors on both sides of the Atlantic for the jointly crafted policy solutions. This in turn contributes to the EU's and the United States' democratic legitimacy

[123] M. Pollack, 'The New Transatlantic Agenda at Ten: Reflections on an Experiment in International Governance' (2005) 43 *Journal of Common Market Studies* 899–919, at 915.

[124] J. S. Shrader, 'Secrets Hurt: How SWIFT Shook Up Congress, the European Union, and the US Banking Industry' (2007) 11 *North Carolina Banking Institute* 397–420, at 408.

[125] H. G. Krenzler and G. Wiegand, 'EU–US Relations: More Than Trade Disputes?' (1999) 4 *European Foreign Affairs Review* 153–80, at 170; H. Paemen, 'Looking Back... and Ahead' (2000) 23 *Fordham International Law Journal* 529–35, at 531. R. Howse, 'Transatlantic Regulatory Cooperation and the Problem of Democracy' in G. A. Bermann *et al.* (eds.), *Transatlantic Regulatory Cooperation: Legal Problems and Political Prospects* (Oxford University Press, 2000), p. 472.

both internally and externally. These are, therefore, the key areas where transatlantic interparliamentarism should be stepped up and where it could yield mutually beneficial outcomes. MEPs could and should make greater use of the Transatlantic Legislators' Dialogue in order to garner support for far-reaching EU initiatives that have global repercussions in diverse fields of action.

However, the constraints facing the Dialogue remain present and contemporary. The interparliamentary forums for EU–US cooperation have no formal status in the EU treaties, their powers are weak and their pronouncements are not legally binding.[126] Their output is not always directly related to the representation of EU citizens but often addresses global problems, whereas parliamentarians are typically elected to further the interests of their constituencies.[127] Consequently, parliamentarians' international efforts do not automatically improve their prospects for re-election.[128] Further disincentives include the lack of parliamentarians' continuity in office, low visibility of their work and the lack of interest.

4 The European Parliament and national parliaments: sombre prospects for collaboration in transatlantic relations?

Like the European Parliament, the national parliaments of the EU Member States have seen their competences in EU affairs grow. In a Union where levels of governance are tightly interlinked, the principle of democracy had to stretch across levels, and this is one of the EU's constitutional idiosyncrasies.[129] In order to redress the loss of power of domestic parliamentarians due to European integration, the EU has since the Treaty of Maastricht attempted to draw them within the Union's institutional framework.[130] It was ultimately the Treaty of Lisbon that envisaged

[126] A.-M. Slaughter, *A New World Order* (Princeton University Press, 2004), p. 122.

[127] Z. Šabič, 'Building Democratic and Responsible Global Governance: The Role of International Parliamentary Institutions' (2008) 61 *Parliamentary Affairs* 255–71, at 255–6.

[128] G. Shaffer, 'Parliamentary Oversight of WTO Rule-Making: The Political, Normative and Practical Contexts' (2004) 7 *Journal of International Economic Law* 629–54, at 643.

[129] See further: D. Jančić, 'Representative Democracy Across Levels: National Parliaments and EU Constitutionalism' (2012) 8 *Croatian Yearbook of European Law and Policy* 227–65.

[130] See essays in: G. Barrett (ed.), *National Parliaments and the European Union: The Constitutional Challenge for the Oireachtas and Other Member State Legislatures* (Dublin: Clarus Press, 2008); J. O'Brennan and T. Raunio (eds.) *National Parliaments within the Enlarged European Union: From Victims of Integration to Competitive Actors?* (Abingdon: Routledge, 2007); O. Tans *et al.* (eds.), *National Parliaments and European*

a number of competences for national parliaments. One of them is to contribute actively to the good functioning of the Union through interparliamentary cooperation with the European Parliament in accordance with Protocol 1 on the role of national parliaments in the European Union.[131]

Protocol 1 provides that 'the European Parliament and national parliaments *shall* together determine the organisation and promotion of effective and regular interparliamentary cooperation within the Union'.[132] The Protocol further sets out the basis for the organisation of a conference of parliamentary committees for EU affairs, which has existed since 1989 in the form of COSAC (Conférence des Organes Spécialisés dans les Affaires Communautaires). COSAC biannually gathers six-member delegations of the European Parliament and of the European Affairs Committees of national parliaments in the Member State holding the EU Presidency. This body may submit non-binding contributions for the attention of the European Parliament, the Council and the Commission. The exchange of information and best practices between national parliaments and the European Parliament is also envisaged, both at the level of the Houses and at the level of sectoral committees.

Protocol 1 also provides for the possibility of organising specific interparliamentary conferences, particularly in CFSP and CSDP matters.[133] This materialised in April 2012 in Warsaw during the Conference of Speakers of EU Parliaments, when the Interparliamentary Conference for CFSP and CSDP was formed, thereby replacing the Conference of Foreign Affairs Committee Chairpersons (COFACC) and the Conference of Defence Affairs Committee Chairpersons (CODACC).[134] According to its Rules of Procedure, the Conference is composed of six-member national parliamentary delegations and a sixteen-member European Parliament delegation, and they convene every six months to exchange information and best practices in the area of CFSP and CSDP, so that both MEPs and MPs are 'fully informed when carrying out their respective roles in this

Democracy: A Bottom-Up Approach to European Constitutionalism (Groningen: Europa Law Publishing, 2008).

131 Article 12(f) TEU.

132 Article 9 thereof (emphasis added). The imperative wording has been opposed by certain national parliaments.

133 Article 10 of the Protocol.

134 Article 1.3 of the Rules of Procedure of the Interparliamentary Conference for CFSP and CSDP.

policy area'.[135] Just as with COSAC, non-binding conclusions may be adopted.[136]

An insight into biannual reports prepared and published by COSAC and the conclusions adopted after the first three meetings of the Interparliamentary Conference for CFSP and CSDP reveal that transatlantic relations between the EU and the USA are not the focal point of the debates of these forums. COSAC contributions rarely address interregional issues in general.[137] Despite the current absence of transatlantic topics in their discussions, these two forums could be used more frequently to appraise those external affairs of the EU that have serious implications for the rights of citizens, such as EU–US international agreements. Such debates could spark interest among both national and European parliamentarians for transatlantic relations and raise awareness of the external dimension of EU affairs. Follow-up meetings at a bilateral level could be organised between MPs and MEPs on an ad hoc basis, depending on the subject matter and the national interests of the Member States. While this would give national parliaments valuable information on the position of and action planned by the European Parliament, the latter could hear the former's arguments in favour of or against the Commission's and the Council's positions in the process of negotiating an international agreement, and also in the process of drafting EU legislation that impacts transatlantic relations, such as the Emissions Trading Scheme.

Other forums that foster cooperation between the European Parliament and national parliaments do not furnish an adequate setting to fill this lacuna of democratic control. Both the Barroso Initiative, which was set in motion by Commission President Barroso in 2006, and the Early Warning System, which became operational in 2009 upon the entry into force of the Lisbon Treaty, are inappropriate for scrutinising the EU's transatlantic affairs, because they concentrate on the Commission's legislative and work programme, and the resulting draft legislative acts, and not on EU international affairs.

[135] Articles 1.1 and 2.1 thereof. [136] Articles 1.4 and 7.1 of the Rules of Procedure of the Interparliamentary Conference for CFSP and CSDP.

[137] An example of when interregionalism was the object of a contribution is that adopted by the 43rd COSAC meeting, which took place in Madrid from 31 May to 1 June 2010. In addition to various other topics, this contribution dealt with regional strategies of the EU, including the relations between the Union and Latin America. See: COSAC Secretariat, *COSAC: Historical Development* (2010), pp. 36–7.

5 Conclusion: implications of the European Parliament's transatlantic 'diplomacy' for the EU constitutional order

This overview shows that the European Union's Parliament endeavours to perform not only the classic constitutional functions but also those that are perhaps less visible to the public eye, such as those sometimes referred to as 'diplomatic' as a result of their similarity to interstate negotiations. The most important characteristic of the 'diplomatic' activities of the European Parliament is that, even though they are loosely and remotely based on the EU treaties, their conduct and development is largely of an informal nature. As such, these activities contribute to an informal constitutionalisation of the European Parliament's powers, because they help hone the existing powers, test their limits and give them a renewed meaning in novel circumstances. This is particularly important for the EU constitutional setting, which Besselink describes as evolutionary, historical and incremental due to its long-term and slow process of step-by-step development.[138] Indeed, in what Curtin refers to as the EU's 'empirical constitution', the polity can also be ordered as a matter of fact, and it is the constitutionally invisible small-scale changes in the legal and institutional practices that can shape the role of institutions.[139] Given the level of interdependence and the sheer number of linkages and interactions in a whole array of policy areas, transatlantic relations represent a vast domain in which this kind of constitutional development can unravel.

While the concrete effects of the European Parliament's transatlantic 'diplomacy' are difficult to measure, the efforts made by MEPs in engaging beyond the narrow remits of their competences and in informing their actions by political discussions with their American counterparts merit support and encouragement. There are solid reasons why MEPs, despite numerous disincentives, should strengthen their 'diplomatic' portfolios and find alleys for scrutinising transatlantic and interregional decision-making. The democratisation of transnational policies and the enhancement of the parliamentary oversight thereof are among the primary advantages of this.

[138] L. Besselink, 'The Notion and Nature of the European Constitution after the Lisbon Treaty' in J. Wouters *et al.* (eds.), *European Constitutionalism beyond Lisbon* (Antwerp: Intersentia, 2009), pp. 272 and 279–80.

[139] D. Curtin, 'The Sedimentary European Constitution – The Future of "Constitutionalisation" without a Constitution' in I. Pernice and E. Tanchev (eds.), *Ceci n'est pas une constitution – Constitutionalisation without a Constitution?* (Baden-Baden: Nomos Verlagsgesellschaft, 2009), pp. 78 and 85.

Precisely because of its non-binding character, which allows greater room for more flexible deliberation and bolder pronouncement, the Transatlantic Legislators' Dialogue should be further exploited to sift through the respective legislative plans of the EU and the USA and, thereupon, to scrutinise them more thoroughly. Concurrently, interparliamentary forums between the European Parliament and national parliaments prove ill-suited for influencing the transatlantic partnership, but could be utilised for inserting it on parliamentary agendas across Europe.

Transatlantic parliamentarism and 'diplomacy' could thus be turned into an important tool for expanding the European Parliament's powers and for bringing influence to bear on both EU and US institutions. The legitimacy of the action of MEPs, and perhaps also of the entire Union, may increase if matters of common interest are discussed and joint positions agreed with international partners. This is where EU–US interparliamentary cooperation can make its major contribution.

4

Transatlantic adjudication techniques

The Commerce Clause and the EU's internal market harmonisation clause in perspective

JOSÉ A. GUTIERREZ-FONS

As one of its essential elements, federalism – understood as the balance of power between the different levels of governance[1] – is devoted to examining the way in which the principle of enumerated powers (the principle of conferral) is enforced by the courts. In the United States, the US Constitution lists the legislative powers that are conferred upon Congress. This means that '[t]he powers not delegated to the [USA] by the Constitution, nor prohibited by it to the States, are reserved to the States respectively, or to the people'.[2] In the same way, by virtue of the principle of conferral, which is enshrined in Article 5(1) of the Treaty on the European Union (TEU), the European Union 'shall act only within the limits of the competences conferred upon it by the Member States in the Treaties to attain the objectives set out therein'. This means that '[c]ompetences not conferred upon the [EU] in the Treaties remain with the Member States'.[3] It follows that both legal orders are governed by the principle of enumerated powers. Moreover, Congress and the EU legislator may respectively pass legislation that seeks to tear down obstacles to interstate commerce. Quantitatively, that grant of power is of paramount importance, as most of US and EU legislation currently in force is grounded in that constitutional authority. However, that power is not unlimited. Otherwise, the principle of enumerated powers would become devoid of purpose.

Legal Secretary at the Cabinet of the Vice-President of the European Court of Justice. All opinions expressed herein are personal to the author.

[1] K. Lenaerts, 'Constitutionalism and the Many Faces of Federalism' (1990) 38 *American Journal of Comparative Law* 204–63.

[2] See the Xth Amendment of the US Constitution.

[3] Article 5(1) TEU. See also Article 4(1) TEU.

In this regard, in the USA, the method of analysis deployed by the Supreme Court of the United States (SCOTUS) when interpreting the Commerce Clause[4] has been of paramount importance when allocating powers between the US Government and its component States. It is true that, from the New Deal to 1995, no federal statute was annulled on the ground that Congress had overstepped its powers to regulate interstate commerce. However, since the late 1990s the SCOTUS has paid a great deal of attention to the 'outer limits' of the Commerce Clause. It follows from cases such as *United States* v. *Lopez* and *United States* v. *Morrison*[5] that the SCOTUS, led by its then Chief Justice Rehnquist, had embarked on a 'federalism revival' that sought to give real meaning to the constitutional mandate according to which the US Government has limited powers. More recently, in *National Federation of Independent Business* ('*NFIB*') v. *Sebelius*,[6] the SCOTUS upheld the Patient Protection and Affordable Care Act (ACA), also known as 'ObamaCare'. In so doing, Chief Justice Roberts, writing for the majority, found that Congress lacked the powers under the Commerce Clause to compel Americans to buy minimum essential health insurance coverage (the so-called 'individual mandate'). However, Congress could do so under its powers to tax. *NFIB* v. *Sebelius* thus shows that the US federal debate over the congressional power to regulate interstate commerce is very much alive.

On the other side of the Atlantic, from 1987 to 2000, the European Court of Justice (ECJ) did not annul or declare invalid legislation adopted pursuant to the EU's internal market harmonisation clause, that is, Article 114 of the Treaty on the Functioning of the European Union (TFEU) (ex Article 95 EC of the Treaty Establishing the European Community),[7] on the ground that the EU legislator had acted *ultra vires*. However, in *Tobacco Advertising I*,[8] the ECJ took that step by annulling Directive 98/43, which prohibited all forms of advertising and sponsorship of tobacco products in the EU.[9] It showed that the EU's internal market harmonisation clause was not a general source of power to regulate the market, but a legal basis

[4] Article I, Section 8, Clause 3 of the US Constitution.

[5] *Lopez*, 514 U.S. 549 (1995) and *Morrison*, 529 U.S. 598 (2000).

[6] *National Federation of Independent Business* ('*NFIB*') v. *Sebelius*, 132 S.Ct. 2566 (2012).

[7] Which provides that 'The European Parliament and the Council shall … adopt the measures for the approximation of the provisions laid down by law, regulation or administrative action in Member States which have as their object the establishment and functioning of the internal market.'

[8] Case C-376/98 *Germany* v. *Parliament and Council* ('*Tobacco Advertising I*') [2000] ECR I-8419.

[9] [1998] OJ L 213/9.

of limited scope. In *Tobacco Advertising II*,[10] the EU legislator proved that it had learned its lesson: Directive 2003/33,[11] the successor to the annulled Directive 98/43, was adopted in accordance with the approach developed by the ECJ in *Tobacco Advertising I*. More recently, in *Vodafone*,[12] the ECJ stressed the importance of the *travaux préparatoires*. If the EU legislator has, in light of a specific factual inquiry, strived to tailor the legislation at issue in a way that respects state autonomy, the ECJ will take into account those legislative findings, giving weight to a 'process-oriented' review.

The purpose of this chapter is to draw some lessons from a comparative study of transatlantic adjudication techniques. It is divided as follows. Section I is devoted to examining the way in which the SCOTUS has applied the principle of enumerated powers in the context of the Commerce Clause. Section II has a similar aim: it focuses on the case law of the ECJ when interpreting the EU's internal market harmonisation clause, that is, Article 114 TFEU. After comparing the method of analysis deployed by both courts when monitoring compliance with the principle of enumerated powers, it is submitted, in Section III, that the latter principle is not by itself capable of containing the 'competence creep' of the central government. The chapter looks at three alternative adjudication techniques capable of striking the right balance between the Union's interests in an integrated market and state autonomy, namely reliance on the political process, the principle of proportionality and the principle of subsidiarity. Finally, a brief conclusion supports the contention that both the SCOTUS and the ECJ should focus on ensuring that, in the vast field of concurrent powers, Congress and the EU legislator take into account 'the values of federalism'. Although protecting enclaves of state sovereignty remains important when reminding Congress and the EU legislator of the limited nature of their powers, it appears that the right balance between different levels of governance can only be struck if courts go beyond the 'borderline federalism' paradigm. Stated differently, courts should also examine the way in which Congress and the EU legislator respectively exercise the constitutional power to regulate interstate commerce. This may be achieved by having recourse to 'process federalism': when exercising their powers of judicial review, both courts should focus on solving failures

10 Case C-380/03 *Germany* v. *Parliament and Council* ('*Tobacco Advertising II*') [2006] ECR I-11573.

11 [2003] OJ L 152/16.

12 Case C-58/08 *Vodafone and Others* [2010] ECR I-4999 (*Vodafone* hereafter).

in federal and EU legislative deliberations that improperly impinge upon state autonomy.

I. The principle of enumerated powers applied to the Commerce Clause

In accordance with settled case law, Congress may regulate three categories of activities under the Commerce Clause, namely (1) the channels of interstate commerce, (2) the instrumentalities of interstate commerce or things and persons therein, and (3) activities having a substantial effect on interstate commerce. From 1937 to 1995 no federal statute was annulled by the SCOTUS on the ground that Congress had exceeded its powers to regulate interstate commerce. This shows that the Commerce Clause was so broadly interpreted that attempts seeking to limit its scope of application were almost futile.

For example, *Wickard* v. *Filburn*,[13] which has been characterised as 'the most far reaching example of Commerce Clause authority over intrastate activity',[14] illustrates this point. In that case the SCOTUS held that, in regulating intrastate activities, not only should effects on interstate commerce be considered on an individual basis, but also in the aggregate (the so-called 'aggregation principle'). For the case at hand, this meant that Congress could regulate wheat for home consumption purposes. Since Congress had sought to increase the price of wheat by controlling its supply, the SCOTUS reasoned that an eventual flow into the market of home-grown and consumed wheat could put at risk that objective.

In addition to regulating activities having a 'substantial effect' on interstate commerce and to the 'aggregation principle', the scope of the Commerce Clause was further expanded by deferring to congressional fact-findings. Insofar as Congress could demonstrate a 'rational basis' in support of its determinations, the SCOTUS would uphold that local activities had a substantial effect on interstate commerce. The ruling of the SCOTUS in *Katzenbach* v. *McClung* provides a good example in this regard.[15] In that case the owner of a restaurant that refused to serve blacks sought the annulment of Title II of the Civil Rights Act,[16] according to which no restaurant could discriminate on grounds of sex, colour,

[13] *Wickard* v. *Filburn*, 317 U.S. 111 (1942).
[14] *Lopez*, 514 U.S. 560 (1995).
[15] *Katzenbach* v. *McClung*, 379 U.S. 294 (1964).
[16] 42 U.S.C. 1971.

national origin or religion, 'if ... it serves or offers to serve interstate travelers or a substantial portion of the food which it serves ... has moved in commerce'. However, by recalling congressional findings, the SCOTUS held that black people would not attend restaurants that discriminated on grounds of race. These restaurants would have fewer customers. Accordingly, '[t]he fewer customers a restaurant enjoys, the less food it sells, and consequently the less it buys [from the interstate commerce]'.[17] Likewise, the SCOTUS did not call into question the fact that racially discriminatory restaurants would render more difficult the interstate travel of black people, given that 'one can hardly travel without eating'.[18] Moreover, cases such as *Katzenbach* v. *McClung* showed that the SCOTUS did not prevent Congress from having recourse to the Commerce Clause as a means of combating racial discrimination.[19] Thus, it favoured the 'indirect' regulation of social matters through the medium of commercial regulation.

From 1937 to 1995 US scholars were divided into two camps when asked about the SCOTUS' case law on the Commerce Clause. Whilst some scholars opined that the SCOTUS was right to follow judicial restraint,[20] others urged the SCOTUS to modify its case law, which had, in their view, excessively eroded the federal model and did not comply with the principle of enumerated powers.[21] Notably, then Justice Rehnquist criticised the SCOTUS' reading of the Commerce Clause, calling for a more tempered interpretation of congressional authority under that constitutional provision.[22] However, it was not until *United States* v. *Lopez*,[23] delivered in 1995, that he finally managed to mobilise the SCOTUS.

A. *Lopez*

In *Lopez* the SCOTUS ruled, in a 5–4 decision, that the Gun-Free School Zone Act (GFSZA)[24] was unconstitutional. Adopted under the Commerce

[17] *Katzenbach* v. *McClung*, 299.

[18] *Ibid.*, 300.

[19] See also *Heart of Atlanta Motel Inc.* v. *United States*, 379 U.S. 241 (1964).

[20] J. H. Choper, 'The Scope of National Power vis-à-vis the State: The Dispensability of Judicial Review' (1977) 86 *Yale Law Journal* 1,552–621. See also *Maryland* v. *Wirtz*, 392 U.S. 183, 204 (1968) (Douglas J, dissenting).

[21] R. A. Epstein, 'The Proper Scope of the Commerce Clause' (1987) 73 *Virginia Law Review* 1,387–455.

[22] *Hodel* v. *Virginia Surface Mining & Reclamation Association*, 452 U.S. 264, 310 (1981) (Rehnquist J, concurring).

[23] *Lopez*, 514 U.S. 549 (1995).

[24] 18 U.S.C. § 922(q).

Clause, this Act criminalised the possession of fire arms in school zones. The US Government supported the validity of the GFSZA by maintaining that there was a close connection between the possession of firearms in a school zone and violent crime. In turn, violent crime adversely affected the national economy in two ways, namely the 'cost of crime' and the 'cost of productivity'. First, through the mechanism of insurance, the financial effects of violent crime are suffered by the entire population. Likewise, violent crime also dissuades people from travelling to areas perceived as unsafe. Second, violent crime is also an obstacle to the educational process. A poorly educated population is less productive, and consequently the national economy is weakened. Thus, the US Government claimed that the GFSZA regulated an activity having a substantial adverse effect on commerce and urged the SCOTUS to uphold that federal statute.

Writing for the Court, Chief Justice Rehnquist held that Congress was bound by the principle of enumerated powers. Although plenary and submitted to no limitations but the ones prescribed by the Constitution, the very wording of the Commerce Clause imposes intrinsic limitations to congressional powers. That constitutional provision is not an unbounded source of federal power. As the GFSZA regulated neither the channels of interstate commerce nor the instrumentalities of interstate commerce or things and persons therein, he went on to examine whether the possession of firearms in school zones had a 'substantial' impact on interstate commerce.

In this regard, he drew a distinction between local economic and local non-economic activities. On the one hand, 'where economic activity substantially affects interstate commerce, legislation regulating that activity will be sustained'.[25] *A sensu contrario*, where Congress sought to regulate non-economic areas traditionally reserved to State sovereignty, such as criminal law, federal legislation will be almost certainly struck down. Consequently, Chief Justice Rehnquist declared the unconstitutionality of the GFSZA, which had 'nothing to do with commerce or any sort of economic enterprise'.[26]

Moreover, he indicated that the GFSZA did not form part of a larger regulation of economic activity, requiring for its effectiveness the inclusion of intrastate non-economic matters. Neither was there a 'jurisdictional hook' that made the application of the GFSZA conditional upon a case-by-case inquiry into the effects of gun possession on interstate commerce.[27]

[25] *Lopez*, 514 U.S., 560 (1995). [26] *Ibid.*, 561.

[27] After *Lopez* Congress limited the scope of the GFSZA to 'a firearm that has moved in or that otherwise affects interstate or foreign commerce'. 18 U.S.C. § 922 (q) (2) (A) (2000). Cf *United States* v. *Dorsey*, 418 F. 3d 10398 (9th Cir. 2005).

Nor were there specific legislative findings indicating the effects of gun possession in school zones on interstate commerce. As to the arguments of the US Government, Chief Justice Rehnquist found that they were no more than 'inferences upon inferences'. If the SCOTUS had followed the appellant's arguments, it would have been very 'difficult to perceive any limitation of the federal power, even in areas such as criminal law enforcement and education where States historically have been sovereign'.[28] As a result, the GFSZA was declared unconstitutional. In the aftermath of *Lopez*, many scholars wondered whether that judgment was an isolated event or whether the SCOTUS was serious about revitalising the federalism debate.

B. *Morrison*

One aspect that was left unresolved in *Lopez* was whether, after undertaking a specific factual inquiry demonstrating that a local non-economic activity had an adverse impact on interstate commerce, Congress could regulate such an activity. In this regard, it is worth recalling that, in *Lopez*, the SCOTUS did not expressly rule out this possibility. As a matter of fact, the absence of congressional fact-finding had led the US Court of Appeals to annul the GFSZA.

However, in *Morrison*,[29] the SCOTUS answered in the negative. There the appellant challenged the constitutionality of Section 13981 of the Violence Against Women Act (VAWA),[30] providing a federal civil remedy for the victims of gender-motivated violence. The appellant argued that Congress had gone beyond its powers under the Commerce Clause and Section 5 of the XIVth Amendment. Unlike the facts in *Lopez*, Congress had, prior to the adoption of the VAWA, carried out exhaustive background research, which proved that gender-motivated violence impinged upon interstate commerce.[31] However, the SCOTUS was categorical: 'Simply because Congress may conclude that a particular activity substantially affects interstate commerce does not necessarily make it so.'[32] The SCOTUS stressed the fact that the US Constitution did not confer on Congress the power to regulate local non-economic activities.

[28] *Lopez*, 564. [29] *Morrison*, 529 U.S. 598 (2000).

[30] 42 U.S.C. §13981.

[31] Congress found that gender-motivated violence deprived potential victims from travelling interstate and from engaging in interstate business, and diminished national productivity.

[32] *Morrison*, 529 U.S. 614 (2000).

To this effect, since gender-motivated violence was a local activity that did not have an economic nature, the SCOTUS ruled that the Commerce Clause could not operate as the constitutional basis for Section 13981 of the VAWA.[33]

C. *Gonzales* v. *Raich*

Lopez and *Morrison* made clear that the scope of the Commerce Clause would depend on how broad the SCOTUS interpreted the notion of 'economic activity'. Accordingly, the federal regulation of local non-economic activities is beyond congressional reach. On the contrary, regarding economic activities taking place within a single State, Congress has a broad leeway to invoke its commercial powers. To this effect, Congress may rely on the aggregation principle enounced in *Wickard* v. *Filburn* to sustain that there is a connection between the local economic activity in question and interstate commerce.

Accordingly, a broad construction of 'economic activity' would render the ruling of the SCOTUS in *Lopez* 'nothing more than a drafting guide'[34] for Congress. Ten years after *Lopez* was delivered, this was precisely the approach followed by the SCOTUS.[35] In *Raich*,[36] with a view to preventing seriously ill patients from suffering from chronic pain, California passed the Compassionated Use Act of 1996 (CUA),[37] which provided an exemption from criminal prosecution for physicians, patients and caregivers who possessed or cultivated marijuana for medical purposes. The respondents were two Californian residents who had relied on the CUA to possess and cultivate marijuana; when, in enforcing the Controlled Substance Act (CSA),[38] federal agents of the Drug Enforcement Administration (DEA) seized and destroyed their cannabis plants. The respondents then filed an injunction against the US Attorney General, alleging that, in relation to the cultivation, distribution and possession of marijuana for medicinal use, the CSA violated the Commerce Clause. On appeal, in light of *Lopez* and *Morrison*, the Ninth Circuit held that the CSA was unconstitutional.

33 *Morrison*, 529 U.S. 627 (2000).

34 *Gonzales* v. *Raich*, 545 U.S. 1, 38 (2005) (O'Connor J, dissenting).

35 Before *Raich* was delivered, the SCOTUS decided not to rule on the constitutionality of two federal statutes, preferring instead to base its ruling on statutory interpretation. See *Jones* v. *United States*, 529 U.S. 848 (2000) and *Solid Waste Agency of North Cook County* v. *United States Army Corps of Engineers*, 531 U.S. 159 (2001).

36 *Gonzales* v. *Raich*, 545 U.S. 1 (2005).

37 California Health & Safety Code Ann. § 11362.5 (b) (West Supp. 2005).

38 21 U.S.C. § 801 *et seq.*

However, in a 6–3 decision the SCOTUS reversed that judgment. Writing for the Court, Justice Stevens stated that the similarities between this case and *Wickard* v. *Filburn* were striking. In both cases the cultivation of a home-grown commodity could put at risk the objectives Congress aimed to achieve. Just as home-grown wheat could threaten federal interests in stabilising the interstate wheat market, the diversion of home-cultivated marijuana could put in peril the congressional intent of eliminating this substance from interstate commerce. 'Be it wheat or marijuana', Justice Stevens wrote, 'home consumption has … a substantial effect on supply and demand in the national market for that commodity'.[39]

Furthermore, the respondents contended that Congress had not itself embarked on an extensive factual inquiry determining the effects of home-cultivated marijuana on interstate commerce. However, Justice Stevens remarked in passing that congressional findings had never been a decisive factor when determining the validity of federal legislation.[40] This was so because judicial scrutiny was limited to ascertaining the existence of a 'rational basis' demonstrating that the federally regulated activity produced substantial effects on interstate commerce, without being necessary to verify if 'in fact' that was the case. To this effect, he concluded that, given the 'enforcement difficulties between marijuana cultivated locally and marijuana grown elsewhere',[41] Congress had acted rationally. Finally, the respondents argued that the possession and cultivation of home-grown marijuana did not have an economic nature and, consequently, the CSA was in breach of the Constitution. Nevertheless, by quoting the broad definition of 'economics' set out in Webster's Dictionary, Justice Stevens replied that 'the activities regulated by the CSA [were] quintessentially economic'.[42]

In light of *United States* v. *Lopez*, *United States* v. *Morrison* and *Gonzales* v. *Raich*, Tushnet observes that the federal vision promoted by Chief Justice Rehnquist limited itself to describing the objective of having a US government with limited powers, and thus missed the opportunity to provide for judicially enforceable standards.[43] This absence prevented the federal judiciary from erecting substantial limitations on the Commerce Clause, whilst giving room for manipulative use of precedent.[44] Put differently,

[39] *Gonzales* v. *Raich*, 16. [40] *Ibid.*, 21.

[41] *Ibid.*, 19. [42] *Ibid.*, 23.

[43] M. Tushnet, 'William Rehnquist's Federalism' in C. Bradley (eds.), *The Rehnquist Legacy* (Cambridge University Press, 2006), pp. 187–204.

[44] R. J. Pushaw Jr, 'The Medical Marijuana Case: A Commerce Clause Counter-Revolution?' (2005) 9 *Lewis & Clark Law Review* 879–941.

the ruling in *Lopez* can be read as a programmatic manifesto that did not provide lower courts with precise guidelines for applying it. Logically, the question was thus whether the Roberts Court would carry on with the Rehnquist legacy so as to improve it or whether the former Chief Justice's federal vision would fall into oblivion.

D. *The Roberts Court and the Commerce Clause*

During the Rehnquist era, a bloc of five Justices led the federalism revival (Rehnquist, O'Connor, Scalia, Thomas and Kennedy). The 'Federalism Five' strived to protect State autonomy. Notably, they limited the powers of Congress under the Commerce Clause, they proclaimed the anti-commandeering doctrine and they gave weight to State immunity.[45] Since 2005 the composition of the SCOTUS has undergone important changes, namely a new Chief Justice (Roberts) and three new Associate Justices (Alito, Sotomayor and Kagan). It is often said that with the arrival of a new Justice, a new court begins, let alone with the arrival of four in less than a decade. In this connection, some scholars have raised doubts as to whether a new majority coalition would be committed to protecting federalism concerns. For example, Shortell observes that an examination of the case law shows that 'since John Roberts was sworn in as Chief Justice in 2005, the Federalism Five bloc of Justices is no longer the dominant paradigm for understanding responses to federalism cases'.[46]

NFIB v. *Sebelius*[47] provided a good opportunity for the Roberts Court to demonstrate whether it would take federalism concerns seriously. In that case the SCOTUS was asked to examine the constitutionality of two provisions of the ACA, namely the so-called 'individual mandate' and the expansion of Medicaid. Since only the individual mandate concerned the powers of Congress under the Commerce Clause, it is to this aspect of the judgment that I now turn.

Congress had observed that the large number of Americans who were unable or unwilling to obtain health insurance had heavily burdened the national healthcare market for decades. Indeed, given that federal and

[45] See, generally, J. A. Gutiérrez-Fons, 'Comparing Supremacy: Sovereign Immunity of States in the United States and Non-Contractual State Liability in the European Union' (2010) 28 *Penn State International Law Review* 199–264.

[46] See C. Shortell, 'The End of the Federalism Five? Statutory Interpretation and the Roberts Court' (2012) 42 *Publius: The Journal of Federalism* 516–37.

[47] *NFIB* v. *Sebelius*, 132 S.Ct. 2566 (2012).

State law require hospitals and physicians to provide care to patients who are in need, regardless of their ability to pay, medical care providers deliver significant amounts of care to the uninsured without receiving compensation. However, hospitals and physicians do not absorb those costs but pass them on to the insurers, which in turn pass them on to their customers. Accordingly, as Justice Ginsburg puts it, 'the uninsured "free-ride" on those who pay for health insurance',[48] inevitably leading to an annual average increase of $1,000 for family premiums.[49] The purpose of the ACA was thus to increase the number of Americans covered by health insurance and to decrease the cost of health care.

To this end, the ACA contained two important reforms of the health care insurance market. In accordance with the 'guarantee-issue' reform, insurers were precluded from denying coverage to individuals suffering from pre-existing medical conditions. As to the 'community-rating' reform, the ACA prohibited insurers from charging unhealthy individuals higher premiums than healthy individuals. However, the problem was that those two reforms did not address the issue of healthy individuals who choose not to purchase insurance. Taken together, those two reforms could actually operate as an incentive for healthy individuals to delay purchasing insurance until they become sick. Moreover, since premiums could not be charged according to pre-existing medical conditions, the pool of unhealthy individuals with insurance would increase, forcing insurers to increase premiums on everyone. In order to counter the undesirable effects of those two reforms, the ACA laid down the so-called 'individual mandate', which required individuals to purchase a health insurance policy providing a minimum level of coverage. If they failed to do so, uninsured individuals had to pay a penalty to the Internal Revenue Service. Thus, the individual mandate sought, in essence, to force healthy individuals to purchase health insurance. Accordingly, since the premiums paid by the latter are on average higher than their health care expenses, their entry into the health care market would allow cross-subsidisation, which would avoid a general increase in the costs of health care, whilst increasing the number of Americans who are insured.

The US Government argued that the Commerce Clause could operate as a constitutional basis for the individual mandate, given that the failure to purchase insurance has a substantial impact on interstate commerce.

[48] *Ibid.*, 2611 (Ginsburg J, concurring).
[49] *Ibid.*, 2585 (Ginsburg J, concurring).

For their part, twenty-six States, as well as private individuals and organisations of independent businesses, argued that the Commerce Clause did not authorise Congress to force individuals to purchase goods that are available in the market, be that health insurance, cars or broccoli. A 5–4 majority agreed with the latter. Chief Justice Roberts, speaking for the Court, held that '[t]he power to *regulate* commerce presupposes the existence of commercial activity to be regulated'.[50] Stated differently, the Commerce Clause focuses on 'existing commercial activity' that substantially affects interstate commerce. This meant that Congress lacked the power to *compel* individuals to enter into the health care market.[51] For the Chief Justice, if Congress could regulate what individuals 'do not do', on the ground that their failure to act has an impact on interstate commerce, the principle of enumerated powers would become devoid of substance.[52] This would 'fundamentally [change] the relation between the citizen and the Federal Government',[53] since 'any police power to regulate individuals as such, as opposed to their activities, remains vested in the States'.[54]

The US Government also posited that uninsured individuals formed a class active in the market for health care, namely the 'self-insured'. However, the Chief Justice took a different view. Congress could not regulate 'a class whose commercial inactivity rather than activity is its defining feature'.[55] In addition, he ruled that, whilst Congress could anticipate the effects on commerce of a commercial activity, it could not 'anticipate that activity itself in order to regulate individuals not currently engaged in commerce'.[56]

In summary, a 5–4 majority ruled that the Commerce Clause did not provide a constitutional basis for the individual mandate. However, recasting the individual mandate as a tax, a different 5–4 majority ruled that, under its taxing powers, Congress could compel individuals to purchase health insurance. Two implications may be drawn from *NFIB* v. *Sebelius*. First, by drawing a distinction between 'commercial activity' and 'commercial inactivity', the SCOTUS endorses a 'formal approach' to imposing an additional limitation on congressional powers under the Commerce Clause. This could give rise to problems since, as Justice Ginsburg pointed out, 'it is possible to restate most actions as corresponding inactions with the same effect'.[57] Second, it appears that the SCOTUS

[50] *Ibid.*, 2586 (original emphasis).
[51] *Ibid.*, 2587. [52] *Ibid.*, 2587.
[53] *Ibid.*, 2589. [54] *Ibid.*, 2591.
[55] *Ibid.*, 2590. [56] *Ibid.* [57] *Ibid.*

sees federalism concerns as a way of protecting individual freedom, and not only State autonomy.[58] However, one may call into question whether the Commerce Clause is the appropriate constitutional venue for protecting individual freedom. Indeed, one may wonder why the Justices did not rely on other constitutional provisions such as the Due Process Clause, as enshrined in the Vth Amendment, in order to determine whether compelling individuals to engage in commercial activity was in breach of their fundamental rights.[59]

Lopez, *Morrison*, *Raich* and *NFIB* v. *Sebelius* show that, in the USA, the federalism debate is very much alive. Let us now examine what happens on the other side of the Atlantic.

II. The principle of conferral applied to the EU's internal market harmonisation clause

A. *The establishment of the internal market*

The EU's internal market harmonisation clause, that is, Article 114 TFEU (ex Article 95 EC Treaty, ex Article 100a EEC Treaty), was introduced by the 1986 Single European Act, with a view to ensuring the establishment and functioning of the internal market as defined in Article 26 TFEU (ex Article 14 EC). In contrast to the original treaty provision governing harmonisation, Article 114 TFEU does not require unanimity, but qualified majority voting (QVM). With the exception of fiscal matters, the free movement of persons and the protection of workers, the introduction of Article 114 TFEU meant that positive integration would take place, even if some Member States raised dissenting voices. Fearing a substantial loss of their sovereignty, Member States introduced two safeguards when drafting Article 114 TFEU. First, this provision may be relied upon 'save where otherwise provided for in [the] Treaty', that is, it has a residual character. Second, it introduces a derogation procedure for those Member States wishing to maintain in force their own provisions, or adopt new measures in the light of new scientific evidence. However, despite those

58 M. Minow, 'Affordable Convergence: "Reasonable Interpretation" and the Affordable Care Act' (2012) 126 *Harvard Law Review* 117–49, at 147.

59 See, J. Greene, 'What the New Deal Settled' (2012) 15 *University of Pennsylvania Journal of Constitutional Law* 265–89 and D. A. Strauss, 'Commerce Clause Revisionism and the Affordable Care Act' (2012) *Supreme Court Review* 1–29. See also *Seven-Sky* v. *Holder*, 661 F3d 1, 19 (DC Cir. 2011).

two safeguards, the EU legislature started a centripetal trend, leading to a proliferation of EU measures.[60]

Originally, the ECJ accepted an expansive use of Article 114 TFEU by embracing a wide interpretation of the concept of 'internal market'. For example, in *Titanium Dioxide,*[61] the ECJ expanded the scope of Article 114 TFEU in two ways. Substantially, the ECJ held that the elimination of distortions of competition was necessary for the establishment and functioning of the internal market. Even in the absence of obstacles to trade, the EU legislator could have recourse to that Treaty provision.[62] Systematically, where Article 114 TFEU and another treaty provision stood on an equal footing, the ECJ seemed to prefer the former. Further, the ECJ again expanded the interpretation of Article 114 TFEU by holding that recourse to that treaty provision was not made conditional upon 'approximating national laws'.[63] On the contrary, where necessary, it can 'lay down measures relating to a specific product or class of products'.[64]

As a result, until 2000 no challenge succeeded in striking down EU legislation adopted under that treaty provision on the ground that it was *ultra vires*.[65] Arguably, some scholars posit that, for the sake of completing the internal market programme launched by the Commission, the ECJ had decided to exercise a pro-integrationist judicial self-restraint.[66] Until 2000, Article 114 TFEU had often been conceived as an unstoppable vacuum of national power. Had the ECJ continued this line of reasoning, some scholars argued that it would have been very difficult to support the contention that the EU was bound by the principle of conferral.[67] In fact, it was argued that Article 114 TFEU had to be read as a general source of power to regulate the market.[68]

[60] Out of the 282 Proposals put forward by the Commission, 250 were approved by 1992, most of which had as their legal basis ex Article 100a (now Article 114 TFEU).

[61] Case-300/89 *Commission* v. *Council* (*Titanium Dioxide*) [1991] ECR I-2867.

[62] Opinion of AG Jacobs in Case C-350/92 *Spain* v. *Council* [1995] ECR I-1985, para. 45.

[63] 'National' here refers to the Member States.

[64] Case C-359/92 *Germany* v. *Council* [1994] ECR I-3685.

[65] *Ibid.*

[66] T. Tridimas and G. Tridimas, 'The European Court of Justice and the Annulment of the Tobacco Advertisement Directive: Friend of National Sovereignty or Foe of Public Health?' (2002) 14 *European Journal of Law and Economics* 171–83.

[67] J. H. H. Weiler and J. Lockhart, '"Taking Rights Seriously": the European Court and its Fundamental Rights Jurisprudence' (1995) 32 *Common Market Law Review* 51–94. See also J. H. H. Weiler, 'The Transformation of Europe' (1991) 100 *Yale Law Journal* 2,403–83.

[68] R. Barents, 'The Internal Market Unlimited: Some Observations on the Legal Basis of Community Legislation' (1993) 30 *Common Market Law Review* 85–109.

B. *Tobacco Advertising I*

With a view to eliminating obstacles to the free movement of advertising media (other than television) and distortions of competition among advertisers, those benefiting from sponsorship of tobacco products and tobacco manufacturers, the Council and the European Parliament relied on ex Article 47(2) EC (now Article 53 TFEU), ex Article 55 EC (now Article 62 TFEU) and ex Article 95 EC (now Article 114 TFEU) as legal bases to adopt Directive 98/43. In principle, that Directive prohibited all forms of advertising and sponsorship of tobacco products in the EU. Nevertheless, its Article 3 allowed the advertising of brand names already used in good faith for both tobacco products and other types of goods or services. In the same way, it excluded from its scope of application communications between professionals in the tobacco trade, advertising in sales outlets or in publications published and printed in third countries but not principally intended for the EU market. Moreover, Article 5 did not preclude Member States from issuing stricter measures in relation to the advertising and sponsorship of tobacco products, that is, it only laid down minimal harmonisation.

As the SCOTUS did in *Lopez*, the ECJ began by stating that, in accordance with Article 5 TEU, Article 114 TFEU cannot be read as vesting upon the EU legislature 'a general power to regulate the internal market'. Neither mere disparities between national rules nor abstract obstacles to free movement can lead to the adoption of EU legislation under Article 114 TFEU.[69] Next, the ECJ ruled that Article 168 TFEU did not preclude all EU measures from having an impact on the protection of public health. Provided that the contested Directive fulfilled the conditions laid down in Article 53 TFEU, Article 62 TFEU and Article 114 TFEU, the fact that the EU legislature had opted for a high level of protection of human health was welcomed. Accordingly, the validity of Directive 98/43 could not be questioned under public health considerations alone. The real question was whether the EU legislator had complied with the conditions laid down in those treaty provisions.[70]

As to the elimination of obstacles to the free movement of goods and to the freedom to provide services, the ECJ drew a distinction between static and dynamic advertising media. Whilst recognising that the choice of Article 114 TFEU was legitimate in relation to the free movement of

[69] *Tobacco Advertising I*, paras. 83–4.
[70] *Ibid.*, para. 88.

dynamic advertising media (e.g. newspapers or magazines), the ECJ concluded that this was not the case for advertising media located in hotels, restaurants, cafes or cinemas (e.g. posters, parasols, ashtrays).[71] It is true that not all provisions contained in Directive 98/43 had to contribute to eliminating obstacles to free movement, as long as they were 'necessary to ensure that certain prohibitions imposed in pursuit of that purpose are not circumvented'.[72] However, that was not the case. In any event, traders complying with Directive 98/43 were not exempt from meeting stricter rules adopted by the host Member States in accordance with Article 5 thereof. In the absence of a 'free movement clause', the Directive did not guarantee the removal of those obstacles. As a result, the ECJ concluded that Directive 98/43 did not eliminate obstacles to free movement.

Regarding the elimination of distortions of competition, the ECJ recalled that those distortions had to be 'appreciable'. It conceded that advertising agencies and producers of advertising products would be economically favoured by Member States imposing fewer restrictions on the advertising of tobacco products. Consequently, those disparities would distort real competition. However, unlike the factual situation in *Titanium Dioxide*, those distortions were 'remote and indirect', that is, they were not appreciable. Although the relocation of sports events, resulting from national disparities concerning their sponsorship by tobacco products, could give rise to appreciable distortions of competition, that finding did not justify an 'outright prohibition of advertising of the kind imposed by the Directive'.

To sum up, since the EU lacked the competences to regulate certain forms of advertising and sponsorship of tobacco products and a partial annulment of the Directive was not possible, the ECJ opted for annulling it entirely. It follows from *Tobacco Advertising I* that the ECJ tried to enforce the principle of conferral. As the SCOTUS held for the Commerce Clause, the ECJ ruled that Article 114 TFEU cannot be read as a '*carte blanche*'.[73] It is not an unlimited source of EU power, but it must comply with constitutional internal and external limits.

Internally, in order to have recourse to Article 114 TFEU, the EU measure must contribute to eliminating a 'real or potential obstacle to free movement' or, alternatively, 'appreciable distortions of competition'. In accordance with the ECJ's decision, static advertising media cannot be considered as an obstacle to free movement. If one considers that

[71] *Ibid.*, paras. 98–9. [72] *Ibid.*, para. 100.

[73] Opinion AG Fennelly in *Tobacco Advertising I*, para. 89.

advertising is a selling arrangement,[74] and that the ban on the advertising of tobacco products in public places does not discriminate against imports,[75] it seems that 'non-discriminatory selling arrangements' fall outside the scope of Article 114 TFEU. Arguably, where a national measure is not an obstacle to EU trade under Article 34 TFEU, the elimination of that measure cannot logically justify the choice of Article 114 TFEU as a legal basis. Thus, one could argue that *Tobacco Advertising I* introduces a parallelism between Article 34 TFEU and Article 114 TFEU.[76] The EU legislator may not expand the scope of the free movement of goods beyond the limits set out in *Keck*.[77] Therefore, harmonisation would focus on national measures that, whilst falling within the scope of Article 34 TFEU, can be justified under Article 36 TFEU or under mandatory requirements, but nonetheless, hinder the completion of the internal market.[78] As recognised by the case law of the ECJ,[79] EU legislation would then focus on limiting the degree of discretion enjoyed by the Member States when invoking the protection of general interests. However, following this approach, several pieces of EU legislation in the field of consumer protection or contract law would qualify as '*ultra vires*'.[80] Still, the ECJ simultaneously introduced an exemption from the overlapping interpretation of Article 34 TFEU and Article 114 TFEU. Activities not considered to be obstacles to the free movement can be harmonised insofar as they are necessary to avoid the circumvention of the aim the EU legislature seeks to achieve. This exemption echoes the SCOTUS in *United States* v. *Lopez* when holding that local non-economic activities may be federally regulated in order for the general economic scheme not to be undercut.

[74] See C-412/93 *Leclerc-Siplec* [1995] ECR I-179.

[75] See C-292/92 *Hünermund* [1993] ECR I-6787.

[76] See J. Usher, 'Case Note on Case C-376/98' (2001) 38 *Common Market Law Review* 1,531–9. See also A. Dashwood, 'The Limits of European Community Powers' (1996) 21 *European Law Review* 113–28; P. J. Slot, 'Harmonisation' (1996) 21 *European Law Review* 378–87; and K. Mortelmans, 'The Relationship between the Treaty Rules and Community Measures for the Establishment and Functioning of the Internal Market – Towards a Concordance Rule' (2002) 39 *Common Market Law Review* 1,303–46.

[77] Joined cases C-267/91 and C-268/91 *Criminal Proceedings against Bernard Keck and Daniel Mithouard* [1993] ECR I-06097.

[78] See Commission White Paper Completing the Single Market, COM (85) 310.

[79] See Case C-1/96 *Compassion in World Farming* [1998] ECR I-1251, para. 47.

[80] Mortelmans, 'The Relationship between the Treaty Rules and Community Measures for the Establishment and Functioning of the Internal Market', 1,326 and W. Van Gerven, 'Harmonization of Private Law: Do We Need it?' (2004) 41 *Common Market Law Review* 505–32.

Unfortunately, the ECJ did not develop this point further, leaving the door open for different interpretations.

As to the expression 'appreciable distortions of competition', the ECJ seems willing to introduce a *de minimis* test, along the lines of that applied in the context of EU competition law. This would seem at odds with its case law pertaining to the fundamental freedoms, where the ECJ has consistently refused to endorse a *de minimis* rule.[81] If distortions on the production costs are sufficiently important to trigger harmonisation, and so are disparities in sponsoring sports events, why is it that divergent national regulatory frameworks on the advertising of tobacco products do not produce such distortions? The ECJ did not provide an exact answer but limited itself to briefly highlighting the differences between the facts of the case at hand and those that gave rise to the judgment in *Titanium Dioxide*.

Externally, the ECJ examined the validity of Directive 98/43 in light of the principle of proportionality as laid down in Article 5 TEU. First, since potential contradictions among national advertising rules of tobacco products constituted obstacles to the free movement of dynamic media, the ECJ went on to assess whether Directive 98/43 was suitable for eliminating those obstacles. Owing to the lack of a free movement clause, Directive 98/43 was manifestly inappropriate to ensure the free movement of dynamic media. Second, as to the appreciable distortions of competition arising from disparities in sport sponsorship rules, the EU legislator had gone beyond what was required to counter those distortions. An outright ban on all types of sponsorship by tobacco products excessively eroded the competence of the Member States. Thus, the ECJ applied the two limbs of the principle of proportionality, stressing its constitutional importance.

C. *Tobacco Advertising II*

After Directive 98/43 was declared invalid by the ECJ in *Tobacco Advertising I*, the EU legislator adopted Directive 2003/33. In so doing, it had recourse to ex Article 47(2) EC (now Article 53 TFEU), ex Article 55 EC (now Article 62 TFEU) and ex Article 95 EC (now Article 114 TFEU) as legal bases. The new Directive also regulated advertising and sponsorship in respect of tobacco products in media other than television.

[81] But see L. Gormley, 'Competition and Free Movement: Is the Internal Market the same as the Common Market?' (2002) 13 *European Business Law Review* 517–22.

Article 3 prohibited the advertising of tobacco products in the press and 'other printed publications', with the exception of publications exclusively intended for professionals in the tobacco market, or printed and published in third countries and not principally intended for the EU market. Directive 2003/33 also extended this prohibition to the information society services (e.g. the Internet). Further, Article 4 prohibited the advertising of tobacco products in radio programmes, as well as their sponsorship by tobacco manufacturers or distributors. Article 5 banned the sponsorship of events or activities by tobacco products taking place in several Member States or having cross-border implications. The free distribution of tobacco products in these events or activities was also prohibited. Finally, Article 8 laid down a 'free movement clause'.

At the outset in *Tobacco Advertising II*, the ECJ rejected that Directive 2003/33 sought to harmonise public health. Referring to *Tobacco Advertising I*, it held that, in so far as Directive 2003/33 eliminated obstacles to trade or removed distortions of competition, the EU legislator was not prevented from protecting public health. On the contrary, Articles 168 TFEU and 114 TFEU required the EU institutions to take into account the protection of public health.

Next, the ECJ went on to acknowledge that there were disparities between the Member States in relation to the advertising and sponsorship of tobacco products. Whilst several Member States had, under certain conditions, allowed the advertising of tobacco products, others did not. Those disparities were not only real, but they were also increasing in importance. In this sense, those disparities impeded the free movement of the press and other printed publications, and restricted the freedom to provide advertising service in three ways. First, because of those disparities, imports had a more restrictive market access than domestic products. Imported publications would have to comply with the two different sets of rules, namely those of the home and those of the host Member States. They would thus have to face a double burden. Second, those disparities prevented service providers from offering space in their publications to advertisers located in different Member States. Finally, the ECJ rejected the '*de minimis*' argument put forward by Germany. 'Even if only by way of exception or in small quantities', it held, the previous findings remained valid regarding publications primarily distributed locally.[82] Thus, the ECJ held that disparities in the national laws constituted an obstacle to trade for the purposes of Article 114 TFEU.

[82] *Tobacco Advertising II*, para. 59.

Moreover, the ECJ examined whether Articles 3 and 4 actually contributed to eliminating those obstacles. As in *Tobacco Advertising I*, the ECJ held that a ban on the advertising of tobacco products facilitated the free movement of printed media and the provision of radio and information society services. Moreover, the inclusion of a free movement clause guaranteed that once publications or radio programmes complied with the provisions of Directive 2003/33, they were free to move or broadcast in the EU. Additionally, the ECJ held that having recourse to Article 114 TFEU was not made conditional upon proving the existence of an interstate element for every situation covered by the EU measure in question, provided that that measure generally contributed to the functioning and establishment of the internal market.

As to the principle of proportionality, Germany argued that the prohibition set out in Articles 3 and 4 was contrary to the freedom of the press, insofar as it restricted the revenue of press products. Moreover, it posited that an exemption should have been granted for press media locally distributed. Nevertheless, the ECJ took a different view. It held that, although the freedom of the press was recognised as a general principle of EU law,[83] it could be proportionally and rationally limited by public interests. Since it facilitated the free movement of press media, whilst ensuring a high protection of human health, the ECJ stated that the solution adopted by the EU legislature was not manifestly inappropriate. Further, in relation to publications targeting a regional or local market, the ECJ ruled that there were no less restrictive options available. Indeed, granting an exemption would have rendered it extremely difficult to distinguish between the exempted publications and the ones violating Directive 2003/33. As a result, the ECJ dismissed the application.

As with all sequels, *Tobacco Advertising II* leaves the reader with a '*déjà-vu*' impression. In *Tobacco Advertising I* the ECJ hinted that it would not oppose the harmonisation of 'dynamic advertising media', such as newspapers, journals and magazines.[84] As the ECJ pointed out in both cases, disparities among national laws could obstruct the free movement of the press. This was precisely what the EU legislator did when adopting Directive 2003/33. Having learned from the mistakes of the past, the EU legislator included a free movement clause, and limited the ban on sponsorship by tobacco products to events having cross-border implications. Moreover, extending the prohibition to radio programmes and

[83] See also Article 11 of the Charter of Fundamental Rights of the EU.

[84] *Tobacco Advertising I*, para. 98.

information societies not only seems reasonable, but it could be considered as completing the legislative framework initiated by Directive 89/552,[85] which prohibits the advertising of tobacco products in order to promote the free broadcasting of television programmes.

However, some scholars argued that when the ECJ examined the existence of obstacles to the freedom to provide radio and internet services, it limited itself to stating that, in the view of 'increasing public awareness', it was likely for future barriers to emerge. Those scholars criticised this part of the judgment on the ground that the ECJ set the probability of new obstacles to free moment at such a low level that it thwarted the accepted internal limits of Article 114 TFEU.[86] Indeed, they argued that the ECJ was caught by an oxymoron: how can mere disparities among national rules not be enough to trigger the application of Article 114 TFEU when 'potential' obstacles are? As the SCOTUS did in *Raich* when defining the expression 'economic activities', the ECJ also appears to follow a broad definition of activities that can be regulated at central level. In its view, the expression 'obstacles to free movement' includes not only 'actual' but also 'prospective' barriers to intra-EU trade.

D. *Vodafone*

More recently, in *Vodafone* the ECJ was asked to examine the validity of Regulation No 717/2007[87] (the Roaming Regulation),[88] in light of EU's internal market harmonisation clause, the principle of proportionality and the principle of subsidiarity. That Regulation lays down maximum charges that mobile operators may levy for voice calls made and received by users outside their own network (the 'Euro-tariff').[89] In addition, the Roaming Regulation lays down the maximum price that the consumer's operator must pay to the foreign operator when that consumer uses the latter operator's network ('wholesale roaming charges'). Moreover, mobile operators are obliged to provide information about roaming charges to customers.[90]

[85] [1989] OJ L 298/23.

[86] M. Ludwigs, 'Note on Case C-380/03' (2007) 44 *Common Market Law Review* 1,159–76.

[87] [2007] OJ L 171/32. Regulation No. 544/2009, [2009] OJ L 167/12, amended Regulation No. 717/2007 so as to extend the imposition of maximum wholesale and retail prices to SMS and data roaming. Accordingly, Regulation No. 717/2007 has been substantially amended, recast by Regulation No. 531/2012, [2012] OJ L 172/10.

[88] See Article 4. [89] See Article 3. [90] See Article 6.

At the outset, the ECJ recalled the conditions under which the EU legislator may have recourse to Article 114 TFEU.[91] Next, the ECJ went on to apply those principles to the case at hand. It began by looking at the situation that existed at the time of adoption of the Roaming Regulation. First, as explained in the explanatory memorandum to the proposal for the Roaming Regulation, consumers faced a high level of charges for international roaming services. The explanatory memorandum and the Impact Assessment Report (IAR) also stated that '[t]he excessive retail charges resulted both from wholesale charges levied by the foreign host network operator and, in many cases, from high retail mark-ups charged by the home provider'.[92] Second, the relationship between costs and roaming prices was not that of a fully competitive market. Third, under Directive 2002/21,[93] the National Regulatory Authorities (NRAs) did not enjoy sufficient tools to take effective and decisive action with regard to the high level of wholesale prices for roaming services.[94] Fourth, Member States faced increasing pressure to solve the high level of retail charges for EU-wide roaming services.[95] As the explanatory memorandum and the IAR pointed out, the adoption of such national measures would have led to a divergent development of national laws.[96] Moreover, in light of Recital 14 of the Roaming Regulation, the ECJ found that 'a divergent development of national laws seeking to lower retail charges only … would have been liable to cause significant distortions of competition and to disrupt the orderly functioning of the [EU]-wide roaming market'.[97] In light of those circumstances, the ECJ held that 'the EU legislator was right to adopt a specific ex ante regulatory measure which would take into account the unique characteristics of the roaming markets and seek to maintain competition among mobile operators, namely the imposition of a price ceiling for the retail and wholesale charges made for roaming services'.[98]

Furthermore, the ECJ was called upon to determine whether, by imposing a Euro-tariff, the Regulation had breached the principle of proportionality. In this regard, applicants urged the ECJ to reply in the negative by reason of the fact that the Regulation did not confine itself to imposing ceilings for the wholesale charge, but also laid down ceilings for

[91] *Vodafone*, paras. 32 to 36. [92] *Ibid.*, para. 39.
[93] [2002] OJ L 108/33. [94] *Vodafone*, para. 42.
[95] *Ibid.*, para. 44 [96] *Ibid.*, para. 45.
[97] *Ibid.*, para. 47.
[98] See K. Lenaerts, 'The European Court of Justice and Process-Oriented Review' (2012) 31 *Yearbook of European Law* 3–16.

retail charges, as well as an obligation to provide information about those charges to roaming customers.

As a starting point, the ECJ recalled that 'the [EU] legislature must be allowed a broad discretion in areas in which its action involves political, economic and social choices and in which it is called upon to undertake complex assessments and evaluations'.[99] This means that the EU legislator is not required to find 'the only or the best possible measure' capable of attaining the objective that it is seeking to pursue. On the contrary, the lawfulness of the EU legislative act in question 'can be affected only if the measure is manifestly inappropriate having regard to the objective which the competent institution is seeking to pursue'.[100] However, the exercise of such discretion must be based on objective criteria.[101] In this regard, the ECJ stressed the fact that the Commission had studied the different options available, namely regulating retail charges only, or wholesale charges only, or both. Referring to those findings, the ECJ noted that the imposition of a Euro-tariff aimed to ensure 'a more reasonable reflection of the underlying costs involved in the provision of those services than ha[d] been the case'.[102] Indeed, as the IAR pointed out, 'the average retail charge for a roaming call was … more than five times higher than the actual cost of providing the wholesale service'.[103] Accordingly, the ECJ ruled that the imposition of a Euro-tariff was an appropriate means of protecting consumers against high levels of charges.

As to the question whether the measure at issue was necessary, the ECJ also referred to the IAR, which stated that 'experience has shown that reductions in wholesale prices for [EU]-wide roaming services may not be reflected in lower retail prices for roaming owing to the absence of [competitive] incentives for this to happen', which necessitated direct regulation.[104] Hence, the EU legislator 'could legitimately take the view that regulation of the wholesale market alone would not achieve the same result as [the Roaming Regulation]'.[105] Moreover, the ECJ added that the scope *ratione temporis* of the measure at issue was limited. Article 13 contained a 'sunset clause', that is, that the Regulation was to expire on 30 June 2010.[106]

[99] *Vodafone*, para. 52. [100] *Ibid.*

[101] *Ibid.*, para. 53. [102] *Ibid.*, para. 57.

[103] *Ibid.*, para. 58. [104] *Ibid.*, para. 66.

[105] *Ibid.*, para. 68.

[106] *Ibid.*, para. 69. However, see Article 22 of Regulation 531/2012, which now provides that the Roaming Regulation is to expire on 30 June 2022. See M. Brenncke, 'Case Note' (2010) 47 *Common Market Law Review* 1,793–814, at 1,811.

As to the question whether the Roaming Regulation complied with the principle of subsidiarity, the ECJ examined the provisions relating to the imposition of price ceilings in the wholesale market and in the retail market. As to the former, given that a Member State lacks the regulatory powers to impose maximum prices on mobile operators located in another Member State, it was clear that the Roaming Regulation complied with the principle of subsidiarity.[107] As to the retail market, the ECJ found that 'any measure seeking to reduce retail charges alone without affecting the level of costs for the wholesale supply of [EU]-wide roaming services would have been liable to disrupt the smooth functioning of the [EU]-wide roaming market'.[108] Hence, a joint regulatory intervention in both markets was required and would be best achieved at EU level.[109]

Lenaerts has argued that '*Vodafone* is an interesting example that shows how the ECJ applies the principle of proportionality in a procedural fashion'.[110] He notes that 'it is the first time ever that the ECJ has expressly relied on the IAR when examining the compatibility of an EU policy measure with the principle of proportionality'.[111] Indeed, he stresses the fact that the ECJ referred to the findings set out in the IAR on six occasions[112] and to those laid down in the explanatory memorandum on five.[113] In so doing, the ECJ does not 'second-guess the merits of the substantive choices made by the EU legislator'. Instead, it 'preferred to make sure that lawmakers had done their work properly'.[114] Brenncke agrees with that reading of *Vodafone*. He posits that '[the] more the [ECJ] requires from the Commission in procedural terms ... the more it will alleviate the marginal judicial review of the substantive issues which a "manifestly inappropriate" standard entails'.[115]

III. Comparing the case law of both courts

Three conclusions may be drawn when comparing the case law of both courts. First, both the SCOTUS and the ECJ have stressed the fact that

107 See also the Opinion of AG Poiares Maduro in *Vodafone*, para. 27.

108 *Vodafone*, para. 77. 109 *Ibid.*, paras. 76 to 78.

110 Lenaerts, 'The European Court of Justice and Process-Oriented Review', 8.

111 *Ibid.* (referring to A. Alemanno, 'A Meeting of Minds on Impact Assessment' (2011) 17 *European Public Law* 485–505, at 502).

112 *Vodafone*, paras. 45, 55, 58 and 65 (three times).

113 *Ibid.*, paras. 39, 43, 45, 59 and 63.

114 *Ibid.* See also Brenncke, 'Case Note', 1,809.

115 Brenncke, 'Case Note', 1,809–10.

the commercial powers of the central government are not infinite, but they must comply with the principle of enumerated powers. To this effect, both courts have respectively sought to identify activities falling outside the scope of the Commerce Clause and Article 114 TFEU. In light of *Lopez*, local non-economic activities do not have a substantial effect on interstate commerce. In the EU, *Tobacco Advertising I* suggests that non-discriminatory selling arrangements are not obstacles to trade. However, neither court provides clear guidance as to the activities remaining 'within' the powers of the federal or EU legislator respectively. *Lopez* did not provide a definition of 'economic activities'. Neither did the ECJ clarify to what extent the scope of Article 34 TFEU and that of Article 114 TFEU overlap, nor did it explain under what circumstances distortions of competition are 'appreciable'. Second, one may argue that, in subsequent developments, these analytical shortcomings favoured the federal and the EU legislatures. Arguably, the Opinion of Justice Stevens in *Raich* provided the broadest possible definition of 'economic activities'. In *Tobacco Advertising II* the ECJ opened the door to 'potential' obstacles. Finally, *Tobacco Advertising I* and *Lopez* introduced an important exception to the regulation of activities falling outside the scope of Article 114 TFEU and the Commerce Clause respectively. Where the inclusion of those activities prevents the general regulatory scheme from being circumvented, Congress and the EU legislature may expand its 'regulatory net'. Besides, in determining whether this is the case, both courts apply a soft standard of review. It is true that in *NFIB* v. *Sebelius* the SCOTUS sought to limit '*Raich*'s regulatory net'. However, Chief Justice Roberts did not provide clear guidance as to why the 'individual mandate' was not a 'proper' means of ensuring the effectiveness of the ACA.

Therefore, the foregoing considerations cast doubts as to whether the principle of enumerated powers may suffice by itself to counter 'centripetal forces'. Perhaps, it would be best to look at other additional or alternative solutions, which would better allocate powers between the centre and the periphery.

IV. Other solutions to counterbalance the centripetal trend

A. *Reliance on the political process*

Some US scholars argued that political safeguards are enough to protect state autonomy. In his seminal article, Wechsler posited that the Senate, the important role played by State legislatures in congressional districting, and presidential rapports with Congress ensure that States' rights are taken into account in the federal decision-making process.[116] *Garcia* echoed this theory, when a majority of Justices ruled that 'the structure of the Federal Government itself was relied on to insulate the interests of the States'.[117] However, not only did *Lopez* suppose a revival of judicial enforcement of federalism, but this approach also fails to capture the modern US political environment.

First, the interests of State governments do not necessarily coincide with those of the States as 'political institutions'.[118] For instance, obtaining federal funding may reduce the incentives of State governments to oppose an *ultra vires* federalisation of extensive areas of law.[119] Second, since Senators are no longer chosen by State legislatures but are directly elected,[120] a Senator will rather support interests geographically concentrated in his State than defend his State's regulatory prerogatives. Federal and State elected officials are 'rivals and not allies', competing for providing the electorate with beneficial regulation. Third, it is very unlikely for the US president to veto popular bills alluding to federalism. For instance, although President Bush raised federalism concerns, he finally did not veto the GFSZA.[121] Fourth, political safeguards do not prevent 'horizontal aggrandisements', that is a coalition of States imposing their preference on a dissenting minority. Last, but not least, since federalism is not a tangible policy objective, Congress may forgo it to benefit more pressing substantive policies.[122]

Drawing on the US experience, Young supports the contention that, in the EU, the political safeguards set out in the treaties have also failed to protect state autonomy.[123] First, although Member States are better represented at the Council than American States are in Congress, success in

[116] H. Wechsler, 'The Political Safeguards of Federalism: The Role of the States in the Composition and Selection of the National Government' (1954) 54 *Columbia Law Review* 543–60; Choper, 'The Scope of National Power vis-à-vis the State', 1,561–7.

[117] *Garcia* v. *San Antonio Metropolitan Transit Authority*, 469 U.S. 528, 551 (1985).

[118] L. Kramer, 'Putting the Politics Back into the Safeguards of Federalism' (2000) 100 *Columbia Law Review* 215–92.

[119] See, in this regard, *South Dakota* v. *Dole*, 483 U.S. 203 (1987).

[120] See XVIIth Amendment of the US Constitution.

[121] Perhaps it was politically unwise to oppose the publicly welcomed 'omnibus' Crime Control Act, of which the GFSZA was part.

[122] Editorial Note, 'The Lesson of *Lopez*: The Political Dynamics of Federalism's Political Safeguards' (2006) 119 *Harvard Law Review* 609–30.

[123] E. Young, 'Protecting Member State Autonomy in the European Union: Some Cautionary Tales from American Federalism' (2002) 77 *New York University Law Review* 1,612–737. However, cf. Opinion of AG Poiares Maduro in *Vodafone*, para. 1.

obtaining substantive policy commitments may overwhelm concerns over institutional interests. Admittedly, the Council prevents radical intrusions into state autonomy, but it leaves the door open to gradual erosions. With a view to obtaining short-term objectives, Bermann suggests that European states have obviated long-term considerations on regulatory competences.[124] In the same way, incentives to protect federalism become less attractive when state executives rely on the Council to circumvent political obstacles at Member State level. Thus, the so-called 'communitarisation' of regulation was seen by state executives as a way of escaping from parliamentary control. Likewise, the shift from unanimity to QMV has facilitated 'horizontal aggrandisements'. Second, Young argues that it is difficult to see how the Commission will protect state autonomy when the Treaty itself prohibits its members from acting in the interests of the Member States.[125] Besides, it is argued that its formal promises to respect subsidiarity have not been followed in practice. Finally, empirical evidence shows that the overwhelming voting pattern of the European Parliament (EP) is explained by 'left–right' politics, whilst national interests, independent of national party positions, have a marginal influence on voting.[126]

Therefore, since all EU political institutions have failed to check the vertical powers of the EU, their 'prevailing institutional incestuousness' has been denounced by some scholars who urge for better competence-monitoring.[127] Perhaps the fact that political safeguards have not protected federalism was due to the absence of the national parliaments in the EU legislative process. As the party most affected by a vacuum of competences, the Treaty of Lisbon now provides for their active involvement in monitoring compliance with the principle of subsidiarity. It introduces an 'early warning' mechanism. National parliaments may manifest their opposition to the presidents of the EU political institutions by issuing a reasoned opinion against proposals that do not comply with the principle of subsidiarity. If at least one third of the votes allocated to the national parliaments favour the withdrawal of the proposal, the Commission must review it. If a simple majority of negative votes is reached but the

124 G. Bermann, 'Taking Subsidiarity Seriously: Federalism in the European Community and the US' (1994) 94 *Columbia Law Review* 331–456.

125 Article 245 TFEU.

126 S. Hix, A. Noury and G. Roland, 'Dimensions of Politics in the European Parliament' (2006) 50 *American Journal of Political Science* 494–511.

127 S. Weatherill, 'Better Competence Monitoring' (2005) 30 *European Law Review* 23–41.

Commission decides to maintain the proposal, the EU legislator must, before concluding the first reading, express its opinion by voting.[128]

In my view, the involvement of national parliaments is a welcomed development that breaks the vicious cycle of the EU institutions.[129] However, it is worth noting that this reform has not been introduced as an alternative to judicial review. On the contrary, in accordance with their own constitutional arrangements, Member States may lodge direct actions on behalf of their national parliaments.[130] Thus, the ECJ would still exercise a key 'ex post' control.

B. *A second layer of competence control*

At the outset it is worth noting that, in the context of the Commerce Clause, there is no US equivalent to the EU principles of proportionality and subsidiarity. As Chief Justice Marshall wrote in *Gibbons* v. *Ogden*, once an activity falls within the scope of the Commerce Clause, congressional power becomes 'complete in itself, may be exercised to its utmost extent, and acknowledges no limitation other than are prescribed in the Constitution'.[131] This absence is explored here next.[132]

1. The principle of proportionality

When having recourse to Article 114 TFEU as a legal basis, the EU legislator must remove obstacles or eliminate distortions of competition. If, in the light of the principle of proportionality,[133] the ECJ considers that the measure adopted is inadequate or excessive, it will have no choice but to annul that measure or declare it invalid. Conversely, subject to compliance with other constitutional provisions such as the Bill of Rights, congressional commercial legislation does not have to take into account whether the federal policy is suitable for the objectives it pursues or, whether it goes beyond what is necessary. The Commerce Clause does

[128] See Article 7 of Protocol (No. 2) annexed to the treaties.

[129] Weatherill, 'Better Competence Monitoring', 39–40.

[130] See Article 8 Protocol (No. 2).

[131] *Gibbons* v. *Ogden*, 22 U.S. (9 Wheat.) 1 (1824).

[132] D. Halberstam, 'Of Power and Responsibility: The Political Morality of Federal Systems' (2004) 90 *Virginia Law Review* 731–834; F. Sander, 'Subsidiarity Infringement before the European Court of Justice: Futile Interference with Politics or a Substantial Step Towards EU Federalism?' (2006) 12 *Columbia Journal of European Law* 517–71; Young, 'Protecting Member State Autonomy in the European Union', 1,677–82; Bermann, 'Taking Subsidiarity Seriously', 403–48.

[133] See Article 5(4) TEU.

not have the 'remedial' justification with which Article 114 TFEU must comply. Time and time again, the SCOTUS has held that these issues pertain to the wisdom of the statute, that is, to the political process. In *Raich* Stevens J expressly excluded from his evaluation whether it was wise for the CSA to prohibit medical marijuana. On the contrary, if the ECJ decided a case similar to *Raich*, it would certainly examine whether prohibiting the therapeutic use of marijuana was compatible with the principle of proportionality. In that factual scenario, one could support the contention that it is an oxymoron to harmonise the marketing of cannabis with a view to achieving a high level of health protection, whilst prohibiting its use to patients suffering from chronic pain. Although judicial review would be limited to verifying that the challenged EU measure is not 'manifestly inappropriate', the EU legislator would still have to demonstrate that available scientific evidence is not conclusive over the positive use of cannabis; that its healing effects do not outweigh its toxicity and addiction; or that other relieving substances less dangerous for public health are available.

Thus, unlike Article 114 TFEU, the Commerce Clause is not subject to a proportionality test. In my view, under the Commerce Clause, Congress is not confined to adopting harmonising measures that seek to remedy unconstitutional behaviour of States, but rather its authority is broader. It is entrusted with defining policies that regulate the interstate commerce. Those policies can be directed towards establishing common standards, but also favouring diversification and even discrimination. The Constitution does not prescribe an objective to be attained by Congress. Accordingly, it would be very difficult for the SCOTUS to start second-guessing congressional policy choices. Provided that Congress complies with other constitutional provisions, it is free to regulate interstate commerce as it pleases.[134] Besides, if the SCOTUS were to evaluate whether federal economic regulation is excessive, that would stir the ghosts of *Lochner*.[135] The open texture of the Commerce Clause renders it very difficult for the judiciary to look for benchmarks facilitating scrutiny of manifest errors.

If proportionality controls the intensity and suitability of EU legislation, subsidiarity operates at an earlier stage. It is to the study of the latter principle that I now turn.

134 Halberstam, 'Of Power and Responsibility', 793.

135 *Lochner* v. *New York*, 198 U.S. 45 (1905).

2. The principle of subsidiarity

With the exception of exclusive competences, the principle of subsidiarity limits the exercise of EU competences to objectives that cannot be sufficiently achieved at Member State level.[136] Thus, that principle seeks to determine at which level of governance a policy objective may be better achieved. However, whilst the ECJ applies a mild version of proportionality under Article 114 TFEU, some scholars argue that subsidiarity may not be non-justiciable at all. Indeed, the ECJ has never annulled an EU measure on that ground. *BAT* may provide some insights as to why. In that case the ECJ briefly stated that, since Directive 2001/37 eliminated obstacles to trade arising from the multifarious developments of national laws, this objective could not be sufficiently attained by the Member States.[137] Put simply, once an objective falls within the scope of Article 114 TFEU, subsidiarity '*va de soi*'. Nevertheless, this reasoning is arguably misleading, given that it fails to explain why obstacles to trade may not be tackled at Member State level.[138] Perhaps the non-justiciability of subsidiarity lies in the fact that it is very difficult for the ECJ to ascertain at which level of governance a policy is more efficiently adopted.[139] Subsidiarity inevitably raises political questions reserved to the legislator.

For Halberstam, in *Lopez* and *Tobacco Advertising I* both the SCOTUS and the ECJ appealed implicitly to the principle of subsidiarity.[140] For example, by holding that local economic activities fall within the scope of the Commerce Clause, the SCOTUS was applying that principle. Unlike the prevention of crime and gender-motivated violence, local economic activities often produce externalities and collective action problems that call for congressional intervention. The same applies in relation to the distinction drawn by the ECJ between static and dynamic advertising media. Whilst there is undeniably great merit in Halberstam's observations, his reading of *Lopez* and *Tobacco Advertising I* appears to integrate

[136] See Article 5(3) TEU.

[137] See, e.g., Joined Cases C-154/04 and C-155/04 *Alliance for Natural Health and Others* [2005] ECR I-6451, paras. 106–7.

[138] T. Tridimas, *The General Principles of EU Law*, 2nd edn (Oxford University Press, 2006), p. 187; Sander, 'Subsidiarity Infringement before the European Court of Justice', 544–5; Weatherill, 'Better Competence Monitoring', 27.

[139] Tridimas, *The General Principles of EU Law*, p. 183; Bermann, 'Taking Subsidiarity Seriously', 391; Sander, 'Subsidiarity Infringement before the European Court of Justice', 569.

[140] D. Halberstam, 'Comparative Federalism and the Role of the Judiciary' in K. Wittington, R. Kelemen and G. Caldeira (eds.), *The Oxford Handbook of Law and Politics* (Oxford University Press, 2008), pp. 142–64, pp. 152ff.

the principles of conferral and proportionality into the principle of subsidiarity. This may, as Halberstam himself acknowledges, be problematic given that, even assuming that subsidiary considerations were taken into account by both courts when deciding those two cases, their legal reasoning lacks transparency.

It is true that both courts may arguably lack the institutional capacity to embark on a technical and complex quest for the level of governance that is better equipped to address a policy issue. That being said, subsidiarity should, in my view, be understood as a 'procedural principle' that requires Congress and the EU legislator to state explicitly the reasons why the legislation at issue satisfies a test of comparative efficiency. By 'enhancing process federalism', both courts would not replace legislative choices with their own preferences. On the contrary, they would limit themselves to verifying that, in their decision-making process, Congress and the EU legislator have respectively reflected upon the preservation of state autonomy. Therefore, the judiciary would undertake a soft review, requiring nonetheless more than an abstract reference to objectives calling for federal intervention and EU harmonisation.[141] Once compliance with the principle of conferral is proven, both courts would respectively press Congress and the EU legislator for supporting quantitative and qualitative information showing that joint or individual action at state level is inadequate.[142]

As with all theories of constitutional adjudication, process-oriented review is not free from criticism.[143] Notably, one could argue that it is difficult, if not impossible, to draw the distinction between 'procedural' and 'substantive' matters. However, this chapter does not seek to demonstrate that a process-oriented review should be embraced by both the SCOTUS and the ECJ as the leading theory of judicial review when deciding federalism cases. In light of the comparative study undertaken above, it is submitted that a process-oriented review may, nonetheless, contribute to better competence-monitoring. In addition to bringing transparency to the legislative decision-making process, a process-oriented review forces Congress and the EU legislator to take into account state autonomy.

[141] See, in this regard, the Opinion of AG Poiares Maduro in *Vodafone*, para. 30.

[142] Needless to say, a statement of reasons consistent with subsidiarity would not excuse the ECJ from verifying compliance with the limits of Article 114 TFEU and the principle of proportionality.

[143] See, e.g., L. H. Tribe, 'The Puzzling Persistence of Process-Based Constitutional Theories' (1980) 89 *Yale Law Journal* 1,063–80.

V. Conclusion

The purpose of this chapter was to demonstrate the difficulties that the SCOTUS and the ECJ have encountered when applying the principle of enumerated powers (or the principle of conferral) to federal and EU commercial measures. To some extent, the adoption of formal tests is not sufficient to counter the competence creep. *Lopez* was weakened by the broad notion of 'economic activity' that the SCOTUS applied in *Raich*. In the same way, in *Tobacco Advertising II* the ECJ opened the door to 'potential obstacles' to trade, which may arguably reduce the impact of *Tobacco Advertising I*. Likewise, both courts introduced an important caveat to the principle of enumerated powers, namely Congress and the EU legislator may regulate activities that, whilst falling respectively outside of the scope of the Commerce Clause and of Article 114 TFEU, are necessary to ensure the effectiveness of a larger regulatory scheme. Still, despite their shortcomings, *Lopez* and *Tobacco Advertising I* canvass the judiciary's commitment to policing the outer limits of federal and EU commercial powers.[144]

In order to counterbalance the competence creep, the principle of enumerated powers must be accompanied by other adjudication techniques that seek to guarantee that the power to regulate the interstate market is properly exercised. Whilst federalism may not rest on political safeguards alone, courts may nonetheless restore failures in the federal legislative process that excessively impinge upon state autonomy. Courts should not limit themselves to protecting enclaves of state sovereignty. In addition, in the vast area of concurrent competences, they should also ensure that the federal legislator provides enough justification as to why state law is displaced. 'Process federalism' would contribute to this end. In *Vodafone* the ECJ was right to check whether the EU legislator had provided enough informative input justifying compliance with the principles of proportionality and subsidiarity. Indeed, the new Protocol on Subsidiarity enhances the federalism debate by incorporating national parliaments into the EU legislative process, but also grants them standing to bring an action for annulment before the ECJ. Accordingly, in light of their limited institutional capacities, one cannot ask either the SCOTUS or the ECJ to second-guess whether a policy may be sufficiently achieved at state level. In my view, the ECJ should focus on verifying that the EU legislator has done

[144] P. Craig, 'The ECJ and *Ultra Vires* Action: A Conceptual Analysis' (2011) 48 *Common Market Law Review* 395–437.

its background work properly and that the (dissenting) voices of national legislators have, where appropriate, been taken into account. In the USA, 'clear statement' rules when Congress regulates local activities would also protect the values of federalism. Finally, 'process federalism' would entail a higher judicial involvement in scrutinising legislative deliberations. However, step by step, when judicial rulings become internalised in the political culture, the role of courts would diminish. In addition to stressing the fact that federal and EU powers are limited, courts on both sides of the Atlantic should protect state autonomy by helping to improve the way in which decisions are made at central level.

5

A 'bottom-up' perspective on EU–US relations

The role of sub-national authorities

JOSEPHINE A. W. VAN ZEBEN

I Introduction

The ever-increasing scope of European competences and the analogous loss in state sovereignty disrupts the delicate balance of power between the European Union and its Member States.[1] However, the effects of this continuous redistribution of power are not limited to the relationship between the EU and its Member States; they trickle down to the sub-national level. Multi-level governance scholarship has provided ample theoretical explanation and empirical evidence on how the combined forces of European integration and regionalism have shattered the regulatory monopoly of the nation states.[2] This is especially true for international relations, which many considered a quintessential sovereign prerogative.[3] This volume explores several aspects of the relationship between the United States and the European Union. In doing so, it emphasizes the legal,[4] rather than political,[5] underpinnings and manifestations of this emergent community.

This chapter greatly benefited from comments by Erin Delaney and other participants of the Indiana University Big Ten Junior Scholars conference, as well as comments from Christiane Ahlborn, Vanessa Casado-Peréz, Brady Cassis, Lucy Chambers, Samuel Cogolati, Hano Ernst, Elaine Fahey, Greig Lamont, Simon Paul and Floran Ponce. I gratefully acknowledge financial support from the Niels Stensen Fellowship 2013. Any remaining errors are my own.

1 E.g. G. Marks, 'Structural Policy and Multilevel Governance in the EC: The State of the European Community' in A. Cafruny and G. Rosenthal (eds.), *The State of the European Community: The Maastricht Debate and Beyond* (Boulder, 1993), pp. 391–411, at p. 392, Lynne Rienner.

2 L. Hooghe and G. Marks, '"Europe with the Regions": Channels of Regional Representation in the European Union' (1996) 26(1) *Publius: The Journal of Federalism* 73–92, at 91.

3 See N. Skoutaris, 'Comparing the Subnational Constitutional Space of the European Sub-State Entities in the Area of Foreign Affairs' (2012) 4(2) *Perspectives on Federalism* 239–67, at 241.

4 See the Introduction to this volume.

5 The role of law, particularly international law, in the transatlantic relationship is complicated by the close relationship between law and politics. In important ways, international

This present-day relationship is preceded by, and builds on, pre-existing relationships between the United States and the EU Member States, which were, and continue to be, sovereign nation states under international law.[6] Any discussion of the transatlantic relationship must therefore go beyond an exclusive focus on the EU's 'federal' level.[7] Any initial impression of a 'bilateral' EU–US relationship quickly gives way to a complex network composed of actors who engage in formal and informal action in a myriad of policy areas. Within this network, the role of sub-national authorities (SNAs) and regions,[8] both in the United States and in the European

law has been explained by, and at times equated to, international politics, for example by Hans Morgenthau who stated that 'what really mattered in relations between nations was not international law but international politics'. Quoted in C. Frei, *Morgenthau: An Intellectual Autobiography* (Los Angeles: LSU Press, 2001), p. 65. See also A-M. Slaughter Burley, 'International Law and International Relations Theory: A Dual Agenda' (1993) 87(2) *American Journal of International Law* 205–39; J. Goldsmith and E. Posner, *The Limits of International Law* (Oxford University Press, 2006).

6 To some, the individual States that later became the United States do represent 'nation states … loosely tied together in an informal confederation'; G. Lawson and G. Seidman, 'The American Experience with Territorial Governance' in D. Kochenov (ed.), *EU Law of the Overseas: Outermost Regions, Associated Overseas Countries and Territories, Territories Sui Generis* (Alphen aan den Rijn: Kluwer Law International, 2011), pp. 417–29, at p. 417. Given the very limited extent of the external relations of these founding States, this historical perspective does not significantly impact our analysis. For more information on the formation of the United States and the position of the States in the pre-constitutional period, see M. Jensen, *The New Nation: A History of the United States During the Confederation, 1781–1789* (New York: Vintage Press, 1950).

7 For the purposes of this chapter, both the United States and the European Union will be referred to as 'federal' systems. This categorization is founded on a conceptual understanding of a federal system as a multi-level hierarchical system of governance rather than a normative constitutional model of government. Even the conceptualization of the more 'traditional' federal systems, such as the United States, is continuously changing; see e.g. N. Aroney, 'Federal Constitutionalism/European Constitutionalism in Comparative Perspective', European Essay No. 45 (Federal Trust, 2009), at 10, describing the US arrangements as an international treaty rather than a constitutional federation ('treaty-based federalism'). See also R. Schütze, 'Federalism as Constitutional Pluralism: Letter from America' in M. Avbeli and J. Komarek (eds.), *Constitutional Pluralism in the European Union and Beyond* (Oxford: Hart Publishing, 2012), pp. 185–212, and A. Dashwood, 'The Relationship between the Member States and the European Union/European Community' (2004) 41 *Common Market Law Review* 355–81. Dashwood suggests designating the Union as a 'federation of sovereign states', at 356.

8 Thus far, the terms sub-national authority (SNA) and region have been used separately, referring to two distinct types of government. SNAs refer to sub-national government that is contained within the territory of a single Member State, whereas the term 'region' implies a cross-border element. European policy-makers, who predominantly use the term 'regions' when referring to sub-national government within one Member State, do not make this explicit distinction. In many policy areas, 'regions' may thus refer to any government 'under' the national level, as well as to cross-border

Member States, has traditionally gone under-theorized.[9] In 2001, Pollack and Shaffer published their tripartite typology of interaction between the EU and the USA focusing on *intergovernmental* action, *transgovernmental* action – dominated by technocratic bureaucrats – and *transnational* action, which is led by civil society and other non-governmental organizations.[10] With respect to transnational action, the United States has long recognized the role of the private sector in advancing regulatory coordination between the EU and the USA.[11] The transnational model therefore presents a building block, rather than a blueprint, on which to construct a broader discussion of the democratic role of SNAs.[12]

This chapter sets out to demonstrate that the current and potential role of sub-central entities in external affairs should form part of the broader European multi-level governance research agenda,[13] and starts by making their role in the EU–US relationship explicit. The autonomy of sub-central authorities in international relations depends on their domestic constitutional status; there are few European sub-national actors that are able to exercise autonomous foreign relations powers, separate from the national level.[14] The relationship of SNAs with the European Union

or Euregions, although the latter is less common. This definitional confusion does not aid in determining the number of European regions and sub-national authorities.

[9] For discussions on the relative competence of the European Union and the Member States with respect to external relations and foreign policy, see e.g. H. de Waele, *Layered Global Player – Legal Dynamics of EU External Relations* (Heidelberg: Springer, 2011); P. Eeckhout, *EU External Relations Law* (Oxford University Press, 2011); A. Dashwood and M. Maresceau (eds.), *Law and Practice of EU External Relations: Salient Features of a Changing Landscape* (Cambridge University Press, 2011); P. Koutrakos (ed.), *The European Union's External Relations: A Year after Lisbon*, CLEER Working Papers 2011/3 (The Hague: T.M.C. Asser Press, 2011); B. Van Vooren, S. Blockmans and J. Wouters (eds.), *The EU's Role in Global Governance: The Legal Dimension* (Oxford University Press, 2013). Notably, none of this literature focuses on the role of EU sub-national authorities or regions.

[10] M. A. Pollack and G. C. Shaffer, 'Who Governs?' in M. A. Pollack and G. C. Shaffer (eds.), *Transatlantic Governance in the Global Economy* (Lanham, MD: Rowman & Littlefield, 2001), pp. 287–305.

[11] G. Shaffer, 'Reconciling Trade and Regulatory Goals: The Prospects and Limits of New Approaches to Transatlantic Governance through Mutual Recognition and Safe Harbor Agreements' (2002) 9 *Columbia Journal of European Law* 29–77. For a more recent discussion on the EU role in this dynamic, see A. Bradford, 'The Brussels Effect' (2012) 107 *Northwestern University Law Review* 1–68.

[12] See Section IV.

[13] On sub-state diplomacy in the EU more broadly, see Skoutaris, 'Comparing the Subnational Constitutional Space of the European Sub-State Entities in the Area of Foreign Affairs'.

[14] A non-exhaustive overview, including Austrian, German and Belgian SNAs, is provided in Skoutaris, 'Comparing the Subnational Constitutional Space of the European Sub-State Entities in the Area of Foreign Affairs'.

and domestic European policy equally depends on the division of power under national constitutional law, which means that the influence of SNAs on European policy differs widely between the Member States.[15] As there is no formal infrastructure for external action by SNAs – for many sub-national authorities and regions even an intra-EU path is missing – it is difficult to measure their presumed influence on international relations. Within the context of the EU–US relationship, it is comparably testing to ascertain whether these parties have too much or too little influence. This raises the question as to whether this overlooked discourse ultimately supplements or undermines the dialogue between the 'federal' EU and US levels.[16]

In order to better understand the potential of diplomatic activism by sub-national actors in the EU–US relationship, this chapter will start European treatment of SNAs and regions. The European Union is the most significant 'external' relationship of many sub-national actors, and their influence on this relationship is highly dependent on their domestic positions and the top-down room provided for sub-national action by the EU (Section II). The chapter then discusses several illustrative examples of sub-central interaction with the United States outside of the formal channels established by the EU and the Member States. The potential for these interactions depends entirely on the domestic constitutional contexts of the relevant SNAs, which are considered in parallel (Section III). This chapter concludes by considering the implications of the status quo and the potential risks of engaging sub-national entities in international relations generally, and in the EU–US relation specifically.

II. The European life of SNAs and regions

The division of power between the European and national level is a source of constant debate, confrontation and compromise between the Member States and the European institutions,[17] as is evidenced by the Treaty of

[15] See Section II.

[16] C. Jeffery, 'Sub-National Mobilization and European Integration: Does It Make Any Difference?' (2000) 38(1) *JCMS: Journal of Common Market Studies* 1–23.

[17] E.g. in early 2013 British Prime Minister David Cameron called for 'a renationalization of European powers', while German Chancellor Angela Merkel made an equally powerful call for the greater 'Europeanization of national powers'. See *The Economist*, 9 February 2013, at 56.

Lisbon's lengthy gestation process.[18] The balancing exercise of European governance is closely linked to the multi-level nature of the European system.[19] Politically, the run-up to the Maastricht Treaty in the 1990s signalled a new dawn for sub-national mobilization in the EU multi-level system:[20] the principle of subsidiarity was formally introduced,[21] the Committee of the Regions was established,[22] and sub-national ministerial access to the Council of Ministers was granted.[23] The term 'Europe of the Regions' has since become ubiquitous in policy documents and discourse,[24] and there have been numerous tangible investments in the European regions.[25] The most visible efforts to remedy these differences can be found within the European 'Cohesion' Policy, which was started with the Development Fund in 1975.[26] The most recent Cohesion Programme, running from 2007 to 2013, assigned €347.4 billion to regions in order to support 'regional growth and job creation, [in order to] boost growth in new Member States by 6% on average and create as many as two million new jobs'.[27] This investment amounts to more than one-third of the EU budget during this period and as such can hardly be considered rhetorical.

[18] Between the 2001 Laeken Declaration and the eventual adoption of the Treaty of Lisbon, the initial attempts at treaty revision failed (Treaty establishing a Constitution for Europe).

[19] E.g. J. van Zeben, 'Research Agenda for a Polycentric European Union' (2013) The Vincent and Elinor Ostrom Workshop in Political Theory and Policy Analysis Working Paper Series, W13-13; Marks, 'Structural Policy and Multilevel Governance in the EC', p. 392.

[20] Jeffery, 'Sub-National Mobilization and European Integration', 4.

[21] Now contained in Article 5(3) TEU.

[22] Articles 189a, 189b, and 189c of the Maastricht Treaty.

[23] Article 146 Maastricht Treaty.

[24] S. Borrás-Alomar, T. Christiansen and A. Rodríguez-Pose, 'Towards a "Europe of the Regions"? Visions and Reality from a Critical Perspective' (1994) 4(2) *Regional Politics and Policy* 1–27.

[25] Already in the Treaty of Rome, the divergent economic and social development of the European regions had been earmarked as problematic for the further development of the EU. See Preamble, Treaty of Rome (stating that one purpose of the foundation of the Union was 'to ensure [a] harmonious development by reducing the differences existing between the various regions and the backwardness of the less favoured regions').

[26] For a brief history of EC Regional Policy, see S. George, *Politics and Policy in the European Community* (Oxford University Press, 1985). For an analysis of the structural fund reform see G. Marks, 'Structural Policy in the European Community' in A. M. Sbragia (ed.), *Euro-Politics: Institutions and Policymaking in the 'New' European Community* (Washington, DC: Brookings Institution, 1992), pp. 191–224.

[27] DG Regio, *Working for the Regions: EU Regional Policy 2007–2013*, January 2008, available at: http://ec.europa.eu/regional_policy/sources/docgener/presenta/working2008/work_en.pdf, accessed 11 February 2014. The EU's regional policy has focused on overcoming income equality between the regions as a way to strengthen solidarity and financial and

In addition, the creation of a strong 'Europe of the Regions' is considered an important 'way to regenerate democracy in Europe and to close the EU's democratic deficit'.[28] Nevertheless, the results of this sub-national mobilization remain ambiguous.[29] This section analyses one specific element of sub-national mobilization: the possibility of SNAs engaging in European policy-making as an expression of autonomy outside of the territory of the Member State. An SNA's influence on European policy and European decision-making is informative for its influence on the EU–US relationship, since the formal and informal channels for exercising foreign relations competences are often identical.[30] Both 'top-down' and 'bottom-up' aspects of sub-national life in Europe are set out below: the EU's regional policy, focused primarily on the Cohesion Policy, and the role and status of regions and sub-national entities 'in' Brussels, respectively.

A. *European regional policy*

Aside from acknowledging their existence, the regions of Europe played little or no part in the 1957 Treaty of Rome. The Community that was established by the Treaty of Rome was one focused on economic development and integration, and the relevance of the regions was limited to this objective.[31] Structural regional policy at the European level was not considered essential to achieving European-wide economic development; the regions were considered the responsibility of the Member States – a matter of national politics.[32] The only direct promotion of regional

social cohesion between the regions. See J. Malais and H. Haegeman, 'European Union Regional Policy' (2009) *School of Doctoral Studies (European Union) Journal* 77–82.

[28] E. Bomberg and J. Peterson, 'European Union Decision Making: The Role of Sub-national Authorities' (1998) 46(2) *Political Studies* 219–35, at 225.

[29] See generally F. Fleurke and R. Willemse, 'The European Union and the Autonomy of Sub-national Authorities: Towards an Analysis of Constraints and Opportunities in Sub-national Decision-making' (2006) 16(1) *Regional and Federal Studies* 83–98.

[30] See e.g. F. Requejo (ed.), *Foreign Policy of Constituent Units at the Beginning of the 21st Century* (Barcelona: Col-lecció Institut d'Estudis Autonòmics, 2010).

[31] As stated in the Preamble of the Treaty, the Community was tasked with 'harmonious development by reducing the differences existing between the various regions and the backwardness of the less favoured regions'. See also Article 2 of Treaty of Rome, which states that the Community was tasked with promoting a 'harmonious development of economic activities' and 'a continuous and balanced expansion'.

[32] See Commission of the European Communities, 'A Regional Policy for the Community', COM (69) 950, 15 October 1969, Brussels, p. 13 ('even more than other branches of economic policy, regional policy is clearly the concern of the public authorities in the member states. The measures it involves fall directly under the political, cultural, admin-

development was through the mandate of the European Investment Bank, which included the granting of loans to 'facilitate the financing of projects for developing less developed regions'.[33] This *laissez-faire* attitude towards regional policy was much criticized,[34] but there was simply no legal basis in the Treaty of Rome on which to base Community action in this area.

In the early 1960s, the European Commission nevertheless started to develop a regional agenda, organizing the 1961 Conference on Regional Economies and eventually publishing its first Communication on Regional Policy in 1965.[35] Despite the increased pressures for a Community-level policy, structural changes only became possible after the creation of the Directorate General on Regional Policy in 1968.[36] In 1969, the Commission published its second Communication on regional policy, which was accompanied by a formal proposal for a Council decision.[37] During this period the financial situation of the Community had changed significantly, which increasingly made regional development a 'European' problem.[38] The debate on the Economic and Monetary Union also stressed the need for regional development intervention.[39] Nonetheless, during the 1960s and

istrative, sociological and budgetary organisation of the States. Regional policy forms an integral part of the system of internal balances on what [*sic*] the State is based').

[33] G. P. Manzella and C. Mendez, *The Turning Points of EU Cohesion Policy* (Glasgow: University of Strathclyde, 2009), p. 5.

[34] *Ibid.*, p. 6.

[35] Commission of the European Communities, 'First Communication of the European Commission on Regional Policy in the European Community', SEC (65) 1170 def., Brussels.

[36] *Ibid.*, 7.

[37] Commission of the European Communities, 'A Regional Policy for the Community', COM (69) 950, 15 October 1969, Brussels.

[38] Economic crises in some of the EU Member States 'drew attention to the close link between declining industries and specific territorial areas'. See Commission of the European Communities, 'A Regional Policy for the Community', COM (69) 950, 15 October 1969, Brussels, at 7.

[39] See Commission of the European Communities, 'Memorandum on the Coordination of Economic Policies and Monetary Cooperation' (12 February 1969) in *Bulletin of the European Communities*, 1969, No. Supplement 3/69, pp. 3–14, and 'Report on the Realisation by Stages of Economic and Monetary Union' (8 October 1970) in *Bulletin of the European Communities*, 1970, No. Supplement 11/70, pp. 5–29, at p. 8 ('[T]he realization of global economic equilibrium may be dangerously threatened by differences of structure. Cooperation between the partners in the Community in the matter of structural and regional policies will help to surmount these difficulties, just as it will make it possible to eliminate the distortions of competition. The solution of the big problems in this field will be facilitated by financial measures of compensation. In an economic and monetary union, structural and regional policies will not be exclusively a matter for national budgets').

early 1970s regional policy continued to be a primarily intergovernmental process monopolized by the Member States.[40] It was not until the late 1970s and the 1980s that the Community's regional policy became increasingly 'Europeanized'.[41] Through legislative reforms in 1979 and 1984, the European Regional Development Fund's (ERDF) budget was consistently increased and the Commission's role grew significantly.[42]

The Single European Act in 1985 introduced the first specific title for 'Economic and Social Cohesion': Articles 130a–c set out the objectives of regional policy ('strengthening economic and social cohesion' and 'reducing disparities between various regions'),[43] together with the key policy instruments for achieving this objective (the ERDF, the European Agricultural Guidance and Guarantee Fund, and the European Social Fund).[44] Against the backdrop of these constitutional changes, the watershed for European regional policy came in 1988 with the adoption of the new Cohesion Policy package.[45]

The adoption of the Maastricht Treaty in 1992 signalled a renewed focus on the role of sub-national governance and an active role for the regions through the application of the subsidiarity principle. The most tangible effect of these changes was a move towards decentralization of implementation and simplification of programming with a view to heightened effectiveness of the programmes, in light of the approaching enlargement of 2004.[46] The 2004 enlargement made its mark through the most recent

[40] Manzella and Mendez, *The Turning Points of EU Cohesion Policy*, p. 10.

[41] This was in part due to the strong criticism levelled against the initial design of the ERDF.

[42] The most significant development during these decades was the adoption of the European Regional Development Fund (ERDF) in March 1975 (Regulation (EEC) No. 724/75 of the Council of 18 March 1975 (OJ L 73, 21 March 1975)). The aim of the ERDF was to support medium- to long-term development in order to bring about self-sustained growth. See 'Report on European Union' in *Bulletin of the European Communities*, 1976, No. Supplement 1, 11–35 (specifically, PART III-C).

[43] Article 130a, Single European Act.

[44] Article 130b, Single European Act.

[45] The package of regulations was approved through Council Regulations (EEC) No. 4253/88 to 4256/88 of 19 December 1988 (OJ L 374/31, 31 December 1988). See Manzella and Mendez, *The Turning Points of EU Cohesion Policy*, p. 13. See also 'Programme of the Commission for 1985', *Bulletin of the European Communities*, Supplement 4/85, at point 15. The Commission's position was supported by the Padoa-Schioppa and Cecchini Reports, which, inter alia, highlighted the 'serious risks of aggravated regional imbalance in the course of market liberalisation' and the corresponding need for 'accompanying measures … to speed adjustment in structurally weak regions and countries'. See T. Padoa-Schioppa, *Efficiency, Stability and Equity: A Strategy for the Evolution of the Economic System of the European Community* (Oxford University Press, 1987).

[46] *Ibid.*, p. 17.

reform of the Cohesion Policy (2007–2013). The regulatory package for this €347 billion programme was approved in July 2006 and put in place several fundamental changes in the structure of EU regional policy.[47] The focus of the policy has shifted from a Cohesion Fund to a Convergence and Restructuring Fund with three main aims: Convergence, Regional Competitiveness and Employment, and Territorial Cooperation. Eighty per cent of the funds are assigned to the Convergence objective, which is focused on the less developed regions with a gross domestic product (GDP) per capita of less than 75 per cent of the EU average.[48]

The EU's Cohesion Fund is undoubtedly the most visible element of regional (inter)action with(in) the EU. The development and implementation of regional policy under the Cohesion Fund (now the Convergence and Restructuring Fund) is, however, not necessarily one of regional empowerment. The Member States and European institutions continue to be the most vocal players, joined only by those regions that actively receive monetary and institutional support for their development; EU regional policy, as discussed thus far, is mostly a top-down process. In fact, some have argued that 'due to European integration there is a redistribution among resources of domestic sectors at [*sic*] the detriment of the regions and at the benefit of the central authorities':[49] the so-called 'disempowerment' thesis, which appears to run contrary to the overall loss of centrality of the nation state in the EU multi-level system.[50] The increased influence of the European Union on sub-national government has been found to have constraining effects, hampering the ability

[47] Council Regulation (EC) No. 1083/2006 of 11 July 2006; Council Regulation (EC) No. 1084/2006 of 11 July 2006; Regulation (EC) No. 1080/2006 of the European Parliament and of the Council of 5 July 2006; Regulation (EC) No. 1081/2006 of the European Parliament and of the Council of 5 July 2006; Regulation (EC) No. 1082/2006 of the European Parliament and of the Council of 5 July 2006 (OJ L 210, 31 July 2006).

[48] Manzella and Mendez, *The Turning Points of EU Cohesion Policy*, p. 19. Several Member States, e.g. the Netherlands and the United Kingdom, have suggested that Cohesion Policy support should be available exclusively to the less developed Member States.

[49] I. Bullain, 'Autonomy and the European Union' in M. Suksi (ed.), *Autonomy: Applications and Implications* (The Hague: Kluwer Law International, 1998), pp. 343–56 as cited in Fleurke and Willemse, 'The European Union and the Autonomy of Sub-national Authorities', 87. See also C. Carter and R. Pasquier, 'The Europeanization of Regions as "Spaces for Politics": A Research Agenda' (2010) 20(3) *Regional & Federal Studies*, 295–314, at 301.

[50] Some scholars find that the EU does not lead to disempowerment per se but rather forces greater cooperation; see e.g. T. Börzel, 'From Competitive Regionalism to Cooperative Federalism. The Europeanization of the Spanish State of the Autonomies' (2000) 30(2) *Publius: The Journal of Federalism* 17–42.

of SNAs to implement, or prepare, their own policies while forcing the implementation of EU-based policy.[51]

Similarly, the principle of subsidiarity has not been able to prevent greater centralization of policy-making at the European level,[52] and little to no mention is made of the role of sub-national entities in subsidiarity discussions. In particular regions that share legislative powers with EU institutions have found themselves moved into a position of 'administration regional agents', implementing EU law and policy rather than exercising primary legislative power over their territories.[53] In addition, empirical research conducted on this issue shows that the European process can lead to the undermining, or even transfer, of traditional regional competences due to the fact that the EU's decision-making process is equipped to deal only with negotiations between Member States and European institutions, to the exclusion of the regions.[54]

B. *Sub-national and regional 'European' policy*

The disempowerment thesis shows that the 'top-down' effects of EU regional policy are not unreservedly positive. This raises the question whether SNAs have been able to influence European policy from the 'bottom up' in order to counterbalance these infringements of their autonomy. Many European Member States provide for some level of SNA and regional autonomy, which manifests itself in differing degrees of foreign policy involvement.[55] There is significant variation both between and within Member States.[56] One of the most important examples of this is the provision, first introduced in the Maastricht Treaty, that a regional

[51] Fleurke and Willemse, 'The European Union and the Autonomy of Sub-national Authorities', 96.

[52] A. Alesina, I. Angeloni and L. Schuknecht, 'What Does the European Union Do?' (2005) 123 *Public Choice* 275–319 (providing empirical evidence on the expansion of the policy-making role of the European Union in the years between 1971 and 2000).

[53] Carter and Pasquier, 'The Europeanization of Regions as "Spaces for Politics"', 300.

[54] Fleurke and Willemse, 'The European Union and the Autonomy of Sub-national Authorities'.

[55] There are also several Member States where such competences are explicitly not provided for in the respective constitutions, such as Croatia and the Netherlands.

[56] Fleurke and Willemse, 'The European Union and the Autonomy of Sub-national Authorities', 86, who find, e.g., that the selection of cases can strongly impact the results, with some findings that even in the British case of a highly centralized state, opportunities are developed by SNAs, whereas others find that hardly any local authority considers itself able to influence the European agenda in the near future.

minister with full negotiating powers may represent a Member State in the Council.[57] This provision applies only to a very limited set of Member States: Germany, Belgium, Austria, Italy (the regions of Trento and Bolzano), Spain (the Autonomous Communities) and the UK (devolved governments of Scotland, Wales and Northern Ireland).[58] Even these relatively 'powerful' regions have divergent experiences with respect to Council representation.[59] The Belgian representatives, for instance, are bound by the 1994 Cooperation Agreement between the Belgian federal government and the regions, whereas the representatives of devolved UK administrations are chosen by the lead UK minister, who also holds final responsibility for the negotiations.[60] This divergence between Member State regions and sub-national authorities permeates every channel of influence in Brussels.

This diversity in terms of access to, and influence on,[61] EU policy-making is protected within the treaties, which explicitly refer to the EU's obligation to respect Member States' 'fundamental structures ... inclusive of regional and local government'.[62] That said, SNA and regional representation does not depend entirely on domestic constitutional arrangements. There are several institutions at the EU level that formally and informally accommodate sub-national and regional influence in Brussels. The main institutions at EU level are the Committee of the Regions (CoR) – a European institution established in 1994 – and the Assembly of European Regions (AER) – an independent network of regions,[63] established in 1987.[64] Aside from these institutions, there

[57] Article 146 EC Treaty (now Article 203(1) TEU).

[58] Hooghe and Marks, "Europe with the Regions", 76. This created the necessity for EU Member States such as Germany and Belgium, which have to involve their regional entities, to pre-formulate their standpoints as a Member State in an internal coordination procedure prior to Council meetings. See M. Suszycka-Jasch and H.-C. Jasch, 'The Participation of the German Länder in Formulating German EU-policy' (2009) 10(9) *German Law Journal* 1,215–56, at 1,238. See also Skoutaris, 'Comparing the Subnational Constitutional Space of the European Sub-State Entities in the Area of Foreign Affairs', 258.

[59] These differences are explored in more detail in Section III. See also Jeffery, 'Sub-National Mobilization and European Integration', 12.

[60] Skoutaris, 'Comparing the Subnational Constitutional Space of the European Sub-State Entities in the Area of Foreign Affairs', 260–1.

[61] See e.g. *ibid.*; H. Hermans, 'Cross-border Health Care in the European Union: Recent Legal Implications of "Decker and Kohll"' (2000) 6(4) *Journal of Evaluation in Clinical Practice* 431–9; and Hooghe and Marks, "Europe with the Regions".

[62] Article 4(2) Treaty of Lisbon.

[63] The AER defines a 'region' as a territorial authority existing at the level immediately below the central government.

[64] The AER started as the Council of the Regions of Europe on 15 June 1985 but was renamed two years later.

are three other main channels for regions and sub-national authorities to influence European decision-making: the Council (as discussed), the Commission and regional offices.[65]

Of the regional institutions, the C. R is the only one that enjoys formal legal status within the treaties.[66] Initially, the CoR's agenda was set mainly by the Commission and failed to be very effective. Writing in 1998, Bomberg and Peterson find that '[w]hile still a young institution, the Committee of the Regions thus far has been a disappointment even for its supporters'.[67] The CoR's influence has increased since then, mostly due to its role in the implementation of regional policies, which makes it difficult to circumvent the institution.[68] Arguably the most influence by the CoR is exercised through those members that are able to directly pressure their national governments through the Council.[69] However, this influence also leads to tensions within the CoR where some regions and sub-national actors are far more powerful than others. This divide is clear both between members from federal or regionalized Member States and unitary Member States, as well as between representatives from northern and southern Member States, which are typically contributors or beneficiaries respectively.[70] Since all CoR members – currently 353 – are appointed by their respective Member States rather than elected, their independence is arguably limited.[71]

The informal channels of SNA influence are primarily based on information exchange with European institutions and other regions.[72] For many sub-national actors, regional offices are the most important expression of such informal influence. There has been a surge in regional offices since their arrival in the 1980s: writing in 2000, Hermans lists 60 official

[65] See Hooghe and Marks, "Europe with the Regions", 74.

[66] Founded on the framework of the Consultative Council of Regional and Local Authorities as set up by the Commission in 1988, the Committee of Regions was formally established by the Maastricht Treaty. See Articles 189a–c, EC Treaty.

[67] Bomberg and Peterson, 'European Union Decision Making', 225.

[68] Hooghe and Marks, "Europe with the Regions", 76.

[69] *Ibid.*

[70] *Ibid.*, 76. See also Bomberg and Peterson, 'European Union Decision Making', 225.

[71] The Treaty of Lisbon set out to improve some of the features of the CoR, most importantly through mandatory consultation with the body at all stages of the legislative process in an increased number of key areas. See inter alia Article 13 TEU. For a list of policy areas, see http://cor.europa.eu/en/about/Pages/key-facts.aspx, accessed 11 February 2014. The CoR has moreover obtained the right to bring actions before the Court of Justice in cases where appropriate consultation was not respected, or in those cases where sufficient weight was not given to the principle of subsidiarity. However, it remains unclear how useful the latter prerogative will be.

[72] See also Hooghe and Marks, "Europe with the Regions".

Euregions and 250 regions within the Assembly of European Regions.[73] Another source lists 300+ regional offices in Brussels in 2009.[74] The Assembly of European Regions is the most influential network of regions and sub-national authorities and currently represents more than 250 regional parliaments from over 35 countries and 16 interregional organizations.[75] Typically, SNAs with strong national autonomy over external affairs continue to invest heavily in this type of influence. For instance, the regional offices of the German Länder are among the best funded and most knowledgeable.[76] Even so, there is no legal right of permanent representation; this lies with the Permanent Representation of Germany as the Member State.[77] For SNAs in Member States without constitutionally protected external representation and influence, informal representation often constitutes one of the only channels for influence.

This discussion of SNA autonomy with respect to European affairs holds several lessons for the role of SNAs in the EU–US relationship. First, it is clear that European experience of SNAs depends on the domestic position, and the extent to which it is subject to, or impacted by, European regulation. Second, for those SNAs where formal representation is constitutionally limited, informal channels and coalition-building with other regions through the CoR and the AER, for example, become vital. For SNAs with constitutionally enshrined representation and external affairs competences, such as Germany, one would expect their strategy with respect to the EU–US relationship to be comparable to their position on the EU. However, even for these Member States, European Union law has a fundamentally different position within the national legal order as compared to 'other' external action. By means of illustration, the German implementation of the Lisbon revisions, specifically the subsidiarity provisions contained within Protocol 2, was a catalyst for revisions to the internal division of competence on EU questions within Germany, which already comprised significant deference to the Länder. In a decision of 30 June 2009, the Bundesverfassungsgericht (Federal Constitutional Court or FCC) held that the role of the Bundesrat (the Federal Council,

[73] H. Hermans, 'Cross-border Health Care in the European Union', 434.

[74] R. Grzeszczak and I. Karolewski (eds.), *The Multi-Level and Polycentric European Union: Legal and Political Studies* (Zurich: Lit Verlag, 2012), p. 66.

[75] The AER has a close working relationship with the Commission, which is in line with the Commission's general coordinating and outreach tasks regarding the Convergence and Restructuring Fund. See Hooghe and Marks, "Europe with the Regions", 88.

[76] M. Keating, *The New Regionalism in Western Europe: Territorial Restructuring and Political Change* (Cheltenham: Edward Elgar Publishing, 1998), pp. 169–70.

[77] Suszycka-Jasch and Jasch, 'The Participation of the German Länder', 1,247.

composed of Länder representatives) needed to be enhanced to the extent that explicit consent would be needed for German 'ratification' of new EU treaties.[78] For less weighty EU-based decisions, the new Article 23 of the German Basic Law sets out that the federal structure of Germany cannot be altered by European influence, protecting the standing of the Länder. Moreover, the Länder shall remain fully informed about *all* EU matters, not only those that directly affect their interests.[79] This integration of EU law into the German domestic order is exemplary insofar that the role of SNAs and regions with respect to the EU is no longer considered a matter of 'external' influence – a position that is supported by the Court of Justice of the European Union.[80]

Regardless of the *de jure* reclassification of European issues as 'domestic' issues, the engagement of SNAs and regions with these issues is still in many cases emblematic of their more general foreign affairs powers, as will be discussed in Section III. Moreover, these formal and informal channels of SNA European action represent direct and indirect methods through which SNAs can influence the EU–US relationship in lieu of autonomous representation powers: first, directly at the EU level, and second, indirectly by influencing their Member State's position on EU external action generally, and the EU–US relationship specifically. Unsurprisingly, external action is a sensitive issue between the Member States and the European Union.[81] The main changes to external relations as introduced by the Lisbon Treaty aim at enhancing the coherence of the Union's external action,[82] specifically through a 'better division and definition of competence'.[83]

[78] *Ibid.*, 1,250–1. See also 2 BvE 2/08 of 30 June 2009, paragraph 414.

[79] Suszycka-Jasch and Jasch, 'The Participation of the German Länder', 1,241.

[80] See M. Pérez Gonzaléz, 'La onda regional en Bruselas y el ámbito del poder exterior (Comentario a la sentencia del Tribunal Constitucional 165/1994, de 26 de Mayo)' (1994) 21 *Revista de Instituciones Europeas* 899–916, as quoted in Skoutaris, 'Comparing the Subnational Constitutional Space of the European Sub-State Entities in the Area of Foreign Affairs', 263.

[81] The European Union now has independent legal capacity, as set out in Article 47 TEU. For an in-depth discussion of the legal instrumentarium of EU external relations, see M. Cremona, 'Defining Competence in EU External Relations: Lessons from the Treaty Reform Process' in Dashwood and Maresceau (eds.), *Law and Practice of EU External Relations*, pp. 34–70. See also S. Blockmans and M-J. Laatsit, 'The European External Action Service: Enhancing Coherence in EU External Action?' in P. J. Cardwell (ed.), *EU External Relations Law and Policy in the Post-Lisbon Era* (The Hague: T. M. C. Asser Press, 2012).

[82] Koutrakos, 'Introduction' in *The European Union's External Relations*, at 8.

[83] Cremona, 'Defining Competence in EU External Relations', p. 36.

Under the status quo, the power to represent the European Union is shared between the President of the Council,[84] the High Representative[85] – supported by the European External Action Service[86] – the Commission[87] and Members of the European Parliament (MEPs). The latter group does not hold explicit representation duties or powers but MEPs are allowed to visit third countries at their own initiative. The Council, together with the European Parliament, holds legislative powers in most areas of external action and in those cases is composed of the Member States' foreign ministers or other competent government officials.[88] In areas of shared competence, these ministers continue to be able to act on behalf of their Member States in international forums.[89] Member State competences on representation continue to exist on those issues that fall within national competences and they can choose to be represented individually or collectively.[90] Given the continued centrality of Member States (or their representatives) in this system, SNA influence at the national level could be seen as an effective indirect control of external affairs at the EU level. Similarly, the increased role for the European institutions provides additional channels for influence.

III. SNAs in the world: their role in the EU–US relationship

Thus far our discussion has focused primarily on the European and Member State rationales, and possibilities in supporting or restricting the role of SNAs with respect to external action and the EU–US relationship. This discourse must be supplemented with the American perspective on

[84] Article 15(6) TEU.

[85] Article 18(4) TEU. Within this mandate, it is particularly noteworthy that the High Representative is the Vice-President of the Commission (as the External Affairs Commissioner) as well as the President of the Foreign Affairs Council. See extensively R. Gosalbo Bono, 'The Organization of the External Relations of the European Union in the Treaty of Lisbon' in Koutrakos (ed.), *The European Union's External Relations*, pp. 13–39, at pp. 22–3.

[86] Article 27(3) TEU and Council Decision 2010/427/EU of 26 July 2010 establishing the organization and functioning of the European External Action Service, OJ 2010 L 201/30.

[87] Gosalbo Bono, 'The Organization of the External Relations of the EU', p. 22. See also Article 17(1) TEU.

[88] See also Gosalbo Bono, 'The Organization of the External Relations of the EU', p. 21.

[89] See Article 216 TFEU on so-called 'mixed' agreements.

[90] Gosalbo Bono, 'The Organization of the External Relations of the EU', p. 35.

the multi-level structure of the European Union and its perception of the EU as 'partner' in the relationship. In one of the most authoritative overviews of the EU–US relationship of recent years, Gunter Burghardt – former ambassador for the European Union in Washington – summarizes the fundamentals of the transatlantic partnership. In his view, the key realities are: (i) the strong transatlantic dimension of the European unification process since the Second World War; (ii) continued interaction on virtually every policy issue – ranging from biotechnology to military intervention – based on shared common objectives for the promotion of peace, stability and economic development; (iii) the need for a more united European Union in order to balance out the relationship.[91] In order to achieve this, institutional and operational capacity geared towards external action need to be strengthened.[92]

Even as the transatlantic relationship has changed, going through times of closer and less close cooperation, it is clear that the success of both the United States and the European Union is interlinked and mutually dependent.[93] Within the scope of this chapter, the United States' interest in a large and unified European Union is particularly noteworthy. The EU's expanded influence on the international stage and an ever-increasing geographical scope, for example by including countries such as Turkey and strengthening relationships with Russia, are to the benefit of the United States as it maximizes the utility of its relationship with the EU.[94] Regardless as to whether one agrees with this vision of EU–US relations (or rather US–EU relations), it is clear that the view of Europe in this relationship leaves little room for sub-national or regional action. Put differently, aside from the aim of strengthening the EU as a whole, the multi-layered aspect of EU external action is not a salient feature of transatlantic thought insofar that it excludes a specific role for regions and SNAs.

From the European perspective, however, there has been an increased emphasis on subsidiarity in the Treaty reform process and the greater role for national parliaments and sub-central entities.[95] Also at the national

[91] G. Burghardt, 'The EU's Transatlantic Relationship' in Dashwood and Maresceau (eds.), *Law and Practice of EU External Relations*, pp. 376–97, at pp. 376–7.

[92] *Ibid.* [93] *Ibid.*, p. 397.

[94] Z. Brzezinski, 'Balancing the East, Upgrading the West: US Grand Strategy in an Age of Upheaval' (2012) 91 *Foreign Affairs* 97–104, at 98–9.

[95] See e.g. Protocol No. 1 on the role of national parliaments in the European Union (OJ 2008 No. C155, 9 May 2008) and Protocol No. 2 on the application of the principles of subsidiarity and proportionality (OJ 2008 No. C155, 9 May 2008).

level, pressure has been placed on governments to allow for greater independence for certain regions, for example in the United Kingdom, or to carve out more influence for sub-national parliaments, for example in Germany and Belgium.[96] Within the European Union the focus of these discussions has been the influence on EU policy specifically, rather than external relations with third parties. Within this discussion the experiences of the German Länder may be placed at one extreme of the continuum, as they enjoy a relative high level of autonomy, also with respect to external relations, as compared to other European SNAs. However, also within the German system, the competence to conduct 'normal' external relations, such as the power to conclude treaties and engage in diplomacy, remains with the federal government.[97] The interference of the Länder is limited to those affairs that directly affect them.[98] In addition, they are authorized to conclude treaties in those policy areas that are delegated to them.[99]

In the United Kingdom, which is traditionally considered a highly centralized Member State,[100] the devolved Scottish Parliament put in place a Cabinet Secretary for Culture and External Affairs in 2011.[101] Despite the upcoming referendum on independence, Scotland continues to be part of the United Kingdom and its positions are typically subsumed under those of the UK within international negotiations.[102] That said, there are three Scottish government offices overseas and twenty-one offices

[96] Although an important and long overdue exercise, an exhaustive overview of the constitutional position of all Member States' SNAs is outside the scope of this chapter. For an exhaustive overview of 27 Member States, see V. Bianchi *et al.*, 'The Participation of European Regions in the Decision-Making and Law-Making Processes of the European Union', May 2010, Promotion 'Victor Hugo' Working Document, available at: http://llet-131-198.uab.es/catedra/images/novetats/regions_project.pdf, accessed 11 February 2014.

[97] Article 32(1) German Basic Law.

[98] Article 32(2) German Basic Law.

[99] Article 32(3) German Basic Law.

[100] For a discussion of the UK's historical discussion on whether or not to become a federal state, and the relationship between Euro-scepticism and (de)centralization, see S. Hix, 'Euroscepticism as Anti-Centralization: A Rational Choice Institutionalist Perspective' (2007) 8(1) *European Union Politics* 131–50.

[101] This was previously a junior position. Currently this is Member of the Scottish Parliament Fiona Hyslop.

[102] See Memorandum of Understanding and Concordats (1999), Scottish Government, Edinburgh, available at: www.scotland.gov.uk/Resource/Doc/283886/0086022.pdf, accessed 11 February 2014. Within the EU, Scotland is able to attend Council meetings if the relevant Secretary of State agrees, but can only speak to the agreed UK line. See Scottish Parliament, *Europe and Foreign Affairs: Taking Forward our National Conversation*, 2009, at 8.

operated by Scottish Development International.[103] As the referendum on independence approaches, the Scottish Parliament has increasingly been promulgating its own international agenda, which has led to tensions between the representation of national and Scottish foreign policy, for instance on the UK's EU membership.[104] The EU–US relationship has specific relevance for the United Kingdom, which is traditionally considered, by itself and others, as the United States' 'closest and most reliable ally'.[105] Since 2002, however, the power balance in this relationship has started to shift, which has caused many to characterize the UK as the 'junior' partner in the relationship, and to note that the relationship has often appeared to be more 'special' to the UK than it is to the United States.[106] From an SNA perspective, a move towards Scottish independence may profoundly affect the transatlantic relationship (both EU–US and UK–US), as it would put into question some important military interests of the United States in the UK in the form of the nuclear submarines currently located in Scotland.[107]

In those Member States where the principle of *in foro interno, in foro externo* is the guideline for SNA autonomy, regions are empowered to maintain and engage in foreign relations in those areas in which they are internally competent, comparable to the situation of the US States.[108] This is also true for Belgium, which is one of the few Member States that have made use of regional Council representation under Article 203 of the Treaty on European Union (TEU).[109] Significantly, the Belgian regions are entitled to independent diplomatic representation.[110] This results in

[103] *Ibid.*, at 8.

[104] At the Doha meeting on 22 May 2013, (then) External Affairs Minister Humza Yousaf said that '[e]ven at the moment, the United Kingdom Government is wanting the UK to leave the European Union but the Scots wish to remain a part of the European Union'. This statement was considered misguided by the Westminster Parliament and most of Mr Yousaf's colleagues in the Scottisch Parliament. See www.heraldscotland.com/politics/political-news/anger-at-ministers-eu-claim-at-doha-meeting.21143504, accessed 11 February 2014.

[105] D. E. Mix, 'The United Kingdom and US–UK Relations' (15 April 2013) *US Congressional Research Service*, at i.

[106] *Ibid.*, 7.

[107] See W. Walker, 'Can Scotland Really Say "No" to Trident? The Nuclear Bases Can't Be Moved South: That Has Huge Implications for the UK and NATO', 29 February 2012, *The Times*.

[108] This is also the case for Switzerland. See Articles 55 and 56 of the Swiss Constitution.

[109] Article 167 §3 of the Belgian Constitution.

[110] See also Skoutaris, 'Comparing the Subnational Constitutional Space of the European Sub-State Entities in the Area of Foreign Affairs', 256.

a unique structure of three formally independent networks of representation: one for the federal Belgian state, one for the Dutch-speaking community in Flanders and Brussels, and one for the French-language community in Wallonia and Brussels.[111]

The most explicit mention of sub-central actors within the EU–US relationship is made with respect to the so-called 'thematic agendas'.[112] Within these areas, bodies such as the Transatlantic Consumers' Dialogue,[113] the Transatlantic Business Dialogue, the Transatlantic Legislators' Dialogue,[114] the EU–US Development Dialogue, the EU–US Education Policy Forum, the EU–US Energy Council and the EU–US Task Force on Biotechnology are, in varying degrees, populated with non-governmental organizations (NGOs) and public interest organizations from both the EU and the USA.[115] Comparably, the European Union has long since developed policies that are geared towards expanded European influence in the areas directly surrounding the EU.[116] As already mentioned, the European influence on border regions is considered an important strength in its transatlantic relationship. The Union for the Mediterranean is a prime example of such a 'transboundary' regional approach. The Union was first

[111] See generally, D. Criekemans, 'Foreign Policy and Diplomacy of the Belgian Regions: Flanders and Wallonia' (2010) *Clingendael Discussion Papers in Diplomacy*. For the federal institution, see http://diplomatie.belgium.be/en/, accessed 11 February 2014.

[112] Part of the overarching New Transatlantic Agenda set out in 1995. On the trade relationship, see T. Takács, 'Transatlantic Regulatory Cooperation in Trade: Objectives, Challenges and Instruments for Economic Governance', Chapter 7 in this volume. On the New Transatlantic Agenda, see generally Pollack and Shaffer (eds.), *Transatlantic Governance in the Global Economy*.

[113] Anu Bradford's recent article 'The Brussels Effect' convincingly argues that much of the European Union's global influence is in fact the result of 'unilateral regulatory globalization' rather than of multilateralism. The European Union has been successfully globalizing its domestic standards by combining its market power with virtually unparalleled regulatory capacity and domestic preferences for strict (consumer protection) rules in product/consumer markets. Commerce is arguably the most important aspect of the transatlantic relationship, and the United States has frequently challenged the unilateral imposition of product standards, privacy relations and/or antitrust laws by the European Union in several international forums.

[114] See D. Jančić, 'The European Parliament and EU–US Relations: Revamping Institutional Cooperation?', Chapter 3 in this volume.

[115] M. Green Cowles, 'Calming the Waters: The Rebirth of the Transatlantic Business Dialogue' in D. Andrews, M. A. Pollack, G. C. Shaffer and H. Wallace (eds.), *The New Transatlantic Agenda and the Future of Transatlantic Economic Governance* (Florence: European University Institute, 2005).

[116] Most notably through the European Neighbourhood Policy Regulation 638/2006, laying down general provisions establishing a European Neighbourhood and Partnership Instrument, OJ [2006] L 310/1.

created through so-called Euromed Agreements (EMAs) in 1995, and has recently been reinvigorated by efforts of the French EU presidency in 2008 when it received its new title.[117] The Union for the Mediterranean (MU) undoubtedly combines the largest single group of countries both within and outside the EU; it currently has forty-three Members, of which twenty-eight are Member States. The other countries include Albania, Algeria, Egypt, Israel, Jordan, Lebanon, the Palestinian Authority, Syria and Turkey.[118] In terms of sub-national and regional action, the initial plans of France to revive and reshape the Union into a different, more powerful body called the Mediterranean Union is informative. France wanted to create this MU in order to provide an alternative to Turkish membership of the EU.[119] In the end, this proposal failed since many considered it a duplication of European institutions in this area, which could undermine EU policy in the region.[120] Tellingly, the United States appears to have had a strong hand in the initial proposal, since it would also help to create a political superstructure over NATO, of which most of the MU's prospective members were already part.[121]

Aside from the constitutional questions that are raised by these instances of SNA action and involvement, they also challenge our conceptualization of the transatlantic relationship more generally. Pollack and Shaffer's framework, as discussed above, identifies three distinct methods of interaction: the *intergovernmental* model, the *transgovernmental* model – dominated by technocratic bureaucrats – and the *transnational* model, where civil society and other non-governmental organizations play an important role.[122] Thus far our focus has been on the intergovernmental elements of the transatlantic relationship, and the more indirect influence of the SNA influence on EU (external) action. More generally, the EU–US relationship may be considered primarily transgovernmental in light of the central role of European bureaucrats within this system. Turning to the future of SNAs within the EU–US relationship, and the

[117] H. de Waele, *Layered Global Player*, p. 131.

[118] *Ibid.*, p. 132. The broad membership may be considered an advantage but has also led to stagnation within the Union since painful political issues are slow to be resolved, such as the Western Sahara problem, the partition of Cyprus and the Middle East peace process.

[119] As first advocated by Nicolas Sarkosy during his presidential campaign.

[120] Germany and the European Commission were particularly negative.

[121] J. Laughland, 'What is Really Behind the Mediterranean Union?' 12 March 2008, available at: www.brusselsjournal.com/node/3083, accessed 11 February 2014.

[122] Pollack and Shaffer, 'Who Governs?', p. 288.

implications of their potential role outside of the formal channels, the transnational aspects of the EU–US relationship become visible.

IV. A future for a bottom-up EU–US relationship?

Writing in 2001, after the third WTO meeting in Seattle, Pollack and Schaffer argued that the USA and EU's attempt to engage civil society in the interdependent relationship between the two actors was aimed at preventing a political backlash.[123] Writing in 2013, the author finds that the issue of a 'disaffected' civil society has arguably worsened, and is now accompanied by an internal European debate on the future of the EU more generally.[124] In lieu of a meaningful interpretation of the subsidiarity principle at the EU level, local actors are nevertheless taking action on issues that impact them. For example, the ongoing economic crisis is a salient issue in international politics with 'high'-level meetings involving the US federal level and European institutions and heads of state. But it is also addressed at the local level.[125] Two recent initiatives under the auspices of the Council of Europe – the 'Local Government in Critical Times: Policies for Crisis, Recovery, and a Sustainable Future' report and the 'Finance Benchmarking' programme – combine expertise from the regional institutions gathered in the Committee of Regions, as well as the Council of the EU.[126] Many of these local initiatives are now geared towards building connections with other local communities, a key example being the outreach efforts and network-building by metropolitan areas such as London and Paris.[127] These efforts are not necessarily accompanied by *legal* competence to take action on these matters – despite the prevalent impression of local autonomy.[128] This chapter confirms that the current positions of European sub-central authorities depend largely on their domestic constitutional status, and to what extent these positions can be leveraged in order

[123] *Ibid.*, pp. 289–90.

[124] See van Zeben, 'Research Agenda for a Polycentric European Union' for a more detailed discussion of the future of multi-level governance and subsidiarity in the EU.

[125] More generally on international local action, see G. Frug and D. Barron, 'International Local Government Law' (2006) 38 *The Urban Lawyer* 1.

[126] Available at: www.coe.int/t/dgap/localdemocracy/default_en.asp, accessed 11 February 2014. These programmes are part of a broader push for stronger local government. See 'The European Outline Convention on Transfrontier Co-operation between Territorial Communities or Authorities', available at: http://conventions.coe.int/Treaty/en/Treaties/Html/106.htm, accessed 20 February 2014.

[127] For instance, consider the C40 city network (www.c40cities.org/c40cities, accessed 11 February 2014).

[128] See Frug and Barron, 'International Local Government Law'.

to (in)directly influence European policy-making in relevant external action areas. In order to ascertain the true effect of SNA actors on EU–US relations, more empirical work would be needed. This lack of quantitative data does not prevent us from considering the theoretical obstacles to, and complications of, SNA action. Put differently, what would be the potential benefits of diplomatic activism by sub-central actors? And what would be its dangers? In sum, what are the risks of engaging sub-federal and sub-state entities in international relations?

First, increased SNA involvement may weaken the 'one-voice' approach of the European Union and the United States, and create 'noise' within their relationship.[129] Despite the outward impression of a 'soloist' president, the power to engage in foreign relations, both in the legal and political sense, is horizontally and vertically fragmented within the United States.[130] The possibility of disaccord between the three branches of government is a real one, as past and ongoing conflicts have shown.[131] This is also true in the vertical relationship between the federal government and the States, which play a supplementary role in foreign affairs,[132] within the limits of the Supremacy Clause, which sets out that federal statutes and treaties trump State law and obligates State judges to respect federal law.[133] Notwithstanding the clear primacy of the federal government over foreign relations, US States have

[129] S. Cleveland, '*Crosby* and the "One-Voice" Myth in US Foreign Relations' (2001) 46 *Villanova Law Review* 975–1,014.

[130] *Ibid.*, 984. At the federal level, the national foreign relations powers are distributed between the three branches of government. In Article I of the US Constitution, the majority of foreign affairs powers are bestowed on Congress, including the power to provide for common defence, to regulate foreign commerce and coin, and to oversee immigration. The diplomatic, treaty and war powers essential to foreign relations are shared between the President (the Executive) and Congress. See US Constitution, Articles II§3 and III§2, cl. 1.

[131] Cleveland, '*Crosby* and the "One-Voice" Myth', 985–9. For a recent example, see M. Trujillo, 'Hoyer: Obama Doesn't Need Approval from Congress to Strike Syria's Assad', 13 September 2013, available at: http://thehill.com/blogs/global-affairs/middle-east-north-africa/322075-hoyer-obama-doesnt-need-congressional-approval-for-syria-strike, accessed 11 February 2014.

[132] US Constitution, Article I§10 prohibits States from entering into treaties or alliances. Conversely, congressional consent is needed before States may tax imports and exports, keep troops or warships in time of peace, or engage in war with foreign states. US Constitution, Article VI, cl. 2.

[133] Cleveland sets out that several commentators debate whether concurrent jurisdiction exists over those foreign relations powers not expressly prohibited by this Clause, but also acknowledges that the federal power to control foreign relations is well established. See Cleveland, '*Crosby* and the "One-Voice" Myth', 990–1.

historically been very engaged in foreign affairs,[134] something which has only fairly recently been curtailed by the courts in several landmark judgments.[135] The importance of State practice with respect to the incorporation of, for example, non-self-executing human rights treaties has long been accepted.[136] Conversely, the federal government has frequently refused to impose treaty obligations upon State and local governments.[137] Despite these domestic fragmentations, the United States has arguably been far better in maintaining the 'one-voice' myth in foreign relations than has the European Union.[138]

The international representation of the European Union was a salient issue throughout the Lisbon revision process. In the Laeken Declaration on the Future of the European Union, which initiated the reform of the EU treaties in December 2001, the question of external representation was explicitly raised: 'Does Europe not, now that it is finally *unified*, have a leading role to play in a new world order, that of a power able both to play a stabilizing role worldwide and to point the way ahead for many countries and peoples?'[139] Similarly, Philip Gordon, the then US Assistant Secretary of State for Europe, said in January 2013 that the USA benefited from a *united Europe*.[140] Is a 'one-voice' approach needed

[134] For State-specific initiatives, see e.g. 'Enterprise Florida', a public–private partnership for Florida's economic development (mission statement available at: www.enterpriseflorida.com, accessed 11 February 2014), Texas' developmental agency (www.texaswideopenforbusiness.com/, accessed 11 February 2014) and Indiana (http://iedc.in.gov/about-the-iedc/international-office-contacts, accessed 11 February 2014) with offices in the UK and Germany.

[135] See Cleveland, '*Crosby* and the "One-Voice" Myth'. See also e.g. L. Wexler, 'Take the Long Way Home: Sub-Federal Integration of Unratified and Non-Self-Executing Treaty Law' (2007) 28 *Michigan Journal of International Law* 1–48, and K. Werhan, 'Regulatory Federalism, Shaken not Stirred' (2013) 21(1) *Journal of Law and Politics* (discussing recent judgments in the cases of *Arizona* v. *United States*, ruling that State law regarding detection and removal of aliens without proper documentation was pre-empted by federal law, and *NFIB* v. *Sebelius*, ruling that the Affordable Care Act fell within federal competence despite its interference with individual choice.)

[136] See extensively Wexler, 'Take the Long Way Home'.

[137] Cleveland, '*Crosby* and the "One-Voice" Myth', at 1,002.

[138] *Ibid.*

[139] European Council, Laeken Declaration on the Future of the European Union, 14–15 December 2001, at 2, as cited in Koutrakos, 'Introduction' in *The European Union's External Relations*, at 7 (author's emphasis).

[140] Review of the Balance of Competences between the United Kingdom and European Union Foreign Policy, July 2013, at 131 (emphasis added), available at: www.gov.uk/government/uploads/system/uploads/attachment_data/file/227437/2901086_Foreign_Policy_acc.pdf, accessed 11 February 2014.

in order to create a powerful European Union on the world stage? Or does the EU's strength lie in its multi-level structure, which should therefore also be incorporated into its external relations?[141] A more fragmented 'divide-and-conquer' tactic that would allow for diffuse and intense lobbying by European SNAs and regions with their American counterparts, for their own and/or European interests, may strengthen European influence, regardless of the lack of 'central' European representation. Already, the Delegation of the European Union to the United States caters to this differentiation by providing information on the presence of European institutions in each individual US State rather than in *the* United States.[142] At the same time, US investment in the EU is discussed as investment per Member State.[143] The real risk of SNA representation is perhaps best considered from an equity perspective: should we worry about over-representation of some groups at the expense of others? Rather than creating a transatlantic and transnational civil society, some commentators worry that instead certain specific interests are able to organize themselves,[144] in partnerships with relevant governmental institutions.[145] At the same time, these dynamics do create room for experiments in new forms of governance in both the USA and the EU,[146] which ties back to the democratic role of SNAs, both nationally and within the European context.[147]

141 Some have argued that the European Union clearly does not attempt, or pretend, to be a unitary actor with one single foreign policy. See de Waele, *Layered Global Player*, p. 19.

142 www.euintheus.org/interactive-map/#!/?map=US&region=473, accessed 11 February 2014.

143 'US investment in the Netherlands from 2000 to 2010 was nine times more than US investment in China during the same period. US investment in the UK was more than seven times more, and in Ireland nearly three times more, than in China.' See www.euintheus.org/what-we-do/eu-us-facts-figures/, accessed 11 February 2014. Tourism and cultural exchange through education, on the other hand, are discussed as EU- and US-wide activities: for 2009/10, more than 188,000 students from the USA and the EU visited each other's country and more than 10 million EU tourists travelled to the USA in 2010 (source: www.euintheus.org/what-we-do/eu-us-facts-figures/, accessed 11 February 2014).

144 Pollack and Shaffer, 'Who Governs?', p. 300 ('International civil society model is that the dialogues are segmented by sector, and their levels of activity and influence are extremely uneven').

145 *Ibid.*, p. 299. See also R. A. W. Rhodes, *Control and Power in Central–Local Government Relations* (Farnborough: Gower, 1981).

146 Pollack and Shaffer, 'Who Governs?', p. 290.

147 Jeffery, 'Sub-National Mobilization and European Integration', 17 ('The credibility of SNA claims for influence in EU decision-making is likely to be enhanced by the perceived legitimacy which SNAs bring with them into the European policy process').

Currently, the Commission's positioning of SNAs in this context 'is principally concerned with reinforcing the democratic credentials of the existing interinstitutional system of governance rather than more radical experiments in direct democracy, in legitimation outside of the context of the European Parliament, or in the transfer of governance activities to civil society'.[148] Moreover, the potential of regions as breeding grounds for active participatory democracy is limited to the extent that it requires civil society actors to conform, for example, to internal standards and codes of conduct in order to be eligible for participation in the EU system.[149] The potential of SNAs as spaces for democracy is thus restricted since the civil society that is stimulated by Europeanization is one that is 'transnationalised and governmentalized' and as such is likely to be successful and active more on the European level, rather than on the regional and local level.[150] As 'local' civil society is becoming increasingly 'global',[151] SNAs are not necessarily the natural, or exclusive, anchor for civil society.[152] At the same time, the recent crises in Europe have left European citizens suspicious of more union, or at least a more central European Union. The idea that the EU will have to reform locally in order to be able to act globally

[148] K. Armstrong, 'Rediscovering Civil Society: The European Union and the White Paper on Governance' (2002) 8(1) *European Law Journal* 102–32, at 115.

[149] *Ibid.*, 129–30.

[150] *Ibid.*, 131. Relatedly, the Committee of the Regions released a report in the run-up to the European Parliament elections to measure the role of the regions and SNAs in distributing information on European issues to their constituents, finding a relatively large willingness to disperse information but also a lack of capacity to do so in some cases. See K. Raube *et al.*, 'Going Local: The Communication Potential of Local and Regional Authorities' (September 2013), available at: http://cor.europa.eu/en/documentation/studies/Documents/2013-Going-Local/2013-Going-Local.pdf, accessed 11 February 2014.

[151] See for instance M. D. Conover *et al.*, 'The Geospatial Characteristics of a Social Movement Communication Network' (2013) 8(3) *PLoS ONE* e55957 (showing that, compared to a network of stable domestic political communication, the Occupy Wall Street network exhibits higher levels of locality and a hub-and-spoke structure, in which the majority of non-local attention is allocated to high-profile locations such as New York, California and Washington DC. In light of social movement theory, these features reflect the movement's efforts to mobilize resources at the local level and to develop narrative frames that reinforce collective purpose at the national level).

[152] E. Ferrara *et al.*, 'Traveling Trends: Social Butterflies or Frequent Fliers?' (2013) *Proceedings of the First ACM Conference on Online Social Networks*, showing that Twitter trends that surface globally emerge from those metropolitan areas that have major air traffic hubs, raising the question of the role of 'visitors' to these streams, rather than diverse inhabitants of metropolitan areas.

is gaining traction.[153] The centrality of the EU–US relationship to the European Union's international position cannot be ignored, but neither should the internal (sub-national) dynamics of the EU's external action. At the very least, more efforts need to be made to understand these forces, and ground them within more general multi-level governance theory,[154] rather than relying on a grey market in sub-central diplomacy.

153 C. Wergin, 'One Europe, Many Europes', *International New York Times* (15 October 2013), at S23.

154 See more generally, van Zeben, 'Research Agenda for a Polycentric European Union'.

PART II

Rule-making between the EU and USA

6

Towards a transatlantic community of law?

The use of law between the EU and US legal orders: questions of legal form and characterisation

ELAINE FAHEY

Introduction

In a review published in 1967 of the textbook by Stein and Hay, *Law and Institutions in the Atlantic Area*, Angelo opined that 'the emergent cross-Atlantic organisations of the 1950s are suffering from internal attacks. To the casual observer there appears to be more conflict than law in Atlantic institutions ... hope for an "Atlantic Community" or even a "partnership" seems to be an ever-receding dream.'[1] Historically, many have doubted the feasibility of transatlantic integration through law. There is still a discernible view in scholarship about the insignificance of law to transatlantic relations, as an 'institutional-light', 'law-light' unfixed scientific entity. However, many distinctive 'interactions' and rule-making exercises take place in contemporary times between the EU and US legal orders, for example the development of the broad adoption of EU rules in the USA,[2] major EU–US rule convergence in data protection,[3] an institutionalised Transatlantic Trade and Investment Partnership (TTIP) or even

Thanks to participants at the workshop 'Transatlantic Relations: The Nature of Rule-Making', January 2013, Amsterdam, the Netherlands, for comments received there. Thanks also to Christina Eckes, Pieter Jan Kuijper, Chantal Mak and Anniek de Ruijter for their helpful remarks and comments. All errors are solely those of the author.

[1] H. Angelo, 'Review of E. Stein & P. Hay (eds.) *Law and Institutions in the Atlantic Area, Readings, Cases, and Problems with Volume of Documents*' (1967) 56 *California Law Review* 923.

[2] A. Bradford, 'The Brussels Effect' (2012) 107 *Northwestern University Law Review* 1.

[3] 'EU Urged to Choose Transatlantic Convergence on Data Protection', *EurActiv* (5 December 2012). Negotiations on a transatlantic data protection framework agreement began in 2010.

the EU intervening frequently before the US Supreme Court.[4] Some of these developments are argued here to indicate the institutionalisation of transatlantic relations. Others are argued to indicate what is termed here as specific degrees of 'proximity' between the EU and US legal orders, that is, closeness of instruments, structures or interactions, formal and informal, more specifically defined than the NATO-esque 'Atlantic Area' considered by Angelo. They (i.e. institutionalisation and close proximity) raise the question of the relationship between them as phenomena. Cumulatively, they form the basis for reflections here, by way of a future research agenda, on what the phenomenon of a 'transatlantic community of law' between the EU and USA actually means in contemporary times. Recent developments also provoke a reflection on our understanding of the character of 'real-world' interactions between legal orders, and perhaps questions of their legitimacy.

More conventional legal analyses of transatlantic relations examine their bilateral agreements *stricto sensu*, especially in sensitive fields such as security. In this perspective, the more conventional template for analysis is the use of mutual recognition and its legitimacy.[5] Arguably, EU–US security rule-making after 9/11 exposed limits of mutual recognition in security cooperation or the limits of proximity between legal orders. Conversely, it can be argued that more recent forms of EU–US security rule-making go beyond mutual recognition, for example EU–US efforts to engage in global rule-making in cybercrime and cybersecurity.[6] Instead, they seem to be the product of the proximity between the two legal orders. It remains to be seen at the time of writing how the EU–US surveillance saga will impact on this state of affairs. Nonetheless, there are many reasons to consider the parameters of proximity between the EU and US legal orders, both within and beyond its conventional forums.

[4] On the TTIP, see M. Bartl and E. Fahey 'A Postnational Marketplace: Negotiating the Transatlantic Trade and Investment Partnership (TTIP)', Chapter 9 in this volume. On EU interventions before the US Supreme Court, see Section II.

[5] See E. Fahey, 'Law and Governance as Checks and Balances in Transatlantic Security: Rights, Redress and Remedies in EU–US Passenger Name Records and the Terrorist Finance Tracking Program' (2013) *Yearbook of European Law*, 368–88; G. Shaffer, 'Reconciling Trade and Regulatory Goals: The Prospects and Limits of New Approaches to Transatlantic Governance through Mutual Recognition and Safe Harbor Agreements' (2002) 9 *Columbia Journal of European Law* 29.

[6] EU–US Working Group on CyberSecurity and Cybercrime, Concept Paper, 13 April 2011 (hereafter WGCC Concept Paper).

Accordingly, this chapter considers these themes using four largely descriptive theses. First, it is intended to show in Section I, following on from accounts in the first part of the volume, how interactions between the EU and US legal orders demonstrate that transatlantic relations can be understood as quasi-institutionalised. This account explores, in Section II, how law serves as a medium for communication between the two legal orders, sometimes outside of the strictly conventional bilateral context of EU–US agreements and conventional dispute resolution forums (termed here 'non-bilateral'), only possible on account of the high quasi-institutionalisation of the relationship or at least very high proximity between the two legal orders. However, it is also shown in Section III that there are boundaries or limitations on this proximity or closeness, and also major legitimacy questions. For example, the limitations of mutual recognition in transatlantic justice cooperation are evident from an analysis of bilateral rule-making in security post 9/11. By contrast, in more recent times the high proximity between the two legal orders results instead in more novel forms of bilateral rule-making, leading to the consideration in Section IV of the movement of rules between the two legal orders in the phenomenon of rule-transfer, and tentatively considers questions of its legitimacy, which warrant future study.

I. The character of law and transatlantic relations

A. *Transatlantic integration through 'law': what is 'law-light'?*

Historically, many have sought an 'Atlantic community of law',[7] a 'Transatlantic Marketplace'[8] or a 'Transatlantic Civil Society'[9] to be forged between the EU and USA. Such entities have been mooted with a view to creating a transatlantic polity of sorts, inter alia for economic, political and even socio-cultural reasons. The recent negotiations between the EU and USA on a Transatlantic Trade and Investment Partnership (TTIP) may signify a new era of legal cooperation between them, if

[7] See Angelo, 'Review of Stein and Hay'.

[8] See L. Britton, 'Europe: The New Tiger? The Shape of Tomorrow's Global Economy', speech delivered at The Kennedy School, Harvard University, Boston, USA (18 March 1998), available at: http://europa.eu/rapid/press-release_SPEECH-98-49_en.htm, accessed 12 February 2014; M. Egan (ed.), *Creating a Transatlantic Marketplace: Government Policies and Business Strategies* (Manchester University Press, 2005).

[9] F. Bignami and S. Charnovitz, 'Transatlantic Civil Society Dialogues' in M. A. Pollack and G. C. Shaffer (eds.), *Transatlantic Governance in the Global Economy* (Lanham, MD: Rowman & Littlefield, 2001), p. 255.

successful.[10] Nevertheless, most scholars of transatlantic relations generally express disappointment and pessimism about the trajectory of transatlantic relations through law, particularly in the area of trade. The relationship between the EU and USA is viewed as having generated many failed agreements, binding and non-binding, often caused by a lack of compliance from the lead actors and plagued by suboptimal remedies.[11] Moreover, the relationship between the EU and USA is viewed by scholars as a 'law-light' and 'institutionally light' scientific entity.[12] In this regard, relations between the EU and USA have been guided by foundational documents such as the Transatlantic Declaration and the New Transatlantic Agenda, which are not legally binding.[13] Yet even optimistic views of transatlantic cooperation through law are appraised by scholars through a language of legal 'pluralism'[14] or the limits of 'rule convergence',[15] language that emphasises a demonstrable political, social and cultural space between the two legal orders. What is important to

[10] See Bartl and Fahey, Chapter 9 in this volume.

[11] E. U. Petersmann, 'Dispute Prevention and Dispute Settlement in the EU–US Transatlantic Partnership' in Pollack and Shaffer (eds.), *Transatlantic Governance in the Global Economy*; M. Egan, 'Mutual Recognition and Standard Setting: Public and Private Strategies for Governing Markets' in Pollack and Shaffer (eds.), *Transatlantic Governance in the Global Economy*; E. U. Petersmann and M. A. Pollack (eds.), *Transatlantic Economic Disputes. The EU, the US and the WTO* (Oxford University Press, 2003); M. Pollack *et al.*, *The Political Economy of the Transatlantic Partnership*, Report (Florence: Robert Schuran Centre for Advanced Studies, 2003), p. 10; Shaffer, 'Reconciling Trade and Regulatory Roles' pp. 73–95.

[12] M. Pollack, 'The New Transatlantic Agenda at Ten: Reflections on an Experiment in International Governance' (2005) 43 *Journal of Common Market Studies* 899. Similarly J. Peterson *et al.*, 'Review of the Framework for Relations between the European Union and the United States: An Independent Study', commissioned by European Commission Director General External Relations Unit C1 Relations with the United States and Canada, 2005. See E. Fahey, 'On the Use of Law in Transatlantic Relations: Legal Dialogues between the EU and US' (forthcoming 20(3)) *European Law Journal*.

[13] The New Transatlantic Agenda (NTA), signed 3 December 1995 in Madrid. See Pollack 'The New Transatlantic Agenda at Ten'.

[14] N. Krisch, 'Pluralism in Post-National Risk Regulation: The Dispute over GMOs and Trade' (2010)1 *Transnational Legal Theory*; see also M. Pollack and G. Shaffer, *When Cooperation Fails: The International Law and Politics of Genetically Modified Foods* (Oxford University Press, 2009).

[15] G. Shaffer, 'Globalisation and Social Protection: the Impact of EU and International Rules in the Ratcheting Up of US Data Privacy Standards' (2000) 25 *Yale Journal of International Law* 1; F. Bignami, 'European Versus American Liberty: A Comparative Privacy Analysis of Antiterrorism Data Mining' (2007) 48 *Boston College Law Review* 609; see also Bradford, 'The Brussels Effect'.

note concerning the role and view of the role of law here is that most scholarly views on the conduct of two of the world's leading global governance actors are built upon views of rule-making in the bilateral legal context, rather than other autonomous conduct or actions.[16] As a result, it is possible to overlook the significance of certain interactions taking place outside of the conventional bilateral context and their significance for our understanding of an Atlantic community of law. The account next considers the institutionalisation of the transatlantic relationship and its genesis.

B. *Institutionalisation and transatlantic relations: why 'institution-light'?*

While there is some dispute in scholarship about the main scientific characteristics of the relationships between the EU and the USA, few suggest that a transatlantic or Atlantic community of law exists.[17] The 'institutionally light' nature of EU–US relations, allied to the novel and innovative capacities that have characterised the transatlantic relationship, constitutes for some a problematic institutional deficit,[18] but for others a strength.[19] Non-legal scholarship on transatlantic relations is generally unambiguous about the extent to which bilateral transatlantic relations are institutionally modest.[20] Such scholarship typically demonstrates how most transatlantic rule-making has been generated by permanent dialogues and by non-institutional actors. However, it can be said from a legal perspective that there are formal and informal aspects of transatlantic relations that indicate that they are at least quasi-institutional, despite their lack of formal legal character, as explored in Part I of this volume.[21] In this regard, a Transatlantic Legislators' Dialogue has been ongoing since 1972, albeit with limited output and only one of the three

[16] See, for example, M. Smith, 'The European Union, the USA and Global Governance', in J. U. Wunderlich and D. J. Bailey (eds.), *The European Union and Global Governance: A Handbook* (London: Routledge, 2011), Chapter 25.

[17] J. Peterson and M. Pollack, 'Conclusion: The End of Transatlantic Partnership' in J. Peterson and M. Pollack (eds.), *Europe, America, Bush: Transatlantic Relations in the Twenty-First Century*: (London: Routledge, 2003), p. 128.

[18] Pollack, 'The New Transatlantic Agenda at Ten'.

[19] J. Peterson and R. Steffenson, 'Transatlantic Institutions: Can Partnership be Engineered?' (2009) 11 *British Journal of Politics and International Relations* 25.

[20] E.g. Pollack, 'The New Transatlantic Agenda at Ten'; Peterson *et al.*, 'Review of the Framework for Relations between the European Union and the United States'.

[21] As I have argued elsewhere: see Fahey, 'On the Use of Law in Transatlantic Relations'.

EU institutional co-legislators participating.[22] Transatlantic annual summits have been held since the 1990s, and continue to generate challenges regarding the appropriate EU institutional representation, even after the Treaty of Lisbon.[23] Also overlooked in non-legal scholarship is the direct contact between the US Supreme Court and the Court of Justice of the European Union, which has been increasing since 2000 in the form of periodic judicial visits.[24]

Historically, most rule-making between the EU and USA has taken place in permanent networks of dialogues. The permanent dialogues include the Transatlantic Business Dialogue, Transatlantic Labour Dialogue, Transatlantic Consumer Dialogue and Transatlantic Environment Dialogue. They have variable degrees of success or failure and comprise public and private spheres, and variable actors and activities.[25] However, it is the Business Dialogue that is claimed to have had the most success as a rule-making instrument.[26] In this regard, the democratic credentials of transatlantic rule-making are not rated highly per se. These dialogues are perceived to have given certain economic actors privileged access to policy-makers at the expense of other sectors of transatlantic society, an assertion that must certainly be the case with respect to the Business Dialogue, which includes over 100 CEOs of leading US corporations.[27] Some have categorically stated that no Transatlantic Civil Society per se exists, yet there has been much cooperation between civil society across the Atlantic for extensive time

[22] That is, the European Parliament. See D. Jančić, 'The European Parliament and EU–US Relations: Revamping Institutional Cooperation?', Chapter 3 in this volume.

[23] See J. Monar, 'EU–US Relations at the Outset of the Obama Presidency: The Potential for Leadership and a New Deal' (2009) 16 *European Foreign Affairs Review* 1; P. Koutrakos (ed.), *European Foreign Policy: Legal and Political Perspectives* (Cheltenham: Edward Elgar, 2011). See also 'EU Settles on Threesome to Collect Nobel Peace Prize', *Reuters.com* (17 October 2012).

[24] See E. Mak, 'The US Supreme Court and the Court of Justice of the European Union: Emergence, Nature and Impact of Transatlantic Judicial Communication', Chapter 2 in this volume.

[25] See M. Green Cowles, 'The Transatlantic Business Dialogue: Transforming the New Transatlantic Dialogue', in Pollack and Shaffer (eds.), *Transatlantic Governance in the Global Economy*, p. 215, on Transatlantic Business Dialogue as the most successful dialogue.

[26] See *ibid.* Others suggest that there are also so-called unofficial transatlantic dialogues, for example on sustainable development, aviation and climate change, and policy networks: Bignami and Charnovitz, 'Transatlantic Civil Society Dialogues', p. 255. However, their composition, tasks, operation and proximity to rule-makers vary considerably, and so the taxonomy of this category is contestable.

[27] See Green Cowles, 'The Transatlantic Business Dialogue'.

periods, not least since the nineteenth century, on topics ranging from peace to slavery. This category of 'unofficial' dialogues must of course be regarded as more complex, subjective and multifarious.[28] Overall, one may say that the prominence of networks of actors and dialogues in rule-making sustains the 'institution-light' thesis of transatlantic relations. However, rule-making networks between the EU and USA, such as the formal and permanent dialogues between the EU and USA, along with High-Level Working Groups, are subject to increasing standards and expectations of participation and transparency, that is, EU standards of good governance.[29] This may operate to alter the traditional shield of 'high' politics surrounding transatlantic relations, which are rooted in its non-institutionalised state.[30] Whether, beyond this, it will incite further and deeper institutionalisation remains to be seen.

The question of institutionalisation has ramifications for our understanding of formal legal cooperation between the EU and USA, and the place of law, legal disputes and interactions between the respective legal orders, which are considered here next.

C. *On bilateral agreements between the EU and US legal orders, and the forums for their disputes*

As a matter of history, relations between the EU and USA have generated considerable amounts of high-profile rather than high-volume conflict.[31] Nevertheless, conflicts generated, for example, through breakdowns in agreement and/or challenges to ostensible attempts by both the EU and USA to regulate each other extraterritorially have usually taken place in conventional forums for the resolution of inter-sovereign disputes, that is in the World Trade Organization (WTO), rather than in each other's respective legal order.[32] For example, in the mid 1990s the European Community (as it then was) enacted legislative measures to prohibit the

[28] See Bignami and Charnovitz, 'Transatlantic Civil Society Dialogues'.

[29] On transparency, take for example the EU–US dialogue on the peaceful use of space, led by the US State Department and the European Commission, which recently fostered a long-term cooperation agreement between two organisations, the National Oceanic and Atmospheric Administration (NOAA) and the European Organisation for the Exploitation of Meteorological Satellites (EUMETSAT). However, see the meagre public information disseminated: www.euintheus.org/events/signature-ceremony-of-the-noaa-and-eumetsat-agreement-on-long-term-cooperation/, accessed 12 February 2014.

[30] See Bartl and Fahey, 'A Postnational Marketplace', Chapter 9 in this volume.

[31] Petersmann, 'Dispute Prevention and Dispute Settlement'.

[32] See Petersmann and Pollack, *Transatlantic Economic Disputes*.

extraterritorial application of the US Helms–Burton Act, in response to legal measures enacted by the USA when Cuba shot down US aircraft,[33] because it purported to allow legal proceedings to be taken against EU citizens and companies involved in the trafficking of property formerly owned by US citizens and confiscated by the Cuban Government. This resulted in WTO proceedings, albeit that these are still without a *de jure* outcome.[34]

There are several disputes still ongoing between the EU and USA before the WTO, relating to breakdowns of agreements between the EU and USA.[35] For example, the Boeing–Airbus dispute concerns subsidies provided to the companies, initially resulting in an EU–US agreement in 1992 on Trade in Large Civil Aircraft. The USA withdrew from this agreement in 2004 on the basis of support given to Boeing and the EU followed suit with claims as to support granted to Boeing. The WTO was asked by the EU to rule on countermeasures in 2012, and hearings commenced in 2013. Similarly, a poultry dispute has been ongoing since 1997, relating to the WTO Agreement on the Application of Sanitary and Phytosanitary Measures (so-called SPS Measures).[36] This aside, other recent bilateral cooperation between the EU and USA in competition law has been spurred by a desire to avoid extraterritorial legislation or direct challenges to authority in such forums as the WTO, even if the success of this cooperation is complex to measure.[37] Overall, however, we may say that disputes between the EU and USA have generally taken place in WTO

[33] Council Regulation (EC) No. 2271/96 OJ L 309/1 (1996), Joint Action of 22 November 1996 OJ L 309/7 (1996). Cuban Liberty and Democratic Solidarity (LIBERTAD) Act (Helms–Burton Act) of March 1996, 22 USC §§6021. See J. Huber, 'The Helms-Burton Blocking Statute of the European Union' (1996) 20 *Fordham International Law Journal* 699.

[34] The EU requested a WTO Dispute Settlement Panel in 1996, and the EU and USA reached an agreement in 1998 not to proceed with its WTO challenge for a quid pro quo undertaking that the USA would not prosecute any EU citizens under the Act. The agreement reached between the EU and USA was never implemented into US law and a de facto truce was reached. See the EC–US Agreement on Trade in Large Civil Aircraft, OJ L 301 of 17 October 1992; Appellate Body Report United States – Measures Affecting Trade in Large Civil Aircraft, 892 WT/DS353/AB/R (12 March 2012).

[35] For a recent survey of the European Parliament, see Library of the European Parliament, 'Principal EU–US disputes' (22 April 2013), available at: www.europarl.europa.eu/RegData/bibliotheque/briefing/2013/130518/LDM_BRI(2013)130518_REV1_EN.pdf and www.wto.org/english/tratop_e/dispu_e/cases_e/ds353_e.htm, accessed 12 February 2014. See Petersmann and Pollack, *Transatlantic Economic Disputes*.

[36] Dispute DS392 United States – Certain Measures Affecting Imports of Poultry from China.

[37] The 1991 EC–US Competition Cooperation Agreement provides for both positive and traditional comity. See J. Griffin, 'EC and US Extraterritoriality: Activism and Cooperation' (1993)17 *Fordham International Law Journal* 353. See the later Agreement between the European Communities and the Government of the United States of

dispute settlement forums, irrespective of how suboptimal such forums may be in terms of outcomes, bindingness or enforceability.[38] Moreover, such disputes have not taken place in each other's legal orders generally, neither before the International Court of Justice, nor any other international body. Nor have individuals been the beneficiaries or originators of claims or disputes. This has operated to contain bilateral disputes in a narrow range of forums of legal activity. Of course, the advent of the TTIP may operate to develop and expand the dispute resolution forums between the EU and USA.

This issue of the forum for the litigation of bilateral disputes also raises the question as to its relationship to litigation in another forum, namely the internal legal orders of the EU and USA respectively. The account here next focuses upon litigation in the EU legal order, thus taking the perspective of EU public law.

D. The litigation of transatlantic relations in the EU legal order

An analysis of the legal effects of transatlantic measures in the case law of the Court of Justice of the EU does not reveal much by way of quantity.[39] The limited amount of case law in this regard is indicative of the contours of EU–US relations in respect of representation and rule-making networks, that is, the actors of bilateral relations, as outlined above. One can observe that the rule-making dynamic of transatlantic relations prior to the Treaty of Lisbon generated little by way of conflict between the EU institutions and its Member States.

A decision of the Court of Justice from 2003 may neatly demonstrate this point.[40] *France* v. *Commission* serves as a rare challenge by a Member State to the authority of the European institutions to enter into transatlantic

America, on the application of positive comity principles in the enforcement of their competition laws OJ L 173, 18 June 1998, p. 28; Bradford, 'The Brussels Effect'.

38 On this issue of suboptimal remedies, see Petersmann, 'Dispute Prevention and Dispute Settlement'.

39 A search in the Curia database for 'transatlantic', that is, EU–US specific references, yields few relevant results. One may more broadly include Case C-233/02 *France* v. *Commission* [2004] ECR I-2759 (EC–US Guidelines on Regulatory Cooperation and Transparency); Case 142/88 *Hoesch AG & Federal Republic of Germany* v. *Bergrohr GmbH* [1989] ECR I-3413 (Arrangement in exchange of letters); Case C-327/91 *France* v. *Commission* [1994] ECR I-3641 1991 (EC–US Competition Cooperation Agreement); see the so-called Open Skies case law, e.g. C-467/98 *Commission* v. *Denmark* [2002] ECR I-9519; Case C-523/04 *Commission* v. *Netherlands* [2007] ECR I–3267.

40 Case C-233/02, *France v. Commission* [2004].

relations prior to the Treaty of Lisbon. In 1998 the EU and USA adopted a statement on Transatlantic Economic Partnership, affirming their intention to concentrate on removing barriers to transatlantic trade. The Partnership had an Action Plan approved by the Council in November 1998, and negotiations began in 1999 between the Commission and US Government on principles/guidelines. The Council had authorised the Commission to undertake negotiations with a view to concluding a bilateral agreement with the USA in the area of technical barriers to trade, and during the negotiations the representatives of the Commission maintained that the principles/guidelines could not create any obligations binding as a matter of international law. By February 2002 the negotiations on the Guidelines on Regulation and Transparency were finally concluded. However, dissatisfaction prevailed in certain Member States with the outcome of the negotiations, and France brought proceedings seeking to annul the decision of the Commission to conclude an agreement with the USA. France contended inter alia that the Commission was not competent to adopt the measures, as the Guidelines amounted to a binding international agreement. By contrast, the Commission argued that the Guidelines were not legally binding and that the intention not to enter binding legal relations or commitments was expressly maintained by the parties throughout the negotiations. Ultimately, the Court held that the Guidelines were devoid of legally binding effects and that the Court would not restrict the right of initiative of the Commission.

The decision may not be regarded as one of any landmark significance, nor as restrictive of EU authority and EU foreign affairs. Nonetheless, the proceedings serve, even if pre-Lisbon, as a reminder of the ability of EU Member States to directly challenge the authority of the EU institutions to enter formally binding transatlantic relations, which they largely do not do. The proceedings also emphasise how transatlantic relations are strikingly under-litigated. One might observe that the role of the Commission in transatlantic relations has been far less contentious than such proceedings might suggest.

The institutional landscape of transatlantic relations post-Lisbon involves the Commission still acting as lead EU negotiator of bilateral agreements, albeit with the European Parliament having consent powers over international agreements, powers which have engendered much discussion on accountability in EU international relations.[41] We may observe

[41] On Article 218(6)(a) TFEU and other relevant provisions, see Jančić, Chapter 3, and Santos Vara, Chapter 12, in this volume.

that recent significant litigation concerning accountability and transparency in transatlantic relations has been generated by an individual Member of the European Parliament before the Court of Justice.[42] Yet previous examples of the litigation of transatlantic relations in EU law concern the European Parliament, collectively, challenging the validity of the EU–US Passenger Name Records Agreement, motivated by rule of law and civil liberties concerns.[43] While such questions of the rule of law – and specifically accountability questions arising therefrom – are outside of the scope of this chapter, this litigation emphasises the layered dynamic of who the actors in transatlantic rule-making are. Nonetheless, the 'institution-light' dynamic of transatlantic rule-making, coupled with historically fragmented European external representation, has not been causative of conflict through law. Nor has it caused more conventional conflict with the EU Member States themselves. One may conclude that such high politics is viewed as beyond the realm of justiciability.[44] However, justiciability is not necessarily a useful template for analysis given the sheer amount of interactions taking place through law outside of bilateral relations.

This account next explores further the forums of and means for interactions between the two legal orders, taking place recently outside of the bilateral context in each other's legal order, which provide a means to examine the contours of an Atlantic community of law.

II. Non-bilateral interactions between the EU and US legal orders

A. *Overview of recent developments*

There are a series of recent non-bilateral interactions that have taken place between the legal orders of the EU and USA and outside of bilateral agreements, which the present author has sought to develop as evidence of specific 'proximity' between the two legal orders that is not conventionally accounted for.[45] For example, there have been a series of regular EU

[42] C-350/12 P *In't Veld* v. *Council*, Judgment of the General Court of 4 May 2012, [2012] ECR II-000, appeal pending.

[43] Joined Cases C-317/04 and C-318/04 *European Parliament* v. *Council and Commission* [2006] ECR I-4721.

[44] See E. Fahey, 'The Justiciability of EU PNR SWIFT Law' in P. Pawlak (ed.), *Beyond Terrorism and Privacy* (Institute for Security Studies, Chaillot Paper, 2012), pp. 55–61.

[45] For a detailed account of the case studies sketched briefly in Section II.A, see Fahey, 'On the Use of Law in Transatlantic Relations'.

amicus curiae submissions made by the European Commission through US-based lawyers before the US Supreme Court in, for example, death penalty cases, even where the EU had no prior involvement or link thereto. These submissions were conducted in support of the EU's long-standing campaign against the death penalty in the EU. Subsequently, the EU submissions were accepted and adopted by the US Supreme Court.[46] The submissions were made prior to the advent of single legal personality in the Treaty of Lisbon, and notably the authority of the Commission to do so on behalf of the EU prior to single legal personality being granted has never been challenged by the Member States, who might have favoured the Council instead, for example, or indeed no such representation.[47] More recently, in late 2012 the European Commission on behalf of the European Union made submissions before the US Supreme Court, seeking to prohibit the application of the US Alien Tort Statute to EU companies for human rights abuses in Nigeria, with less success.[48]

We may also note that in 2011 the EU took upon itself to include aviation within the scope of EU Environmental Emissions Trading Scheme rules, having failed to see an agreement reached at international level.[49] It thus adopted a series of rules that were perceived to have a considerable impact on foreign airlines, even when they were outside EU airspace. While further consideration of these events and details has been conducted elsewhere,[50] for present purposes the most significant event was that the US House of Representatives passed legislation to prohibit the impact of EU Environmental Trading Emission (EU-ETS) rules upon the US legal order.[51] It also supported the litigation by certain US airlines before the Court of

[46] See M. Cremona, 'Values in EU Foreign Policy' in M. Evans and P. Koutrakos (eds.), *Beyond the Established Legal Orders: Policy Interconnections between the EU and the Rest of the World* (Oxford: Hart Publishing, 2011), p. 275. Interventions accepted in earlier rather than later submissions: for example, not in *Sosa* v. *Alvarez-Machain*, 542 US 692 (2004), on the Alien Tort Statute.

[47] Except see W. Pryor, 'Foreign and International Law Sources in Domestic Constitutional Interpretation' (2006) 30 *Harvard Journal of Law and Public Policy* 173, at 174.

[48] *Kiobel* v. *Royal Dutch Petroleum et al.*, 133 S.Ct. 1659 (2013), on the effects of, inter alia, the Alien Tort Statute 28 USC §§1350.

[49] Directive 2008/101/EC, amending Directive 2003/87/EC.

[50] See J. Scott and L. Rajamani, 'EU Climate Change Unilateralism' (2012) 23 *European Journal of International Law* 469; E. Fahey, 'The EU Emission Trading Scheme and the Court of Justice: The "High Politics of Indirectly Promoting Global Standards" (2012) 13 *German Law Journal* 1,247.

[51] See Case C-366/10 *Air Transport Association of America* v. *Secretary of State for Energy and Climate Change* [2011] ECR I-000. See also the European Union Emissions Trading Scheme Prohibition Act of 2011 (HR 2594).

Justice to challenge the rule. However, the Court of Justice rejected the challenge, making no reference to the US legislation in its decision. Nonetheless, the decision of the Court is widely regarded as a landmark ruling on the limitations of regulation and global governance. In particular, it exposed the transatlantic divide on the boundaries of such regulation and governance. Additionally, however, it exposed both the indirect and direct nature of interactions between the EU and US legal orders.

Many now study the phenomenon of EU–US 'rule-transfer'[52] epitomised recently in the account of Bradford on the so-called 'Brussels effect'.[53] This phenomenon involves charting a vast transfer of EU regulatory standards into the US legal order, in areas ranging from genetically modified foods, antitrust rules and data privacy standards to chemical safety rules. Some suggest that the EU has indirectly forced such rule-transfer onto the USA on account of its market size and force.[54] Others suggest that it is a far less obvious and more nuanced process of rule-transposition.[55] Nevertheless, we may note that the extent to which EU legal rules are actually transposed into US law is increasing, in whole or in part: for example, the partial transposition of EU environmental rules in California, Maine and Boston State law,[56] because of the desirability of these rules.[57] This particular 'transfer' phenomenon is developed in greater detail in Section IV.[58]

In addition, the USA recently intervened informally and anonymously in the formulation of EU Data Protection legislation against the backdrop of the EU and US negotiations on a General Data Protection Regulation that had been taking place since 2010.[59] Furthermore, a more coherent

[52] On the use of this term, see Section IV.

[53] Bradford, 'The Brussels Effect'.

[54] *Ibid.*

[55] See e.g. J. Scott, 'Extraterritoriality and Territorial Extension in EU Law', 62 *American Journal of Comparative Law*, available at: http://ssrn.com/abstract=2276433, accessed 12 February 2014.

[56] 'Reach Regulation': Council Regulation (EC) No. 1907/2006 amending Directive 1999/45/EC and repealing Council Regulation (EEC) No. 793/93 and Commission Regulation (EC) No. 1488/94 as well as Council Directive 76/769/EEC and Commission Directives 91/155/EEC, 93/67/EEC, 93/105/EC and 2000/21/EC.

[57] J. Scott, 'From Brussels with Love: The Transatlantic Travels of European Law and the Chemistry of Regulatory Attraction' (2009) 57(4) *American Journal of Comparative Law* 897; see also US Government Accountability Office, *Chemical Regulation. Comparison of US and Recently Enacted European Union Approaches to Protect against the Risks of Toxic Chemicals* (August 2007) GAO-07-825, available at: www.gao.gov/assets/270/265550.pdf.

[58] See Section IV.

[59] 'Informal Note on Draft EU General Data Protection Regulation' (December 2011), available at: http://edri.org/files/12_2011_DPR_USlobby.pdf, accessed 12 February 2014. See also 'US Lobbying Waters Down EU Data Protection Reform', *Euractiv.com* (21 February

EU foreign policy post-Lisbon is asserted to have given rise to a more ready 'harmonisation' of EU law vis-à-vis US foreign policy, for example in relation to secondary sanctions applied to Iran.[60] Such interactions demonstrate the significance of examining the use of law outside of the conventional bilateral context, and the dimensions of the phenomenon of proximity between legal orders, the significance of which is developed further in the next section.

B. *Why are non-bilateral interactions of significance?*

The next question to probe is why these interactions are of significance to the present account. One might begin by noting that the submissions made by the EU before the US Supreme Court in death penalty cases show the EU indirectly engaging in rule-making in the USA using US institutions as the forum for their intervention. In this way, the intervention by the EU in formal court proceedings constitutes 'compliant' conduct on the part of the EU with the authority of the US legal order in order to further its own policy goals before a judicial forum. On account of the prominence of this forum, participation by the EU in it has a global impact and allows the EU to impart its message broadly. In the same vein, the use of legislation in the EU-ETS dispute and the deployment of EU institutions and procedures by political actors supported by their governments both within and outside their own legal systems is a distinctive form of interaction between legal orders. The US legislation was not binding upon the EU and had no authority in the EU legal order. Nevertheless, there was a compliance with the EU legal order, or its legal procedures through the initiation of litigation in its legal order.

The 'Brussels effect' indicates practices of flexible 'rule-transfer', rule convergence or rule migration between legal orders.[61] As a result, we may observe the malleability of the space between the EU and US legal orders to accommodate direct and indirect variants thereof. More concretely, it demonstrates the openness of transatlantic relations to each other's legal

2012); 'Informal Comment on the Draft General Data Protection Regulation and Draft Directive on Data Protection in Law Enforcement Investigations', available at: www.edri.org/files/US_lobbying16012012_0000.pdf, accessed 12 February 2014.

[60] See the analysis of EU–US relations in the several accounts given in 'Developments in the Law – Extraterritoriality' (2011)124 *Harvard Law Review*, 1,226. See also Memorandum of Understanding concerning the US Helms–Burton Act and US Iran and Libya Sanctions Act, EU–US, 11 April 1997, 36 ILM 529.

[61] See further in Section IV.

norms. In the case of data transfer, the informal or unofficial advocacy by non-specific US agencies in the EU legislative process resulted in detailed input into EU rules. These unofficial interventions, in the non-bilateral context, are not legally binding yet provide evidence of entry points into formal rule-making processes so as to pursue their lawmaking objectives. EU foreign policy responsiveness to the US remains in the realm of high politics. However, similar to the Brussels effect, it also indicates that empirically a high degree of proximity actually exists between the legal orders. The interactions demonstrate the centrality of the use of law by many actors in various institutional locations between the EU and US legal orders in recent times, including at the highest possible levels, beyond mere diplomacy.

We may say that, evidently, direct and indirect legal dialogues, both official and formal or unofficial and informal, between the EU and USA are observable outside of the conventional bilateral context of Transatlantic Relations, a contention supported and sustained by the findings of Mak in Chapter 2 of this volume. The actual locations of these interactions, however diverse, are particularly distinctive for a number of reasons. We may note that the EU does not usually communicate its norms using advocacy in third countries, last instance courts. Rather, the EU usually communicates its norms or engages in the promotion of its norms, such as the rule of law and the promotion of fundamental rights, in clauses of agreements with neighbouring countries, candidate countries and trade partners.[62] Alternatively, the EU issues local statements: for example, in Gaza the EU recently expressed its views on the local use of the death penalty in a public statement.[63] More usually, the promotion of EU norms is communicated to the subjects and objects of the agreement with legal authority and by agreement, albeit that it rarely enforces its suspension rights for breach thereof in the context of trade.[64] And overall, we may say that the EU does not

[62] For example, European Commission, Inventory of Agreements Containing the Human Rights Clause, DG RELEX/B2 – Treaties Office, 7 July 2011, available at: http://ec.europa.eu/world/agreements/viewCollection.do, accessed 12 February 2014.

[63] For a list of locally issued EU views on the death penalty, see the website of the EEAS, available at: http://eeas.europa.eu/human_rights/adp/index_en.htm, accessed 12 February 2014.

[64] See B. De Witte, 'The EU and International Legal Order: The Case of Human Rights' in Evans and Koutrakos (eds.), *Beyond the Established Legal Orders*, p. 127, at p. 143; L. Pech, 'Rule of Law as a Guiding Principle of the European Union's External Action', 2012/3 CLEER Working Paper; M. Cremona, 'The Union as a Global Actor: Roles, Models and Identity' (2004) 41 *Common Market Law Review* 553.

usually communicate its norms in the legal orders of these countries in the same way that it does with the USA. Instead, it usually communicates formally with third countries, through clauses of specific agreements. The EU also maintains a transparent treaty register, where it formally categorises the types of norms that it promotes in its external relations.[65] This renders its communications with the USA all the more distinct, less routine and less conventionally formal. The interactions are not limited to specific formal legal instruments, for example bilateral legal agreements between sovereign actors. They are thus taking place outside of conventional bilateral constraints, practices and legal instruments.

One specific example from practice possibly demonstrates the reasons for such non-bilateral interactions, and ties together the strands of the outline developed in Sections I and II. As noted above, in 2012 the European Commission made *amicus curiae* submissions on behalf of the European Union in proceedings before the US Supreme Court, as did two EU Member States, concerning the extraterritoriality application of the US Alien Tort Statue to European companies.[66] However, this practice is striking as one might have thought that, post-Lisbon, only the EU would intervene as the main external institutional representative, whereby it would through the European External Action Service (EEAS) negotiate a position in accordance with the views of its Member States, which would be advocated by the European Commission on behalf of the EU alone.[67] One can say that the institutional evolution of EU external relations post-Lisbon does not appear to have limited EU Member State interventions through law before the US Supreme Court in recent times, in order to propose a pan-European perspective. The prevailing fluidity of the (institutional) status quo might simply be said then to incite the EU to directly take action in the US legal order using law to obtain a desirable outcome in the political process, conducted outside of the conventional bilateral processes.

The above sections have considered the character of bilateral relations, institutionalisation and forums for interactions between the EU and USA (in Section I), explored the idea of non-bilateral interactions between legal orders (in Section II), and examined proximity between the EU and US legal orders in various ways. The next section explores the limits of proximity between the EU and US legal orders in the area of bilateral justice and home affairs.

[65] See n. 62.

[66] In *Kiobel* v. *Royal Dutch Petroleum* (i.e. Netherlands, United Kingdom).

[67] Interviews by the author conducted in late 2012 indicate that EEAS officials, particularly individuals regularly used to making submissions before the US Supreme Court, were not aware of the submissions being made by the individual Member States.

III. Transatlantic bilateral rule-making in justice and home affairs: the character of law

A. *Overview*

Transatlantic security cooperation received its most prominent rule-making impetus after the September 2001 (9/11) terrorist attacks, when a raft of EU–US Justice and Home Affairs Agreements were enacted.[68] Rule-making from this particular period may be considered to demonstrate the limitations of mutual recognition of each other's legal order or the shortcomings of adequacy presumptions in law.[69] Over a decade after 9/11, cooperation is ongoing and also planned in new areas, for example cybersecurity and cybercrime, with a striking shift in legal form. Even if the impetus for terrorism legislation in the transatlantic context has abated, the effectiveness of transatlantic rule-making has been lauded as a reason to engage in transatlantic 'rule-convergence' in data protection. Moreover, this rule-making has inspired the EU to engage in 'replica' rule-making of policies, programmes and agreements.[70] The recent National Security Agency (NSA) surveillance saga has placed EU–US Justice and Home Affairs cooperation centre stage once more.[71] These developments invite an analysis of the character of law in contemporary rule-making.

[68] See J. Santos Vara, 'Transatlantic Counterterrorism Cooperation Agreements on the Transfer of Personal Data: A Test for Democratic Accountability in the EU', Chapter 12, and V. Mitsilegas, 'Transatlantic Counterterrorism Cooperation and European Values: The Elusive Quest for Coherence', Chapter 13 in this volume. See K. Archick, 'EU–US Cooperation Against Terrorism', Congressional Research Service 7-5700 (21 May 2012); Fahey, 'Law and Governance as Checks and Balances'.

[69] See Fahey, 'Law and Governance as Checks and Balances'; Shaffer, 'Reconciling Trade and Regulatory Roles'; M. Cremona, 'Justice and Home Affairs in a Globalised World: Ambitions and Reality in the Tale of the EU–US SWIFT Agreement', Institute for European Integration Research Working Paper No. 4/2011 (Austrian Academy of Social Sciences, 2011).

[70] For example, 'Proposal for a Directive on the Use of Passenger Name Record Data for the Prevention, Detection, Investigation, and Prosecution of Terrorist Offences and Serious Crime', COM(2011)32, Commission Communication, *A European Terrorist Finance Tracking System Available Options*, COM(2011)429 final. See Mitsilegas, Chapter 13 in this volume.

[71] See 'EU–US Counterterrorism Pacts at Risk over Snooping Affair', *EUObserver.com* (5 July 2013); 'MEPs Raise Suspension of EU–US Bank Data Deal', LIBE Press release (24 September 2013), available at: www.europarl.europa.eu/news/en/news-room/content/20130923IPR20604/html/MEPs-raise-suspension-of-EU-US-bank-data-deal, accessed 12 February 2014. See also 'Intervention of Commissioner Malmström during This Event on the Use of TFTP Dispute Resolution Clauses' SPEECH/13/742 (24 September 2013).

The legal form of rights, redress and remedies in such rule-making is indicative of a particular imbalance of powers in transatlantic relations in this period, borne out in many accounts.[72] A particular agreement may be underpinned by formulations of mutual recognition of each other's legal order: access to it, and assumed and expressed similarities. Mutual recognition in justice inevitably involves the acceptance of aspects of the content and form of the legal system of another legal order. This phenomenon has proven to be particularly complex among the EU Member States themselves, where mutual recognition in justice is recognised as having both substantive and procedural components.[73] However, the imbalance evident overall arguably reflects the impossibilities of actual transatlantic mutual recognition in justice.

By way of illustration, two of the most prominent agreements entered into by the EU with the USA in the post 9/11 period, designed to communicate air passenger data and to target the financing of terrorism, are the EU–US Passenger Name Records (EU–US PNR) Agreement and EU–US Terrorist Financial Tracking Programme (EU–US TFTP) Agreement, a phenomenon considered here next.[74] These two agreements have generated much controversy on account of their limitations on redress and their uneven application of US law to EU citizens, not enabling the latter to fully realise their rights to redress and review. The formulation of the character of rights, remedies and redress is distinctively replicated in both agreements in a broad timeframe, extending well after a decade post 9/11.[75] Their genesis and operation is exhaustively analysed here in Part III of this volume, and this account conducts a particularly brief analysis of only specific aspects of one such agreement as a result.

[72] See further Fahey, 'Law and Governance as Checks and Balances'; Mitsilegas, Chapter 13 this volume. B. De Witte, 'Too Much Constitutional Law in the European Union's Foreign Relations?' in M. Cremona and B. De Witte (eds.), *EU Foreign Relations Law: Constitutional Fundamentals* (Oxford: Hart Publishing, 2008), p. 11; Cremona, 'Justice and Home Affairs in a Globalised World'.

[73] See Shaffer, 'Reconciling Trade and Regulatory Roles'; V. Mitsilegas, 'Constitutional Implications of Mutual Recognition in Criminal Matters in the EU' (2006) 43 *Common Market Law Review* 1,277.

[74] See Agreement between the United States of America and the European Union on the Use and Transfer of Passenger Name Record Data to the United States Department of Homeland Security of 17 November 2011, COM (2011) 807 final, approved by the European Parliament in April 2012 (hereafter EU–US PNR Agreement); Agreement between the European Union and the United States of America on the Processing and Transfer of Financial Messaging Data from the European Union to the United States for the Purposes of the Terrorist Finance Tracking Program, OJ L 195 (hereafter TFTP Agreement).

[75] On the background to the EU–US PNR Agreement see Santos Vara, Chapter 12 in this volume, and Fahey, 'Law and Governance as Checks and Balances'.

The most recent so-called 'Second-Generation' EU–US PNR Agreement was intended to represent, over a decade after 9/11, an improved agreement with the USA to transmit air passenger data to the USA in the name of fighting serious crime and terrorism,[76] but remains very similar in form and in substance to the 'First-Generation' EU–US PNR Agreement. The Second-Generation Agreement now provides for a default 'push' system in Article 15 thereof, with a 'pull' system provided for in exceptional circumstances in Article 15(5), indicating that the legal character of the Agreement still is significantly disposed towards US concerns.

In the EU–US PNR Agreement rights of redress, access to personal information and rights of correction and rectification are provided in Articles 11–13. Article 13 expressly provides that any individual, regardless of nationality, country of origin or place of residence, whose personal data and personal information has been processed and used in a manner inconsistent with that Agreement, may seek effective administrative and judicial redress in accordance with US law. Moreover, it provides that any individual is entitled to seek to administratively challenge the Department of Homeland Security (DHS) decisions related to the use and processing of US law. EU citizens can petition for judicial review under an express list of US Acts in Article 13(3), including the Freedom of Information Act, the Computer Fraud and Abuse Act, and the Electronic Communications Privacy Act. However, the US Privacy Act of 1974 is not one of the listed acts and is an intentional and significant omission, limited as it is to US citizens only. This thus deprives EU citizens of important legal protections. The Agreement provides in Article 14, simply entitled 'Oversight', that compliance with privacy safeguards in the Agreement will be subject to independent review and oversight by Department Privacy Officers, such as the DHS Privacy Officer, expressed to have a 'proven record of autonomy', who will exercise inter alia 'effective powers of oversight, investigation, intervention and review'. In turn, the Agreement expresses itself to be subject to independent review and oversight by the DHS Office of the Inspector General, the Government Accountability Office and the US Congress. Thus considerable administrative discretion is accorded to a variety of US agencies

[76] Improving upon the Agreement between the European Community and the United States of America on the Processing and Transfer of PNR Data by Air Carriers to the United States Department of Homeland Security (DHS), Bureau of Customs and Border Protection ([2004] OJ L 183/ 83, and corrigendum at [2005] OJ L 255/168); Agreement between the European Union and the United States of America on the Processing and Transfer of Passenger Name Record (PNR) Data by Air Carriers to the United States Department of Homeland Security (DHS) (2007 PNR Agreement), OJ 2007 L 204/18.

that are checked in turn by further agencies and government. The extent to which an EU citizen will be in a position to challenge their effectiveness seems problematic. Moreover, Article 21 expressly provides that the Agreement shall not inter alia create any right or benefit for any person, arising from the standpoint of the USA in negotiations that the Agreement would not create new rights under US law.[77] This reinforces how mutual recognition or equivalence seems far from apparent in this area.

A critical view of the evolution of the EU–US PNR Agreement may be readily adopted, given that the expressed improvements of the Agreement appear as piecemeal changes without any fuller integration of the two legal orders. Overall, the formulation of rights and remedies therein appears singularly deficient for EU citizens, even when expressed to the contrary. The specific character of legal rights in the EU–US PNR Agreement is especially novel and qualified, but arguably highly imbalanced as regards EU citizens. In this way, the use of law in transatlantic relations is revealing as much about the proximity between the legal orders as the state of transatlantic relations in the post 9/11 era, even a decade thereafter. The controversy of NSA surveillance in 2013 put the spotlight on their deficiencies and structural imbalances once again.

However, newer forms of bilateral cooperation offer an alternative perspective on justice and home affairs in transatlantic relations, for example in the area of EU–US cybercrime and cybersecurity, which is the latest form of transatlantic bilateral security cooperation. They offer a different perspective on the boundaries of bilateral cooperation precisely because they indicate closeness between the legal orders. They are much more indicative of the contours of what might be understood in contemporary terms as an 'Atlantic community of law', explicable alongside the many non-bilateral interactions through law identified here.

B. *EU–US cybercrime and cybersecurity cooperation*

The latest transatlantic cooperation in justice and home affairs is in cybercrime and cybersecurity, in the form of the EU–US Working Group on Cybercrime and Cybersecurity (WGCC), which was established after the EU–US Summit in November 2010.[78] However, the origins of this

[77] See EU-US data protection negotiations during 2011, Council Doc. 5999/12, Annex note from Commission DG Justice.

[78] WGCC Concept Paper, Annex 1. E. Fahey, 'The EU's Cybercrime and Cyber Security Rule-Making: Mapping the Internal and External Dimensions of EU Security' (2014) 1(1) *European Journal of Risk Regulation* 46.

cooperation date back a decade earlier to the Joint EC-US Task Force on Critical Infrastructure Protection.[79] Also around this time the Council of Europe Cybercrime Convention was adopted, which now forms a central legal element of EU–US cooperation as well as internal EU rule-making in this field.[80] The EU–US cooperation goals are predominantly in four areas: (1) the expansion of cyber-incident management response capabilities jointly and globally, through a cooperation programme culminating in a joint-EU–US cyber-incident exercise by the end of 2011; (2) to broadly engage the private sector using public–private partnerships, sharing good practices with industry, and to launch a programme of joint awareness-raising activities; (3) to remove child pornography from the Internet; and (4) to advance the international ratification of the Council of Europe Convention by the EU and Council of Europe Member States, and to encourage pending non-European countries rapidly to become parties.

From its distinctive legal objectives, it seems apparent that the WGCC had first and foremost 'global' rule-making objectives. The WGCC Group mentions specific countries to be 'encouraged' to become parties to the Convention, countries within and outside the EU.[81] However, while during 2012 Belgium, Malta and Austria ratified it, there are several EU Member States still 'resisting' ratification on various grounds. In this regard, of note is that the USA is not a member of the Council of Europe but took part in the drafting of the Convention and has signed and ratified it. Also of note is that in 2008 the European Commission suggested that its redrafting or modernisation had become unachievable, but nonetheless promoted both international and EU ratification, as it currently does.[82] Another notable and global-esque expected goal of EU–US cooperation includes the endorsement of EU–US 'deliverables' in cybercrime by the Internet Corporation for Assigned Names and Numbers (ICANN), a notable US-based entity engaging in significant postnational rule-making.[83] And further evidence of the nature of the 'global' objectives of rule-making and policy development is provided by the minutes of a 2011 meeting of EU–US Senior JHA Officials, where it was stated that the EU and USA would work together in the UN to avoid

[79] 'Creating a safer Information Society by improving the security of information infrastructures and combating computer related crime', COM(2000)890 final.

[80] See *Cyber-security Strategy of the European Union: An Open, Safe and Secure Cyberspace*, JOIN(2013)1final, Brussels (7 February 2013).

[81] WGCC Concept Paper, 4.

[82] COM(2010) 517 final, 2.

[83] WGCC Concept Paper, 3.

dilution of the body of international law on cybercrime.[84] Similarly, the European Commission has been oriented towards global-like objectives, seeking global cybersecurity policies before its own internal policy at EU level had been conceived.[85] And well in advance of the adoption by the EU of its internal rule-making objectives in this area, in particular its Cybersecurity Strategy published only in 2013, and thus after the EU–US cooperation, the European Parliament in 2012 advocated an EU framework on cybersecurity, with a view to the policy being 'brought up' at G8 and G20 levels.[86]

This latest EU–US cooperation may be said to indicate new boundaries in the transatlantic relationship on account of its global rule-making ambitions, notwithstanding first, formal limitations on the conduct of the USA as an actor outside of the Council of Europe, and second, the unwillingness of certain EU Member States to cooperate in bilateral rule-making.[87] There are of course other precedents for the USA acting as a vocal and active observer, even if it is not a member of a specific international organisation. For example, in the Convention on Biodiversity, while only an observer, the USA still played a major role in the drafting process of a Protocol, so as to ensure a particular relationship of the Convention with WTO law.[88] Yet it is the regional territorial limits or boundaries of the Council of Europe as an organisation in addition to its regional goals as an organisation,[89] juxtaposed alongside the goals of the EU and US cyber cooperation, that indicate the irrelevance of territory. Instead, it suggests considerable proximity between the legal orders

[84] 'Summary of Conclusions of the EU–US JHA Informal Senior Officials Meeting of 25–26 July', Council Doc. 13228/11, p. 3.

[85] See 'Critical Information Infrastructure Protection – Achievements and Next Steps: Towards Global Cyber-security', COM (2011)163 final.

[86] See the account in 'Parliament Demands Single EU Voice on Cyber-Security', *EUObserver.com*, 13 June 2012.

[87] See the European Commission's advocacy of the Convention, emphasising how the Convention had been signed by 25 out of the 27 Member States and ratified by only 15 of them: COM(2010) 517 final, p. 2. See the ratification table at: http://conventions.coe.int/Treaty/Commun/ChercheSig.asp?NT=185&CM=&DF=&CL=ENG, accessed 12 February 2014.

[88] E.g. the 1992 Convention on Biological Diversity (CBD) and process of the adoption of the Cartagena Protocol on Biosafety to the Convention. See N. Krisch, *Beyond Constitutionalism: The Pluralist Structure of Postnational Law* (Oxford University Press, 2010), p. 194.

[89] On the objectives of the Council of Europe, which specifically identify its Member States as its objects, see its website: www.coe.int/aboutcoe/index.asp?page=nosObjectifs, accessed 12 February 2014.

using law. The WGCC indicates that the boundaries of traditional bilateral cooperation are not fixed, that their rule-making objectives form a striking context of cooperation beyond the nation state. The goals of the WGCC suggest that they will lead eventually to the adoption of a global-like cyber policy or at the very least global standard-setting, through their promotion of the primacy of external norms.

In conclusion, unlike earlier bilateral rule-making, this newer rule-making appears to have joint shared 'global' objectives. An imbalance in legal form is not apparent – the current bilateral legal goals are not weighted or disposed towards the USA. Instead, this newer bilateral rule-making is distinctive because it does not seek to engage in mutual recognition in justice and home affairs but rather has 'larger' global-like legal goals. While there are specific curiosities to these goals, particularly when contrasted with the EU-ETS rule-making, a newer era of greater proximity between the two legal orders seems apparent. Whether the latest saga of NSA/PRISM surveillance will alter this remains to be seen.

Section IV considers the phenomenon of rule-transfer between the EU and US legal orders and its relation to the idea of proximity in transatlantic rule-making considered here throughout. This section draws from one specific case study in justice and home affairs, thus developing the themes considered in Section III.

IV. Transatlantic rule-transfer: the effects of the bilateral relationship in justice and home affairs

As outlined briefly above in Section II, there is an emerging legal scholarship on actual rule-transfer, that is the movement of rules between legal orders, from the EU legal order to the US legal order, which suggests that it is far-reaching and widespread. The so-called 'Brussels effect' is the subject of recent US-based scholarship, assessing the perceived 'spill-over' effect of EU regulatory standards on US rules.[90] Equally, accounts consider the extent to which EU legal rules are actually transplanted or physically replicated in the USA is increasing – for example, EU environmental rules.[91] These (legal) accounts conceptualise the actual transfer of rules from the EU to the USA. Of course, this phenomenon may bear some similarities to the concept of a legal transplant, a principle of

[90] Bradford, 'The Brussels Effect'; Scott, 'Extraterritoriality and Territorial Extension in EU Law'; Scott, 'From Brussels with Love'; Shaffer, 'Globalisation and Social Protection'; Bignami, 'European Versus American Liberty'.

[91] Scott, 'From Brussels with Love'.

comparative law, where a rule is transplanted into another legal order, different to its country of origin.[92] Moreover, there is also a body of non-legal scholarship describing the diffusion of values from the EU to the US legal order, focusing more upon the reasons for this diffusion rather than the process itself or its conceptualisation. However, this scholarship is not couched in terms of rule-transfer or less still transposition.[93] Nor does such scholarship focus upon legal aspects of the process of rule-transfer.

Rule-transfer may thus be described as a means or process by which legal rules are adopted in other legal orders. It is a term deployed in non-legal scholarship on governance and policy development, often focusing upon the reasons for the adoption of rules or promotion of the adoption of rules by the EU.[94] However, while it has a central and distinctive legal component as a concept, given that it depicts legal rules and/or legislative measures, it is not so conceptually fixed or certain. This process of the adoption of EU rules elsewhere, particularly in the USA, is sometimes referred to as 'rule-transfer', 'sideways rule-transfer' or 'rule-migration'.[95] Such accounts conceptualise the actual transfer of rules from the EU to the USA, and less so the process, and offer limited normative explanations other than economic power or alternatively assume a 'horizontality' in the legal relationship between the two legal orders without offering a normative perspective thereon.[96] Moreover, some draw a distinction between

[92] See H. P. Glenn, *Legal Traditions of the World*, 4th edn (Oxford University Press, 2010).

[93] D. Bach and A. Newman, 'Self-Regulatory Trajectories in the Shadow of Public Power: Resolving Digital Dilemmas in Europe and the United States' (2004) 17 *Governance* 387; W. Rees and R. Aldrich, 'European and US Approaches to Counterterrorism' in R. Tiersky and E. Jones (eds.), *Europe Today: A Twenty-First Century Introduction*, 3rd edn (Lanham, MD: Rowman & Littlefield, 2007), p. 437; Z. Laïdi, 'European Preferences and their Reception' in Z. Laïdi (ed.), *EU Foreign Policy in a Globalized World: Normative Power and Social Preferences* (London and New York: Routledge, 2008), p. 1.

[94] See, for example, its use without any formal definition by F. Schimmelfennig and U. Sedelmeier, 'Governance by Conditionality: EU Rule Transfer to the Candidate Countries of Central and European Europe' (2004) 11 *Journal of European Public Policy* 669. See M. Rousselin, 'But Why Would They Do That? European External Governance and the Domestic Preferences of Rule Importers' (2012) 8 *Journal of Contemporary European Research* 470, examining the reasons for the process of rule-transfer.

[95] Bradford, 'The Brussels Effect'; Scott, 'Extraterritoriality and Territorial Extension in EU Law'; Scott, 'From Brussels with Love'.

[96] See Scott, 'Extraterritoriality and Territorial Extension in EU Law'.

the EU's transfer of legal rules and governance practices externally.[97] In doing so, some argue that rule-transfer constitutes an exportation of rules. However, this is not necessarily the case, given that it implies only the form of development discussed here next. Others define transnational law itself as the 'migration of norms, rules and models across borders',[98] distinguishing 'rule mimicry', which takes place out of 'convenience' or because of the economic weight of the rules, from 'rule diffusion', based upon market dominance of sets of rules in a jurisdiction. However, this arguably blurs the conceptual and the methodological question of why rule-transfer occurs, and is rooted in assumptions about the normative character of transnational law.[99]

The impact of transatlantic rules upon and in the EU legal order is argued here to be relevant to the theorisation of rule-transfer, as a useful means to consider the place of and phenomena of law in transatlantic relations. For example, there are several EU security policies being pursued that have clear imprints of EU–US policies: for example, an EU Passenger Name Records Directive and an EU Terrorist Finance Tracking System, mirroring in form, context and lexicon the EU–US PNR Agreement and EU–US TFTP Agreement.[100] We may observe that EU 'internal' security readily embraces 'external' transatlantic security. Put another way, EU security rules under development may be said to demonstrate the migratory effects of EU–US legal rules by way of some form of rule transposition or 'rule-transfer'. Moreover, the adoption of transatlantic measures in EU law, particularly in a more stringent format, may be evidence of the highly fluid importation and exportation of values. The EU frequently imports values and norms, and itself often acts as a model for values.[101] However, EU value importation through law is far from uncontroversial. For example, there is a view that in the realm of terrorist financial transactions the EU has largely adopted international law measures wholesale,

[97] E.g. G. De Búrca, 'EU External Relations: The Governance Mode of Foreign Policy' in B. Van Vooren, S. Blockmans and J. Wouters (eds.), *The EU's Role in Global Governance: The Legal Dimension* (Oxford University Press, 2012) pp. 39–58.

[98] See D. Bodansky and G. Shaffer, 'Transnationalism, Unilateralism and International Law' (2012) 1 *Transnational Environmental Law* 1.

[99] See P. Zumbansen, 'Transnational Legal Pluralism' (2010) 1(2) *Transnational Legal Theory* 141.

[100] See above, n. 70.

[101] Cremona, 'Values in EU Foreign Policy', p. 285. The European Convention on Human Rights and the Geneva Convention on the status of refugees are examples of the former; the evolution of the legal order of ASEAN might represent the latter. See also Cremona, 'The Union as a Global Actor'; Pech, 'Rule of Law as a Guiding Principle'.

which has been critiqued as an unduly 'blind' absorption.[102] Of course, the use of international norms in internal EU policy-making in the realm of counterterrorism is far from unprecedented or unprincipled. The normative reasons for such adoption are usually well intentioned, for example ostensibly high legal standards or benchmarks from best international practice, or a desire to establish compliance at international level by using standards from such a forum.[103]

The theme of exportation of EU values has a very broad interpretation and considerable span of subject areas beyond security.[104] For example, all forms of EU trade agreements contain value commitments and value exportations, but they are controversial and have been haphazardly applied.[105] Legal scholarship asserts across a broad range of subject areas that there is much fluidity and uncertainty concerning the importation and exportation of values in EU law. Seen in this light, the transposition of transatlantic rules into EU law seems entirely comprehensible, or at the least similarly fluid. Nevertheless, in the area of security, transatlantic relations represent a tricky balance of powers, where the EU has jointly agreed to particular value commitments, similarly entered into by the USA. Legal scholarship has engaged with this phenomenon of the balance of powers in transatlantic relations in security more readily than rule-transfer.

Many have provided accounts mapping specific imbalances or unevenness of the rule-making between the EU and US legal orders in the post 9/11 period as considered here. This specific context renders any effort to subsequently transpose transatlantic standards, de facto and *de jure*, into EU law all the more challenging. As discussed above, transatlantic security rules derived from the post 9/11 period are perceived to have emanated from a peculiarly complex legal and political context. While a future problem, the legal review of the emerging EU internal security law with its origins in EU–US relations remains problematic. Evidently, the appropriate place for redress, justiciability and fundamental rights generally in security rules is far from settled. The phenomenon of rule-transfer possibly adds a significant dimension to our understanding of transatlantic

[102] E.g. O. Bures, *EU Counterterrorism Policy: A Paper Tiger?* (Aldershot: Ashgate, 2011).

[103] E.g. M. Scheinin (ed.), *European and United States Counter-terrorism Policies, the Rule of Law and Human Rights*, EUI RSCAS Policy Papers (2011/03).

[104] See also S. Lucarelli and I. Manners (eds.), *Values and Principles in EU Foreign Policy* (London: Routledge, 2006).

[105] The EU has suspended agreements on fundamental grounds only in a minority of instances: see De Witte, 'The EU and International Legal Order', p. 143.

relations outside of the bilateral context and proximity between the legal orders of the EU and USA. It is suggested here that it warrants being part of a future research agenda, one that is only canvassed here rather than developed. It indicates a richer context to transatlantic relations outside the strictly bilateral context, but one also in need of close analysis and reflection, especially in security. In this regard, the interactions between the EU and US legal orders outside of the bilateral context operate in the background to the ambiguity and malleability of transatlantic rule-transfer. It is yet again a significant aspect of contemporary transatlantic relations outside of the bilateral context and further reason to adopt a larger view of what could be considered to be a contemporary Atlantic community of law.

Conclusion

This account has explored what the phenomenon of an Atlantic community of law actually entails in contemporary times. The account has sought to develop its exploration descriptively and perhaps rather tentatively, as part of a future research agenda. It has sought to show how there are many recent interactions and rule-making exercises between the EU and US legal orders that demonstrate that transatlantic relations could be understood as quasi-institutional rather than law-light and institution-light. Many recent interactions between the legal orders of the EU and USA take place in unconventional forums and ways, explicable through and even as a result of quasi-institutionalisation and/or, at the very least, high proximity existing between the two legal orders. However, there are boundaries to this proximity. A more conventional analysis of bilateral agreements in post-9/11 justice and home affairs cooperation suggests serious limits to the idea of proximity between legal orders, along with major legitimacy issues. Paradoxically, newer cooperation suggests higher proximity between the legal orders of the EU and USA. Such a thesis is echoed by the development of transatlantic rule-transfer and borne out in particular in new EU security measures, the latter warranting further exploration. This account also forms the basis for reflections on our understanding of the character of real-world interactions between legal orders, not least across the Atlantic, and possibly also their legitimacy.

7

Transatlantic regulatory cooperation in trade

Objectives, challenges and instruments for economic governance

TAMARA TAKÁCS

1 Introduction

The European Union and the United States have the largest bilateral trade relationship in the world, and the transatlantic economy is regarded as the world's most integrated economic relationship between two trading blocs.[1] This is due to the remarkable extent of mutual investment relations, and the volume of exports and imports between these two trading blocs, amounting to roughly a third of global trade and over half of the world's gross domestic product (GDP). In addition to their significant bilateral economic relationship, both the EU and the USA are pre-eminent actors within the World Trade Organization (WTO) system, and as more or less balanced market powers within this system, their cooperation largely shaped the multilateral rule-based trade system.[2] Their role as frontrunners in the multilateral arena has manifested in the various trade negotiation rounds through the impact of their respective positions in further shaping and reforming multilateral trade relations within the General Agreement on Tariffs and Trade (GATT) framework and its successor, the WTO. In such a strong bilateral economic relationship, each partner's trade policy will impact and

This chapter is an extended and revised version of a chapter in M. Cremona and T. Takács (eds.), *Trade Liberalisation and Standardisation: New Directions in the 'Low Politics' of EU Foreign Policy*, 6 CLEER Working Papers 2003, pp. 75–96 and EUI Working Paper AEL 2014/1, pp. 71–86.

[1] See European Commission DG Trade at: http://ec.europa.eu/trade/creating-opportunities/bilateral-relations/countries/united-states/, accessed 13 February 2014.

[2] S. Woolcock, 'In the Shadow of the Eagle: The Pervasive and Continued Influence of the United States on European Trade Policy', prepared for delivery at the 2008 Annual Meeting of the American Political Science Association, 28–31 August 2008, at p. 1.

shape the other's, as can be seen, for example, in the influence of the USA's market power and normative power over the development of EU trade policy.[3]

While the transatlantic market is today a highly integrated one, and tariffs are set at a relatively low rate (an average of three per cent), substantive regulatory differences, non-tariff, 'behind the border' trade barriers, such as technical regulations, standards and conformity assessment requirements, and differences in regulatory approaches and philosophies hinder the development of an even tighter and more integrated marketplace, and have, in fact, impeded market access. Substantive regulatory differences in particular are the cause of some of the most politically sensitive bilateral trade disputes. While the EU and the USA take pride in the fact that only 2 per cent of their bilateral trade is encumbered by actual litigation in Geneva before the WTO dispute settlement mechanism,[4] some of the trade irritants arising out of regulatory differences since 2000 have strained trade relations, highlighting seeming irreconcilable differences between the trading partners, and their respective retaliations have been viewed by some as 'mini trade wars'.[5] In 2000 Pascal Lamy, the EU Trade Commissioner at the time, noted that trade-related 'problems seem to get worse, not better' between the EU and USA.[6] As a consequence of these increasingly intractable differences, both the EU and USA resorted to the formal dispute settlement mechanism at the WTO on various occasions, but maintained parallel to this legal process close bilateral conciliation and coordination channels to attempt to settle disputes. In this context, it has been observed that the formalistic and legalistic dispute settlement system of the WTO is 'incapable of ensuring wholly amicable EU–US trade relations'.[7]

Indeed, regulatory barriers have long been recognized as the *most significant impediment* to trade and investment between the EU and

[3] *Ibid.*

[4] http://ec.europa.eu/trade/policy/countries-and-regions/countries/united-states/, accessed 13 February 2014.

[5] F. Breuss, 'Economic Integration, EU–US Trade Conflicts and WTO Dispute Settlement', (2005) 9 *European Integration Online Papers* 2, available at: http://eiop.or.at/eiop/pdf/2005-012.pdf, accessed 13 February 2014.

[6] R. J. Ahearn, 'US–European Union Trade Relations: Issues and Policy Challenges', 17 March 2006, CRS-2, available at: http://fpc.state.gov/documents/organization/64460.pdf, accessed 13 February 2014.

[7] N. Kuehler, 'Trans-Atlantic Trade Disputes – From Conflict to Crisis?', *EurActiv* 17 July 2002, available at: www.euractiv.com/trade/trans-atlantic-trade-disputes-conflict-crisis/article-116970, accessed 13 February 2014.

the USA.[8] Eliminating non-tariff barriers (NTBs) would imply not only reduction of costs for businesses, but also an overall increase in GDP, the volume of exports and national income. A study commissioned by the EU has indicated that eliminating even half of the NTBs to trade caused by regulatory divergences could increase transatlantic GDP by 163 billion EUR until 2018 on both sides of the Atlantic.[9] Regulatory convergence in the form of harmonized standards and norms would assist the transatlantic economy in presenting itself as a 'common normative power *vis-à-vis* third countries, in particular China'.[10] Given the importance of the USA's market access to the EU internal market, the condition of which is to comply with EU regulations and standards, the so-called 'Brussels effect' reveals that it is in the power of the EU to project its regulatory autonomy in commerce globally, in our case vis-à-vis a crucial trading partner, the USA.[11] In addition, given the USA and EU's still very substantial joint volume and share of global trade, they are also well positioned to promote common regulatory approaches or positions on which they agree on a global scale.[12]

Regulatory divergence and non-tariff, 'behind the border' barriers are among the most timely and controversial issues on the transatlantic economic agenda and have been identified as the main challenge in negotiating an EU–US trade agreement. Peter Mandelson, the former EU Trade Commissioner, stated at the World Economic Forum in Davos in 2012 that any EU–US trade deal 'would have to focus not on tariffs but on very many non-tariff barriers, technical specifications, differences in regulation … They are the hardest things to agree and those two negotiating partners are the hardest to find an agreement.'[13]

In these circumstances, and accompanied by added pressure from business organizations on both sides of the Atlantic, the tackling of regulatory

[8] European Commission, European Commission DG Enterprise and Industry – International Affairs, EU–USA Regulatory Cooperation, available at: http://ec.europa.eu/enterprise/policies/international/cooperating-governments/usa/regulatory-cooperation/index_en.htm, accessed 13 February 2014.

[9] Non-Tariff Measures in EU–US Trade and Investment, Final Report, ECORYS, 2009, available at: http://trade.ec.europa.eu/doclib/docs/2009/december/tradoc_145613.pdf, accessed 13 February 2014.

[10] European Foreign Policy Scorecard, 2010 Report, p. 65, available at: www.ecfr.eu/page/-/ECFR_SCORECARD_2010_PDF.pdf, accessed 13 February 2014.

[11] On the Brussels effect, see A. Bradford, 'The Brussels Effect' (2013) 107 *Northwestern University Law Review* 1.

[12] R. J. Ahearn, 'Transatlantic Regulatory Cooperation: Background and Analysis', Congressional Research Service, RL34717, 24 August 2009, USCRS, p. 6.

[13] T. Vogel, 'Crisis Leads to Push for a Transatlantic Trade Deal', *EuropeanVoice*, 6 May 2012.

differences is and will continue to be at the centre of the project for a more formally integrated transatlantic economy.

The present chapter aims to look at the nature of regulatory cooperation in transatlantic trade relations. It looks at such cooperation in the context of the ongoing discussion of strengthening economic integration and designing a comprehensive free trade agreement that includes methods of reducing or eliminating regulatory barriers. While it is difficult to predict the impact of the EU–US trade negotiations on the diverging regulatory environments on both sides of the Atlantic, it is nevertheless worthwhile to look at challenges these two regulatory regimes present for closer transatlantic economic integration so as to assess regulatory interactions in this specific area of transatlantic cooperation and gauge their impact on EU–US relations. The chapter then detects the underlying rationale for regulatory cooperation between the EU and USA. Next, it offers a review and assessment of regulatory initiatives and policy instruments, as well as their defined objectives since the New Transatlantic Agenda in 1995 to date, and the structural frameworks along which cooperative efforts were conducted by regulators from both sides of the Atlantic. The ensuing general evaluation of approaches to transatlantic regulatory cooperation will distil the suggested and possible forms of regulatory cooperation in a further integrated transatlantic economic relation, as has been placed in the Transatlantic Trade and Investment Partnership (TTIP) negotiations ongoing at the time of writing.

2 Regulatory cooperation in the context of transatlantic economic relations

Despite the significant volume of trade and the connectedness of the two economies, until recently no serious consideration has been given at the political level to a comprehensive liberalization of transatlantic trade in the form of a free trade agreement. In 2006 the European Parliament (EP) suggested a legal regime in the form of a Transatlantic Partnership Agreement and called for 'a more visionary and strategic approach to design a new Transatlantic Partnership Agreement that leads to the achievement of a "barrier-free transatlantic market" by 2015' and in it the establishment of a bilateral dispute settlement mechanism.[14] In its reaction to the EP's report,

[14] EP Resolution on Improving EU–US Relations in the Framework of a Transatlantic Partnership Agreement of 1 June 2006, available at: www.europarl.europa.eu/document/activities/cont/201004/20100427ATT73598/20100427ATT73598EN.pdf, accessed 13 February 2014.

the Commission rejected the sense of necessity for such institutionalized forms to address removal of trade barriers. Opposing the EP's call for a formal dispute resolution mechanism, the Commission stood firmly by the multilateral enforcement system of the WTO, and stated the view that the formal bilateral trade dispute settlement mechanism proposed in the EP's report was not necessary. The Trade Commissioner at that time, Peter Mandelson, noted that none of the parties had an appetite for a comprehensive 'big bang EU–US scheme' in the form of an agreement.[15] Another recurring argument against a transatlantic free trade agreement was the concern about the fate of the multilateral trade system, in the event of an advanced liberalization between the two biggest trading blocs, while others rejected the idea of a North Atlantic Free Trade Area, claiming that such concession and concentration between the two major trading powers signal their isolation and in particular abandonment of concerns towards poor countries, 'a nightmare scenario for "anti-West" movements'.[16] In contrast, according to Petersmann, protection of general consumer interests and general welfare interests in transatlantic economic relations calls for the 'citizen-oriented international dispute prevention and settlement methods', as would be established in a Transatlantic Free Trade Agreement that provides for dispute settlement bodies with direct access for citizens in transatlantic economic relations.[17]

However, with the severe negative impact of the 2008 economic crisis on both sides of the Atlantic, and the waning hope for a successful revival of the Doha negotiation round, the idea for deeper transatlantic economic integration has become more attractive,[18] and explicitly supported by commentators and (past and current) politicians at the

[15] Meeting on the European Parliament Transatlantic Relations Report, Commissioner Mandelson at the EP Plenary Debate, Brussels, 31 May 2006, available at: http://trade.ec.europa.eu/doclib/docs/2006/june/tradoc_128914.pdf, accessed 13 February 2014.

[16] A. Taylor, 'Economic Tensions between the European Union and the United States', EUI, Florence, p. 8, available at: www.eui.eu/RSCAS/Research/Transatlantic/Taylor.pdf, accessed 13 February 2014.

[17] See E. U. Petersmann, 'Prevention and Settlement of Transatlantic Economic Disputes: Legal Strategies for EU/US Leadership' in E. U. Petersmann and M. A. Pollack (eds.), *Transatlantic Economic Disputes: The EU, the US and the WTO* (Oxford University Press, 2003), pp. 3–64 at p. 64.

[18] See B. Stokes, 'An Idea Whose Time Has Come', *EuropeanVoice*, 23 March 2012; J. Ewing, 'Trade Deal between US and Europe May Come to The Forefront', *New York Times*, 25 November 2012.

highest levels.[19] It was indeed with a view to responding to the impact of the economic crisis and to maximizing bilateral trade that the two trading partners wished to boost growth and jobs, and in November 2011 established a High-Level Working Group on Jobs and Growth (HLWG) 'to identify policies and measures to increase EU–US trade and investment to support mutually beneficial job creation, economic growth, and international competitiveness' and assess the feasibility of a comprehensive transatlantic trade agreement, as well as to identify opportunities for enhancing the compatibility of regulations and standards, and for the reduction, elimination or prevention of unnecessary non-tariff barriers.[20]

In its interim report of June 2012, the HLWG suggested that a comprehensive agreement, including trade and investment but also, importantly, regulatory issues and non-tariff barriers, would be beneficial for reciprocal market access. The interim report noted the need for a balance between a more integrated transatlantic marketplace and national regulatory autonomy for public policy purposes, such as health, safety and the environment. It suggested an 'SPS-plus' and a 'TBT-plus' chapter, both functioning with a bilateral forum for improved dialogue on relevant SPS (sanitary and phytosanitary) issues, and technical regulations, conformity assessment procedures and standards for the technical barriers to trade (TBT)-related issues. Furthermore, the interim report recommended horizontal disciplines on regulatory coherence and transparency, including early consultations, impact assessment, upstream regulatory cooperation and good regulatory practices. The HLWG also called for a wide consultation with involvement of stakeholders to suggest proposals to address the impact on trade of those differences, so as to better prepare negotiations towards a system of enhanced regulatory compatibility while

[19] See J. Solana, 'Transatlantic Free Trade?', Project Syndicate, 28 December 2012, available at: www.project-syndicate.org/commentary/why-the-us-and-the-eu-need-a-free-trade-agreement-by-javier-solana, accessed 13 February 2014; M. Barroso, 'A EU–US Partnership for Growth and Jobs', AECA Brussels, 26 April 2012, available at: http://europa.eu/rapid/press-release_SPEECH-12-305_en.htm, accessed 13 February 2014; H. Clinton, 'US and Europe: A Revitalized Global Partnership', Brookings Institution, Washington DC, 29 November 2012, available at: www.brookings.edu/~/media/events/2012/11/29%20clinton/20121129_transatlantic_clinton, accessed 13 February 2014.

[20] European Commission DG Enterprise and Industry – International Affairs, EU–US High-Level Working Group on Jobs and Growth, available at: http://ec.europa.eu/enterprise/policies/international/cooperating-governments/usa/jobs-growth/index_en.htm, accessed 13 February 2014.

respecting legitimate regulatory objectives.[21] The envisaged enhanced trade policy and strengthened economic ties correspond with the trade policy aspiration that the Commission had set out in its Communication on Trade, Growth and World Affairs in 2010, having proposed to develop stronger ties with strategic partners, such as the USA.[22]

Taking these suggestions further, the Final Report of the HLWG highlighted what the parties saw as the key elements and objectives of regulatory cooperation:

> addressing 'behind-the-border' obstacles to trade, including, where possible, through provisions that serve to reduce unnecessary costs and administrative delays stemming from regulation, while achieving the levels of health, safety, and environmental protection that each side deems appropriate, or otherwise meeting legitimate regulatory objectives; identify new ways to prevent non-tariff barriers from limiting the capacity of US and EU firms to innovate and compete in global markets; seek to strengthen upstream cooperation by regulators and increase cooperation on standards-related issues; putting processes and mechanisms in place to reduce costs associated with regulatory differences by promoting greater compatibility, including, where appropriate, harmonization of future regulations, and to resolve concerns and reduce burdens arising from existing regulations through equivalence, mutual recognition, or other agreed means, as appropriate.[23]

The specific recommendations in the Final Report offer more detail than the interim report concerning the form of cooperation in various areas of trade and regulatory cooperation. With respect to sanitary and phytosanitary issues, it calls for SPS measures that are based on international standards and global (WTO) principles, and application following scientific risk assessment, in accordance with proportionality and transparency.[24] Similarly, TBT issues should be tackled in light of cooperative

[21] Interim Report to Leaders from the Co-Chairs, EU–US High-Level Working Group on Growth and Jobs, 19 June 2012, available at: http://trade.ec.europa.eu/doclib/docs/2012/june/tradoc_149557.pdf, accessed 13 February 2014.

[22] Commission Communication on Trade, Growth and World Affairs, 9 November 2010.

[23] Final Report of the High-Level Working Group on Growth and Jobs, 11 February 2013, p. 3, available at: http://trade.ec.europa.eu/doclib/docs/2013/february/tradoc_150519.pdf, accessed 13 February 2014.

[24] The HLWG takes note of the (public policy) sensitivity of SPS measures on both sides of the Atlantic and recommends closer cooperation in this area, next to the bilateral negotiations involved in the comprehensive agreement. Accordingly, the Report calls on the parties to 'seek to make early and continuing progress on SPS measures affecting bilateral trade, taking into account the priorities of either side, and their respective institutional frameworks'.

efforts between regulators, in transparent and coordinated processes, and for enhanced confidence in conformity assessment procedures and standards. As to horizontal regulatory issues, methodological rapprochement is called for by highlighting the importance of early consultations, use of impact assessment, periodic reviews and application of best practices. With respect to specific sectors, the final report calls for a plan of commitments in sector-specific cooperation and the approaches applied to create more convergence. Finally, the HLWG emphasize the need for a (permanent) institutional framework within which future regulatory cooperative steps can be explored and processed.[25]

With such detailed and ambitious recommendations in sight, the negotiations of the comprehensive trade agreement were announced in February 2013[26] (in the State of the Union address delivered by President Barack Obama),[27] and shortly afterwards the European Commission drafted the EU's draft negotiating mandate for the negotiations towards ostensibly the biggest bilateral trade agreement ever negotiated.[28] Assessing the upcoming negotiations, commentaries singled out the importance attached to: the removal of regulatory barriers to trade;[29] the focus on aligning rules and technical product standards that form the 'most important barrier to transatlantic trade',[30] which were seen as 'potentially "making or breaking" the agreement';[31] the dismantling of unnecessary regulatory barriers; and the inclusion in the agreement of mechanisms (including upstream regulatory cooperation) aiming at preventing future trade barriers.[32]

[25] *Ibid.*

[26] Press Release, 'European Union and United States to Launch Negotiations for a Transatlantic Trade and Investment Partnership', 13 February 2013, available at: http://europa.eu/rapid/press-release_MEMO-13-95_en.htm, accessed 13 February 2014.

[27] www.nytimes.com/2013/02/13/us/politics/obamas-2013-state-of-the-union-address.html?pagewanted=all&_r=0, accessed 13 February 2014.

[28] Press Release, 'European Commission Fires Starting Gun for EU–US Trade Talks', 12 March 2013, available at: http://europa.eu/rapid/press-release_IP-13-224_en.htm, accessed 13 February 2014.

[29] 'A New EU–US Free Trade Agreement Will Provide an Invaluable Shot in the Arm for Exporters and Workers', 15 April 2013, available at: http://eu2013.ie/news/news-items/20130415brutonsbpopedeu-ustrade/, accessed 13 February 2014.

[30] 'Progress Made on New EU–US Trade Agreement at the EU Trade Informal', 18 April 2013, available at: http://eu2013.ie/news/news-items/20130418post-tradeinformalpr/, accessed 13 February 2014.

[31] www.fas.org/sgp/crs/row/R43158.pdf, accessed 13 February 2014.

[32] European Parliament Resolution of 23 May 2013 on EU Trade and Investment Negotiations with the United States of America, INTA/7/12078, available at: www.europarl.europa.eu/sides/getDoc.do?type=TA&language=EN&reference=P7-TA-2013-227, accessed 13 February 2014.

3 The rationale for regulatory cooperation and convergence for transatlantic economic integration

It has been widely acknowledged that despite the expansive volume of trade and investment, and the low level of tariff barriers, regulatory barriers can still seriously impede transatlantic trade, as has been shown by some of the past decades' memorable trade disputes before the WTO, which proved and still prove to be especially hard to resolve, because they involve wider issues of political concern or public interest unlike traditional protectionist trade measures.[33] It is apparent that WTO dispute resolution does not reach the regulatory convergence in every case, therefore bilateral regulatory policy coordination can be a useful mechanism. Many bilateral disputes involve clashes in domestic priorities, larger societal values, and public preferences and interest, favouring domestic regulation in the absence of international standards, which render dispute resolution all the more difficult.[34] One example of a highly politicized regulatory policy (which resulted in a full-blown trade dispute in beef hormones, the GMO disputes and the still ongoing poultry dispute) is the USA's relatively science-based system of risk management and regulation only in case of identified risk. This is in contrast with the EU's oft-cited precautionary principle,[35] allowing for regulation before a problem has been scientifically proven where there are reasonable grounds for concern about the harm that may be caused. The 'sensitive political balance' between legitimate public policy choices and regulatory autonomy on the one hand, and the market access prescribed by trade liberalization on the other has on multiple occasions strained transatlantic economic relations.[36]

The rationale for regulatory cooperation, therefore, is to minimize divergences and reduce necessary regulatory burdens so as to facilitate

[33] M. Johnson, 'US–EU Trade Disputes: Their Causes, Resolution and Prevention', EUI, 2001, available at: www.eui.eu/RSCAS/Research/Transatlantic/Johnson.pdf, accessed 13 February 2014.

[34] See Ahearn, 'US–European Union Trade Relations'.

[35] The precautionary principle is to be relied upon when 'scientific information is insufficient, inconclusive, or uncertain and where there are indications that the possible effects on the environment, or human, animal or plant health may be potentially dangerous and inconsistent with the chosen level of protection'. See Communication from the Commission on the Precautionary Principle, COM/2000/0001 final.

[36] See M. A. Pollack, 'The Political Economy of Transatlantic Trade Disputes' in Petersmann and Pollack (eds.), *Transatlantic Economic Disputes*, pp. 65–118.

trade and minimize trade frictions, while respecting the regulatory autonomy of each party. With the expansive scope of regulatory divergences, regulatory cooperation should promote compatible transatlantic regulatory approaches so as to enhance economic ties. In addition, regulatory cooperation is important so that the EU and the USA can establish joint approaches to common global challenges and promote global trade. As will been seen in the next section, multiple efforts have been undertaken to dismantle existing regulatory NTBs and prevent new ones from emerging.

4 Approaches to transatlantic regulatory cooperation

The chronological overview of instruments and objectives of regulatory cooperation below will indicate that, until now, the extent of regulatory cooperation has extended to consultation, dialogue, exchange of information and sharing of best practices with respect to sector-specific issues as well as horizontal matters (methodology), with a few mutual recognition agreements (of conformity assessment certification). No standardization or harmonization has been achieved, or aimed at by the instruments considered below, and they lack legally binding character. Some of these instruments are directed in a general sense to 'reinforce' regulatory cooperation; others – such as the early warning mechanism, standard systems and initiatives in new technologies – focus on cooperation in specific areas. What can be noted is the instruments' increasingly specific focus in scope, and that the more specific their focus becomes, the more useful they are for regulatory cooperative efforts, and they may provide clear(er) guidance to regulators and follow up on achievements.

4.1 *Soft law instruments, policy initiatives and their objectives*

Transatlantic initiatives in trade and economic matters began in the 1980s with declarations of good intent that lead to the Transatlantic Declaration in 1990.[37] The initial impetus for a transatlantic dialogue on regulatory standards was the intensive harmonization process that the establishment

[37] The Transatlantic Declaration of 22 November 1990 states that the European Community and the United States 'will inform and consult each other on important matters of common interest, both political and economic, with a view to bringing their position as close as possible, without prejudice to their respective independence'. Bulletin of the European Communities, 23 (11), point 1.5.3 (1990). Official title: Declaration on Relations between the European Economic Community and the United States.

of the EU's internal market entailed, and the concomitant concerns of US exporters with respect to impediments to market access and competitive disadvantages that such EU-aligned standards would mean.[38]

The New Transatlantic Agenda (NTA) (1995) aimed to reinvigorate and upgrade the bilateral relationship, foster transatlantic bilateral economic relations and work towards expansion of world trade, albeit without specific commitments and deadlines, and thus with no political or legal force. Part of the NTA, a joint declaration adopted at the 1995 Madrid Summit, added political support for strengthened regulatory cooperation, in particular by encouraging regulatory agencies to give high priority to cooperation with their respective transatlantic counterparts, so as to address technical and non-tariff barriers to trade resulting from divergent regulatory processes, and by conclusion of mutual recognition of conformity assessment (including certification and testing procedures) for certain sectors as soon as possible.[39] The Transatlantic Marketplace so envisaged was meant to be promoted by such regulatory cooperation.

The subsequent Transatlantic Economic Partnership (TEP) was agreed in 1998 with the explicit aim to further bilateral economic and trade relations. The TEP included a call for action to address technical barriers to trade in goods,[40] an 'ambitious programme of regulatory cooperation designed to reconcile, if not eliminate, regulatory barriers to trade',[41] and cooperation among regulators to intensify economic ties and approach trade irritants, along the traditional process of trade negotiations and dispute resolution.[42]

The NTA's regulatory cooperation ambitions resulted in the adoption of a mutual recognition agreement (MRA) in 1998. Mutual recognition agreements, in general, go beyond regulatory dialogue and can entail either recognition of conformity assessment certification (certification

[38] See Ahearn, 'Transatlantic Regulatory Cooperation', p. 5.

[39] EC Delegation to the US, New Transatlantic Agenda, 3 December 1995, EC–US Summit, Madrid.

[40] European Commission DG Enterprise and Industry – International Affairs, EU–US Regulatory Cooperation, available at: http://ec.europa.eu/enterprise/policies/international/cooperating-governments/usa/regulatory-cooperation/index_en.htm, accessed 13 February 2014.

[41] M. Pollack, 'The New Transatlantic Agenda at Ten: Reflections on an Experiment in International Governance' (2005) 43 *Journal of Common Market Studies* 899–919, at 907.

[42] See G. Shaffer and M. Pollack, 'The Future of Transatlantic Economic Relations: Continuity Amid Discord' in D. Andrews, G. Shaffer, M. Pollack and H. Wallace (eds.), *The Future of Transatlantic Economic Relations: Continuity Amid Discord* (Florence: EUI 2006), pp. 3–9.

tests) or mutual recognition of relevant standards. In the first, much less ambitious case this does not involve harmonization and aligning of substantive standards, rather the recognition only of each other's testing and certification of production processes with the aim that the product is tested only once. The MRA from 1998 covered recognition of the results of conformity assessment procedures by identified certification bodies in the exporting country that could assess the conformity of goods in these sectors with standards in the destination country, albeit without being legally binding and enforceable agreements between the EU and the USA – and in reality with a limited economic impact. The Annexes to this Agreement covered six sectors (telecommunications and ICT equipment, pharmaceuticals, electronics, electromagnetic compatibility, sport boats and medical devices), and conformity assessment procedures required that regulators of one party accept the competence of the other party to conduct product testing, inspection or certification. While in theory this method is of considerable significance for market access and is relatively easy to implement, as it does not concern the substance of regulation,[43] the implementation of these MRAs was problematic in a few sectors, with the slow process of recognition by some independent US regulatory agencies such as the Food and Drug Administration Agency (FDA), and Occupational Safety and Health Administration (OSHA) of the European laboratories' certification of pharmaceuticals, medical devices and electrical safety standards.[44] As a result, 'tensions grew when the USA failed to implement the agreement with respect to three of the sectors which were initially of greatest interest to the EU (electrical safety, medical devices and pharmaceutical good manufacturing practices)'.[45]

Following the EU–US Summit in Bonn in 1999 a Joint Statement on Early Warning and Problem Prevention Mechanism was adopted. This framework included an early warning system so as to help avoid non-tariff barriers to trade by identifying regulations that might result in a trade irritant, preferably at an early stage of the regulation drafting process. However, subsequent emergence of disputes indicated that the required

[43] R. von Borries, 'Transatlantic Regulatory Initiatives in Europe' in G. A. Bermann *et al.* (eds.), *Transatlantic Regulatory Cooperation: Legal Problems and Political Prospects* (Oxford University Press, 2000), pp. 451–65, at p. 460.

[44] See Pollack, 'The New Transatlantic Agenda at Ten', 909.

[45] G. Shaffer, 'Managing EU–US Trade Relations through Mutual Recognition and Safe Harbour Agreements: "New" and "Global" Approaches to Transatlantic Governance?' in Petersmann and Pollack (eds.), *Transatlantic Economic Disputes*, pp. 297–325, at p. 303.

economic coordination was not successful in preventing trade irritants and rows. This was apparent with the instigation of the GMO dispute at the WTO in 2006, as biotechnology was exactly one of the areas where structured dialogue among regulators had already been initiated in 2000, within the Consultative Forum on Biotechnology, with the aim of gradual convergence of regulatory standards and prevention of trade disputes.

Consecutive soft law initiatives still lacked actual political commitment and clearly set deadlines or binding goals. Adopted at the 2002 EU–US Summit, the Guidelines on Regulatory Cooperation and Transparency encouraged dialogue between EU and US regulators and agencies in government-to-government consultations on a voluntary basis in the form of regular consultation, and exchange of data and information, as well as informing one another at an early stage on planned new regulation, so as to enhance cooperation between regulators. In lacking any legal binding force, the primary function of the Guidelines is to 'enshrine political commitment to dialogue between EU and US regulators', though it has been noted that so far 'little effort has been made to implement them'.[46]

The MRA for Marine Equipment, adopted in 2004, went further than the 1998 MRA by providing mutual recognition of certificates of conformity for marine equipment. Under its terms, designated products that comply with EU requirements will be accepted for sale in the USA without any additional testing or certification and vice versa, and the parties' procedures are regarded as 'equivalent' for the purposes of assessment conducted by conformity assessment bodies in either country (Articles 3 and 4).[47]

At the June 2005 EU–US Summit, the United States and European Commission issued the Roadmap for EU–US Regulatory Cooperation to provide a framework for cooperation on a broad range of important horizontal and sector-specific areas. Under this ongoing multi-year initiative, US and European authorities aim to build effective mechanisms to promote better quality regulation, minimize unnecessary regulatory divergences to facilitate transatlantic trade and investment, and increase consumer confidence in the transatlantic market. This Roadmap set a

[46] A. Meuwese, 'EU–US Horizontal Regulatory Cooperation: Mutual Recognition of Impact Assessment' in D. Vogel and J. Swinnen (eds.), *Transatlantic Regulatory Cooperation: The Shifting Roles of the EU, the US and California* (Cheltenham: Edward Elgar Publishing, 2011), pp. 249–64, at p. 255.

[47] Shaffer, 'Managing EU–US Trade Relations', p. 306. (Shaffer notes the pre-existing harmonization of standards in this sector under the International Maritime Organization, which allowed for mutual recognition of 'equivalence' of each others' standards.)

framework for specific regulatory activities in fifteen sectors.[48] Regulatory cooperation featured as the main objective of transatlantic cooperation in the Communication on 'A Stronger EU–US Partnership and a More Open Market for the 21st Century' in 2005, suggesting a reinforced approach to regulatory policy cooperation.[49] The EU–US Declaration 'Initiative to Enhance Transatlantic Economic Integration and Growth' promoted regulatory cooperation and standards by identifying cooperation and coordination mechanisms in order to improve regulatory quality and reduce divergences; exchanges of experience and the sharing of knowledge are encouraged through a high-level dialogue in accordance with the Roadmap for EU–US Regulatory Cooperation.[50]

The EU–US Regulatory Cooperation Best Cooperative Practices of 2006 distilled a set of suggested best practices to complement the EU–US Guidelines on Regulatory Cooperation and Transparency as a guide for regulators to use in cooperative approaches or informally.[51]

To provide impetus and boost regulatory cooperation, in 2007 the Framework for Advancing Transatlantic Economic Integration between the EU and the USA aimed to foster cooperation and reduce regulatory burdens, 'to achiev[e] more effective, systematic and transparent regulatory cooperation', and to reinforce the existing transatlantic dialogue structures by intensifying sector-by-sector regulatory cooperation in a defined set of areas as well as 'lighthouse projects', and reinforcing dialogue on methodological issues.[52] As will be discussed below, the Transatlantic Economic Council (TEC) was established so as to give high-level political support to the government-to-government cooperation. In 2010 a

[48] Pharmaceuticals, automobile safety, ICT standards in regulations, cosmetics, consumer product safety, unfair commercial practices, nutritional labelling, food safety, marine equipment, eco-design, chemicals, energy efficiency, telecommunications and radio-communications equipment, electromagnetic compatibility and medical devices.

[49] Communication from the Commission to the Council, the European Parliament and the Economic and Social Committee, 'A Stronger EU–US Partnership and a More Open Market for the 21st Century', Brussels, 19 May 2005. Available at: http://trade.ec.europa.eu/doclib/docs/2005/may/tradoc_123438.pdf, accessed 13 February 2014.

[50] OJ 2005 No. 10305/5 of 20 June 2005, available at: www.europarl.europa.eu/document/activities/cont/201004/20100427ATT73625/20100427ATT73625EN.pdf, accessed 13 February 2014.

[51] EU–US Regulatory Cooperation: Best Cooperative Practices, June 2006, available at: http://trade.ec.europa.eu/doclib/docs/2006/july/tradoc_129223.pdf, accessed 13 February 2014.

[52] Framework for Advancing Transatlantic Economic Integration between the European Union and the United States of America, available at: http://ec.europa.eu/enterprise/policies/international/files/tec_framework_en.pdf, accessed 13 February 2014.

Memorandum of Understanding was signed on e-health and the harmonization of electronic health records and education programmes for IT and health professionals in the context of the TEC; however, implementation has reportedly been slow.[53] In April 2011 an agreement laid down a set of fundamental regulatory principles for trade in information and communication technology (ICT) services. The Common Understanding on Regulatory Principles and Best Practices,[54] drafted by the High Level Regulatory Cooperation Forum in 2010, reaffirmed the shared joint commitment to regulatory principles of evidence-based policy-making, transparency and openness, analysis of relevant alternatives, monitoring and evaluation of the effectiveness of existing regulatory measures, and use of approaches that minimize burden and aim for simplicity. However, the document indicates that these best regulatory principles are not binding on the regulators, and are to be considered only as much as the applicable laws in each jurisdiction allow. Furthermore, for the EU they serve as 'an aid to better lawmaking' and do not bind the EU institutions.

Initiatives to apply international standards and already existing international harmonization faced difficulties, as in the USA the regulatory agencies are required to use international standards only to the extent that is prescribed by the TBT Agreement, but are not prevented from taking measures they consider necessary to reach a public policy objective (such as human, animal, plant life or environment) at the level they deem necessary. The 'voluntary', private-sector and marketplace-driven character of the US standards system differs from the EU's intensive implementation of international standards in its domestic regulatory practice.[55] To foster cooperation in and recognition of standards, the TEC encouraged regulatory agencies, services and standardization bodies to implement recommendations from the new document on 'Building Bridges between the US and EU Standards Systems'.[56]

[53] European Council for Foreign Relations Scorecard, 2010.

[54] United States–European Commission: High Level Regulatory Cooperation Forum, 'Common Understanding on Regulatory Principles and Best Practices', available at: www.whitehouse.gov/sites/default/files/omb/oira/irc/common-understanding-on-regulatory-principles-and-best-practices.pdf, accessed 13 February 2014.

[55] 'Report on the Use of Voluntary Standards in Support of Regulation in the US', October 2009, p. 11, available at: http://gsi.nist.gov/global/docs/Voluntary_Standards_USRegs.pdf, accessed 13 February 2014.

[56] 'Building Bridges between the US and EU Standards Systems', available at: www.whitehouse.gov/sites/default/files/omb/oira/irc/us-eu-standards-bridges.pdf, accessed 13 February 2014.

With the aim of stimulating economic growth and job creation, the Transatlantic Innovation Action Partnership coordinates US and EU activities aimed at strengthening innovation and ecosystems, and promoting the commercialization of emerging technologies and sectors. The Innovation Action Partnership established two new sectoral work streams in priority areas – raw materials and bio-based products – that were not sufficiently addressed through the then-existing cooperation.[57]

Most recently, in 2012 two mutual recognition agreements were adopted between US regulators and the EU. First, the EU and US Organic Trade Partnership and Equivalence Arrangement established mutual recognition of conformity assessment for organic products, eliminating the need to obtain separate certifications with reference to two standards, and thus improving market access, and reducing red tape and related costs.[58] Through this arrangement, the EU and USA agreed on a mutual recognition of their respective Organic Standards legislation, namely Council Regulation 834/2007 on organic production and labelling of organic products and the Organic Foods Production Act. The next MRA covered 'trusted traders', authorized economic operators, whose certification will now be recognized by both parties thereby allowing these companies to benefit from faster controls and reduced administration during customs clearance. Under this agreement the EU and the USA will recognize each other's security-certified operators. Authorized economic operators in the EU will receive benefits when exporting to the US market, and the EU will reciprocate for certified members of the US Customs–Trade Partnership Against Terrorism (C–TPAT).[59]

4.2 Assessment of regulatory cooperation approaches and convergence initiatives

While they can be useful tools of regulatory cooperation, the MRAs adopted in the above-mentioned cases are not to be construed as entailing mutual acceptance of standards or technical regulation of the parties, only the recognition of conformity assessment procedures. The adopted

[57] Transatlantic Innovation Action Partnership Work Plan, available at: http://trade.ec.europa.eu/doclib/docs/2011/january/tradoc_147174.pdf, accessed 13 February 2014.

[58] See http://www.usda-eu.org/trade-with-the-eu/trade-agreements/us-eu-organic-arrangement/, accessed 3 March 2014.

[59] European Commission Press Release, 'Customs: EU and USA Agree to Recognise Each Other's "Trusted Traders"', available at: http://europa.eu/rapid/press-release_IP-12-449_en.htm, accessed 13 February 2014.

MRAs contain an Article on preservation of regulatory autonomy, stating that 'nothing in this Agreement shall be construed to limit the authority of a Party to determine, through its legislative, regulatory and administrative measures, the level of protection it considers appropriate for the relevant public policy area'. Among the adopted MRAs, one finds safeguard clauses (see Pharmaceutical Good Manufacturing Practices Article 21, 1998 MRA) or transitional periods (Medical Device Article 5), during which parties engage in confidence-building activities for the purpose of obtaining sufficient evidence to make determinations concerning the equivalence of Conformity Assessment Bodies of the other party with respect to the ability to perform quality, system and product evaluations or other reviews resulting in reports to be exchanged (joint confidence-building programme). The latest MRAs from 2012 (and the one on marine equipment from 2004) are, arguably, less 'protective' than the one from 1998, as much as they entail an 'equivalence arrangement'.[60]

As Morrall suggests:

> a review of the regular progress reports on the Roadmap sectors issued between 2005 and 2008 finds the reports mostly speaking in terms of the 'enhanced' dialogue, 'expanded' information exchanges and 'deepening' collaboration. By 2008, despite monthly meetings held by the Office of the US Trade Representative with the regulatory agencies with roadmap responsibilities, there was little to showcase, except in the financial and securities sectors, and both sides stopped reporting on progress on the roadmaps. Emphasis shifted back again to methodological and horizontal issues such as risk assessment, regulatory impact analysis, voluntary standards, and early warnings of new regulations.[61]

Others note that even though 'initiatives to removing or reducing transatlantic regulatory barriers to trade since the NTA have made some progress towards reducing regulatory burdens, many US and European companies heavily engaged in the transatlantic marketplace maintain that the results have not been materially significant'.[62] It is apparent from the infamous disputes before the WTO panels that the most controversial regulatory differences emanate from 'diverging regulatory philosophies', different risk assessment systems, public policy considerations,

[60] See Bartl and Fahey, Chapter 9 in this volume.

[61] J. F. Morrall, 'Determining Compatible Regulatory Regimes between the US and the EU, US Chamber of Commerce, Advancing Transatlantic Business', at p. 39, available at: www.uschamber.com/sites/default/files/legacy/reports/Determining%20Compatible%20Regulatory%20Regimes.pdf, accessed 13 February 2014.

[62] See Ahearn, 'Transatlantic Regulatory Cooperation', p. 1.

and regulatory approaches of 'principal character', and make it difficult or seemingly impossible to establish harmonization or mutual recognition of standards without complex legislation changes (for example in consumer protection, health and food standards).[63]

As we have seen, numerous political declarations have called for regulatory convergence and harmonization, but enacting changes into laws that would move regulatory approaches to converge have been limited. Stakeholders have criticized such slow progress, and the US Chamber of Commerce brought up the idea of a binding Agreement on Regulatory Cooperation that would oblige regulators on both sides to operate under a common set of regulatory principles and beliefs, and assess the cost impact of forthcoming regulations on transatlantic commerce, adopt each other's best practices, and utilize similar methodology to assess costs and benefits of proposed regulations.[64]

5 The structural framework of transatlantic regulatory cooperation

As can be seen from the previous section, the subsequent regulatory cooperation initiatives – all of them in the form of non-binding soft-law instruments – increasingly reiterated the need for regulatory dialogue. Substantially speaking, no harmonization or standardization resulted (or was even targeted) by these initiatives, and (the impact of) recognition of the equivalence of conformity assessment has been limited to a few sectors, with varying success in actual implementation. One can, however, note that regulatory cooperation initiatives also placed important emphasis on creating dialogue and formalizing networks so as to enhance regulatory information flow, and exchange of ideas and best practices, so that regulators can better understand the differences in their regulations or standards or regulatory practices, preferably before regulations become effective. As will be shown below, because of the non-binding character of the instruments and consequent resistance to regulatory changes, as well as the diversity of ad hoc, informal and structured dialogue, the political and strategic leadership in consultations is important. Such strategic direction is provided by the TEC and the Forum, streamlining regulatory

[63] S. Mildner and O. Ziegler, 'A Long and Thorny Road: Regulatory Cooperation under the Framework for Advancing Transatlantic Economic Integration' (January/February 2009) *Intereconomics* 49–58, at 49.

[64] See Ahearn, 'Transatlantic Regulatory Cooperation', p. 12.

and government-to-government sector-specific discussions. The following overview will highlight the main features of such an institutional framework of transgovernmental bodies engaged in regulatory dialogue in EU–US regulatory policy cooperation and formalized networks of stakeholders.[65]

5.1 *Sector-specific bilateral regulatory dialogues*

The 2002 Guidelines on Regulatory Cooperation and Transparency addressed government-to-government consultation, encouraged information exchanges and facilitated a more effective dialogue in areas through consultation and data-sharing, for example. Sector-specific cooperative objectives were laid down in the Roadmap for EU–US Regulatory Cooperation, involving the USA, European Commission and, where relevant, EU regulators, promoting a broad range of sector-specific arrangements including those that permit the sharing of non-public information between regulators in important areas such as pharmaceuticals, medical devices and food safety.

5.2 *Methodological dialogues between the OMB and European Commission*

The Roadmap for EU–US Regulatory Cooperation initiated an informal dialogue led jointly by the US Office of Management and Budget (OMB) and relevant experts in the European Commission (led by its Secretariat General) to address horizontal regulatory management issues (e.g. transparency provisions, risk assessment, impact assessment and public consultation) in order to improve understanding of each other's regulatory systems and practices of mutual interest. Based on such methodological dialogues, regulators discussed good regulatory practices, with a focus on transparency provisions and public consultation, and compared respective impact assessment methodologies.[66] Such informal dialogues at the highest regulatory level were clearly aimed at preventing trade irritants, signalling potential divergences, and sharing of regulatory philosophies and approaches.

[65] See Bartl and Fahey, Chapter 9 in this volume.
[66] Joint Report on the Roadmap for EU–US Regulatory Cooperation, June 2006, Annex 2 to Progress Report on Economic Initiative.

5.3 *High-Level Regulatory Cooperation Forum*

A more formal dialogue on horizontal regulatory issues is conducted in the frame of the High-Level Regulatory Cooperation Forum (the Forum), which was set up by the EU–US Summit in 2005 and brings together senior officials from all areas of the government to discuss regulatory policy matters of mutual interest. The Forum is co-chaired by the Director-General of the Directorate General for Enterprise and Industry and the Administrator of the Office of Information and Regulatory Affairs in the Office of Management and Budget. The Forum 'lends senior-level support and visibility to the concrete activities of informal dialogue',[67] and as a more institutionalized dialogue on good regulatory practices aims to improve the quality of regulation on both sides, through sharing regulatory best practices such as risk and impact assessments, and techniques related to reducing the costs to business and consumers that arise from unnecessary differences in regulatory requirements. The Forum has contributed significantly to the discussions of high-level political bodies engaged in regulatory policy dialogue, such as the Transatlantic Economic Council (discussed in following section), with reports, including common understanding of best regulatory practices, as well as opportunities for cooperation on specific sectoral issues, with particular attention given to early engagement on new emerging regulatory issues.

5.4 *Transatlantic Economic Council*

The 2007 EU–US Summit launched the Transatlantic Economic Council (TEC), a platform to help further strengthen EU–US economic integration, bringing together those members of the European Commission and US Cabinet Members who carry the political responsibility for the policy areas covered by the Framework for Advancing Transatlantic Economic Integration. The TEC is the political body that oversees and accelerates government-to-government cooperation with the aim of advancing economic integration and was expected to have the kind of high-level political support that previous efforts at economic integration may have lacked, and which 'is perceived as necessary to persuade domestic regulators to yield some of their authorities or to better cooperate with their counterparts across the Atlantic in the harmonizing regulatory approaches'.[68]

[67] See Meuwese, 'EU–US Horizontal Regulatory Cooperation', p. 256.

[68] See Ahearn, 'Transatlantic Regulatory Cooperation', p. 18.

The TEC's initially more precise focus on trade and prevention of trade disputes has by now shifted to ensure transatlantic regulatory convergence by preventing barriers and sharing best practices, and to develop joint principles with the aim of promoting maximum compatibility of regulations and the freest possible transatlantic flow of ideas, products and services, albeit with a limited agenda for regulatory harmonization in selected areas.[69] The TEC meets at least once a year at the level of Commissioners and members of the Administration (for example, heads of agencies such as the Environmental Protection Agency) to identify possible directions of regulatory cooperation.

The TEC's function is viewed to rest heavily on the regulatory exercise and creation of synergies in standard-setting, taking stock of compatibility in bilateral economic relations.[70] However, both in its efforts to resolve a number of long-standing bilateral trade disputes, or to prevent new ones, as well as its efforts to harmonize regulations on a sector-by-sector basis, the TEC's mission proved difficult due to 'political and bureaucratic resistance on both sides to revise existing laws and regulations'.[71] It appears that the TEC's ambition to create regulatory convergence has its inherent limitations: existing barriers stay, new ones have arisen (despite the intent to coordinate), and the political leaders on both sides (from the executive branch) have not managed to pull their weight towards the regulators to make them yield to convergence, let alone harmonization. Consequently, it is the pre-emption of future trade irritants to which the TEC seems to have shifted its activities, and it has refocused its work towards 'upstream regulatory cooperation' so as to help preclude unintended trade barriers and prevent new trade irritants, with the 'potential to develop into a genuine strategic instrument focusing on dispute prevention through upstream regulatory cooperation and convergence'.[72] Focusing on compatible approaches for the regulation of new and innovative sectors in the Innovation Action Plan allows more effective prevention of regulatory divergence and has resulted in the focus of regulatory cooperation

[69] See F. Erixon and G. Pehnelt, 'A New Trade Agenda for Transatlantic Economic Cooperation', ECIPE WP 9/2009 at p. 2.

[70] Interview with official at EU Delegation to the US, February 2011.

[71] See Ahearn, 'US–EU Trade and Economic Relations: Key Policy Issues for the 112th Congress', 18 January 2012, p. 5, available at: www.fas.org/sgp/crs/row/R41652.pdf, accessed 13 February 2014.

[72] Speech by Catherine Ashton, EU Trade Commissioner, 'The Transatlantic Challenge: Working Together to Shape the Rules of Globalisation', US Chamber of Commerce, Washington DC, 26 October 2009, available at: http://europa.eu/rapid/press-release_SPEECH-09-499_en.htm?locale=fr, accessed 13 February 2014.

on emerging technologies and specific sectors such as electronic health records, nanotechnology, energy-saving products and electric vehicles, so as to pre-empt unnecessary obstacles to exports and reduce costs.[73]

5.5 Stakeholder participation in regulatory cooperation through advisory bodies

Structurally, the government-to-government cooperation and transgovernmental dialogue between regulators from agencies and corresponding executive levels have been complemented by stakeholder involvement and input. The Transatlantic Business Dialogue (TABD) has been the principal business interlocutor with the US Government and the European Union on transatlantic economic relationships, being a prime drive behind barrier-free trade and transatlantic economic (as well as regulatory) promotion. Both the TABD and the Transatlantic Consumer Dialogue (TCD) were created in 1995 as part of the NTA that set up the 'people-to-people dialogue system', to canvass input from consumers and labour, environmental and business organizations towards the regulators,[74] out of which the Transatlantic Business Dialogue (being part of the Transatlantic Business Council) and the Transatlantic Consumers Dialogue have provided particularly useful and constructive input. The Transatlantic Consumer Dialogue is a forum of US and EU consumer organizations that develops and agrees on joint consumer policy recommendations to the US Government and European Union, to promote consumer interest in EU and US policy-making, and which serves as an important platform for regulatory discussions on various issues (consumer protection, food etc.).

The involvement of stakeholders, especially that of the TABD, a transatlantic coalition of big businesses from the EU and USA, 'developed into an effective framework for enhanced cooperation between the transatlantic business community and the governments of the EU and the US', and is an important source of inspiration and information for negotiators.[75]

[73] Transatlantic Innovation Action Partnership, available at: http://trade.ec.europa.eu/doclib/docs/2011/january/tradoc_147174.pdf, accessed 13 February 2014.

[74] Mildner and Ziegler, 'A Long and Thorny Road', 49.

[75] M. Green Cowles, 'Calming the Waters: The Rebirth of the Transatlantic Business Dialogue' in D. Andrews, M. A. Pollack, G. C. Shaffer and H. Wallace (eds.), *The New Transatlantic Agenda and the Future of Transatlantic Economic Governance* (Florence: European University Institute, 2005), p. 278. See Bartl and Fahey, Chapter 9 in this volume.

Both the TABD and TCD have developed joint EU–US trade policy recommendations, working together with the European Commission and US administration to promote the interests of their respective stakeholders. Next to the TABD and TCD, the Transatlantic Legislators' Dialogue serves as advisory body to the TEC, and with the increasing competences of the EP in trade policy, its role and function may be heightened.

5.6 Assessment of dialogue as form of regulatory cooperation

The institutional structure that was sketched out and called for in the Transatlantic Economic Partnership was 'strictly intergovernmental in nature'.[76] Transatlantic regulatory dialogue in economic matters has been conducted in a primarily executive-driven fashion, which can be seen in the composition of all actors participating in the various platforms of co-operation and dialogue: regulators from the higher political stances as well as agencies and relevant authorities. Accordingly, the High-Level Regulatory Cooperation Forum brings together senior officials from the European Commission and regulatory agencies of the US administration to discuss horizontal regulatory issues and share best practices, as well as to discuss sector-specific issues in closed government-to-government sessions, followed traditionally by open sessions where the regulators meet with stakeholder organizations.

The executive plays a major role in the TEC as well, since the Commission, or more specifically, delegations from the Directorate General for Trade, Enterprise and Industry (DG Trade) and any other Directorate General represent the EU, next to the US Trade Representative (USTR) or OMB. For the EU, however, considering that the European Commission is the only institution represented at these dialogues, but not the only actor in the EU's regulatory and decision-making processes, the risk arises that despite the regulatory dialogue with the US regulators and commitments undertaken at the TEC, any EU legislative acts (involving the EP and the Council, as well as other relevant bodies such as the Economic and Social Committee) that are eventually adopted may carry such divergence from US regulation that they would potentially become a trade barrier. This materialized into an actual problem and full-blown trade dispute initiated at the WTO in the case of the poultry dispute, where the Commission put

[76] See W. H. Roth, 'Building the "Transatlantic Economic Partnership": Are New General Institutions Needed?' in Bermann *et al.* (eds.), *Transatlantic Regulatory Cooperation*, pp. 601–13, at p. 603.

forward a proposal to the Council to lift the 1997 EU ban on the import of US chlorine-washed poultry – in line with its earlier promise to the TEC – but the Council rejected the proposal.[77] Assessing this point, Sapir argues that only in policy areas where the Commission is the (internal) regulator can it negotiate and deliver to its foreign partners in regulatory matters, noting the successful agreement in competition policy where the European Commission as sole regulator also acted as the EU's external voice.[78] In the case of trade, but also other areas of interest for transatlantic regulatory cooperation, this risk has become even more prominent since the entry into force of the Lisbon Treaty, which prescribes the coequal participation of the European Parliament in decision-making along with the Council, thereby creating another actor whose position must be taken into account in the decision-making process.

The Agreements and discussions within the TEC and other regulator-to-regulator forums have primarily dealt with non-tariff barriers to trade in certain specific areas following a case-by-case approach, and regulatory agendas seem to aim low. While the general methodological cooperative efforts on principles and guidelines are of an overall horizontal scope (such as transparency, openness etc.), the actual regulatory initiatives in bilateral regulatory talks have always focused on a sectoral, case-by-case approach. The relatively modest success of transatlantic initiatives has been attributed by some to the absence of economic guidance and lack of clear direction,[79] limited agenda, 'small-scale incrementalism' and the too-low aim that the regulatory cooperation efforts took within the TEC and otherwise.[80] While it is understandable that complex technical discussions need to be precisely framed, and constitutional structures for negotiations respected, the economic benefits have to match the political costs, and real political commitment needs to fuel negotiations.[81] Although it was established to create regulatory harmonization and to

[77] See R. Johnson, US–EU Poultry Dispute, Congressional Research Service, R40199, 9 December 2010, available at: www.fas.org/sgp/crs/row/R40199.pdf, accessed 13 February 2014.

[78] A. Sapir, 'The Political Economy of Transatlantic Regulatory Cooperation and Competition: A (Unofficial) View of Europe' in S. J. Evenett and R. M. Stern (eds.), *Systemic Implications of Transatlantic Regulatory Cooperation and Competition* (Singapore: World Scientific Publishing, 2011), pp. 47–61, at p. 52.

[79] F. Erixon and L. Brandt, 'Ideas for New Transatlantic Initiatives on Trade', Transatlantic Task Force on Trade Working Papers, p. 2, available at: www.ecipe.org/media/publication_pdfs/ideas-for-new-transatlantic-initiatives-on-trade.pdf, accessed 13 February 2014.

[80] See Erixon and Pehnelt, 'A New Trade Agenda', p. 5.

[81] *Ibid.*

steer and evaluate regulatory cooperation, the TEC seems to have fallen short of expectations. Despite the declarations, with ambitious wording of intent focusing on exchanging views, best practices, and shaping common principles and frameworks, the TEC's performance can hardly be viewed as successful in light of its mission 'to streamline regulations, eliminate non-tariff barriers to trade and investment so as to enhance compatibility of standards and regulations'. The TEC has been noted for its 'discussion rather than action' nature and modest language of commitments, where officials negotiated toothless agreements.[82]

The limitations of the regulator-to-regulator dialogue as a form of regulatory cooperation emerge in food issues, which constitute a 'ground zero in the transatlantic dialogue' delivering no result, while consumer protection issues such as product safety, exchange of information on scams and dangerous product recalls also show slow results.[83] In these dialogues, exchanges and consultations, structured dialogue has fallen short of any results early on in regulatory cooperation efforts concerning the GMO dispute, despite the fact that biotechnology was one of the areas where structured dialogue among regulators was initiated for the gradual convergence of regulatory standards and prevention of trade disputes.

A clear disregard for regulatory cooperation commitments for dialogue – and especially the mutually accepted early warning system – was apparent in legislation introduced unilaterally by both the EU and the USA. The EU adopted the REACH Directive without much input from US stakeholders, and the USA adopted the Sarbanes–Oxley Act, which reformed public accounting standards, without taking into account EU views,[84] both regulatory acts creating an important barrier to commerce. The obvious lack of convergence efforts thus raises the questions of just how effective the structures for dialogue and exchange of views are, and why there was no coordination in these important regulatory areas despite the reiterated commitment in the earlier mentioned documents.

[82] See Erixon and Brandt, 'Ideas for New Transatlantic Initiatives on Trade', p. 5.

[83] European Foreign Policy Scorecard 2012, p. 66, available at: www.ecfr.eu/page/-/ECFR_SCORECARD_2012_WEB.pdf, accessed 13 February 2014.

[84] See Ahearn, 'Transatlantic Regulatory Cooperation', p. 19, available at: http://fpc.state.gov/documents/organization/64460.pdf, accessed 13 February 2014.

6 Options for regulatory cooperation in a transatlantic free trade agreement

The HLWG on Jobs and Growth identified in its final report that a comprehensive free trade agreement, in which regulatory cooperation would feature prominently for the elimination, reduction or prevention of unnecessary 'behind the border' non-tariff barriers to trade in all categories, with opportunities for enhancing compatibility of regulations and standards, would increase EU–US trade and transatlantic economic relations.[85] As noted, reduction and negotiation of non-tariff barriers and regulatory differences is expected to be the hardest area to negotiate between the EU and the USA, with regulatory autonomy and culture being perceived as part of sovereignty.

Surrounding the ongoing discussion on further integrating bilateral economic relations, various suggestions for regulatory features were put forward in the frame of an initial public consultation and a subsequent consultation process with all relevant stakeholders. The Impact Assessment that DG Trade prepared from the detailed views gathered during the public consultation assisted in the designing of a negotiation plan and draft mandate. The views thus presented generally confirmed that regulatory barriers are perceived as major obstacles to trade and investment. The overall opinion unequivocally supported an ambitious approach to transatlantic economic integration, one that would enhance the transatlantic regulatory environment in both the goods and services sectors. The options suggested show that the preferred approach to regulatory cooperation depends on the policy context, the purpose and function of regulations in that sector. Among the various suggestions for eliminating NTBs one can find the call for intensified dialogue, and sharing of information and experience to produce more efficient regulatory mechanisms. In addition, preference for the further adoption and implementation of mutual recognition agreements in an extended number of sectors is called for. Some suggest carrying further earlier developed initiatives, such as the inclusion in the agreement of core regulatory best practices that are embodied in the 2011 Common Understanding on Regulatory Principles and Best Practices, as well as the April 2002 Guidelines on Regulatory Cooperation and Transparency. Focus and enhanced efforts

85 Interim Report to Leaders from the Co-Chairs EU–US High-Level Working Group on Jobs and Growth, 19 June 2012, available at: http://trade.ec.europa.eu/doclib/docs/2012/june/tradoc_149557.pdf, accessed 13 February 2014. On the normative dimensions of a future agreement, see Bartl and Fahey, Chapter 9 in this volume.

toward convergence are called for with respect to new and relatively unregulated areas and aligning regulations in emerging technologies, such as nanotechnology and electric cars, where both the EU and USA are developing regulatory approaches and where dialogue can prevent divergent regulatory action. These are the innovative, new areas in which the transatlantic axis can also feed into global norm-setting.

7 Conclusions

Looking at the initiatives of regulatory policy cooperation so far, one can note their limited scope and underlying lack of political will for binding commitment. However, the currently ongoing developments project is a strong political momentum for a potential comprehensive free trade agreement and partnership, in which addressing regulatory divergence and NTBs are identified to be the main challenge.[86] The overall liberalization in goods and services – despite the already relatively low tariffs – will certainly bring economic gains,[87] but what businesses and stakeholders call on their regulators to address is remarkably the multitude of regulatory barriers and beyond-the-border requirements that increase costs for operators or otherwise hinder market access.

In the absence of an institutionalized bilateral dispute settlement system within the transatlantic economic relation, regulatory cooperation has become an important mechanism for addressing regulatory divergences. If the comprehensive free trade agreement includes dispute settlement mechanisms, just as in the North American Free Trade Agreement, this would enhance constitutional empowerment of the citizen, offering direct access to justice[88] and at the same time confirming disciplines on regulatory convergence.

The political and strategic directions that the TEC and the Forum have provided remain essential in a system where non-binding initiatives and instruments 'govern' key regulatory convergence features, where sector-specific convergence and dialogues on horizontal matters are separated, and the framework of dialogues varies between ad hoc, informal and structured formats. Strong strategic leadership of the TEC and Forum is

[86] C.-C. Cîrlig, 'EU–US Trade Agreement: The Issues of Consumer Protection and Food Safety', Library Briefing, 5 December 2012.

[87] See F. Erixon and M. Bauer, 'A Transatlantic Zero Agreement: Estimating the Gains from Transatlantic Free Trade in Goods', ECIPE Occasional Paper, 4/2010.

[88] See the discussion in Petersmann, 'Prevention and Settlement of Transatlantic Economic Disputes'.

indispensable for a successful interplay with the institutionalized stakeholder network, and the canvassing of suggestions (bottom-up) should be fed into all levels of regulatory dialogue (top-down). Regulatory cooperation should build on achievements, such as the Common Understanding on Regulatory Principles and Best Practices, as well as the Regulatory Cooperation Best Cooperative Practices, making these agreed documents central in regulator-to-regulator discussions. The limitations of sector-specific regulatory convergence show that legal harmonization of standards and regulations is not realistic, yet the EU and USA can, together, set standards even at the global level in emerging, new technologies where regulation is not yet set in stone unilaterally. In addition, mutual recognition agreements covering not only testing and certification but also standards would boost the confidence of regulators and consumers in the EU and the USA. The details of regulatory cooperation, its mechanisms and guiding approaches negotiated under the TTIP will most certainly draw the attention of regulatory authorities, businesses and stakeholders alike. There appears to be political commitment to address the issues, and even if the eventual agreement may not address every issue of regulatory cooperation and convergence, or set deadlines and guiding approaches, methods or defining of sectors – defined in legally binding terms – and an institutional structure that is permanent, transparent and effective, it would nonetheless constitute a substantive step forward in transatlantic economic relations.

8

Addressing transatlantic regulatory barriers

Can the USA and the EU create an effective equivalency instrument?

JAMES MATHIS

1 Introduction

The stage for this chapter is set by the history of regulatory cooperation between the USA and EU (recounted in Tamara Takács' contribution to this volume)[1] and the new initiative again on the horizon of establishing a transatlantic regional trade agreement between them. Since 1995 the two have established almost a dozen efforts constituting agendas, roadmaps, partnerships and dialogues to facilitate regulatory convergence, conformity assessment frameworks, cooperative early warning systems, 'upstream' regulatory convergence and so on. In fact, a view of the overall transatlantic regulatory terrain gives the impression of a very busy 'roadmap' carrying all sorts of cooperative regulatory vehicles. There is likely no other example of two territories in the international trading system that have established more dialogues at various levels of government engaging more lawmakers and regulators, economic operators and civil society than these two. The chapter by Takács also reviews the assessments that have been made of these multiple efforts of regulatory cooperation.[2] With a few noteworthy successes,[3] the results of completed regulatory harmonization,

[1] T. Takács, 'Transatlantic Regulatory Cooperation in Trade: Objectives, Challenges and Instruments for Economic Governance', Chapter 7, this volume.

[2] See also, M. Bartl and E. Fahey, 'A Postnational Marketplace: Negotiating the Transatlantic Trade and Investment Partnership (TTIP)', Chapter 9 this volume.

[3] For example, the 2012 mutual recognition agreements for organic products and for certified 'safe traders'. See T. Takács, Chapter 7 Section 4.1 this volume. The European Commission notes that the 1998 Mutual Recognition Agreement has been successful in two areas: telecommunications and electromagnetic compatibility. European Commission, EU–US Transatlantic Trade and Investment Partnership, Technical Barriers to Trade, Initial EU Position Paper, 2013, 6, available at: http://trade.ec.europa.eu/doclib/docs/2013/july/tradoc_151627.pdf, accessed 14 February 2014.

convergence or equivalency recognition for the alleged numerous non-tariff barriers of interest have been disappointing.[4]

These efforts are now directed under an initiative to establish a transatlantic regional trade agreement that, if successful, would include a free trade area for goods and an economic integration agreement for services.[5] That a high emphasis will remain on resolving regulatory barriers is reflected in the final report of the US–EU High-Level Working Group on Jobs and Growth (HLWG), which calls for a 'comprehensive trade and investment agreement' that would include the 'elimination, reduction, or prevention of unnecessary "behind the border" non-tariff barriers to trade in all categories'.[6]

As for mechanisms, the HLWG calls for – among other things – 'ambitious' sanitary and phytosanitary (SPS) and technical barriers to trade (TBT) 'plus' chapters with ongoing mechanisms 'for improved dialogue and cooperation', early consultations on significant regulations, and additional commitments to promote approaches relating to 'regulatory harmonization, equivalence or mutual recognition'.[7]

Perhaps there is something inherent in the architecture of a regional trade agreement, as compared to bilateral declarations of cooperation and dialogue, which might put some flesh on these well-trodden cooperative bones, but one is sceptical when seeing these same ideas recirculated, albeit in a different package. There is little common institutional power to be located in a typical free trade area or economic integration agreement, and if there is such an institutional innovation coming for this one, its model has not emerged in other recent regional trade agreements

[4] T. Takács, Chapter 7 Section 4.2 this volume, and citing R. J. Ahearn, 'Transatlantic Regulatory Cooperation: Background and Analysis', 2009, Congress Research Service, available at: www.dtic.mil/cgi-bin/GetTRDoc?AD=ADA506415, accessed 14 February 2014. Ahearn notes on p. 17: 'Based on the premise that enhanced regulatory cooperation, particularly through mutual recognition, will never happen if matters are left to individual regulatory agencies, high-level political pressure is commonly prescribed.' For an assessment of the 1997 EC–US Conformity Assessment Mutual Recognition Agreement, see G. Shaffer, 'Reconciling Trade and Regulatory Roles: The Prospects and Limits of New Approaches to Transatlantic Governance through Mutual Recognition and Safe Harbor Agreements' (2002) 9 *Columbia Journal of European Law* 29–77.

[5] As defined by GATT Article XXIV and GATS Article V respectively. It is not clear whether investor protection issues would be incorporated in a GATS V agreement or as a separate chapter dealing only with those aspects.

[6] HLWG Final Report, 11 February 2013, Introduction, available at: http://trade.ec.europa.eu/doclib/docs/2013/february/tradoc_150519.pdf, accessed 14 February 2014.

[7] *Ibid.*, Section B, Regulatory Issues and Non-Tariff Barriers.

initiated by either of these transatlantic parties.[8] This is evidenced by the lack of detail in the HLWG report, which, while asking for provisions that provide an 'institutional basis for future progress', is not suggesting one or even a set of alternatives or an outline. That degree of specificity is perhaps not its task either, but overall one finds more of the same dialogue and cooperation in which the parties have already been engaging, but this time it is to be more ambitious and improved.[9]

In the absence of a meaningful, that is stronger, institutional instrument, one doubts if the next round of cooperation is going to be any more satisfying than the previous ones. The emphasis on voluntary approaches, such as cooperation and dialogue, while of course understandable, is not going to yield an advanced marketplace concept nor be a pattern-setter in the international trading system. This is because the problem of overcoming regulatory barriers resides in the legal character of the parties' operable and mandatory laws. These laws are not themselves in violation of the origin territories' constitutional frameworks, nor do they violate the rules of the World Trade Organization (WTO). While cooperation and dialogue are valuable transnational processes on their own terms, they do not rise to the level of a legal instrument that would operate according to guiding presumptions capable of exercising the balancing tests necessary to weigh the demands of the market with a state's legitimate regulatory objectives. At the core of it, only a regional institutional instrument can determine (or compel) a process of recognition that one territory's regulation, while different from another territory's regulation, is yet essentially and functionally equivalent to it, according to its established level of protection and its mechanisms for insuring application and compliance.

Accordingly, this chapter examines the possibility of an arbitral or mediational instrument for determining the equivalency of existing regulations affecting trade in goods and services. Section 2 makes the case for focusing on equivalency, either as a preferred approach or one formulated in addition to those based on the administrative processes

[8] J. Mathis, 'Regulatory Regionalism in the WTO – Are 'Deep Integration' Processes Compatible with the Multilateral Trading System?' in S. Lester, B. Mercurio and L. Bartels (eds.), *Bilateral and Regional Trade Agreements: Commentary and Analysis* (Cambridge University Press, 2014). Two exceptions may be noted: the EU–Korea NTM Mediation Mechanism (discussed in Section 2.2 and cited in n. 19 below) and the US–Panama Agreement provision requiring unilateral recognition by Panama of US certified food products, cited in n. 15 below.

[9] HLWG Final Report, Section B, Regulatory Issues and Non-Tariff Barriers.

of negotiated harmonization or gradual convergence. Brief reference is made to the role of equivalency in both the US and EU systems, and to the recognition processes employed in the transatlantic parties' most recently concluded regional trade agreements with another developed country – Korea. Section 3 turns to the possible outline of such an equivalency instrument, and the choices to be made in its design and relationship to the existing system of transatlantic cooperation. This includes considerations of the legal tests to be applied, the parties to proceedings, and the legal effect of an equivalency determination and its relationship to governing political bodies and other societal actors. Finally, Section 4 addresses the non-discrimination rules of the WTO and whether or not a regional trade agreement containing such an instrument would be excused from them.

2 Harmonization and equivalency recognition

2.1 EU and US regional/national harmonization

In regional regulatory harmonization the parties either together establish a new regulation or one party adopts the regulation of the other. For new regulations, harmonization requirements may be either 'strict', as in specifying requirements that must be met without variation, or they may be more flexible by requiring states to meet a designated minimum level of protection, and then allowing them to set 'higher' levels above that established floor. The higher level applies to domestic goods and services of origin while the minimum constitutes the entry requirement for foreign products and providers. This minimum harmonization approach was established in the internal market legislation of the European Communities in order to fulfil the European Court of Justice (ECJ)'s judgments in *Dassonville* and *Cassis de Dijon*.[10] It was the legislative and executive response to the Court's mandate for Member State

[10] Case 8/74, *Procureur du Roi* v. *Dassonville*, [1974] E.C.R. 837; Case 120/78, *Rewe-Zentrale* v. *Bundesmonopolverwaltungfur Branntwein* (*Cassis de Dijon*), [1979] ECR 649. In *Cassis* the Court enunciated the principle that what is lawful to produce and market in one Member State should be able to be introduced into any other Member State. For a review of the legal impact of these and following judgments, see E. L. White, 'In Search of the Limits to Article 30 of the EEC Treaty' (1989) 26 *Common Market Law Review* 253–80. For a more recent review of the EU mutual recognition doctrine as it has evolved and as it is applied to the assimilation of third-country goods, see L. Ankersmit, 'What if Cassis de Dijon Were Cassis de Quebec? The Assimilation of Goods of Third-Country Origin in the Internal Market' (2013) 50 *Common Market Law Review* 1,387–410.

recognition across the market.[11] The USA has no constitutional mandate for the removal of non-tariff barriers between the States, and thus no court interpretation mandating a minimum form of harmonization across the US internal market.[12] However, the Commerce Clause of the Constitution does empower Congress to act to pre-empt State regulations by federal action. The resulting federal administrative agency regulations can and do assume forms of either strict or minimum styles of harmonization.[13]

While both the EU and USA (and other states and territories) can accommodate or mandate forms of legislative harmonization and recognition internally, such devices for addressing non-tariff barriers remain somewhat rare on the international plane of regional trade agreements. Where found, the mechanism for establishing a harmonized level, to be used as a basis for recognition, is not a common-created institutional authority or even a federalized approach reflecting elements of centrality and subsidiarity. With few exceptions,[14] what occurs instead in a small number of regional trade agreements is that one party acts as a 'rule-taker' of the other.[15] A variation used by the both the USA and EU is found in their external trade agreement chapters for intellectual property protection. Here the other country is adopting the protection levels applied by the USA or the EU; however, the point of legal reference is not made to the domestic regime of either country, but rather to an international treaty

[11] Council Resolution of 7 May 1985, on a new approach to technical harmonization and standards (85/C 136/01).

[12] The US Constitution prohibits tariff duties among the States. US Constitution, Article I, Section 10.

[13] US Constitution, Commerce Clause, Article I, Section 8, Clause 3: 'The Congress shall have Power … To regulate Commerce with foreign Nations, and among the several States, and with the Indian Tribes'. The congressional power is said to be inherently 'corrective' rather than 'affirmative'. A. Abel, 'The Commerce Clause in the Constitutional Convention and in Contemporary Comment' (1941) 25 *Minnesota Law Review* 332–4.

[14] The EU itself is an example, of course, but so are Australian and New Zealand Mutual Recognition Arrangements (MRAs). In respect of the latter, and suggesting a similar negative listing approach for the USA and EU, see Transatlantic Task Force on Trade and Investment, 'A New Era for Transatlantic Trade Leadership', 2012, 22, available at: www.gmfus.org/wp-content/blogs.dir/1/files_mf/tatf_report_2012.pdf, accessed 14 February 2014.

[15] Examples of this can be found in EU trade (association) agreements with accession-oriented countries where the third country agrees to align its domestic regulations with Community internal market law. Another European example is the EEA (European Economic Area) Agreement, the EEA parties align to EU internal market law. A US trade agreement example is found in the US–Panama Agreement, in which Panama agrees to recognize US sanitary, phytosanitary and related regulatory systems; Agreement Regarding Certain Sanitary and Phytosanitary Measures and Technical Standards Affecting Trade in Agriculture Products, dated 20 December 2006, paras. 2, 4.

regime – World Intellectual Property Organization (WIPO) intellectual property agreements, for example.[16]

It is not difficult to spot the troublesome sovereignty and constitutional issues that emerge for either a 'rule-taker' or a mutual legislative harmonization approach. The first suggests that one party sublimate its domestic authority to the rules of another domestic authority. The second may call for both parties to sublimate their domestic authorities to a created 'supra' legislative and/or executive power. As a practical matter, where each territory has already determined its own lawful level of protection, even a negotiated process of convergence towards harmonization – if it might alter this choice of protection – would also not likely be welcomed by a number of stakeholders in the domestic system. While such reluctance might suggest an opening for the more flexible forms of minimum harmonization and recognition, the problem inherent in them is that a territory with a higher level of protection would then be allowing products meeting a lower level of protection into its market ('race to the bottom'). Or, if that is unacceptable, then the territory with the lower level of protection must raise it to a new minimum level ('cost-raising'). This perhaps explains in part why more recent transatlantic regulatory efforts focus on 'upstream' regulations for new and emerging subject areas that have not yet been crystallized into existing domestic protection levels.

2.2 *Equivalency provisions in US and EU trade agreements*

Equivalency recognition also relies on a certain level of underlying harmonization. But rather than placing the emphasis on the processes of how goods and services are certified (conformity assessment) to meet an approximate harmonized or converged level of protection, it assesses whether the substantive protection levels of different regulations can be recognized as functionally the same. In most regional trade agreement settings, as in the case of the transatlantic relationship to date, this is operated as a voluntary process of agency and trade association negotiations with some prioritized encouragement possibly generated from the agreement's signatories. The USA and the EU have both used this approach in their respective agreements with Korea for certification or authorization

[16] This international referencing style is also found in those positive harmonization provisions that occur in the WTO agreements for technical barriers to trade (TBT Agreement Art. 2.4) and for intellectual property (TRIPS Agreement, Art. 9.1, among other TRIPS provisions).

of foreign professional service suppliers. In the KORUS (US–Korea) Agreement, when the Joint Committee of the parties agrees on a service sector, it can then choose to encourage their respective professional associations to develop recommendations for mutual recognition to be provided to a professional services working group. A positive decision by the Joint Committee would then encourage their respective bodies to implement the recommendation for recognition.[17] The EU–Korea Agreement takes the similar initial approach of encouraging the respective professional bodies to develop recognition recommendations, with a somewhat stronger conclusion requiring the negotiation of a mutual recognition agreement by the competent authorities of the parties if the recommendations are approved by the Trade Committee.[18]

Neither the USA nor the EU establishes any voluntary frameworks or processes for equivalency recognition of existing product standards in their respective agreements with Korea. Rather, the approach is more centred on transparency and participation for new and amending regulations. The EU–Korea Agreement does, however, contain a 'Mediation Mechanism for Non-Tariff Measures', allowing the parties to request and receive an advisory opinion with proposed solutions for measures 'adversely affecting trade' between the parties.[19] In this state-to-state procedure the mediator is neither permitted to consider whether the measure is consistent with the Agreement nor to question the legitimacy of the state's policy objective.[20] The standard of 'affecting trade' might be equated with a 'restrictiveness' standard,[21] but in any case there is no reference made in the instrument to the 'unnecessary obstacle to international

[17] KORUS Agreement, Art. 12.2. Free Trade Agreement between The United States Of America and the Republic of Korea (KORUS Agreement), ratified in 2011, USTR, available at: www.ustr.gov/trade-agreements/free-trade-agreements/korus-fta/final-text, accessed 14 February 2014.

[18] EU–Korea Agreement, Art. 7.21(4): 'the Parties shall, with a view to implementing that recommendation, negotiate, through their competent authorities, an agreement on mutual recognition'. Free Trade Agreement between the European Union and its Member States, of the one part, and the Republic of Korea, of the other part (EU–Korea Agreement) OJ L 127/6, 14 May 2011.

[19] Mediation Mechanism for Non-Tariff Measures, EU–Korea Agreement, Annex 14-A, L 127/1336-37. The agreement does employ an international-standard reference for auto vehicles and parts equivalency. Annex 2-C, L 127/1142-1144, 14 May 2011.

[20] *Ibid.*, Annex 14-A, Art. 5.3.

[21] Farrah's proposal for a transatlantic non-tariff barrier (NTB) resolution mechanism centres on 'restrictiveness' rather than 'legality'. He also reviews similar proposals made in the Non-Agricultural Market Access Negotiations (NAMA) in the WTO. J. E. Farrah, 'Resolution of Non-Tariff Barriers in Bilateral Trade Agreements: Lessons from the US–Korea Free Trade Agreement and a Model for Market Access in the Twenty-

trade' standard that is used in the TBT Agreement.[22] The EU–Korea Mechanism does not prescribe the possible solutions for the mediator to consider, but it is not inconceivable that the mediator could recommend that a trade-affecting measure be resolved by an act of recognition. In this sense only, the Mechanism might be considered to be incidentally a vehicle for formulating recognition.

This very brief overview of the two Korea agreements shows that recognition frameworks are either non-existent or, when present, are based on voluntary encouragement and cooperation. With the single exception of the EU–Korea Trade Committee's ability to order that a recognition agreement be formed, the approaches are similar to elements already employed in the existing transatlantic relationship. They rely strongly on associations (or standard-setting bodies) and regulating agencies to 'bubble up' the details as to how recognition might occur. The role of the parties is primarily the identification of sectors, and encouraging the bodies and regulators to offer a recognition approach.

3 Equivalency in a transatlantic regional trade agreement

3.1 How much equivalency is there?

The role of standard-setters and agencies is of course essential to the process of recognition, but it raises the question of whether the inevitable resulting attention to the details of institutional certification and qualification procedures – conformity assessment – is actually the appropriate centrepiece for US and EU recognition. In other words, if there is a considerable degree of actual substantive equivalency between the two, then perhaps the process should be driven by equivalency at the outset.

From the Commission's point of view, the prevalence of equivalency appears to be the case. While regulatory measures are said to be the greatest obstacles between the EU and USA, most of these barriers are claimed to stem from the 'dissimilarity of regulatory structures … although the level of consumer/user protection can be considered similar in many areas of regulation'.[23] The same opinion is offered for a number of service sectors for which 'regulators on both sides of the Atlantic

First Century', 2010, available at: http://papers.ssrn.com/sol3/papers.cfm?abstract_id=1571364, accessed 14 February 2014.

[22] WTO Agreement on Technical Barriers to Trade (TBT Agreement), Art. 2.2.

[23] EU Commission Impact Assessment, Report on the Future of EU–US Trade Relations, COM(2013) 136 final 47, 12 March 2013, 17–18, noting also that one dissimilarity is the

seek to achieve similar outcomes in terms of prudential oversight and consumer protection'.[24]

Where there is an underlying substantive equivalence, the voluntary approaches used in the Korea agreements would not actually be sufficient to clear the administrative differences in the application of these regulations. One can conceive of an outcome to the Transatlantic Trade and Investment Partnership (TTIP) negotiations in which several key goods and service sectors would be prioritized for a similar voluntary approach undertaken by associations and agencies. However, something more would be required to evolve it beyond the sort of results the parties have seen on other occasions when sectors were prioritized and then handed over to the associations and agencies to fill in the details.[25]

3.2 *Equivalency instruments*

A possible candidate for this 'something more' would be a negotiated provision in the trade agreement establishing equivalency as the leading legal presumption. As in the Australia–New Zealand Trans-Tasman model, this would declare equivalency in effect except for those subject areas exempted by a negative list,[26] or included as a positive list.[27] The legal effect of this provision would be to shift the burden of demonstrating equivalency for the various certification systems, and clear the field to accept the goods and services for all of those systems that share an underlying similarity (equivalency) in their level of protection. It might not eliminate the possibility of demonstrating that a certification or conformity assessment system did not return the outcome of an equivalent level of protection, but the burden of demonstrating that point is decidedly distinct from one where there is an operating presumption that the systems are not

difficulty with existing mutual recognition agreements 'as to their actual effectiveness and implementation'. The author has not located an independent study assessing the degree of substantive equivalency between the transatlantic parties for either goods or services.

[24] *Ibid.*, 21, and again referring to the absence of recognition of equivalence between different regulatory frameworks.

[25] The 1997 US–EU Mutual Recognition Agreement remains a leading example of this approach.

[26] See n. 14. See also generally, Council of Australian Governments, Committee on Regulatory Reform, 'A Users' Guide to the Trans-Tasman Mutual Recognition Arrangement (TTMRA)', 1998, available at: www.dfat.gov.au/geo/new_zealand/ttmra_users_guide.pdf, accessed 14 February 2014.

[27] A positive list would retain a certain continuing political control over equivalency. The parties would add subjects as they agreed upon them over time.

sufficiently functional to ensure equivalent outcomes until proven (negotiated) to be so. This is as if to say to the agencies, 'rather than requesting you to come up with something positive that might form the basis of an agreement, please explain why the principle of equivalency cannot apply at the outset'.

A less dramatic possibility stems from Ahearn's notation that more 'high-level political pressure' is commonly prescribed for motivating regulatory agencies to establish mutual recognition.[28] Perhaps this would be fulfilled where the trade body of the regional trade agreement is given the authority to mandate that a recognition agreement be formed, as in the EU–Korea Agreement for services example. However, the low threshold of expectations on agencies and associations operating in a voluntary environment to return a plan in the first place retains the deficient elements of the weaker approach. While a trade committee itself could initiate its own negotiations to designate mandated sectors, perhaps that possibility would be strengthened by a more independently moving body that had the legal capacity to render a finding of equivalency as a result of a proceeding, within which the agencies would of course make their representations. On a positive determination based on a credible proceeding, a resulting order to form a recognition agreement by a trade committee would then be a directive to the agencies to either recognize the certification process of the other party or return an objection showing why the underlying certification process in question does not in fact yield the same substantive level of protection, that is, that the *differences* in the conformity systems in question somehow undermine the already determined substantive equivalency of the regulations.

Here the burden-shifting is somewhat different from both the treaty provision described above and cooperative negotiating processes. The initial burden for demonstrating equivalency may be tacitly upon the moving party, but not in the setting of a voluntary negotiation. Rather, the environment is more factually oriented and limited to a proceeding where parties would provide their materials for or against an equivalency recommendation (or finding). A positive finding treated as a direct mandate for recognition, or as above, tied to a later approval by the trade committee, would result in the presumption of equivalency taking effect and thereby a shifting of the burden.

This aspect of making a finding in a proceeding raises the mediation approach used by the EU and Korea for identifying trade-affecting non-

[28] Ahearn, 'Transatlantic Regulatory Cooperation'.

tariff measures. This also uses a combination of independent findings and political control. However, the orientation is different in that the test in an equivalency proceeding would not be about affecting trade or restrictiveness but rather about equivalency itself. The first recognizes a 'problem' and then forwards recommendations the parties can use to resolve it. The second determines a 'status' that goods or services are already circulating in their respective home markets according to substantially the same levels of protection.

3.3 Equivalency elements

Having raised the notion of a transatlantic equivalency proceeding, this section treats a number of the choices that can be considered in its composition and operation.

3.3.1 Scope of coverage

The standard-setting universe presents a plethora of diversity, including mandatory regulations and voluntary standards, public and private bodies, and central and sub-central bodies, with these possibilities operating in all possible combinations. Thus, a sub-central private body may be setting delegated mandatory regulations while a central public body may be engaged in setting voluntary standards. Presumably, wholly voluntary standards, however set, would not operate as a non-tariff barrier to goods or services and would therefore not be of interest on the issue of equivalency.[29] For the other categories of private or public, or central and sub-central, we also know that there are significant differences in the US and EU approaches to these systems and that these differences have been highlighted as a significant issue for concluding recognition agreements.[30] This acknowledged, the key threshold here is the point at which these varying systems assume a mandatory character, either by promulgation or selection by the regulators.

3.3.2 Equivalency as a legal test

An equivalency examination remains outside the scope of existing agreements in the WTO. While the WTO has several provisions regarding

[29] It is understood that the dividing line between mandatory regulations and voluntary standards has been a point of contention in WTO case law. See panel dissent and the Appellate Body ruling in *US – Tuna II*, WT/DS381.

[30] Commission Impact Assessment, Report on the Future of EU–US Trade Relations, 18.

equivalency for goods in the TBT and SPS Agreements and for services in the General Agreement on Trade in Services (GATS),[31] they do not specify any legal test or procedures for the formulation of equivalency, other than the notification and participation provisions in respect of other WTO members.[32] This contrasts with the EU–Korea mechanism's test for 'affecting trade' or the proposal for a transatlantic non-tariff barrier mechanism to assess 'restrictiveness', both of which share some elements of the test contained in TBT Article 2.2 for challenging 'unnecessary obstacles to trade'. In varying degrees, each of these tests is a type of 'hindering trade' test. While there may be distinctions between the first two and the WTO TBT test, the line of demarcation is evidently not clear at the outset. While the possibility of multiple forums addressing similar obligations is present in most regional trade agreements,[33] the equivalency test avoids any overlap and leaves to the WTO what is already in the WTO.

3.3.3 Parties

Common dispute settlement provisions in regional trade agreements are ubiquitously limited to state-to-state (party-to-party) proceedings, as is the EU–Korea Non-Tariff Measure Mechanism. For the EU and Korea, this exclusivity might make a degree of sense where the measure in question is that of one of the parties and the determination to challenge it as 'affecting trade' is assessed by the other party in considering the position of its own economic operators and balancing its other interests. In an equivalency determination, the moving party is not only addressing the other party's regulatory system, but rather seeking a finding that would address the operation of both parties' systems. If two separate regulations were found to be equivalent, then any resulting recognition would be 'bilateral' in nature, as each party would recognize the other. This raises a role for economic operators to initiate proceedings that are addressed to both parties, that is, a right of private action.[34] An additional

[31] Respectively, WTO, Agreement on Technical Barriers to Trade (TBT Agreement), Agreement on the Application of Sanitary and Phytosanitary Measures (SPS Agreement), General Agreement on Trade in Services (GATS).

[32] WTO equivalence provisions: SPS Agreement, Art. 4, TBT Agreement Art. 2.7, GATS, Art. VII.

[33] For example, regional trade agreements commonly recite national treatment obligations.

[34] Farrah also proposes private rights of action on the rationale that the private sector will have confidence that barriers can be addressed, to build pressure in the system and encourage compliance. 'Resolution of Non-Tariff Barriers in Bilateral Trade Agreements', 24.

argument for rights of private action is in the consideration of small and medium enterprises (SMEs). The government-controlled processes that prioritize key sectors for negotiation (for market access or for recognition frameworks) tend to reflect the larger producer and service interests in the economy. This is understandable, but there is a substantial SME presence even in the larger trade sectors.[35] For both goods and services there are many sectors that do not operate in large transnational business organizations. How smaller sectors and their operators not as omnipresent in the international system can attain access to an equivalency determination may be somewhat daunting. However, an opening for private rights at least allows the possibility of such a strategy to be formulated by them and their associations.

A final question regarding parties is the effect of an equivalency determination or a trade committee mandate for recognition on private parties, and whether they might derive legal rights as a result of a process. An examination of the direct effect possibilities of an international agreement and its institutional processes is not going to be explored here, except to note that residual political control over whether an arbitral process, as suggested here for the role of a trade agreement committee, would seem to add the political element, which has been noted before by the ECJ in its examinations of whether General Agreement on Tariffs and Trade (GATT) panel recommendations could generate direct effect.[36]

3.3.4 Confidentiality/legitimacy

The EU–Korea Mechanism prescribes a confidential proceeding. Given the position taken above on private rights of action, confidentiality would be patently inconsistent with the participation of private parties. More importantly, it would undermine the legitimacy of transatlantic mutual recognition. An equivalency assessment of a regulatory system's level of health and consumer protection touches the core societal values that are encompassed in the established level of protection and that have a strong and clearly evident impact on consumers. Their interest is thus core to the process. A determination of equivalency should be as open as the participation processes employed by the governments when they

[35] 'SMEs are prominent in the sectors most benefiting from a potential EU–US FTA.' EU Commission Impact Assessment, 'Resolution of Non-Tariff Barriers in Bilateral Trade Agreements', 47.

[36] As in Case C-149/96 *Portuguese Republic* v. *Council of the European Union* [1999] ECR I-8395, 23 November 1999.

formulated their regulations in the first place. Diversity in participation would enhance the material upon which a determination was made and contribute to the legitimacy of its outcome. The consumer and legislative dialogues that are already a long-functioning feature of the transatlantic relationship would certainly have a role to play in any question regarding equivalency.[37]

3.3.5 Arbitration or mediation?

The choice of either mediation or arbitration is not a central question for an instrument. Arbitration systems can be designed as 'soft' and mediation systems can be designed as 'hard'. Both can make factual findings and pose recommendations, and neither need necessarily be binding upon the parties for further action. Mediation is often characterized in the zone of a 'good offices' effort to bring the parties together and can be cast as more solution-oriented rather than judicial. However, the mediation process can certainly contain the formulation of an independent factual report that is at the core of the consideration here.

3.3.6 Selection of arbitrators/mediators

Due to the technical nature and variance of each proceeding, a standing body would not seem to be a realistic possibility, nor would it be typical of trade agreement arbitration systems. An expert panel selected for the determination at hand would be more appropriate. The default procedure is well known: each party chooses one panellist and either agrees on the third or the governing body appoints the third panellist. Because of the relationship to the trade agreement committee, an alternative procedure would be for all the panellists to be chosen by that committee, irrespective of the moving party in the proceeding.

There are other elements of arbitral or mediation bodies that could be considered, but are not taken up here. These include remedies for failure to implement recognition if a proceeding ultimately results in an agreement, and whether (and how) parties could generate an appeal if there was disagreement with a recommendation or a finding.

[37] For a statement of the consumer interest in regulatory issues in the transatlantic agreement negotiations, see Transatlantic Consumer Dialogue (TACD), 'EU and US Consumer Groups' Initial Reaction to the Announcement of a Transatlantic Trade and Investment Partnership', 5 March 2013, available at: http://www.citizen.org/documents/TACD-TAFTA-letter-3-5-13.pdf, accessed 20 February 2014.

4 WTO considerations

4.1 Sequence of examination and initial considerations

The subject of how WTO obligations and exceptions for regional trade agreements relate to recognition is well-travelled turf, though not all commentators are in accord on each point along the way. The main elements of WTO legal reference for equivalency or conformity assessment recognition are understood and set the sequence for this section. These include: the application of general most-favoured nation (MFN) rules for goods and services to recognition, and the possible relationship between these general obligations and the recognition provisions contained in the TBT and SPS agreements for goods, and the GATS for services. If these rules (separately or in combination) apply to recognition so as to suggest a possible WTO violation, then the final question is whether the WTO regional trade agreement exceptions for goods or services could excuse it.

In applying the WTO rules for equivalency recognition, there is an initial distinction to be drawn between a preferential recognition of another country's certifications (country-based), and a more restrictive form of recognition that is further limited to only the certificates for the goods or services of national origin of the recognized territory (origin-based).[38] Both types raise issues of application for the MFN obligation. For the second and more restrictive type, there should be general agreement that any recognition limited only to the products or services of national origin of the recognized territory is a red flag for a WTO MFN violation.[39] For the less restrictive form of country-based recognition, there appears to be some agreement that MFN is not violated, either by application of the general GATT rules alone or as they might be interpreted together

[38] Throughout, country-based recognition is referred to as 'open' while origin-based recognition is referred to as 'closed'. Other authors may be using the term 'closed' to refer to recognition that is not open for participation by other countries. See J. P. Trachtman, 'Toward Open Recognition? Standardization and Regional Integration Under Article XXIV of GATT' (2003) 6 *Journal of International Economic Law* 459–92.

[39] 'Should', because it is not always clear in the literature whether the discrimination finding being made is referencing conformity assessment or equivalence, or is based on a violating advantage being given to a country or to its products of origin. But for origin-based examples, see L. Bartels, 'The Legality of the EC Mutual Recognition Clause under WTO Law' (2006) 8 *Journal of International Economic Law* 691–720, at 696–7; P. Mavroidis, 'Transatlantic Regulatory Cooperation: Exclusive Club or "Open Regionalism"' in G. Bermann, Linsdseth and Herdegen (eds.), *Transatlantic Regulatory Cooperation: Legal and Political Prospects* (Oxford University Press, 2000), pp. 263–72, at p. 267 (Japan products example).

with the relevant SPS or TBT Agreement provisions. There is less clarity as to the participation rights of other WTO members to either join such an arrangement or be entitled to form a similar one.[40] Finally, if a closed recognition system contained in a regional trade agreement is found to violate GATT MFN rules, there is agreement that GATT Article XXIV will not provide a justification for that violation.[41]

4.2 *WTO MFN rules as applied to an equivalency recognition*

Since the subject of this chapter is equivalency recognition, one first inquires whether this form in practice operates in an open or closed manner for the purpose of applying the WTO MFN rules. Conformity assessment recognition is commonly portrayed as open since a national system that receives products for testing operates on a non-discriminatory basis, testing submitted foreign as well as domestic products. When the results of that testing process are recognized by another territory, it does not only recognize the testing data for products of origin from the territory of the conformity assessment.[42] This may be the same for equivalency

[40] J. P. Trachtman, 'The Limits of PTAs: WTO Legal Restrictions on the Use of WTO-Plus Standards Regulation in PTAs' in K. Bagwell and P. Mavroidis (eds.), *Preferential Trade Agreements: A Law and Economic Analysis* (Cambridge University Press, 2011), pp. 115–49, at p. 136 and sources cited in his n. 62, including Mavroidis, 'Transatlantic Regulatory Cooperation', p. 266. Trachtman's phrase is 'artificial, PTA-based limitations on the right to "qualify" for recognition'. Mavroidis is quoted in the note as saying: 'Any interpretation ... that the MFN principle precludes MRAs must be rejected, because it runs counter to the principle of "effective interpretation"'.

[41] The signatories of such a regional trade agreement would likely argue otherwise. The question has not been extensively treated for economic integration agreements under GATS Art. V, but see J. Mathis, 'Multilateral Aspects of Advanced Regulatory Cooperation: Considerations for a Canada–EU Comprehensive Trade Agreement (CETA)' (2012) 38 *Legal Issues of Economic Integration* 73–91. See also, GATS Art. V.6, defining service suppliers as juridical persons rather than on the basis of nationality. To the point of whether recognition qualifies under GATT Article XXIV, see J. Mathis, 'Regional Trade Agreements and Domestic Regulation: What Reach for "Other Restrictive Regulations of Commerce"?' in L. Bartels and F. Ortino (eds.), *Regional Trade Agreements and the WTO Legal System* (Oxford University Press, 2006), pp. 79–108, at p. 96. For EU mutual recognition, see Bartels, 'The Legality of the EC Mutual Recognition Clause', 713. A trending view based on analogous cases would also suggest that Article XXIV, limited as it is to the GATT, is not available for any violation based solely on an SPS or a TBT provision. B. Rigod, 'TBT-Plus Rules in Preferential Trade Agreements' (2013) 40 *Legal Issues of Economic Integration* 247–70, at 270.

[42] See WTO, 'The WTO and Preferential Trade Agreements: From Co-existence to Coherence', 2011, Economic Research and Statistics Division, 169, available at: www.wto.org/english/res_e/reser_e/wtr_e.htm, accessed 14 February 2014: 'In other areas, such

recognition. Using an example for services, if recognition is made of professional licences granted by another territory, it may well be that the territory's system of receiving applications for consideration and approval is not limited to its own nationals of origin. Thus, a foreign graduate of a US law school may qualify to take a State bar exam and receive a licence to practise law in that granting State. The law school is not limited to applications only from US nationals and neither is the bar examination. Since that system is not closed to foreigners, recognition of the law licence would, if the analogy to conformity assessment holds, also not be closed and, therefore, arguably not actionable on that basis alone according to WTO MFN rules.[43] This line of argument says that even while a benefit (recognition of certificates) may be conferred on another territory on a wholly preferential basis, the absence of an origin-based limitation in the system being recognized renders it consistent with MFN. For goods, GATT Article I refers to an advantage 'granted to any product originating in ... any other country' and requires that it be 'accorded immediately and unconditionally to the like product ... originating in ... all other contracting parties'. The interpretation above would consider this phrase as stating a product origin requirement in the act of recognition in order to trigger the MFN obligation to extend the advantage to the products of all other WTO members.[44]

4.3 *WTO rules as applied to an equivalency process*

This analysis of recognition focuses on the substantive act of granting it as either open or closed in respect of the origin of the products or the persons who may qualify for the benefit. The attention in this chapter has been more oriented to the institutional process of a regional equivalency

as mutual recognition agreements (MRAs) on testing, RoOs are absent.' 'RoOs' refers to Rules of Origin.

43 The analysis does not consider the possibility of a de facto origin-restricted national certification system. For services, national origin restrictions might also not even be effective in closing foreign participation, since foreign enterprises engaging in substantial business operations receive the same treatment as national enterprises in an economic integration agreement. See GATS Art. V.6.

44 This reasoning can be drawn from the AB Report in *Canada – Autos*, WT/DS142/AB/R, para. 86. The MFN obligation was found to apply de facto as well as *de jure*, but the point of the inquiry (and the found violation) was that the advantage was granted to products *of some countries* but not to others. The comparable GATS Article II 'Most-Favoured-Nation Treatment' text refers to treatment to be accorded to 'services and service supplies of any other Member no less favourable than it accords to like services and service suppliers *of any other country*' (author's emphasis).

instrument, assumedly operating on a purely bilateral basis. If the process underlying a recognition agreement may also constitute a measure, in the sense of applicable WTO rules and exceptions, then a more general question is raised as to how regional trade agreement exception rules in the WTO apply to regional institutional processes. If MFN can reach the more favourable treatment granted to one territory's product – and while a regional trade agreement exception may or may not validate this preferential treatment – does the same violation and exception apply in the same manner to the institutional process underlying that treatment granted, or are those processes somehow severable for treatment under the rules?

The view can be taken that the process is so inherently tied to its resulting act that the act of recognition should be examined solely under WTO rules, and its complementary institutional process should be validated or not according to the results of the act. For example, trade agreements commonly provide for a dispute settlement mechanism in the event that a party violates the agreement by failing to eliminate or reduce a tariff duty according to the committed plan and schedule of the parties. The preferential elimination of the duty is a violation of GATT MFN, but is also understood to be validated by GATT Article XXIV if it is part of a qualified customs union or free trade area. Since the elimination of the duty is covered by the scope of Article XXIV, this view would argue that the corresponding mechanism insuring compliance for that duty elimination is also covered by the regional exception. In other words, if the preference is not accessible to other WTO members by the operation of Article XXIV, then the process establishing that preference is also not accessible. To apply this reasoning to recognition, if an act of recognition violated GATT MFN and was validated by a WTO regional exception, then the process used to determine that act of recognition would also arguably be validated. If the preference was not validated by the WTO regional exception, then it is owed to all other WTO members immediately and unconditionally, and so is its process.

But what if the process itself is exclusively the subject of the action irrespective of its resulting act; that it is the preferential benefit of participating in a regional regulatory instrument or system that is viewed by a non-member as the advantage not being accorded to all other WTO members? This raises, in a different context, the same initial distinction made above (Section 4.1), of MFN's possible application to preferential recognition being accorded to one territory irrespective of an origin-based restriction.

As a general point of WTO law, an institutional process can, by itself, certainly be an actionable measure and the subject of a WTO trade dispute.[45] On this aspect alone, one could conclude that a preferential territory recognition, even if open as to the origin of the recognized products, could be analyzed as an advantage or benefit in the sense of GATT Article I MFN. However, as also noted above, the GATT's MFN obligation also requires that the advantage be accorded to a '*product originating in* ... any other country' (author's emphasis). The conclusion would then be that while the process is severable from the final act of recognition for the purpose of framing a WTO claim, the terms of MFN Article I would necessarily require a consideration of whether the process itself was directed to an origin-based benefit.

4.4 An equivalency institutional process as subject to other WTO equivalency provisions

If one uses effective or harmonious interpretation to bring in the TBT, SPS and GATS recognition provisions in conjunction with general MFN rules, the results may be the same. In GATS MFN the general obligation applies for any measure affecting the supply of a service.[46] GATS Article VII for 'Recognition' details how MFN applies to a recognition agreement for services. It requires notification 'as far in advance as possible' of prospective negotiations of an agreement, and requires that other members have adequate opportunity to negotiate an accession to it or to form a comparable agreement.[47] Thus, GATS allows *inter se* recognition agreements, but requires early transparency and a certain type of openness to other WTO members. The TBT Agreement does not have any explicit notation for equivalency agreements, but for agreements 'related to technical regulations' it requires notification to the WTO, and 'encourages' the members to be open to allowing participation in the agreement or to negotiate

[45] GATT national treatment rules have long been applied to institutional processes, as in *US – Section 337* (L/6439 – 36S/345), 7 November 1989, para. 5.10: 'For these reasons, the Panel found that the procedures under Section 337 come within the concept of "laws, regulations and requirements" affecting the internal sale of imported products, as set out in Article III of the General Agreement.' GATT Article I applies to those matters covered by GATT Article III.4.

[46] GATS Article II MFN applies to 'any measure covered by this Agreement'. GATS Article I says that '(t)his Agreement applies to measures by Members affecting trade in services'. Article II thus applies to any measure affecting trade in services.

[47] GATS Art. VII, paras. 2 and 4(b).

comparable ones.[48] Equivalency recognition is explicitly noted in the TBT Agreement's provision requiring members to give positive consideration to accepting as equivalent the technical regulations of other members, if they are satisfied that the regulations adequately fulfil the objectives of their own regulations.[49] The SPS Agreement does not mention recognition agreements but requires the acceptance of the SPS measures of other members on an objective demonstration that the measures achieve the importing member's appropriate level of protection.[50]

While all three of these provisions require a member to be receptive in varying degrees to recognizing another member's regulations, they do not clearly stamp the MFN obligation on equivalency recognition and are silent on any processes to be undertaken to consider that equivalency. Only the GATS provision refers to equivalency recognition agreements in its requirement that a member 'shall afford adequate opportunity' to negotiate accession to the agreement or negotiate a comparable one. It does not, however, appear to accord a right to enter that first negotiation being notified, nor to become a member in that agreement's system that is being used to generate later recognition agreements. What can be drawn from this is that when an equivalency determination between the transatlantic parties is commenced for services, since this could result in recognition, WTO notification would occur, and other members would have a right to have their certificate system recognized, but not necessarily by that same regional process. For the TBT, WTO notification would occur on the conclusion of the agreement, but the parties are only encouraged to consider the inclusion of other WTO members in the recognition. The TBT Agreement's Article 2, which contains the reference to equivalency in Article 2.7, is titled 'Preparation, Adoption and Application of Technical Regulations by Central Government Bodies'. One can argue that the 'positive consideration' required in Article 2.7 should be extended to the 'preparation', that is the process of that equivalency consideration, but the object of the Article is the recognition itself and it does not refer to the process by which it is made. This is similar to the SPS provision, which also only refers to the act of recognition on an objective showing of equivalency.

One can draw contradictory inferences from these provisions. If the TBT and SPS Articles are viewed as superseding the general MFN

48 TBT Agreement, Art. 10.7. The TBT Agreement explicitly encourages conformity assessment agreements, but without noting any participation requirements for other WTO members. TBT Agreement, Art. 6.3.

49 TBT Agreement, Art. 2.7.

50 SPS Agreement, Art. 4.1.

rules, then their silence on a WTO member's rights in respect of another member's recognition agreement could be viewed as terminating those rights to claim MFN for agreements falling within the scope of SPS or TBT equivalency recognition. If, however, a harmonious interpretation is considered, in which both sets of provisions are operable to the extent that one does not exclude the other, then all residual rights not modified by the specialized provisions would be in force and effect. This would mean that to the extent an institutional recognition process is captured by general MFN rules, either because of its preferential territorial treatment or because of its closed origin, then there is nothing in the TBT and SPS equivalency provisions that would affect that general MFN application.

4.5 *WTO regional trade agreement exceptions applied to an equivalency process*

Section 4.3 raised the possibility of institutional processes being captured by WTO MFN rules and considered how those processes would be validated or not by a regional trade agreement exception. The idea was raised that the process could be linked to its resulting act and be validated or not accordingly. If that is accepted, then only a short summation is necessary to consider how equivalency recognition does or does not fall within the scope of the WTO regional trade agreement exceptions. For a trade agreement dealing with goods, the question is whether Article XXIV's term 'other restrictive regulations of commerce' is broad enough to capture preferential recognition. The exception is only available for aspects that are required (necessary) to be enacted in order to fulfil the definition of a qualified regional trade agreement.[51] That definition provides that a free trade area or customs union 'shall be understood to mean' that 'duties and other restrictive regulations of commerce are eliminated with respect to substantially all trade between the constituent territories'. If recognition is an elimination of a barrier to trade that falls within the scope of 'other restrictive regulation of commerce' (ORRC), then the preferential recognition would come within the scope of Article XXIV for the purpose of the exception. A narrow reading of the term suggests that

[51] *Turkey – Textiles*, WT/DS34/AB/R, para. 58: '... that the measure at issue is introduced upon the formation of a customs union that fully meets the requirements of sub-paragraph 8(a) and 5(a) of Article XXIV. Second, the party must demonstrate that the formation of that customs union would be prevented if it were not allowed to introduce the measure at issue.'

the underlying barrier of a varying product regulation, it being itself neither discriminatory nor an internal quantitative restriction, would not qualify as an ORRC to be eliminated.[52] To suggest otherwise would infer that it would be 'necessary' for all qualifying regional trade agreements to engage in equivalency recognition in order to eliminate these types of non-tariff barriers.

The analysis for GATS Article V (Economic Integration) is similar. Members are permitted to engage in an economic integration agreement provided that the agreement has substantial sector coverage and eliminates discrimination in the sense of GATS Article XVIII (National Treatment).[53] The act of 'covering sectors', though not made explicit in the text, suggests that the action required for the sectors is to eliminate market access restrictions, in the sense of those listed in GATS Article XVI (Market Access). The listing there mainly refers to quantitative-type restrictions, including the number of service providers, the value of service transactions, the number of service operations and so on.[54] Similar to the result for GATT Article XXIV's reference to 'other restrictive regulations of commerce', the Article XVI restrictions to be treated do not appear to include the types of non-tariff barriers that are addressed by equivalency recognition.

Although the scope of GATS Article V does not provide for additional substantive qualification requirements, the two requirements that are contemplated by the Article fall within the section of GATS Part III dedicated to 'Specific Commitments'. GATS Article XVIII 'Additional Commitments' is also part of that section, which could suggest that what qualifies as an 'additional commitment' for the purpose of making specific commitments in the GATS might also be a part of an economic integration agreement for the purpose of qualifying for the GATS Article V exception. The scope of scheduling possibilities under Article XVIII could at least contemplate including regulatory recognition.[55] This would, however, require an interpretation of GATS Article VII (Recognition)

[52] As cited for the scope of ORRC, see n. 41.

[53] GATS Art. V, paras. 1(a) and (b).

[54] GATS Art. XVI, paras. (a)–(f). Paragraph (e) does refer to measures restricting types of legal entity or joint venture, a non-quantitative restriction.

[55] WTO, Guidelines for the Scheduling of Specific Commitments under the General Agreement on Trade in Services (GATS), S/L/92, 28 March 2001, 7: 'Such commitments can include, but are not limited to, undertakings with respect to qualifications, technical standards, licensing requirements or procedures, and other domestic regulations that are consistent with Article VI.' This is also discussed in Mathis, 'Multilateral Aspects of Advanced Regulatory Cooperation', 85–6.

that would 'carve out' economic integration agreements from recognition agreements as referred to in that Article.

For both goods and services, a broader argument is required to make the case for excusing closed equivalency recognition as a part of a qualified regional trade agreement. This view would emphasize that a qualified trade agreement's legitimate and recognized purpose is to facilitate trade, as noted in GATT Article XXIV.4. To limit the scope of what trade-facilitating activities may be permitted on a preferential basis within a trade agreement to a narrow set of border and discriminatory measures not only undermines the reality of how liberalization proceeds in the current international economic order, but also renders the WTO Agreement's interpretation in a wholly static manner. The WTO regional agreement provisions should not be interpreted as a straitjacket confining bilateral liberalization agreements to only the border measures of interest in the original 1947 GATT Agreement. Rather, since the condoned purpose of a trade agreement is to facilitate trade, then any aspect that furthers that objective in a bilateral trade agreement should also fall within the scope of the regional exceptions.

One can chisel away at the issue of the static or dynamic character of the Vienna Convention rule on the interpretation of a treaty provision and whether the WTO Appellate Body has viewed it one way or the other. Prospective speculation aside, one cannot foretell how restrictively or expansively the term 'other restrictive regulation of commerce' would be interpreted in a WTO case.[56] What might be more constructive is for WTO members to get on with a discussion clarifying that term, with the purpose of reaching an understanding that would set the balance between preferential non-tariff barrier instruments and the rights of WTO members. So far there has been little guidance from the WTO members that could be applied as a point of reference by a panel or the Appellate Body.[57]

5 Conclusion

The point of this balance may be found in the distinction between permitting preferential territorial recognition and not permitting preferential

[56] Vienna Convention on the Law of Treaties, 23 May 1961, Article 31, 'General rule of interpretation ... 1. A treaty shall be interpreted in good faith in accordance with the ordinary meaning to be given to the terms of the treaty in their context and in the light of its object and purpose.'

[57] As indicated by the Chairman of the Negotiating Group on Rules in 2010, work cannot advance on regional trade agreement systemic issues in the absence of text-based proposals. Report of the Chairman, TN/RL/24, 22 March 2010.

origin-based restrictions. Allowing the first but not the second would permit the treatment of non-tariff barriers in a more intensive regional institutional process. This would facilitate trade, but without overly restricting the current open character of conformity assessment systems. While the territorial process would remain preferential to the parties of the agreement, the results could nevertheless be viewed as 'multilateralizing' the benefits of recognition for the goods and services of third countries. This might be a satisfactory outcome that allows the experimentation offered by a more intensive regional instrument.

While this chapter has called for this more intensive and effective instrument, the other side of the coin is that such an instrument also suggests a more preferential treatment of non-tariff barriers. While the United States and the European Union may be uniquely qualified to seek out such an instrument, its implementation would also have effects on the multilateral trading system. There, the transatlantic parties are also somewhat unique, not only for the size of their markets but also for their role in facilitating (or not facilitating) legal developments in the WTO.

This leads us to ask: could a well-functioning regional instrument set an example for more universal participation? If shifting the process of recognition from the intractable issues of conformity assessment negotiations to a functional equivalency determination is an effective means of addressing these types of barriers, then there is an additional benefit to be gained by refining such an instrument and bringing it to the attention of others who might wish to join it. The softer mediation and recommendation style of the EU–Korea non-tariff measures instrument discussed earlier has also been proposed for consideration in the WTO. That is a constructive step that the transatlantic parties can support even as they explore their own regional approach. It can be hoped that the results of that exploration can also contribute to a more productive discussion in the WTO on how to address non-tariff barriers in international trade.

9

A postnational marketplace: negotiating the Transatlantic Trade and Investment Partnership (TTIP)

MARIJA BARTL AND ELAINE FAHEY

Introduction

Transatlantic regulatory cooperation has in general been a 'swift' rather than a 'deep' affair, unlike its disputes, which often appear to run longer than its agreements.[1] Arising from its last major framework, the New Transatlantic Agenda (NTA) of 1995, nine formal binding and non-binding regulatory cooperation agreements had been entered into between the EU and USA in areas as diverse as competition, privacy, customs and veterinary standards by 2003.[2] Nonetheless, at whatever stage of its development, transatlantic cooperation has posed major challenges for regulatory independence, transparency and administrative law requirements, confidentiality, multilevel governance and regulatory sovereignty.[3]

These themes have come to the fore in recent times since the G8 Summit in Lough Erne in June 2013, which saw the launch of the agreement by the USA to begin negotiations between the EU and USA on a Transatlantic Trade and Investment Partnership (TTIP hereafter). The scale of the collaboration between two of the world's leading economies with an

Thanks to Christina Eckes, Martijn Hesselink, Machiko Kanetake, Chantal Mak, Eljalill Tauschinsky, Maria Weimer and Jonathan Zeitlin for their comments on an earlier draft of this chapter. The chapter reflects the state of affairs as to the first round of TTIP negotiations only.

1 See the summary by the Library of the European Parliament, 'Principal EU–US Disputes', 22 April 2013, available at: www.europarl.europa.eu/RegData/bibliotheque/briefing/2013/130518/LDM_BRI(2013)130518_REV1_EN.pdf, accessed 15 February 2014.

2 On the NTA, see M. Pollack *et al.*, *The Political Economy of the Transatlantic Partnership*, EUI Report (Florence: Robert Schuman Centre for Advanced Studies, 2003).

3 See M. Pollack and G. Shaffer (eds.), *Transatlantic Governance in the Global Economy* (Lanham, MD: Rowman & Littlefield, 2001).

ambitious timeframe for negotiations is unparalleled, with the aim to be completed before the end of 2014. With the combined economies of the EU and USA accounting for almost 40 per cent of global gross domestic product (GDP) and approximately a third of global economic trade, the TTIP has thus been touted as a dramatic kick-start to the global economy. The opening of negotiations on a TTIP was commenced after the Report of the EU–US High-Level Working Group on Jobs and Growth.[4] There, the suggestion was developed that the negotiations would explore market access, regulatory issues and non-tariff barriers, and rules, principles, and new modes of cooperation, to address shared global trade challenges and opportunities.

The TTIP purports to develop a multi-level postnational marketplace that would deepen and prospectively *institutionalise* EU–US relations in a range of fields – such as pharmaceuticals, chemicals, public procurement or motor vehicles – and also through a Regulatory Cooperation Council with rule-making capacity.[5] The TTIP negotiations expressly involve the discussion of the prospective revision and renegotiations of a broad range of existing EU laws, rules and standards of the *acquis communautaire* and will thus progress far beyond the technical scope of the last EU–US Mutual Recognition Agreement from 1997.[6] This form of institutionalisation and prospective renegotiation of EU laws, rules and standards is unprecedented in an EU international trade agreement. It is an exercise that is also strikingly legally complex if brought to its full fruition, not

[4] Established after the EU–US Summit in 2011, followed by an Interim Report on 19 June 2012. See Final Report, High-Level Working Group on Jobs and Growth, 11 February 2013, available at: http://trade.ec.europa.eu/doclib/docs/2013/february/tradoc_150519.pdf, accessed 15 February 2014.

[5] See Article 43 of the leaked Directives for the negotiation on the Transatlantic Trade and Investment Partnership between the EU and US (Brussels, 17 June 2013): 'The Agreement will set up an institutional structure to ensure an effective follow-up of the commitments under the Agreement, as well as to promote the progressive achievement of compatibility of regulatory regimes.' See Suggestion for a Regulatory Cooperation Council by Commissioner de Gucht, placing institutionalisation as the third pillar of the EU's negotiation goals: speech delivered in Czech Republic, 10 October 2013, No. 13/801.

[6] The 1997 Agreement is viewed as having a very limited scope and as having been hampered by a multiplicity of actors involved in its implementation: see G. Shaffer, 'Reconciling Trade and Regulatory Roles: The Prospects and Limits of New Approaches to Transatlantic Governance through Mutual Recognition and Safe Harbor Agreements' (2002) 9 *Columbia Journal of European Law* 29; K. Nicolaidis and G. Shaffer, 'Transnational Mutual Recognition Regimes: Governance Without Global Government' (2005) 68 *Law & Contemporary Problems* 263.

least because of its multi-level nature.[7] The TTIP differs from historical EU–US regulatory cooperation, where the EU and USA could often learn from each other and in theory 'compete' to produce the best result. Some have argued that such regulatory competition between the EU and US legal orders has historically accorded legitimation to its rule-making. Of course, this is no longer relevant in deeper integration and evolving institutionalisation.[8] The TTIP raises the issue, then, whether it may legitimately be classified as a conventional international trade instrument at all, not least for the purposes of the procedures that apply to its approval and ratification, pursuant to Article 218 of the Treaty on the Functioning of the European Union (TFEU). Furthermore, it poses the question as to *who* sets the normative agenda for these far-reaching negotiations and *how* this specific agenda reflects EU values and standards as a postnational democracy.

Much emphasis has been placed both at the outset and during the TTIP negotiations on the substantive and procedural consent of the European Parliament and US Congress, along with Member State parliaments. From an EU perspective, EU international trade agreements post-Lisbon are formally legitimated in a new dynamic of European Parliament scrutiny and enhanced transparency practices of heightened involvement, pursuant to Article 218 TFEU and an Inter-Institutional Framework Agreement. In this regard, two specific issues of this institutional context of and for legitimation must be remarked upon. First, the European Parliament recently voted down the Anti-Counterfeiting Trade Agreement (ACTA) on fundamental rights grounds after battling to procure transparency in its negotiation.[9] One may question what kind of precedent this creates for the TTIP – in particular when it comes to the questions of transparency raised by this chapter.[10] Yet having received the information, in its view

[7] For example, the outcome of EU Member States raising cultural 'exemptions', e.g. French audiovisual exemptions, or the existence of Buy America Laws on the statute books of twenty US States: 'Buy America Laws Raise Hurdles in European Talks', *Financial Times*, 26 June 2013. EU cultural 'exceptions' were supported by the European Parliament and were included in Article 9 of the (leaked) negotiating mandate and European Parliament Resolution of 23 May 2013 (2013/2558(RSP)).

[8] R. Howse, 'Transatlantic Regulatory Cooperation and the Problem of Democracy' in G. Bermann *et al.* (eds.), *Transatlantic Regulatory Cooperation: Legal Problems and Political Prospects* (Oxford University Press, 2000).

[9] See C. Eckes, E. Fahey and M. Kanetake, 'International, European and US Perspectives on the Negotiation and Adoption of the Anti-Counterfeiting Trade Agreement (ACTA)' (2012) 20 (2) *Currents* 20.

[10] See D. Curtin, 'Official Secrets and the Negotiation of International Agreements: Is the EU Executive Unbound?' (2013) 50 *Common Market Law Review* 423.

too late, the European Parliament voted against the Agreement. Whether this ameliorates its political or legal input into international trade agreements still seems an open question.

Second, the recent US surveillance saga has brought to the surface the place of norm-setting and parliamentary accountability in EU–US relations. The European Parliament inquiry on the affair ongoing at the time of writing has been explicitly linked to the TTIP.[11] It has threatened to refuse to consent to the TTIP Agreement in the event of an unsatisfactory outcome to its inquiry, building upon its efforts to meaningfully influence the content of EU–US relations, as it did in the recent EU–US Passenger Name Records Agreements and the EU–US Terrorist Financial Tracking Programme, as a norm-setter.[12] In respect of the TTIP, such an institutional context is indeed a significant one. However, taken together with the treaty provisions in Article 218 TFEU, it may be said to comprise largely *ex post facto* input, which is not necessarily of benefit to the unique nature of the TTIP. It is argued here that the emphasis placed in the negotiations on parliamentary legitimation serves to shield and obscure the role of other actors involved in the setting of the normative agenda of this new (multi-level) postnational marketplace.[13]

Accordingly, Section 1 of this chapter focuses upon the manner in which the Commission has employed 'knowledge' to justify the TTIP, and singles out the role of private actors and independent contractors in this exercise. Section 2 investigates the emergent institutions of the TTIP. Analysing the institutional chapter of the 'non-papers', the section examines both the implications of the proposed institutional framework as well as the implications of the less advertised investor–state dispute settlement mechanism (ISDS). We turn then to discuss the horizontal chapter of the non-papers. Establishing the TTIP as a new level of functional market integration carries specific democratic and epistemic risks. These risks

[11] 'Key US–EU Trade Pact under Threat after More NSA Spying Allegations', *Guardian*, 30 June 2013, available at: www.theguardian.com/world/2013/jun/30/nsa-spying-europe-claims-us-eu-trade, accessed 15 February 2014.

[12] E.g. A. Ripoll Servent and A. MacKenzie, 'The European Parliament as a "Norm Taker"? EU–US Relations after the SWIFT Agreement' (2012) 17 *European Foreign Affairs Review* 71. Nonetheless, as this surveillance saga unfolded, the EU and USA reached a temporary agreement on financial derivatives instruments worth $500 trillion, emphasising the sectoral autonomy of EU–US cooperation. See 'US and EU Seal Landmark Derivatives Deal', *Financial Times*, 11 July 2013.

[13] In making this distinction and general contention, we do not necessarily espouse the views of, e.g., P. Lindseth, *Power and Legitimacy: Reconciling Europe and the Nation State* (Oxford University Press, 2011) on the character of the EU polity and its legitimacy.

are further enhanced by the stress on international standards and 'scientific' evidence, while at the same time the Commission's non-papers lack reference to the precautionary principle. As a result, the operation of the European Parliament's right to approve or reject such an agreement must inevitably be seen to be highly circumscribed and 'after the fact'. We argue in Section 3 that parliamentary approval powers cannot neutralise or limit the shortcomings in the general conduct of the negotiations in their first and opening round, as the subject and object of the analysis here. The chapter concludes with a call for more thorough and meaningful democratic scrutiny.

1 Crafting the TTIP

1.1 Who formulates the agenda?

The evolution of the TTIP commenced in 2011 with the establishment of the EU–US High-Level Working Group on Jobs and Growth (HLWG) hereafter. The HLWG was tasked with identifying policies and measures to increase EU–US trade and investment, to support mutually beneficial job creation, economic growth and international competitiveness. In particular, it was asked to work closely with all public and private sector stakeholder groups, and to draw on existing dialogues and mechanisms as appropriate.[14] This group has produced an influential six-page report, widely deployed in public discourse and drawn upon by the Commission's 'non-papers'. The report is an ode to the benefits of economic integration – both *in abstracto* as well as in the case of EU–US relations. The main message of the report is that the deepest possible economic integration between the two partners should be preferred. It states that:

> an agreement of this kind [most comprehensive trade agreement] could generate new business and employment by significantly expanding trade and investment opportunities in both economies; pioneer rules and disciplines that address challenges to global trade and investment that have grown in importance in recent years; and further strengthen the extraordinarily close strategic partnership between the United States and Europe.[15]

[14] European Commission, 'EU–US High-Level Working Group on Jobs and Growth', available at: http://ec.europa.eu/enterprise/policies/international/cooperating-governments/usa/jobs-growth/, accessed 15 February 2014.

[15] HLWG Final Report, 2.

In order to analyse the content of the report, it is necessary to reflect upon the membership and the task of the group. Thus, who has participated in this group? The first significant issue worthy of reflection is that the membership of the group is not made public on the website of the EU Commission, just the names of two chairs, the EU Trade Commissioner and the US Trade Representative. This secrecy seems to be a deliberate decision: the Brussels-based non-governmental organisation (NGO) Corporate Europe Observatory has tried on numerous occasions to obtain this information from the European Commission pursuant to freedom of information requests. The Commission has responded to the requests by saying that '[t]here is no full membership list of High-Level Working Group on Jobs and Growth (HLWG)' or '[u]nfortunately we are not in a position to provide you with the information requested as your request does fall outside the purpose of Regulation No. 1049/2001 regarding public access to European Parliament, Council and Commission documents. As mentioned before, there is no document containing the list of authors of the reports prepared by the High-Level Working Group on Jobs and Growth (HLWG).'[16] Finally, the information has been made available to the NGO and the public by the US administration. This emphasises the place of transparency in the negotiations, considered further below in Section 3.

As already mentioned, the HLWG has been chaired by the highest EU and US trade officials. The ordinary members of the HLWG were the executive officials of the European Commission and US administration. A notable issue is that – unlike the US – the European Commission has not nominated any representatives of the Labour and Environment Directorates General to take part in the preparation of the report. One can readily argue that the representatives of the Directorate General for Trade, Enterprise and Industry (DG Trade) and the Directorate General for Internal Market and Services (DG Internal Market) should have defended these normative concerns.[17]

Vast scholarship addresses the question of disciplinary or functional bias of 'trade' officials (broadly construed), the institutions

[16] www.asktheeu.org/en/request/high_level_working_group_on_jobs, accessed 15 February 2014.

[17] The list of members of the HLWG is not accessible on the website of the Commission. It can be found at the website of Corporate Observatory Europe, which was unsuccessful in claiming the documents from the European Commission, and received them only from the US administration: http://corporateeurope.org/sites/default/files/hlwg-members.pdf, accessed 15 February 2014.

committed to the 'free trade'/'open markets' mandate (such as the World Trade Organization (WTO), International Monetary Fund (IMF), World Bank (WB) or the EU) as well as the mechanisms of the entrenchment of this bias.[18] This line of critique holds that the normative commitment to free trade and open markets will tend to shunt other normative concerns to a secondary status – reinterpreting these as a 'by-product' of the primary normative concern.[19] This tendency may be observed in the report presenting labour and environmental goals as a by-product of market integration.[20]

1.1.1 To whom does the HLWG listen?

The second question that we need to address is stakeholder participation in the preparation of the HLWG Report. The HLWG Report claims that the group 'has engaged intensively with key stakeholders – including business, environmental, consumer, labor, and other representatives'.[21] First, let us offer some crude numbers here. In the initial consultations on the TTIP, out of the 48 stakeholders consulted, 3 stakeholders were the representatives of states, 2 stakeholders were private parties and finally 43 stakeholders were the industry representatives or their representative organisations.[22] In the latest consultations, out of 52 submissions, only one submission did not come from industry.[23] To be sure, the information regarding the so-called 'public consultation', both the stakeholders'

[18] We cannot do justice to a broad literature that stands behind this claim, and even less to larger socio-theoretical literature on which it builds. Thus we provide a few select examples: A. L. St. Clair, 'The World Bank as a Transnational Expertised Institution' (2006) 12 *Global Governance: A Review of Multilateralism and International Organizations* 77; D. Kennedy, 'Challenging Expert Rule: The Politics of Global Governance' (2005) 27 *Sydney Law Review* 2; P. C. Schmitter, 'Neo-neofunctionalism' in A. Weiner and T. Diez (eds.), *European Integration Theory* (Oxford University Press, 2004); M. Bartl, 'Internal Market Rationality, Private Law and the Direction of the Union: Resuscitating the Market as the Object of the Political in the EU', *European Law Journal* (forthcoming).

[19] As the above-cited paragraph of the HLWG Report suggests, the employment is an automatic product of more free trade: it does not require a self-standing consideration.

[20] The HLWG, in spite of its name, makes only a general sweeping statement regarding the benefit of trade integration at the level of employment. The non-papers on the other hand posit that the possible environmental costs of the TTIP will be offset by trade in environmental goods.

[21] HLWG Final Report, 2

[22] http://trade.ec.europa.eu/consultations/documents/consul_147.pdf, accessed 15 February 2014.

[23] http://ec.europa.eu/enterprise/policies/international/cooperating-governments/usa/jobs-growth/consultation-on-regulatory-issues_en.htm, accessed 15 February 2014.

submissions and the Commission's summary or report, again is not available on the Commission's website.[24] Industry participation and support also continue to be a crucial source of ideas and legitimacy in the Commission's non-paper, which states that:

> The purpose of this paper is to present some possible elements for a TTIP annex on pharmaceutical products. *It is based on ideas put forward by EU and US industry and builds on existing cooperation between EU and US regulators in this area.* It is anticipated that stakeholders will continue to support the process and could play an active role towards the implementation of some of the identified objectives.[25]

'Industry' is hardly a uniform group with a common interest, raising the question as to which industry is then supplying ideas to the rule-makers. The participants in the consultations were mainly lobbying firms, industry associations or large industry. The empirical question as to whose interests these entities represent goes well beyond the scope of this chapter, yet the link with the mentioned 'Business Dialogue' may ground an informed intuition. The account of transatlantic dialogues by Green Cowles posits that the Business Dialogue had given a 'privileged access' to the European Commission to the largest EU and US industries.[26] Thus, aside of the consideration that the highest resources and highest incentives available to large industry influence the process, this previously established proximity may further tilt the balance towards furthering their particular interests.

One may also wonder whether we should base the regulation on the ideas provided by the industry. The regulatory mixture of industry and regulators equally falls short of the optimal mix that would represent the common citizens of either the EU or the USA. While industry can hardly be considered as an impartial representative of the common interest, a large body of literature on 'regulatory capture' demonstrates that groups and individuals with high stakes in the outcome of regulatory decisions can gain influence over the regulatory agencies.[27] They do so through lobbying, 'revolving doors' whereby the officials come from/go to industry

[24] http://trade.ec.europa.eu/consultations/index.cfm?consul_id=169, accessed 15 February 2014.

[25] Non-papers, Pharmaceuticals, 14 (authors' emphasis). See the full list at http://trade.ec.europa.eu/doclib/press/index.cfm?id=943, accessed 15 February 2014 (hereafter non-papers).

[26] M. Cowles, J. Caporaso and T. Risse-Kappen (eds.), *Transforming Europe: Europeanization and Domestic Change* (Ithaca: Cornell University Press, 2001), p. 163.

[27] This literature goes back to G. Stigler, 'The Economic Theory of Regulation' (1971) 2 *Bell Journal of Economics* 3.

and, most importantly, through intellectual capture. The 'understanding' among industry and regulators is hence enhanced as a consequence of dependency on industry for information, cooperation, or shared professional, social or educational background.[28] The threat of regulatory capture increases with the growth of regulatory units.[29] As we learn from the accompanying documents, the TTIP would be the greatest market in the world. In this light, the sole fact that the Commission is presenting the ideas of 'industry and regulators' as a one self-supporting intellectual unit should be considered as problematic.

1.1.2 Who is to assess the impact of the TTIP?

A significant democratic concern regarding the process comes from yet another corner. While consulting stakeholders has so far usually implied listening to industry, assessing the impact of the TTIP has been contracted out to 'independent contractors'. The much-publicised and disseminated report of the London-based think tank CEPR, commissioned by the DG Trade,[30] has supplied the basic hard data, for example, the economic growth of €119 billion a year for the EU, for the discourse of the Commission and other political actors. This practice of outsourcing appears in the TTIP in other ways. For example, the Commission has stated that:

> Now that the negotiations have begun, the European Commission will launch a trade sustainability impact assessment (Trade SIA). The Trade SIA will look particularly at the potential environmental and social impacts of the TTIP. It will be done by *an independent contractor* and will include a representative consultation process involving stakeholders and civil society from both the EU and the US. The process will provide genuine opportunities for consultation, information gathering, and dissemination of results.[31]

[28] Many attribute the latest financial crisis to the (multi-level) regulatory capture of the financial regulators. A. Baker, 'Restraining Regulatory Capture? Anglo-America, Crisis Politics and Trajectories of Change in Global Financial Governance' (2010) 86 *International Affairs* 647.

[29] A. Hamilton, 'Small Is Beautiful, at Least in High-Income Democracies: The Distribution of Policy-Making Responsibility, Electoral Accountability, and Incentives for Rent Extraction', World Bank Policy Research Working Paper No. 6305 (2013), available at: http://papers.ssrn.com/sol3/papers.cfm?abstract_id=2197676, accessed 15 February 2014.

[30] 'Independent Study Outlines Benefits of EU–US Trade Agreement', 12 March 2013, available at: http://europa.eu/rapid/press-release_MEMO-13-211_en.htm, accessed 15 February 2014.

[31] The Frequently Asked Questions to the TTIP, available at: http://ec.europa.eu/trade/policy/in-focus/ttip/questions-and-answers/, accessed 15 February 2014 (authors' emphasis).

'Outsourcing' impact assessment is democratically problematic, but is not exceptional practice for the European Commission. However, it becomes very troubling in the case of the TTIP, where we are not faced with a conventional treaty or routine legislation but rather the emergence of a new institutional framework that should put in place a new layer of functional market integration. We pose the question, is outsourcing the analysis of 'impact' truly appropriate in such a case?

One of the reasons for outsourcing a task is the procurement of 'impartial expertise'. Yet there are number of concerns in respect of the 'impartiality' of these contractors. A lack of conflict of interest is normally ensured through a 'no conflict of interests' declaration and/or the declarations of professional honesty and diligence. Yet one may doubt the sufficiency of such guarantees. The financial dependency of consultancies on the contractee (the European Commission in this case) renders any declarations of the lack of conflict of interest rather futile. Surely no one will be surprised that CEPR has brought forward the results entirely in line with what the contractee (the European Commission) sought.

More importantly, however, the 'outsourcing' suggests that the information regarding the benefits and costs of the TTIP is an uncontroversial and objective set of facts, which only needs to be collected and calculated by – essentially – anyone. Yet this operates to misrepresent the political nature of the information on which these reports are based: it is not natural facts, but rather interpretative, controversial and political concepts or economic theories that ground these data.[32] Outsourcing the impact assessments, along with the 'technical' presentation of data, aims to avoid the problematisation of the information that underpins the reports. This is a major concern, for both epistemic and democratic reasons.

As a result, we now turn to examine the precise recommendations and calculations of this contractor.

1.2 The benefits of the TTIP

The CEPR report has so far served as a main justificatory tool for asserting the overwhelming positive impact of the TTIP. The report's main conclusions are that, first, the most comprehensive trade deal with the EU will bring an economic benefit of €119 billion a year for the EU, and €95 billion a year for the USA. This benefit, according to the report, translates to an extra €545 in disposable income each year for a family of four in the EU.

[32] See, for instance, R. Dworkin, *Justice for Hedgehogs* (Harvard University Press, 2011).

Second, it reports that the TTIP will benefit the rest of the world, increasing global GDP by €100 billion per year.

Several issues are raised by the 'marketed' or touted €119 billion a year benefit to be generated by the TTIP. First, this prediction is based on the deepest integration scenario considered by the report. This impact can be achieved only through the most comprehensive level of economic integration imaginable. As the previous history of transatlantic relations suggests, to achieve such level of integration is far from simple.[33]

More importantly, however, one has to inquire whether the knowledge on which the report is based is reliable – and thus whether the promised positive impacts will actually take place. There is indeed little certainty that the 'best available' knowledge has come to the fore in the preparation of the report. In fact, the report relies on methodology, which as a matter of principle always confirms the benefits of trade liberalisation,[34] while the CEPR's study in particular is based on several problematic assumptions.[35]

The other crucial question is the redistribution of the benefits of the TTIP – not mentioned in any of the documents accompanying the negotiations. The report touches on this issue when it expounds TTIP benefits as bringing €545 for a family of four in the EU. While such information may sound attractive to some European citizens, it is misleading. The estimate is based on the arithmetic average of the expected benefits of the TTIP – thus entirely circumventing the question of the real redistributory impact. Such use of 'arithmetic' data then underpins a broader structure in the

[33] See F. De Ville, 'Deconstructing the Transatlantic Trade and Investment Partnership Rationale: A Game Changer, but in What Way?' (unpublished manuscript), on file with the authors.

[34] See, for instance, the account produced for Oxfam: L. Taylor and R. Von Arnim, *Modelling the Impact of Trade Liberalisation: A Critique of Computable General Equilibrium Models* (Oxford: Oxfam International, 2007).

[35] EuroMemorandum Report 2014, available at: www.euromemo.eu, accessed 15 February 2014: 'The CEPR study feeds the results from the ECORYS study into a computable general equilibrium model. This raises a number of further questions about the final results obtained, not least on who would gain from the new arrangement. Firstly, the changes in wages projected by CEPR, for both the EU and the US, are almost exactly the same as the changes in GDP, which means that labour (wages) shares proportionally in productivity gains with capital (i.e. gross profits). This would require a major historical change of direction, as it is entirely out of line with the historical experience over the last decades. Both in the US and the EU wages continually lost share from the mid-1970s, e.g. in the EU the wage share declined more or less steadily from 67% of GDP to 57% before the crisis. Secondly, the study assumes that there is no long-term unemployment. In other words, it is assumed that all those who are unemployed will find jobs in the other sectors. This is completely unrealistic for a variety of reasons including that there is in fact a high

discourse of the European Commission. The discourse of the 'common interest' that permeates the EU political rationality disguises the diversity of interests among various groups of citizens and the EU Member States, as well as various regions within Member States.[36] The original assumptions of EU integration – free trade and market integration – are difficult to reconcile with the idea that interests could possibly differ to the extent that market integration with the USA may harm, for instance, the peripheral EU Member States.[37] Such ideas are also foreclosed from consideration in the TTIP framework.

A third pillar of the TTIP justificatory benefits are those for third countries. Thus the report of the CEPR suggests that the TTIP will benefit third countries and increase their GDP by €100 billion. Yet the 'alternative' scenarios of future economic integration may dilute, or even harm, third countries. The HLWG Report suggests that the mutual recognition framework may not be applicable to third countries:

> Instead, the expected approach to be followed in the negotiations with the US would focus on regulatory coherence and a degree of mutual recognition between the EU and the US standards, particularly in the field of safety regulation relevant for electrical and electronic equipment. Sector experts assume that bilateral negotiations with the US would mainly lead *to bilateral and not erga omnes recognition of standards*. This in turn would mean, contrary to the 20% general spillover effect assumed, a significantly more limited spillover effect in this sector, or even none at all.[38]

According to De Ville, this paragraph may suggest that third countries would still have to comply with *two* sets of rules, depending on the market

and growing level of long-term unemployment in Europe, and that the new jobs may be, for example, in Eastern EU countries with much lower wage levels than in the countries losing jobs, and resulting mobility to these countries is most unlikely. Thirdly, further assumptions in the model are that perfect competition is assumed in 15 out of the 20 sectors in the model, including, remarkably, in finance, insurance and motor transport equipment. Perfect competition means that any gains in costs are passed on to customers, and most of the gains from the deal as projected in the model are assumed to be in that form. Much more prevalent in modern capitalism, however, is oligopolies, including in the sectors mentioned above, where much of the savings through productivity increases are not passed on to consumers.'

[36] A more general critique has been very powerfully raised by D. Kukovec, 'A Critique of the Rhetoric of Common Interest in the EU Legal Discourse', SSRN Scholarly Paper (Rochester, NY: Social Science Research Network, 13 April 2012), available at: http://papers.ssrn.com/abstract=2178332, accessed 15 February 2014.

[37] See G. Myrdal, *Economic Theory and Under-developed Regions* (New York: Harper and Row, 1957).

[38] See European Commission, Impact Assessment Report on the Future of EU–US Trade Relations, SWD(2013) 68 final, p. 41 (authors' emphasis).

to which they export. They would be thus disadvantaged in this way in comparison with EU/US companies.[39] We conclude, then, that the economic benefits of an agreement, that is the redistributory impact of the TTIP, as well as its impact upon third countries – often developing countries – needs to be problematised if the agreement is to be based upon truly solid knowledge.

2 Emerging institutions

The 'institutional' questions are dealt with in the Commission's non-papers in two separate chapters. The institutional chapter deals with the bodies and procedures that should be put in place. The horizontal chapter puts forth, one may say, 'constitutional' provisions, such as the objectives of the TTIP, which are relevant for the whole economic integration enterprise and across various specific sectors. We address both chapters in turn.

2.1 The institutions of the TTIP

In the institutional chapter, the European Commission has proposed an institutionalised framework for the TTIP, which should have '[s]trong institutions … [which are] … key to making the TTIP a living agreement that promotes greater compatibility of our regimes and accelerates the development of global approaches'.[40] It envisages a threefold structure: the institutionalisation of the consultation in market regulation, a streamlined procedure for amending the sector-specific annexes without ratification, and eventually the establishment of the Regulatory Committee, assisted by sector-specific advisory committees.[41] The envisaged 'consultations' between the EU and the USA shall play a significant role in the review of current legislation and non-necessary behind-the-border barriers, as well as timely consultation about future regulatory initiatives. Even if it may appear to be the instrument that intrudes least into 'domestic' regulatory environments, the HLGW as well as the Commission ascribe a large significance to the enhanced consultations. According to the Commission, the TTIP institutions should be equipped with powers

[39] De Ville, 'Deconstructing the Transatlantic Trade and Investment Partnership Rationale'.

[40] See de Gucht, Suggestion for a Regulatory Cooperation Council.

[41] *Ibid.*

to amend the sectoral annexes of the agreement without recourse to the domestic ratification procedures.[42]

The most important TTIP institution will be a body with regulatory competences. The breadth of competences, the membership of the regulatory body or its relations to the 'ordinary legislative procedure', has not been made clear so far. Commissioner de Gucht proposes a body 'that brings together the heads of the most important EU and US regulatory agencies'.[43] This body should be assisted by various sectoral working groups, staffed by the members of the regulatory agencies. The sectoral working groups will be charged with overseeing the implementation of the regulatory provisions of the TTIP and making recommendations to the body with decision-making power under TTIP.

The European Commission has sought to appease concerns regarding the potential breadth of powers of this regulatory body, and has asserted that the decisions of the body will not enjoy supremacy. Yet supremacy is not the only democratic challenge that the decisions of such a body may pose. So far it is not clear what the relationship between the new institutions and the legislative procedures is going to be. However, we are certainly witnessing a new configuration that will favour executive and technocratic decision-making at the expense of legislative and democratic processes. Experiences from previous transatlantic relations suggest that regulatory agencies strengthen in such constellation.[44] Moreover, this 'set-up' increases the threat of regulatory capture, on account of growing regulatory units and the concentration of powers in expert agencies.[45]

Finally, it is important to address perhaps the most crucial element of the TTIP – the investor–state dispute settlement mechanism (ISDS). We can indirectly infer from the 'non-papers' that such mechanism is at least considered.[46] Another leaked document clarifies the objectives of the Commission. The Commission argues for the broadest investor–state dispute arbitration mechanism, which would provide investors with the highest possible level of legal protection and certainty in the EU.[47] Also

[42] See Non-papers, Horizontal Chapter.

[43] De Gucht, Suggestion for a Regulatory Cooperation Council.

[44] Shaffer, 'Reconciling Trade and Regulatory Roles'.

[45] Hamilton, 'Small Is Beautiful'.

[46] The Directorate General for Competition has acquiesced to subsuming it within the dispute settlement mechanism: 'Provisions on antitrust/mergers shall not be subject to the general dispute settlement mechanism of the agreement' (Non-papers, 44).

[47] The leaked document is accessible at: https://netzpolitik.org/2013/leak-aktueller-entwurf-des-verhandlungsmandates-zum-eu-usa-freihandelsabkommen/, accessed 15 February 2014.

a recently published fact sheet, which aims to justify such dispute resolution mechanism, clearly shows that such a mechanism is envisaged by the Commission.[48] A proposal for the ISDS, advocated strongly by the EU and US businesses,[49] has triggered significant criticism from consumers, environmentalists and lobbying monitoring NGOs for its far-reaching protection asserted therein.[50] The Commission has responded by stating the importance of 'increasing attractiveness' of the EU or providing the level playing field. Yet doubts can be raised regarding either of these objectives. First of all, the courts in both parties to the TTIP ensure a very high degree of independence and impartiality: in fact, foreign investment in either the EU or USA is not usually seen as deterred by the quality of their institutional and legal frameworks.

The second argument is even more questionable: the level playing field for whom and how? Both inclusion and non-inclusion of such a mechanism ensures a level playing field. To the extent that the Commission refers to the existence of the various bilateral agreements among the Member States and the USA, one may wonder – why should the TTIP adversely affect countries that have avoided such agreements so far? Perhaps the experience of some EU Member States, such as the Czech Republic, should serve as a warning sign – entailing significant pro-investor bias, as well as ruinous awards.[51] More recently, looking at the disputes against crisis measures taken against countries such as Greece or Argentina, it already appears that the economic risks are to be borne by the host states.[52]

The experience with ISDS reveals that these instruments are increasingly serving as a means to penalise public policy choices of implicated

[48] The document is available at: http://trade.ec.europa.eu/doclib/docs/2013/october/tradoc_151791.pdf, accessed 15 February 2014.

[49] ISDS is an important element of the various inputs that businesses have into the proceedings. One of the greatest is Chevron – a company itself trying to avoid damages for large-scale pollutions in Ecuador through the ISDS mechanism – which devotes an entire submission to the ISDS alone.

[50] Significant criticism has been raised within the Transatlantic Consumer Dialogue of this. See: 'Resolution on Investor–State Dispute Resolution in the Transatlantic Trade and Investment Partnership', Doc. No. Trade 15/13, available at: www.consumersinternational.org, accessed 15 February 2014.

[51] O. Chung, 'Lopsided International Investment Law Regime and its Effect on the Future of Investor–State Arbitration' (2006) 47 *Virginia Journal of International Law* 957. With regard to the level of awards, see the discussion in the UNCTAD latest report on the ISDS at: http://unctad.org/SearchCenter/Pages/Results.aspx?k=investor%20state, accessed 15 February 2014.

[52] See UNCTAD report.

states in a considerably investor-friendly environment.[53] The exponential increase in investor–state disputes shows the saliency of the threat.[54] ISDS impinges upon the space for democratic policy choices: even if the TTIP can be drafted in a way that protects public policy choices, this will less likely be the case for the investor–state dispute resolution (ISDR) mechanism.[55] This is underscored by the EU–Canada Trade Agreement Impact Assessment, which instead recommends state-to-state dispute resolution.[56]

2.2 The rationale of economic integration: horizontal provisions of the TTIP

While the institutions are to be specified in the 'institutional chapter', the competences of the newly established institutions are to be set out in a 'horizontal' chapter to the TTIP, which means they should be applicable across the whole regulatory field. According to the Commission, the horizontal chapter should have three building blocks. It should start with so-called 'underlying principles', which will likely serve as interpretative guidance for the TTIP. These include the right of each party to pursue public policy objectives as well as the focus of the agreement on the sector-specific regulation. The function of the TTIP is then set out as the 'overall objective':

> The overall objective of the regulatory provisions of the TTIP will be to eliminate, reduce or prevent unnecessary 'behind the border' obstacles to trade and investment. In general terms (although this may not be applicable in all cases), the ultimate goal would be a more integrated transatlantic market where goods produced and services originating in one party in accordance with its regulatory requirements could be marketed in the other without adaptations or requirements.[57]

[53] See T. Cheng, 'Power, Authority and International Investment Law' (2005) 20 *American University International Law Review* 465.

[54] UNCTAD reports: 'with fewer than 50 litigated from the 1950s until 2000 but now there are 514 known cases as of the end of 2012'. UNCTAD report, available at: http://unctad.org/SearchCenter/Pages/Results.aspx?k=investor%20state, accessed 15 February 2014.

[55] For an analysis of the interests and the stakes of the investor–state dispute resolution mechanism, see Corporate Observatory Europe and Transnational Institute publication 'A Transatlantic Corporate Bill of Rights', available at: http://corporateeurope.org/sites/default/files/publications/corporate-bill-of-rights.pdf, accessed 15 February 2014.

[56] EU–Canada SIA Final Report, 19, available at: http://ec.europa.eu/trade/policy/policy-making/analysis/sustainability-impact-assessments/assessments/index_en.htm, accessed 15 February 2014.

[57] EU Non-paper, 3.

The objective of the TTIP is to create a supranational instance of functional market integration.[58] However, such functional integration carries specific epistemic and democratic risks, which need to be articulated. The main epistemic challenge is that the functional orientation skews epistemic processes in these entities. Through endowing institutions with an objective to pursue one primary goal, they prioritise that goal against other public policy objectives.[59] This may result in flawed policies to the extent that these entities marginalise important concerns that are not harmonious with the main objective. Moreover, over time these entities accumulate knowledge that is justificatory for their functional vision of the world, yet that narrows down the space for the problematisation of its premises.[60] This epistemic limitation turns into a major democratic challenge. Democracy requires problematisation of the politically controversial questions. Yet the functional integration combines several legal and institutional mechanisms that push out such politicisation. First, the juridification of the main objective and other 'specifying' purposes takes these out of the sphere of the political. Second, technocratic 'expert' institutions are put in place that should further these goals, be they regulatory body or adjudicatory bodies, which further perpetuates the functional bias. Finally, when the integration of these entities is so deep that we call for democratisation, that becomes very difficult since the remaining space for democratic politics is considerably reduced.

The 'partial objectives' of the TTIP further reinforce this trend. The first partial objective is promoting cooperation between regulators from both sides at an early stage. The second partial objective is to promote compatible regulations by achieving increased compatibility/convergence in specific sectors, including – through recognition of equivalence – mutual recognition. Finally, the last partial objective of the TTIP should

[58] De Gucht, Suggestion for a Regulatory Cooperation Council.

[59] In the context of the EU, a large body of scholarship critically notes this institutionally embedded 'peculiarity'. Most prominently, see F. Scharpf, 'The European Social Model' (2002) 40 *Journal of Common Market Studies* 645: F. Scharpf, 'Monetary Union, Fiscal Crisis and the Preemption of Democracy', (2011) LEQS Working Paper No. 36; G. Brueggemeier *et al.*, 'Social Justice in European Contract Law: A Manifesto' (2004) 10 *European Law Journal* 653; C. Joerges and F. Rödl, 'Informal Politics, Formalised Law and the "Social Deficit" of European Integration: Reflections after the Judgments of the ECJ in Viking and Laval' (2009) 15 *European Law Journal* 1. In the international context, the most prominent critique has been voiced by Koskenniemi, e.g. M. Koskenniemi and P. Leino, 'Fragmentation of International Law? Postmodern Anxieties" (2002) 15 *Leiden Journal of International Law* 553; M. Koskenniemi, 'The Fate of Public International Law: Between Technique and Politics' (2007) 70 *The Modern Law Review* 1.

[60] Bartl, 'Internal Market Rationality'.

be, according to the Commission, to affirm the particular importance and role of international rule-making as a means to achieving increased compatibility/convergence of regulations. The European Commission thus suggests that endorsing the normative power of the 'international disciplines' should become an objective of the entire agreement. While this term covers the instruments of international law, it more importantly covers so-called 'international standards', thus empowering private or public–private bodies, not infrequently dominated by large industry, to become a major source of normativity within the TTIP and eventually also globally. However, as Trebilcock *et al.* have shown in the case of the WTO,[61] this has prompted functional institutions to interpret available material so as to further their primary objective. The public impetus towards the privatisation of lawmaking in the international arena may thus result in the imposition of further disciplines on the democratic processes in TTIP countries – possibly at the expense of pursuing 'other' policy objectives.

An impetus towards the privatisation of lawmaking is further embedded in the Commission's emphasis on scientific evidence as a condition for justifying the behind-the-borders barriers to trade. The Commission proposes that phytosanitary-related import requirements and certification conditions for all commodities should be available up front, grounded in scientific evidence or the relevant international standards, and applicable to the entire territory of the exporting party. It is perplexing that the EU, which alone has been fined by the WTO because it has refused to let genetically modified organisms (GMOs) into its territory on the basis of the precautionary principle and citizens' preferences,[62] essentially advocates the opposite here: restriction based solely upon scientific evidence or international standards. First of all, if a reference to the precautionary principle is to remain absent in this international instrument, the agreement may be open to challenge.[63] One may ask, however, if the principle ought not to be infringed by the TTIP, why should it be absent from the EU negotiation position? Second, from a policy perspective, the position of the Commission is strongly deregulatory, which has significant redistributory implications. If a default position is pro free trade, the burden of

[61] M. Trebilcock, R. Howse and A. Eliason, *The Regulation of International Trade* (London: Routledge, 2012), pp. 295, 317.

[62] N. Krisch, 'Pluralism in Post-National Risk Regulation: The Dispute over GMOs and Trade' (2010) 1 *Transnational Legal Theory* 1.

[63] The precautionary principle is a general principle of EU law. See P. Craig and G. De Búrca, *EU Law: Text, Cases, and Materials*, 5th edn (Oxford University Press, 2011), p. 550.

proof lies with public authorities to show a potential harm that thus serves as a reason to regulate. Such a step shifts the costs of proving harm from businesses to the public. Yet it also greatly enlarges the number of issues that should be investigated and funded from public resources, adding the costs of selection. Most importantly, however, it indirectly redirects public resources from potentially more socially useful purposes to investigating the harm posed by various new technologies.

Needless to say, 'harm' is sometimes impossible to establish, in particular if *longue durée* is concerned. This is the case, for example, with regard to the impact of GMOs in our biosphere. Any assessments would be a guess at best, depending in their content more on a normative commitment of a scientist than on existing evidence. For this reason, many of the 'risk-related' questions at the frontiers of scientific knowledge cannot be justifiably transferred from the hands of the democratic collective into the hands of experts.[64]

Finally, the horizontal chapter of the TTIP should be concluded, according to the European Commission, by 'substantial elements' of the institutional framework. The first two elements – best practice and transparency on the one hand, and the requirement of impact assessment on the other – have been discussed earlier in this chapter. What interests us here is a third substantial element of the horizontal chapter – cooperation towards increased compatibility/convergence of regulations. According to the Commission, while many issues will be resolved in the TTIP, a number of issues will remain unresolved: the so-called in-built agenda. If the TTIP is to become a 'living' agreement, TTIP institutions have to be afforded competences to deal with this in-built agenda. In particular:

- Provision of a general mandate, understood as a legal authorisation and commitment, for regulators to engage in international regulatory cooperation.
- Provision to launch, upon the request of either party, discussions on regulatory differences with a view to moving towards greater compatibility. The request could be based on substantiated proposals from EU and US stakeholders.

The 'general mandate' may indeed serve as a gate for the expansion of the TTIP framework. The Commission's non-paper suggests that it should be private actors (stakeholders) who will be the main motor of change

[64] D. Winickoff *et al.*, 'Adjudicating the GM Food Wars: Science, Risk, and Democracy in World Trade Law' (2005) 30 *Yale Journal of International Law* 81.

in the TTIP. Judging by the EU experience, we can expect that EU–US economic integration will be driven by businesses, and most notably big businesses.[65] The activity of large industry so far also suggests that the TTIP may become a rapidly evolving entity.

This leads us to the penultimate point in our analysis, in respect of the actual legitimation processes of the TTIP, and the place of information and knowledge therein.

3 Transparency and democratic accountability in the TTIP negotiations

The European Parliament's new right of veto on international agreements is specifically linked to a right of information in Article 218 (10) TFEU. This new power has exposed a conflict between EU executive actors and the European Parliament in international negotiations of trade: from norm-setting to input.[66] More specifically, however, the recent ACTA affair has rendered salient what Article 218 TFEU mandates as regards transparency in the conduct of EU international relations.[67] What is significant about the ACTA affair is that there it prompted the European Commission to take measures to dispel 'myths' and publish information catalogues. But this was only after a bout of interinstitutional conflict between the European Commission and European Parliament at political and judicial levels. Notably, the agreement was voted down by Members of the European Parliament (MEPs) because of a lack of information.[68] Moreover, an individual MEP, Sophie in't Veld, sought public access to

[65] A. Stone Sweet and W. Sandholtz, 'European Integration and Supranational Governance' (1997) 4 *Journal of European Public Policy* 297.

[66] Council Regulation (EC) 1049/2011 of the European Parliament and of the Council, of 30 May 2001, regarding public access to European Parliament, Council and Commission documents (OJ 2001 L 145, p. 43).

[67] See Council Decision on the conclusion of the Anti-Counterfeiting Trade Agreement between the European Union and its Member States, Australia, Canada, Japan, the Republic of Korea, the United Mexican States, the Kingdom of Morocco, New Zealand, the Republic of Singapore, the Swiss Confederation and the United States of America, No. 12195/11, 23 August 2011. It was negotiated and signed by the EU and was vetoed by the European Parliament in July 2012 for reasons related to the failure to inform it 'adequately and on time': see Curtin, 'Official Secrets and the Negotiation of International Agreements'.

[68] Eckes, *et al.*, 'International, European and US Perspectives on the Negotiation and Adoption of the Anti-Counterfeiting Trade Agreement (ACTA)'. See European Commission, *10 Myths about ACTA*, 1, 1–3 (2012), http://trade.ec.europa.eu/doclib/docs/2012/january/tradoc_148964.pdf, accessed 15 February 2014. See also Curtin, 'Official Secrets and the Negotiation of International Agreements'; Cf. B. Driessen,

the negotiating mandate for ACTA through litigation. The document was subsequently leaked and then was placed by the EU in the public domain. The General Court recently ruled against her on the ground that the interest in shielding the EU's negotiation strategy had to prevail.[69] ACTA as a case study suggests that the European Parliament's role is to ask for and the Commission's to offer relevant knowledge, yet one may question the nature of this dynamic. However, we may also say that its precedential value remains unclear, given that the Court's decision is so heavily qualified and is also under appeal.

In respect of the ACTA decision, Curtin has argued that the mere 'listing' of EU interests in a negotiation mandate for an international agreement is not in any sense a strategy.[70] This constitutes an issue of significance for the TTIP because the leaked TTIP negotiation mandates contain a vast range of EU interests, most of which one can readily say are general 'EU concerns' or interests not warranting secrecy. This aside, the question we pose here is whether the General Court's interpretation of 'strategy' applies to a wholly non-conventional trade agreement. We suggest that transparency should prevail in such a context.

Two issues of openness and information in the conduct of the negotiations are noteworthy here – the formal place of transparency in the negotiations and the application of transparency to participation in the negotiations. On the formal place of transparency rules, the EU Chief Negotiator in mid 2013 outlined in detail the application of the EU access-to-documents system to the TTIP negotiations, specifically Council Regulation (EC) 1049/2001.[71] He maintained that all documents relating to the negotiation or development of the agreement would be held in confidence according to EU law, and all documents not classified under EU law had to be held in confidence, subject to the EU seeking to increase its level of protection of documents. However, as many such documents

Transparency in EU Institutional Law: A Practitioner's Handbook, 2nd edn (Alphen aan den Rijn: Kluwer Law, 2012).

69 T-301/10, *In't Veld* v. *European Commission*, decision of the General Court of 19 March 2013, [2013] ECR II-000, appeal pending. See also its confirmation in part by the General Court in Case C-331/11 *Besselink* v. *Council*, decision of 12 September 2013, [2013] ECR I-000 (Council decision authorising European Convention on Human Rights accession negotiations), paras. 70, 72.

70 Curtin, 'Official Secrets and the Negotiation of International Agreements'.

71 This leaked document is available on the civil liberties observatory of www.statewatch.org, accessed 15 February 2014. Contrast its absence from the Commission's extensive listing of transparency information: http://trade.ec.europa.eu/doclib/docs/2013/june/tradoc_151381.pdf, accessed 15 February 2014.

have been consistently leaked since the beginning of the negotiations, there is a sense of (post-ACTA) *déjà vu*. Also, the membership of the group tasked with producing the founding document of the TIIP negotiations was shrouded in secrecy, and formal requests for disclosure pursuant to Council Regulation (EC) 1049/2011 for the full membership of the HLWG were officially refused, but then subsequently leaked, as outlined here above. As regards the more substantive application of transparency, by contrast, both the European Commission and the US Trade Representative have published lists of negotiators in the talks.[72] This begs the question as to why the HLWG should be concealed given that this unduly shrouds the normative agenda of the TTIP. Moreover, while the EU Trade Commissioner and US Trade Representatives have been jointly leading the negotiations, the Commission alone has published a fact sheet on the accountability of the negotiations, indicating its intention to take the lead in this field.[73] It appears considerably less defensive than its ACTA counterpart document, yet in some respects unduly simplistic on its legal effects.[74] This entails that there are substantive and procedural shortcomings in the application of transparency, compounded by the precedent of ACTA. They detract from, and significantly impinge upon, the legitimacy of the agreement pursuant to Article 218 TFEU. Finally, it should be noted that the leaked TTIP mandates also contain provisions on transparency in Article 40, including a particularly brief commitment to consult stakeholders on the impact of measures on transparency and investment. However, it appears to constitute a rather formalist commitment to transparency, one that even suggests privileges to economic *actors*, rather than a fulsome effort to deal progressively with the ACTA precedent.

3.1 TTIP and parliamentary accountability

The new powers of the European Parliament and the existing powers of US Congress to consent to and thereby approve and legitimise international agreements have played an important part of the 'marketed' legitimacy of the TTIP. Indeed, the European Parliament endorsed the TTIP early in

[72] See http://trade.ec.europa.eu/doclib/docs/2013/july/tradoc_151668.pdf, accessed 15 February 2014. On the US side, see www.ustr.gov/ttip, accessed 15 February 2014.

[73] http://ec.europa.eu/trade/policy/in-focus/ttip/; http://trade.ec.europa.eu/doclib/docs/2013/june/tradoc_151381.pdf; http://ec.europa.eu/trade/policy/in-focus/ttip/questions-and-answers/, all accessed 15 February 2014.

[74] It lists a series of questions, including 'What will the TTIP change in my life?' and 'Will the TTIP automatically trump EU laws?'

the process of securing a Council mandate.[75] The subsequent US surveillance scandal, however, and the inquiry of the European Parliament set to take place, may alter the context for the use of its powers, as suggested here above.[76] The traditional debate regarding the powers of the European Parliament in international trade agreements has been largely concerned with the balance of powers between the Council and the European Parliament. Pursuant to Article 218(3) TFEU, it is the Council that shall authorise the opening of international relations negotiations and adopt negotiating directives, and it may authorise the signing and conclusion of agreements.[77] Eeckhout, for example, considers this process to exclude the European Parliament.[78] Similarly, Schütze contends the Council is not *primus inter pares* with the Parliament but instead is *primus* in relation to the negotiation of international agreements, which renders the process executive-dominant.[79] While these questions dominate the debate regarding the democratic legitimacy of EU international trade law-making, as the ACTA case also suggests, a less exposed yet democratically crucial conflict may be found at an *earlier* stage: namely, the relations of the European Commission and the European Parliament during negotiations. The underlying problem relates to who produces the knowledge that frames the political debate and on which the Parliament should/will base its conclusions regarding the desirability of the TTIP, and how and why this is done.

The main sources of 'knowledge' on which the European Parliament has relied and is to rely is the report of the HLWG, staffed by the members of the European Commission. Further, the impact assessments have been outsourced to 'independent' contractors by the European Commission – a not uncommon practice. Other supporting documents, such as non-papers, further self-referentially refer to the HLWG Report as a source authority. Of course, the 'stakeholders' deemed worth listening to during the process were also chosen by the Commission. Overall, the majority of TTIP-relevant knowledge is produced under the directorship of

[75] Resolution of 15 May 2013 P7_TA(2013)0227.

[76] See the non-binding vote on the surveillance saga of 24 October 2013: European Parliament Resolution of 23 October 2013, on the suspension of the TFTP Agreement as a result of US National Security Agency surveillance (2013/2831(RSP)).

[77] See R. Schütze, *European Constitutional Law* (Cambridge University Press, 2012), at p. 207; See also H. de Waele and J. Kuipers (eds.), *The European Union's Emerging International Identity: Views from the Global Arena* (Leiden: Martinus Nijhoff, BRILL, 2013).

[78] See P. Eeckhout, *EU External Relations Law*, 2nd edn (Oxford University Press, 2011) at p. 199.

[79] See Schütze, *European Constitutional Law.*

the European Commission, thus reflecting its normative commitments. One may wonder at the extent to which the European Parliament may be 'trapped' in such a set-up. If the European Parliament mainly has access to knowledge that exalts the benefits of EU–US market integration as the cheapest way to economic growth in crisis-tormented Europe,[80] the space for the politicisation of agreement may be considerably narrowed down. The European Parliament may indeed produce its own knowledge, yet that requires considerable resources and the incentives may be lacking. This is thanks to the special position of the European Commission in the EU institutional framework: as an independent, technical and apolitical apparatus, the Commission can be expected to produce the best available knowledge.

According to the Inter-Institutional Framework Agreement, the Commission shall take due account of the Parliament's comments throughout the negotiations.[81] One may question how the European Parliament is in fact effectively and capably able to have an input throughout the negotiations. For instance, was the European Parliament informed about the members of the HLWG, and in particular that the EU labour and environment representatives would not be present in the HLWG? The ratification of (consent to) international treaties poses further problems for parliamentary accountability. In particular, the 'take-it-or-leave-it' situation does not endow much space for political deliberations in parliaments. A very small number of highly resourced national parliaments are undertaking large-scale independent inquiries into the TTIP, for example the UK, but this can be considered neither to constitute the norm nor suffice of itself.[82]

To conclude, leaving 'democracy' – here meant to extend to legitimation and meaningful political debate – to the last stage of creation of the TTIP, and to the deliberations in front of the European Parliament, is hardly satisfactory from a democratic perspective. The European Parliament has limited resources and incentives to produce alternative knowledge, which could be a basis for the problematisation of the normative standpoint of the European Commission. The 'independent' position of the European

[80] See de Gucht, Suggestion for a Regulatory Cooperation Council.

[81] See Framework Agreement on Relations between the European Parliament and Commission, 2010; Inter-Institutional Agreement on Classified Information Held by the Council, 2012.

[82] See the UK House of Lords Call for Evidence: www.parliament.uk/documents/lords-committees/eu-sub-com-c/TTIP/FinalCallforEvidence26July.pdf, accessed 15 February 2014.

Commission in the EU institutional structure then triggers far too little opposition in the Parliament, creating a serious democratic vacuum. And even where there is political opposition – for example as on ACTA – a negative vote pursuant to Article 218 TFEU neither compensates nor neutralises its limited access to knowledge prior to this point in time.

Conclusion

This chapter has considered who has set the normative agenda in the negotiation of the TTIP, reflecting upon both the actors and processes thereof. It has been argued here that the TTIP places the EU and USA at the edge of creating a new level of functional market integration. It thus necessitates that democratic institutions test the soundness of this step. This chapter has drawn attention to several problematic aspects of the TTIP that should be part of such discussion: participation, the use of knowledge to legitimise the TTIP, the issue of transparency and the new institutions that are being built. Of course, this analysis has been conducted at the exclusion of many substantive questions not the subject of consideration here.

The impact on the TTIP on the balance of powers between the EU institutions, and the de-democratising potential of the agreement, remains of much significance. Tilting regulatory power over and beyond the hands of the EU executive will significantly affect the capacity of the European Parliament to affect the shape of the internal market. The TTIP has the potential to unwind the powers of the Commission, with considerably less oversight from the side of the political institutions.[83] The cumulative effect of the TTIP could yet operate to further decrease Member State power to influence the regulation of the internal market and their national markets. Parliamentary legitimation of this entity, through approval and information rights, must be viewed as inadequate in light of the institutionalisation process that forms the goal of the TTIP.

Whatever the impacts of the TTIP may or could be, its formation warrants serious democratic scrutiny, scrutiny that its initial stages of negotiation suggest is seriously wanting.

[83] Notably, Monsanto, a GMO corporation, is reported to have halted lobbying and the applications for the authorisation of GMOs, pending the outcome to the TTIP negotiations. See http://opendotdotdot.blogspot.nl/2013/07/what-has-monsanto-quit-europe-answer-is.html, accessed 15 February 2014.

PART III

Security and transatlantic relations

10

Transatlantic relations and security

Reflections from a politician, practitioner and litigator

SOPHIE IN'T VELD

I am Vice Chair of the European Parliament Committee for Civil Liberties, Justice and Home Affairs. I was a member of the Transatlantic Legislators' Dialogue and was also a member of the committee investigating the CIA renditions and black sites. I am currently a member of the parliamentary inquiry into mass surveillance by the National Security Agency (NSA), and programmes such as Prism and Tempora. I am rapporteur for the evaluation of EU counterterrorism policies and for the international agreements for the exchange of Passenger Name Records. I have equally been involved in the discussions on the so-called 'SWIFT' Agreement on the transfer of bank data,[1] as well as the controversial Anti-Counterfeiting Trade Agreement (ACTA) and the current review of the EU data protection framework. I am rapporteur for the annual report on transparency and access to documents. In addition to my parliamentary work, I have pursued some of these matters in court, both in the USA and in the EU, and have also taken some cases before the European Ombudsman.

One of my main observations on contemporary transatlantic relations would be that the European Union needs to shape up in the transatlantic relationship. In the area of law enforcement, security and counterterrorism,

The following text in the main body of this contribution replicates the content of a speech delivered by its author on 21 January 2013 in Amsterdam. The text has been reproduced almost in full with minimal alteration to reflect the fact that it is the reflections of a practitioner, negotiator and litigator of contemporary transatlantic relations rather than an academic contribution to this volume in respect of its origins. It represents a thematic reflection for Part III. The volume editors thank in particular Thomas Van der Valk for his assistance with various aspects of its publication.

[1] Agreement between the European Union and the United States of America on the Processing and Transfer of Financial Messaging Data from the European Union to the United States for the Purposes of the Terrorist Finance Tracking Programme (hereafter TFTP), 2010 OJ L 195.

the relationship is very unequal. Europe will need to get its act together and become a real partner for the USA. In recent years we have often criticized US policies. And with good reason. But have we offered a real alternative? Have we provided any meaningful counterweight? Have we ever stuck to our guns and refused to support the policies we publicly denounced? We have not. Europe meekly accepts that its own laws are overridden by US laws on its own territory. And in some cases Europe and its Member States have, while publicly denouncing US policies, secretly cooperated with the USA on those same policies. We can rightfully condemn many of the US policies in this area. But that is not enough. The real answer lies in a stronger, more self-assured and more assertive Europe.

A second important observation that I would make is that the parliamentary dimension of transatlantic cooperation needs to be strengthened urgently. Most transatlantic contacts are between civil servants, diplomats and government officials. The relations between elected representatives on both sides of the 'pond' are close to none. This means that the transatlantic dialogue lacks proper democratic oversight and legitimacy. The recent revelations about massive surveillance by the NSA and related scandals have demonstrated how the activities of intelligence services escape the regular arrangements for democratic scrutiny, not least because of the increasingly cross-border nature of surveillance, and cooperation and exchange between national intelligence services. The so-called Transatlantic Legislators' Dialogue (TLD), a joint committee, composed of Members of the European Parliament and members of the US Congress, does not work very well in practice. In my experience, the composition of the TLD does not allow for an in-depth exchange, as it is a cross-section of all policy committees on both sides, and rarely includes the actual experts on specific topics. I have more positive experiences with visits from specific European Parliament policy committees. That allows for a more meaningful dialogue. Secondly, the interest from the US side is considerably weaker than from the EU side. Although, as a rule, the US administration is open and available for meetings with the European Parliament, it has proven to be very difficult to get to speak with members of the US Congress, even in Washington. Thirdly, there is no full symmetry of powers between the European Parliament and Congress. The European Parliament may have legislative powers that in the USA are strictly for the US administration, and vice versa. Notably, international agreements have to be approved by the European Parliament under the Lisbon Treaty, whereas such agreements are considered executive acts by the USA. So we are not necessarily each other's direct interlocutors on all subjects. A fourth observation is the duplicity in the position of governments of the EU Member States. Although they publicly condemn excesses of the US counterterrorism policies, they simultaneously cooperate with the USA, or they benefit from data collection by the USA. Europe has formally condemned Guantánamo Bay and the CIA's extraordinary renditions programme, but to date no European government has admitted to its own role, despite overwhelming evidence of Europe's complicity. European leaders reacted with outrage to the reports on Prism and massive snooping by the NSA, conveniently overlooking the fact that European intelligence services operate similar programmes and often cooperate with the NSA without scruples.

I want to focus here more closely on a few concrete cases on transatlantic relations that I have dealt with in the past ten years – first of all, the so-called 'SWIFT' Agreement, on the transfer of bank data to the USA. As is well known, SWIFT is a Belgian-based company that facilitates international bank transfers. In 2006 the US media revealed that for years US authorities had been secretly obtaining access to a SWIFT database in the USA. After a bit of legal toing and froing, it was decided to move the database to Europe. However, in 2009 European governments decided (during the summer break, when inquisitive parliamentarians were supposed to be at a safe distance, somewhere on a beach) to grant the USA access to the data after all and started negotiations. The European Parliament, using its new powers under the Lisbon Treaty, rejected a first version of an EU–US agreement, but in summer 2010 – reluctantly – endorsed a revised version on condition that, within a year, a system for the extraction of data on European soil would be set up. In other words: if the Americans ask for a needle, we would no longer send them the entire haystack, but find the needle they requested and send it to them. In addition, Parliament stated it would *closely monitor* the application of the Agreement. Europol was put in charge of the verification of the US requests for data. The legal service of the Council prepared an Opinion on the legal base for the EU–US SWIFT Agreement; however, it was immediately classified by the Council. This would seem to confirm suspicions that the Council Legal Service is of the view that the Agreement lacks a solid legal base.

I requested access to this document, but it was denied. I challenged the decision in the General Court, and the Court ruled in my favour in May 2013.[2] The Court considered the exception to the transparency rule

[2] T-529/09 *Council* v. *in't Veld*, [2012] ECR II-000, Judgment of the General Court of 4 May 2012.

for international relations cannot be interpreted as an automatic classification of all documents with a bearing on international relations. The Council has appealed, and we expect a final ruling of the European Court of Justice (ECJ) in the course of 2014.[3] If the 2013 ruling is upheld, that will be a major victory for transparency in international relations.

So where are we today on the SWIFT Agreement? Every year a joint review is being conducted by the European Commission and the US authorities. In addition, the Joint Supervisory Board, composed of national data protection authorities, oversees the implementation of the Agreement by Europol. The 2011 review revealed fundamental flaws in the application of the Agreement; for example there were several examples of oral requests by the USA for data – in other words a simple phone call to obtain large batches of personal data from EU citizens. The fact that the requests for data are made on a highly regular, monthly basis, suggests that they are systematic and not 'targeted' as prescribed by the Agreement. The 2012 report of the Joint Supervisory Board suggests that the problems have not been solved; indeed there does not seem to be any limit to the data the USA gets. The report itself has not been published, but a three-page summary has been posted on the Internet. Instead of starting an urgent in-depth investigation, the Director of Europol decided simply to classify the document as secret. He claims the classification was done 'at the request of the Americans'. This way, the USA essentially determines the transparency standards in the European Union.

I have asked for access to the implementation report under the EU Transparency Regulation, the equivalent of the US Freedom of Information Act, but again access was denied. The responsible parliamentary committee, of which I am Vice Chair, has also asked for access. However, if we do get access, it will be in a secure room; we will not be allowed to take notes or discuss the contents in public. Thus Parliament is essentially gagged. We cannot exercise any meaningful parliamentary oversight, and I have taken proceedings challenging this before the European Ombudsman. As to the European Parliament demand for a European system for the extraction of data: it never materialized. Instead the Commission proposed a system for the collection and storage of SWIFT data within Europe. This met with a frosty reaction from the Parliament and now it has been shelved. Adding insult to injury, we recently learned from the Snowden leaks that the NSA has hacked the SWIFT servers, or at least reserves the right to access the SWIFT servers, without authorization. Apparently data

[3] C-350/12 P *In't Veld* v. *Council*, appeal pending.

can be retrieved and used for a wide range of unspecified purposes. The fact that the USA may tap into the SWIFT databases directly, and the fact that data are used for purposes other than the fight against terrorism, are both clear breaches of the terms of the SWIFT Agreement. Nevertheless, the European Commission has so far not initiated a suspension or termination of the Agreement, but merely asked the US administration for an explanation. So far, the Commission has stated it is not satisfied with the answers provided by the USA. If no satisfactory answers are provided, the Commission might indeed submit a proposal for the suspension or termination of the SWIFT Agreement, but it is doubtful that the Member States would adopt such a proposal. An additional question might be if the direct retrieval of the data was already taking place back in 2010, at the time of the transatlantic negotiations on SWIFT. That would be a clear act of bad faith and extremely damaging for trust in transatlantic relations.

In conclusion, we can say that the EU has concluded a transatlantic agreement on a very shaky legal base at best: the implementation is botched, democratic oversight is non-existent, there is zero transparency and the Commission failed to deliver on its promise of a system for the extraction of data on European soil. The whole Agreement may actually turn out to be a farce, if the NSA is tapping into the SWIFT database directly, disregarding the Agreement. The Parliament has been sidelined, as the Lisbon Treaty had not foreseen any role for it once an international agreement has been *concluded*. It is a bit like signing a blank cheque, and so this results in it not being an entirely confidence-inspiring example of transatlantic cooperation. But I stress once again that Europe has only itself to blame for not being more assertive.

I can be fairly brief on the EU–US Agreement on the Transfer of Passenger Name Record (PNR) Data: after nine years of negotiations, renegotiations and court cases, in 2012 Parliament ended up endorsing an agreement that was worse than the one we challenged in the Court of Justice in 2004.[4] There are many reasons why Europe gave in to US pressure. One is that the USA made the transfer of passenger data one of the conditions for EU countries to get into the US Visa Waiver Programme (or to stay in, for those countries that were in already). In other words: a rejection of the EU–US PNR Agreement might have led to EU countries losing visa-free travel to the USA. Of course, theoretically, Europe could have applied a tit-for-tat strategy and withdrawn visa-free travel

[4] Joined Cases C-317/04 and C-318/04, *European Parliament* v. *Council and Commission* [2006] ECR I-4721.

for US citizens, but that was never a real option. So we accepted being blackmailed into endorsing an agreement on the transfer of data that is considered to be a violation of our own laws.

In the case of the Anti-Counterfeiting Agreement, ACTA, the European Parliament showed a bit more backbone. Public opinion played a major part in the decision to reject ACTA. The massive protests against ACTA swayed the mood, and Parliament voted against it, despite urgent appeals by the European Commission to endorse it. In 2008 I sought access to all documents relating to ACTA and my request was denied. I challenged the refusal in the General Court and, unfortunately, the Court decided that international relations took precedence over transparency and citizens' rights.[5] I see this as entirely contrary to the earlier decision by the EU General Court in my other litigation against the Council, which considered that transparency is essential for the democratic process. In any case, litigation takes a long time and ACTA had been signed in the meantime. Thus the Commission decided to release a few of the minutes of negotiating rounds. The papers were redacted but, entirely by mistake, the parts that were supposed to be blacked out were actually highlighted, thus drawing attention to what the Commission wanted to keep from us. No major state secrets or vital information, but merely parts that are embarrassing for the Commission, showing how a weak and submissive EU loses out against an assertive USA. There is irony in the fact that the Court considered transparency a threat to the negotiations, but in the end it was not transparency but the lack of it that sounded the end of ACTA.

One of the most shocking examples of the unbalanced transatlantic relations is of course the issue of renditions and CIA black sites. To date, not a single European government has been held to account over this shameful violation of human rights and international law. It is not good enough to point at the USA: European governments and EU institutions have given their full support to the US counterterrorism strategy, turning a blind eye to the excesses. The scandal was brought to light by Human Rights Watch and the *Washington Post* and not by Europeans. Indeed, we seem reluctant to accept our share in the guilt. We happily depict the Bush Administration as those riding roughshod over human rights and international law, but we fail to shed any light on our own role. Another issue is the extraterritorial application of US law. One of the most worrying examples is the Foreign Intelligence and Surveillance Act of 1978 (FISA),

[5] T-301/10 *In't Veld* v. *European Commission* [2013] ECR II-000, judgment of the General Court of 19 March 2013.

amended by the US Patriot Act 2001, which now allows the USA to intercept any communication in the cloud, without proper court orders, as long as it does not relate exclusively to US citizens. Requests for warrants under FISA are assessed by a secret court, the Foreign Intelligence and Surveillance Court. The Court has come under heavy criticism recently, not only against the principle of secret court hearings, but also because individual (former) judges have come out expressing their unease or outright disagreement with the way the Court fails to exercise any meaningful scrutiny of the requests for warrants. And so essentially, US authorities have unlimited access to anything we store in the cloud. But there are also other ways in which the Patriot Act (or any US legislation for that matter) is being applied to European data stored on European soil. The USA considers its jurisdiction extends not only over companies established on US soil, but also data held by that company or its branches elsewhere in the world. An example is the company that produces Dutch passports, including the fingerprints stored in them. The company, Morpho, is part of a wider cluster of companies with activities in the USA. US authorities could gain access to Dutch biometric data – fingerprints – and even oblige the company to keep silent about any subpoena it may get.

The European Commission and Member State governments have so far failed completely to address this problem. Clearly they feel no responsibility for protecting the interests and rights of European citizens. We meekly accept that US law takes precedence over EU law … on EU territory. I wonder if we would be as complacent if Mr Putin or the Chinese were to do the same. And given the growing number of European companies setting up offices in China, that is not an imaginary risk. Regarding transatlantic data-sharing in the private sector, there are several ways of legally transferring personal data of EU citizens to the USA. One way would be through binding corporate rules, guidelines on the protection of personal data that are adopted within a multinational company and have been consented by a European national data protection authority. Another way is the so-called US Safe Harbour programme. Safe Harbour rests on the decision by the European Commission that US companies fulfilling the requirements are considered adequate for the processing of personal data of EU citizens. The enforcement and supervision of Safe Harbour have not lived up to the legal requirements. In December 2010 I tabled Parliamentary Questions with the Commission on this issue. No action has been undertaken by the Commission up until the time of writing. Yet false claims by US companies on Safe Harbour compliance and the lack of proper redress remain problematic. Furthermore, national security is outside the protective scope of the programme, while no guidelines exist on how exactly national security is defined. With the recent reports on mass surveillance it has been revealed that US authorities indeed access data of non-US citizens on a large scale. The EU should suspend the Safe Harbour programme until satisfactory solutions have been established.

Lack of action on the EU side can be observed in other policy areas as well, for example the (US) Foreign Account Tax Compliance Act (FATCA) of 2010, which obliges financial institutions such as banks, insurers and investment firms to disclose the data stored in Europe on their US customers to the US authorities. If they fail to do so, they have to pay a withholding tax of 30 per cent. The transfer of data is a violation of EU law, but again, Commission and Member State governments remain passive. With all its shortcomings, there is transatlantic cooperation in the area of law enforcement and security. However, when it comes to the other side of the coin – the protection of fundamental rights – there is little to nothing. The only example is an EU–US Agreement on Data Protection for which talks have been going on for many years now, without much result. The main sticking point is granting non-US citizens the right to judicial redress. One of the main differences between our respective systems is that the USA distinguishes between US citizens and aliens, whereas EU fundamental rights apply generally, regardless of nationality.

Transparency and access to documents are not only key democratic rights, they are also essential to create trust in government bodies. In this area the USA is clearly ahead of the EU. The FOIA is not perfect, but it has proven to be a strong instrument enabling citizens to scrutinize their governments. I made use of the procedure in 2008, in order to find out if US agencies held any records on me. The replies to my FOIA requests were not very satisfactory, and with help of the Electronic Frontier Foundation, I challenged them in Court proceedings in the USA.[6] I did not find out much more – the most intriguing answer being that one particular agency could 'neither confirm nor deny' it held any records on me – but the procedure is easy and accessible. This is in contrast to the cumbersome, time-consuming equivalent in Europe. However, there are concerted attempts to reduce transparency as much as possible. In the case of international agreements such as ACTA, the EU and USA have concluded a non-disclosure agreement before the negotiations. It would seem to me that such an

[6] *In't Veld* v. *Department of Homeland Security*, Civil Action No. 08-1151 (RMC), United States District Court, 15 December 2008, available at: www.eff.org/files/filenode/foia_travelinfo/20081215opinion.pdf, accessed 15 February 2014.

agreement is a violation of the – already weak – EU transparency rules, which prescribe that any restriction of transparency must be specifically justified. *Ex ante* automatic blanket exemptions from the transparency rules are a rather unsavoury example of transatlantic cooperation. In addition, the attempts to maintain government secrecy are rather futile in the internet era, as WikiLeaks and various whistle-blowers have demonstrated. The British secret services smashing hard disks of a newspaper that had revealed secrets is a particularly curious example of how they seem to fight 'yesterday's war'. Information can be spread very rapidly once it has been leaked or disclosed. Although at each new revelation, governments make alarming statements how such leaks are threatening national security, in most cases they are just very embarrassing for the governments in question. The general public is getting more sceptical, and trust in governments is affected. 'Good' transatlantic cooperation is vital in a world with ever more open borders; therefore, the inequality between the two partners is a reason for concern. If we want European values to be better protected and promoted, we should become a more serious partner for the USA. A united Europe, speaking with a single voice, can achieve more. And a united Europe will also be less frustrating for Americans, who are occasionally driven to despair by the intricacies of European policy-making and the elusive, fluid balance of power between EU bodies.

Europe should also be more self-confident and represent the interests of its citizens more proactively with the Americans. The USA has a very strong, at times even aggressive, lobby in the area of law enforcement and security policies. In the case of the new Data Protection Regulation and Directive, it seems to have a 24/7 presence in the European Parliament in order to monitor and lobby. The US Mission was actually involved in the drafting stage, before the submission of proposals to Council and Parliament (a degree of interference in domestic lawmaking they would probably never accept in their own country). The USA, however, was very quick to acknowledge the new role of the European Parliament with the new powers conferred upon it by the Treaty of Lisbon. Immediately after the vote on SWIFT, it invested heavily in its unit for relations with the European Parliament – something many EU Member State governments have yet to grasp.

In conclusion: in my portfolio of Civil Liberties, Justice and Home Affairs, transatlantic cooperation has been very unequal. Europe has to rapidly become a mature political union in this area, become an equal and reliable partner for the USA, and better represent the interests and rights of European citizens. I am sure the USA will appreciate a stronger ally.

11

Obstacles to transatlantic security cooperation in the 'War on Terror'

WYN REES

Introduction

The 9/11 attacks made the countering of international terrorism the USA's foremost security concern. It became necessary, in the view of the US Government, not only to target terrorist organizations that threatened its security directly but also those states that aligned themselves and provided material support to terrorist groups. Interventions in Afghanistan and Iraq were undertaken on the pretext that threats needed to be pre-empted and dealt with as far from its shores as possible. The USA mobilized all of its national security resources and proved to be willing to use its unparalleled military power to strike its adversaries. The 9/11 attacks also changed the attitude of the USA towards its own domestic vulnerability. It set about overhauling its 'homeland' security provisions in fields such as transportation and borders, as well as enhancing the powers of its law enforcement agencies.

This transformation in the US security agenda had important implications for its European allies. It created a new field of transatlantic security cooperation in which internal and external security were closely interconnected. It led the USA to demand new forms of cooperation from Europe.[1] These demands caused Europe to confront the questions of whether they agreed with US priorities and how they could most appropriately respond. For its own part, Europe has advocated a law enforcement strategy to combat terrorism, one that has emphasized the use of police, judicial and intelligence resources.[2] It has been willing to tolerate a degree of

[1] W. Rees, *The US–EU Security Relationship: The Tensions between a European and a Global Agenda* (Basingstoke: Palgrave Macmillan, 2011).

[2] J. Argomaniz and W. Rees, 'The EU and Counter-Terrorism' in S. Biscop (ed.), *The Routledge Handbook of European Security* (London: Routledge, 2013), p. 225; W. Rees

risk based upon past experiences of countering terrorist threats. Only a few countries, such as the UK, have been willing to partner the USA in robust military activities overseas.

It was perhaps inevitable that this reordering of the transatlantic security relationship resulted in a range of tensions. Many European countries felt alienated by the unilateralism of the Bush Administration and its pursuit of narrow US interests.[3] They regarded themselves as being pushed into measures that they had played little role in determining. The two sides have proceeded to develop new patterns of cooperation, but progress has been patchy and slow. The starkest tensions were in the foreign policy domain because these presented the greatest danger in terms not only of loss of life but also financial costs. The determination of the USA to counter terrorism resulted in notable disagreements with Europe over the treatment of 'enemy combatants', over practices to extract intelligence from detainees and over the transfer of prisoners to the jails of other countries. These impacted on Europe's sense of what was both legal and legitimate in international relations.[4]

The homeland security agenda also presented a series of issues that were felt to impact on the legal order and conceptions of proportionate responses to terrorism among European countries. At the core were different perceptions of the balance between security and citizens' rights. Europe has perceived itself as trying to safeguard civil liberties and matters of individual privacy, while the concerns of the USA seem to have been directed towards improving security and preventing the repeat of another major attack on the US mainland.[5] This interpretation of its

and R. Aldrich, 'European and US Approaches to Counterterrorism' in R. Tiersky and E. Jones (eds.), *Europe Today: A Twenty-First Century Introduction*, 3rd edn (Lanham, MD: Rowman & Littlefield, 2007), p. 437; W. Rees, 'The External Face of Internal Security' in *International Relations and the European Union* (Oxford University Press, 2005), p. 205; T. McCrisken, 'Ten Years On: Obama's War on Terrorism in Rhetoric and Practice' (2011) 87 *International Affairs* 781.

[3] W. Rees, 'Securing the Homelands: Transatlantic Co-Operation after Bush' (2009) 11 *British Journal of Politics and International Relations* 108.

[4] W. Rees, 'Transatlantic Relations and the War on Terror' (2003) 1 *Journal of Transatlantic Studies* 76; W. Rees, 'International Cooperation in Counter-Terrorism' in D. Mahncke and J. Monar (eds.), *International Terrorism: A European Response to a Global Threat?* (Brussels: Peter Lang, 2006).

[5] W. Rees and R. J. Aldrich, 'Contending Cultures of Counterterrorism: Transatlantic Divergence or Convergence?' (2005) 81 *International Affairs* 905; W. Rees, 'Justice and Internal Security' in J. Peterson and M. Pollack (eds.), *Europe, America, Bush: Transatlantic Relations in the Twenty-First Century* (London and New York: Routledge, 2003), p. 47.

priorities has been rejected by US officials, who argue that security is a vital precondition for the enjoyment of liberty.

Tensions in the foreign policy domain

For a variety of reasons, Europe was much less involved than the United States in the campaign that has been waged overseas against al-Qaeda and countries sympathetic to terrorism. Many individual countries have lacked the capabilities to be able to fight at long distance from their home territories, while Europe as a whole has proved insufficiently cohesive to agree upon a collective effort. The Bush Administration was disdainful of the benefits of working with allies and preferred to work bilaterally with countries that could make a meaningful contribution. This has meant that many European countries had not had to confront the same complex challenges as those that have faced the United States, and this has enabled them to critique the actions of the superpower. The disdain that they experienced from the first Bush Administration led them to have little compunction in exposing the inability of Washington to live up to its moral authority.

There have been four major issues on which the Europeans have criticized the way in which the USA has prosecuted its overseas War on Terror – quite apart from US decisions to invade Afghanistan and Iraq.[6] These issues have proved to be obstacles when the USA has asked its European allies for their assistance. The first of these issues has concerned the way in which the US Government designated those enemies whom it captured in the course of its military efforts. It chose to label them as 'enemy combatants' and thereby excluded them from the provisions of the 1949 Geneva Convention. Under President Bush, individuals were transported to the Guantánamo Bay detention facility that was deliberately chosen as it lay outside the jurisdiction of US federal courts. Intelligence information led the US authorities to conclude that these combatants were a threat to national security, but placing them in such a military facility meant that they could be held in perpetuity and their right of *habeas corpus* could be denied. The standards by which these prisoners were held and interrogated were the subject of considerable criticism from human rights organizations as well as from governments on the other side of the Atlantic.

[6] W. Rees, *Transatlantic Counter-Terrorism Cooperation: The New Imperative* (Abingdon: Routledge, 2006).

When President Obama came to power, he acknowledged that criticism of Guantánamo Bay had damaged the legitimacy of US counterterrorism efforts in the eyes of the world. It had also undermined the willingness of European governments to work with the USA. He contended that Guantánamo Bay had dented America's reputation for justice and he committed his administration to close the facility. One of his first acts as president was to sign an order mandating its closure within a year.

Nevertheless, two factors have meant that although Guantánamo Bay has been reduced in size, it has not been closed. Some 170 high-risk prisoners remain there.[7] The first problem was that many governments, including ones in Europe, refused to accept the return of detainees. Having made the case that prisoners were being held because of the risk that they posed, countries were unwilling to accept their return. The second problem was that the transfer of prisoners to the US mainland faced stiff opposition from Congress. Politicians in Washington were reluctant to damage their own popularity in their constituencies by making the case for suspected militants to be housed in mainland prisons. Instead, President Obama was forced to revert to the practice of using military tribunals in order to bring some of the accused before a court. This was a return to a policy that had been initiated by the first Bush Administration under the Military Order passed by Congress in November 2001.[8] Once again the contrast with European practices was demonstrated as no European state has used military tribunals in countering terrorism.

A second area of transatlantic tension has been over the application of so-called 'enhanced interrogation' techniques.[9] The Bush Administration embarked upon the War on Terror with an acknowledged disadvantage: it was fighting a sub-state organization on which it had limited information. Although the threat from al-Qaeda had been appreciated during the latter part of the 1990s, human intelligence sources (HUMINT) were practically non-existent, and the traditional focus upon high-technology espionage meant that the USA was ill-prepared for the new challenge. Allied to the fact that the 9/11 attacks had inflicted massive psychological harm, in addition to the loss of life and material damage, the US determination to retaliate was overwhelming. While this does not excuse the path the USA

[7] See http://projects.nytimes.com/guantanamo, accessed 15 February 2014, for a 'count' of the remaining detainees.

[8] Military Order of 13 November 2001.

[9] On their origins, much public discussion has been focused upon a manual leaked by a civil liberties watchdog, *Truthout*, available at: www.dod.gov/pubs/foi/operation_and_plans/Detainee/PREAL%20Operating%20Instructions.pdf, accessed 15 February 2014.

chose to take, it does help to explain why it acted in the way that it did. The rapid acquisition of intelligence was deemed vital not only to facilitate US action but also to forestall the risk of future attacks.

To this end, the White House authorized the reinterpretation of America's own rules forbidding torture, based upon the 1948 Universal Declaration of Human Rights and the 1984 UN Convention Against Torture and Other Cruel, Inhuman or Degrading Treatment. It approved the use of interrogation techniques, providing that the pain inflicted upon the subject was less than that which accompanied organ failure or death. Khalid Sheikh Mohammed, the alleged planner of the 9/11 attacks, suffered water-boarding (simulated drowning) 183 times while in US custody.[10] The Defense Secretary, Donald Rumsfeld, presided over a military establishment that employed such interrogation techniques and, inadvertently, this formed the backcloth against which further abuses of human rights were perpetrated at facilities such as Abu Ghraib in Iraq. Vice-President Richard Cheney later argued that substantive intelligence gains had resulted from what critics called the embrace of torture by US personnel.

President Obama appreciated the damage that accusations of torture had done to the legitimacy of US counterterrorism policy. The use of such methods undermined US claims to moral authority in fighting al-Qaeda and made many of its European allies recoil in revulsion. Obama signed Executive Order 13491, which rescinded the legal guidance on which the use of enhanced interrogation had been based.[11] Four secret memos from the Department of Justice in 2002 had made the case for these methods and the memos were placed in the public domain. All US federal agencies, henceforth, were instructed to comply with the guidelines on interrogation contained within the Army's field manual.

A third source of transatlantic tension centred upon the issue of 'extraordinary rendition'. This was a practice begun during the first Bush Administration by which terrorist suspects were transported to countries outside the United States where more extreme forms of interrogation could be inflicted upon them. The USA flew detainees to so-called 'ghost prisons' in countries such as Egypt, Jordan and in Central Europe where they tortured, held for long periods and, in some instances, killed these detainees. A diplomatic storm about these US practices blew up in

[10] See http://projects.nytimes.com/guantanamo/detainees/10024-khalid-shaikh-mohammed, accessed 15 February 2014.

[11] Executive Order 13440 of 20 July 2007.

December 2005 when the nature of these Central Intelligence Agency flights began to become public knowledge. It became apparent that thousands of such flights had taken place.

Despite the fact that many European governments expressed their indignation when the practice of extraordinary rendition was revealed, it subsequently became clear in an inquiry led by the European Parliament that many had been complicit, to a greater or lesser extent, in these activities. At one end of the spectrum, some governments asked no questions when flights transited their territories. At the other end, some governments were aware of what the CIA were doing and benefited from the intelligence that was obtained. The Obama Administration announced the cessation of rendition flights, and this was confirmed by CIA Director Leon Panetta in April 2009.

Those European governments that actively complied with the USA over rendition have found that the issue has returned to haunt them. The opprobrium that has attached itself to the USA has also smeared onto some of its allies. European countries have been drawn into legal cases where victims of the process have tried to obtain damages from the perpetrators. The ability of governments to defend themselves has been weakened by the fact that they have been dependent on the level of intelligence information that the USA has been willing to release in such cases. Britain, for example, was accused of being involved in the case of Binyam Mohamed, who was rendered by the USA to Morocco and Afghanistan and ended up in Guantánamo Bay.[12] Mohamed claimed that his interrogators were fed information by intelligence officers from the UK. After his release from US custody, the British Government paid Binyam Mohamed substantial damages to drop the legal case that he was pursuing against them. As British courts have demanded to see intelligence material in such cases, Washington responded by threatening to downgrade its level of intelligence cooperation with Britain. Ken Clarke, the then-Justice Minister, had to intervene to prevent an embarrassing hiccup in the US–UK 'special relationship'.

The fourth obstacle within transatlantic foreign policy cooperation has related to the use of Unmanned Aerial Vehicles (UAVs), or 'drones', in targeted killings. The USA has employed UAVs to kill its enemies in inaccessible regions without putting the lives of its own service personnel at risk. This has been a different issue to the preceding three discussed above.

[12] *The Queen (On application of Binyam Mohamed)* v. *Secretary of State for Foreign & Commonwealth Affairs* [2010] EWCA Civ 65.

First, although the practice was initiated by the Bush Administration, it has been expanded dramatically under the Obama Administration. For example, in 2008 there were 36 drone attacks but in 2010 this had climbed to a record of 122 attacks.[13] Second, it is part of a policy designed by the USA that does not seek to elicit cooperation from allies. While the USA has traditionally sought assistance from Europe in counterterrorism, this policy reflects US determination to continue to prosecute its fight against terrorism remotely from the safety of its own shores.

The ability to execute this strategy remotely has been one of the causes of tension between the USA and its European critics. CIA operatives attacking targets from bases in the US homeland have caused people to fear that the process will become desensitized. Furthermore, there are concerns that the USA is using force on the sovereign territory of other countries and that this is of questionable legitimacy. Most of the drone strikes have been on the territory of Pakistan, in its Federally Administered Tribal Areas. Attacks have even been extended to the territory of Yemen. European allies have warned that the USA risks alienating allies such as Pakistan and Yemen, who have experienced considerable domestic turmoil over this issue. The USA has justified these attacks as self-defence and argued that it is at war with al-Qaeda and its affiliates. The extent to which civilians have been the victims of these attacks is another source of contention. Human rights organizations have alleged that there are large numbers of casualties, whereas the USA responds that the strikes are highly accurate and great care is taken to avoid the deaths of civilians.

In all of these ways, US action within the War on Terror has fallen short of the standards that its European allies expected. The USA had claimed the moral high ground against its enemies, arguing that it represented the forces of human progress and freedom, yet over time the dark side of its behaviour has been revealed. The USA has aligned itself with authoritarian regimes, such as Uzbekistan, in order to secure bases in its operations in Afghanistan, and the actions of its own personnel have belied its ideals. As a result, European governments have been wary of cooperating with the USA for fear of being tarred with the same brush. In addition, US policies have been viewed on this side of the Atlantic as counterproductive. They have been seen to fuel a radical discourse that has impacted on the security of European states. Small numbers of Muslims living within

[13] See the remarks of John Brennan, 'The Ethics and Efficacy of the President's Counter-Terrorism Strategy', Speech of the Assistant to the President for Homeland Security and Counter-terrorism at the Woodrow Wilson Center, Washington DC, 30 April 2012.

Europe have been radicalized by the misdeeds of the USA in the Arab world.

Homeland security

Foreign policy cooperation has been the most high-profile aspect of the transatlantic security agenda since 2000, but it has not been the only facet of counterterrorism collaboration. A less high-profile, but nevertheless vital, aspect of the relationship has been *internal* security cooperation. Two sorts of tensions have characterized this dimension of the relationship. In the first place, the USA was requesting its European allies to engage in innovative forms of security: intelligence agencies, police forces and judiciaries have been called upon to share information and collaborate against a common enemy. Such bodies have little experience of working across international boundaries and this in itself has caused a number of difficulties, as new ways of interacting have needed to be worked out. The second factor has compounded the problem, namely that it has been necessary to construct this new pattern of cooperation against a backcloth of European mistrust of the attitudes of the USA towards human rights and civil liberties. Sharing information and acquiescing to US demands has been made more problematic by suspicions of its intentions.

This suspicion has been driven by some of the domestic policy initiatives adopted by the Bush Administration. The PATRIOT Act, for example, served to endow US security agencies with powers that exceeded many of their European counterparts.[14] US law enforcement organizations were given authority to gather personal data about citizens, acquire bank account and medical information, conduct 'roving' interception of telecommunications and carry out surveillance. European governments were critical of the extent of the powers that the USA had invested in its law enforcement agencies. Contrary to their expectations, President Obama proceeded to renew, rather than overturn, much of this legislation when he came to office.

Sensitivities around data-sharing have exemplified this absence of US–European trust.[15] Ever since 9/11 and the resulting US demands for law enforcement data from Europe, there has been disquiet at US procedures for handling confidential data. With comprehensive EU

[14] USA Patriot Act of 2001.

[15] See the contributions of J. Santos Vara and V. Mitsilegas in this volume. See P. Pawlak (ed.), *The EU–US Security and Justice Agenda in Action*, Chaillot Paper 127, December, EU Institute for Security Studies, Paris (2011).

directives on data issues, there were fears that the USA allowed data to be shared among a plethora of agencies at both state and federal levels. Across several policy areas, ranging from information-sharing agreements with the European Police Office (Europol), to the exchange of Passenger Name Records (PNR) collected by airlines flying to the USA, fears arose concerning the way data would be disseminated and stored. The European Parliament has taken a lead role in championing the cause of data security with the US authorities. It secured the overturning of the original Agreement between the US Government and the European Commission on the exchange of PNR data. In May 2010 it demanded that the European Commission renegotiate a framework agreement designed to serve as a blueprint for future transatlantic cooperation that involved data exchange. The revised Agreement was not passed until April 2012. It limits data retention to a five-year period and provides a mechanism by which citizens can obtain judicial redress for inaccurate information held by the USA. For its part the USA has become increasingly frustrated by what it has regarded as its allies' obsession with data privacy.

A further source of tension related to the handling of financial information. The Obama Administration inherited from its predecessor a debate about US access to electronic financial transactions carried out by means of international telecommunications: so-called SWIFT data. The Bush Administration had accessed banking information from 2001 to 2006 as part of its Terrorist Financial Tracking Programme (TFTP) but had not informed its allies. The fact that the USA was intercepting this data, based in Belgium, was not revealed until the *New York Times* exposed the practice in June 2006.[16] The USA then undertook to find an agreement with the EU on this subject, and the negotiations outlasted the Bush presidency. A draft agreement was reached in 2010, but the European Parliament rejected it in February on the grounds that they were dissatisfied with US data protection provisions. A second version of the document was not agreed until later that same year when safeguards were added that restricted the amount of data that could be transferred and provided the basis for judicial redress of erroneous information. Even the revised Agreement has been subject to criticism from the Joint Supervisory Board of Europol, the EU agency given responsibility to oversee US compliance

[16] E. Lichtblau and J. Risen, 'Bank Data Is Sifted by US in Secret to Block Terror', *New York Times*, 23 June 2006, available at: www.nytimes.com/2006/06/23/washington/23intel.html?pagewanted=all&_r=0, accessed 15 February 2014.

with the Agreement.[17] These measures reinforced European perceptions of a growing divide between the two sides of the Atlantic over civil liberties and human rights. European governments argued that the sort of cooperation that they could extend to the USA was constrained both by their own national laws as well as by the European Convention on Human Rights. Issues over the death penalty and concerns about human rights have made European states more reluctant to extradite individuals who have been accused of terrorist offences to the USA. Thus, US behaviour has actually undermined the level of cooperation it has been possible to expect from its allies.

Conclusion

European countries have varied in the depth of their criticism of US policy within the War on Terror. There have been differences over the legality of what the USA has been doing as well as criticisms of the moral authority it has sacrificed by actions of questionable legitimacy. These criticisms have discouraged many European governments from responding positively to US requests for cooperation. They have been reluctant to become associated with the policies of the superpower. They have also perceived that their own security has been adversely affected by US actions that have increased the radicalization of Muslims both inside and outside of Europe.

Transatlantic differences were at their sharpest during the period of the two Bush administrations. The inauguration of President Obama marked a sharp upturn in European optimism that there would be a major change in US counterterrorism policy. This optimism has not been fulfilled. European governments misunderstood the priority that any US government would devote to counterterrorism, even a decade after the 9/11 attacks. They also underestimated the legacy of issues that Obama inherited and the constraints under which his administration has operated.

[17] T. Wetzling, 'What Role for the Rule of Law in EU–US Counter-Terrorism' in Pawlak (ed.), *The EU–US Security and Justice Agenda in Action*, p. 29, at p. 35.

12

Transatlantic counterterrorism cooperation agreements on the transfer of personal data

A test for democratic accountability in the EU

JUAN SANTOS VARA

Introduction

Transatlantic security relations are still characterized by the difficulty in finding a balance between the need to fight effectively against terrorism and organized crime, and the need to safeguard fundamental rights and, in particular, the protection of personal data.[1] However, the conclusion of transatlantic agreements to facilitate the transfer of personal data for the purpose of combating terrorism and organized crime is an essential tool in addressing the challenges the EU and the USA face in this area.[2] The

This chapter has benefited from the support of Research Project DER2011–28459 and DER2012–36703, financed by the Spanish Ministry of Economy and Competitiveness. It substantially develops a working paper published by the Centre for the Law of EU External Relations ('The Role of the European Parliament in the Conclusion of the Transatlantic Agreements on the Transfer of Personal Data after Lisbon', CLEER Working Paper 2013/2). The author wishes to express his gratitude to Elaine Fahey for her comments on the earlier version of this chapter. Any remaining errors are my own.

[1] The EU–US Declaration on Counterterrorism of 2010 states that 'the EU and the US share a deeply rooted fundamental value in the protection of personal data and privacy, and that our information sharing and cooperation in preventing, investigating, and prosecuting terrorism takes place with full respect for our obligations under applicable international and domestic constitutional law'.

[2] See M. Cremona, 'Justice and Home Affairs in a Globalised World: Ambitions and Reality in the Tale of the EU–US SWIFT Agreement', Institute for European Integration Research Working Paper No. 4/2011; D. Curtin, 'Official Secrets and the Negotiation of International Agreements: Is the EU Executive Unbound?' (2013) 50 *Common Market Law Review* 423–58; V. Mitsilegas, 'EU–US Co-operation in Criminal Matters Post-9/11: Extradition, Mutual Legal Assistance and the Exchange of Police Data' (2003) 8 *European Foreign Affairs Review* 515–36; P. Pawlak (ed.), *The EU–US Security and Justice Agenda in Action* (Paris: EUISS Chaillot Paper, 2011); V. Pfisterer 'The Second SWIFT Agreement between the European Union and the United States of America – An Overview' (2011) 11 *German Law Journal*, 1,173–90.

different perspectives of the USA and the EU with regard to the protection of personal data were present in the negotiations of the agreements between the USA and Europol,[3] the agreements on extradition and mutual legal assistance of 2003,[4] the agreements on the processing and transfer of financial messaging data of 2009 and 2010 (SWIFT Agreements),[5] and the EU–US Passenger Name Records Agreements (PNR Agreements) of 2004, 2006, 2007 and 2011.[6]

It is true that the EU has clearly stated the incompatibility of some of the measures proposed by the USA with the protection of human rights and fundamental freedoms. However, it has ended up accepting a system that focuses mainly on the establishment of and access to personal data information systems, and it has fostered the development and implementation of certain similar measures by the EU.[7] Perhaps the most evocative example of the process of internalizing US demands in the area of transatlantic security relations can be found in the PNR Agreements. The transfer of PNR was introduced into the European agenda as a result of the unilateral demand by the USA to require passenger name records from airlines for their flights from the EU to the USA. Before this, transfer of PNR data did not form part of the EU's antiterrorist agenda. The EU's reaction was motivated more by the need to provide a solution to the difficult situation for the airlines than by a desire to intensify antiterrorist cooperation in this area. Finally, the EU is attempting to develop its own PNR directive, following the US model.[8] In the processing and

3 Agreements between the United States of America and the European Police Office of 6 December 2001 and 20 December 2002, available at: www.state.gov/documents/organization/170982.pdf, accessed 15 February 2014.

4 Agreements on Extradition and Mutual Legal Assistance of 2003, OJ 2006 No. L181/27 and OJ 2006 No. L181/34.

5 Agreements between the European Union and the United States of America on the Processing and Transfer of Financial Messaging Data from the European Union to the United States for Purposes of the Terrorist Finance Tracking Programme of 2009 (OJ 2010 No. L/9) and 2010 (OJ 2010 No. L195/3) (hereafter 2010 SWIFT Agreement).

6 Agreements on the Use and Transfer of Passenger Name Records (PNR) to the US Department of Homeland Security (DHS) of 2004 (OJ 2004 No. L183/84), 2006 (OJ 2006 No. L298/29), 2007 (OJ 2007 No. L204/18) and 2011 (OJ 2012 No. L215/1).

7 J. Argomaniz, 'When the EU is the "Norm-taker": The Passenger Name Records Agreement and the EU's Internalisation of US Border Security Norms' (2009) 31 *Journal of European Integration* 119–36, at 121. See also P. Pawlak, 'Made in the USA? The Influence of the US on the EU's Data Protection Regime', Center for European Policy Studies, 2009, available at: http://aei.pitt.edu/15102/1/made-usa-influence-us-eus-data-protection-regime.pdf, accessed 24 October 2013.

8 Proposal for a Directive on the Use of Passenger Name Record Data for the Prevention, Detection, Investigation and Prosecution of Terrorist Offences and Serious Crime, COM

transfer of financial messaging data, the EU also seems to be following the same pattern observed in the case of PNR data. Thus, at the request of the Parliament, the Council committed itself to establishing the legal and technical framework that would permit the future extraction of data in the EU. In mid July 2011 the Commission presented a preliminary study on the different options available to develop its own Terrorist Financial Tracking Programme (TFTP).[9] The European system of monitoring terrorist financing would have two main objectives: to aid in the fight against terrorist financing within the EU and to reduce significantly the volume of data transferred to the United States

In the past, the European Parliament was strongly opposed to the US demands for data transfers. The Parliament sought to strike a balance between the fight against terrorism and other serious crimes, and the protection of civil liberties and fundamental freedoms. However, the role attributed to the European Parliament in the conclusion of international agreements in the area of freedom, security and justice (AFSJ) was marginal. The application of the ordinary legislative procedure to the adoption of Acts in the area of police and judicial cooperation in criminal matters, since the entry into force of the Treaty of Lisbon, enhances the role of the European Parliament in the conclusion of international agreements.[10] The new powers vested in the European Parliament by the Lisbon Treaty have enabled it to influence the negotiation of agreements in the area of police and judicial cooperation in criminal matters, and in particular in the field of data processing. The European Parliament seems willing to use the new powers conferred on it by the Lisbon Treaty in the conclusion of international agreements in this area. The refusal to give its consent to the EU–US SWIFT Agreement in February 2010 and the deferral of its consent on the PNR Agreements with the USA and Australia in December 2010 are good examples. If the Parliament must give its consent to this kind of agreement, it will need to be involved at early stages of the negotiation process. This chapter will aim to examine the implications arising from the Parliament's involvement during the negotiation process of international agreements in the area of police and judicial cooperation in criminal matters.

(2011) 32; EU-PNR Commission Staff Working Paper Impact Assessment COM (2011) 32 final.

[9] Commission Communication, A European Terrorist Finance Tracking System: Available Options, COM (2011) 429 final, 13 July 2011, available at: www.csm.it/Eurojust/CD/19.pdf, accessed 24 October 2013.

[10] See Art. 218 TFEU.

The PNR and SWIFT Agreements fall within the scope of the current negotiations for an agreement between the EU and the USA on the exchange of personal data in the framework of police and judicial cooperation in criminal matters.[11] On 3 December 2010 the Council authorized the opening of negotiations for an agreement between the EU and the USA on the protection of personal data when transferred and processed for the purpose of preventing, investigating, detecting or prosecuting criminal offences, including terrorism, in the framework of police and judicial cooperation in criminal matters. This proposal was included in the Action Plan Implementing the Stockholm Programme.[12] The objective was to negotiate an umbrella agreement that would provide for a coherent set of data protection standards in the relations between the EU and the USA. However, this agreement would not constitute the legal basis for any specific transfers of personal data. A specific legal basis for such data transfers would always be required. The conclusion of this agreement would not provide for a higher level of protection of personal data if it did not contain additional rules to the specific agreements on data transfer. It would also be required to ensure the effective application of data protection rules and their supervision by independent authorities. Unfortunately, the negotiations have advanced very slowly.[13]

In June 2013 the press revealed that the US authorities have accessed and processed on a large scale the personal data of EU citizens using online service providers. The EU institutions expressed serious concerns over PRISM and other such programmes implemented by the National Security Agency (NSA), since these initiatives may entail a serious violation of the fundamental rights of EU citizens and residents, and called on the US authorities to provide the EU with full information on such

[11] See European Commission, 'European Commission Ready to Start Talks with US on Personal Data Agreement to Fight Terrorism or Crime', Press Release, 3 December 2010, available at: http://europa.eu/rapid/press-release_IP-10-1661_en.htm, accessed 24 October 2013.

[12] Communication from the Commission to the European Parliament, the Council, the European Economic and Social Committee, and the Committee of the Regions, Delivering an Area of Freedom, Security and Justice for Europe's Citizens, Action Plan Implementing the Stockholm Programme, COM(2010) 171 final, available at: http://eur-lex.europa.eu/LexUriServ/LexUriServ.do?uri=COM:2010:0171:FIN:EN:PDF, accessed 24 October 2013.

[13] See Chapter 10 of this volume by S. in't Veld, 'Transatlantic Relations and Security: Reflections from a Politician, Practitioner and Litigator'.

programmes.[14] The European Parliament opened an investigation into the matter in order to assess the impact of the US surveillance programmes regarding fundamental rights, in particular the right to respect for private life and communications, freedom of expression, the presumption of innocence and the right to an effective remedy. Some Members of the European Parliament (MEPs) raised the possibility of suspending or even terminating the SWIFT and PNR Agreements during the hearings on the NSA surveillance programmes.[15] The Parliament was due to finish its report by the end of 2013, at the time of writing. At the moment it does not seem that the majority of MEPs are willing to ask the Commission and the Council to adopt this serious decision, which could negatively affect transatlantic relations and, in particular, the negotiations on the transatlantic trade agreement. The NSA scandal further reaffirms the need to negotiate a transatlantic framework agreement on the protection of personal data that ensures access for EU citizens to the US judicial system and a right to redress under the same conditions as US citizens.[16]

The aim of this contribution is to analyze to what extent the European Parliament is in practice using its new powers to influence the substantive content of the transatlantic agreements or to assert its new role on the conclusion of international treaties. This chapter focuses on the agreements concluded in the area of police and judicial cooperation in criminal matters, in particular the SWIFT and PNR Agreements. The inquiry into the US surveillance activities constitutes an unprecedented test for democratic accountability in the EU. The analysis of the role played by the Parliament in the negotiation of the SWIFT and PNR Agreements would also be useful in exploring what could be expected from the parliamentary investigation into the NSA scandal.

[14] See Commissioner Reding, letter to the US Attorney General, Eric Holder, 10 June 2013, available at: www.edri.org/files/holder.pdf, accessed 24 October 2013; Statement by the President of the European Council, 11 July 2013, available at: http://europa.eu/rapid/press-release_SPEECH-13-625_en.htm, accessed 24 October 2013; European Parliament Resolution of 2 July 2013, on the US National Security Agency surveillance programme, surveillance bodies in various Member States and their impact on EU citizens' privacy.

[15] European Parliament, 'MEPs Raise Suspension of EU–US Bank Data Deal', Press Release, 24 September 2013; European Parliament Resolution of 23 October 2013, on the suspension of the TFTP Agreement as a result of US National Security Agency surveillance (2013/2831(RSP)), footnote 11.

[16] The access to justice and the redress system is very weak in the SWIFT and PNR Agreements. See E. Fahey, 'Law and Governance as Checks and Balances in Transatlantic Security: Rights, Redress and Remedies in EU–US Passenger Name Records and the Terrorism Finance Tracking Program' (2013) 1 *Yearbook of European Law* 368–88.

This contribution examines, first, the practical implications arising from the new role played by the European Parliament in the conclusion of agreements in the area of police and judicial cooperation in criminal matters (Section 1). In the following section, the operation of parliamentary scrutiny is analyzed with regard to the negotiation of the SWIFT Agreements. It will be shown how the transfer of substantial powers to the European Parliament is affecting the field of data processing in the external dimension of the AFSJ. Finally, Section 3 assesses the influence of the European Parliament in the PNR Agreements concluded with the United States on the basis of the 2004, 2006, 2007 and 2011 Agreements. The vote of the European Parliament on the SWIFT and PNR Agreements will have significant implications for EU external relations and, in particular, for cooperation with the USA in the fight against terrorism.

1 An enhanced role for the European Parliament in the conclusion of agreements in the area of police and judicial cooperation in criminal matters

The role that the former Treaty on European Union (TEU) attributed to the European Parliament in the third pillar was wholly marginal, within both the internal and the external dimensions of the AFSJ.[17] In a Resolution from 2007 the European Parliament advocated the need to improve democratic accountability in the external dimension of the AFSJ.[18] The Parliament had also urged the Council Presidency and the Commission to consult the Parliament when agreements would affect the fundamental rights of Union citizens and the main aspects of judicial and police cooperation with third countries or international organizations.[19] However, there is no doubt that the Parliament managed to make intelligent use of the mechanisms of political and judicial control provided for in the TEU in order to try to influence the content of third-pillar Acts.[20] For example, the European Parliament was not involved in the

[17] In the past, the Parliament was merely informed of the conclusion of third-pillar agreements. The Treaty of Lisbon introduced the innovations that were already included in the Constitutional Treaty.

[18] European Parliament Resolution of 21 June 2007, on an area of freedom, security and justice: Strategy on the External Dimension, Action Plan Implementing the Hague Programme (2006/2111(INI)).

[19] *Ibid.*, paras. 1 and 2.

[20] See J. Martín y Pérez de Nanclares, 'La posición del Parlamento Europeo en el espacio de libertad, seguridad y justicia' in E. Barbé Izuel and A. Herranz Surrallés (eds.),

negotiations of the agreements on extradition and mutual legal assistance between the EU and the USA. Nonetheless, the European Parliament exploited the possibilities for political control bestowed upon it by former Articles 39(1)–(2)TEU to try to influence the content of the agreements.[21] As will be shown in the second section of this chapter, the Parliament has also been very critical of the conclusion of the PNR Agreements and the SWIFT Agreements with the USA.

The entry into force of the Treaty of Lisbon has led to major progress that contributes to alleviating the deficiencies that characterized European cooperation in this field from a democratic perspective.[22] The application of the ordinary legislative procedure to the adoption of Acts in the area of police and judicial cooperation in criminal matters has strengthened the EU's democratic accountability, and this democratic enhancement is obviously having repercussions on the external dimension of all policies included in the AFSJ. The new powers vested in the European Parliament by the Lisbon Treaty enable it to influence the implementation of the actions undertaken by the EU both in policies on border checks, asylum and immigration, and in police and judicial cooperation in criminal matters.[23] The Parliament will also be able to influence the content of any agreement on the exchange of personal data with third countries.[24]

Política Exterior y Parlamento Europeo: Hacia el Equilibrio entre Eficacia y Democracia (Barcelona: Oficina de Información del Parlamento Europeo, 2007), pp. 67–83.

[21] According to former Art. 39 TEU, the Council had to consult the Parliament before adopting framework decisions, decisions and conventions among the Member States. Also, the Parliament was to be kept fully informed by the Commission and the Council about the discussions in the area of police and judicial cooperation in criminal matters. See the European Parliament Recommendation B5-0540/2002, requesting the Council to inform it as well as national parliaments on the progress of the negotiations, and Resolution B4-0813/2001, in which the Parliament insisted on safeguards such as not allowing extradition if the defendant could be sentenced to death in the USA.

[22] See European Parliament, Report on the Treaty of Lisbon (2007/2286(INI)), 29 January 2008, and Resolution of 20 February 2008 on the Treaty of Lisbon, Doc. A6-0013/2008.

[23] For thorough comments on the institutional implications of the Treaty of Lisbon for the external dimension of the AFSJ, see S. Poli, 'The Institutional Setting and the Legal Toolkit' in M. Cremona, J. Monar and S. Poli (eds.), *The External Dimension of the European Union's Area of Freedom, Security and Justice* (Brussels: Peter Lang 2011), pp. 25–75; J. Santos Vara, 'The External Dimension of the Area of Freedom, Security and Justice in the Lisbon Treaty' (2008) 10 *European Journal of Law Reform* 577–97.

[24] H. Hijmans and A. Scirocco, 'Shortcomings in EU Data Protection in the Third and Second Pillars. Can the Treaty of Lisbon Be Expected to Help?' (2009) 46 *Common Market Law Review* 1,485–525, at 1,522.

Whereas in the past there was no parliamentary involvement in former third-pillar agreements whatsoever,[25] the consent of the European Parliament is required in a wide range of international agreements, including those concerning domains subject to the ordinary legislative procedure in the internal sphere of the Union.[26] According to Article 218(6) of the Treaty on the Functioning of the European Union (TFEU), the Council shall conclude the agreements on police and judicial cooperation on criminal matters after obtaining the consent of the European Parliament in the case of agreements covering fields to which either the ordinary legislative procedure applies, or the special legislative procedure applies where the consent of the European Parliament is required. This means that the Council shares with the Parliament the power of *concluding* international agreements in the whole AFSJ.[27]

Since the conclusion of the international agreements in this area depends on the consent of the European Parliament, it seems logical to consider its involvement from the early stages of the negotiations. Article 218(6) TFEU states that 'the European Parliament shall be immediately and fully informed at all stages of the procedure'. The involvement of the European Parliament is not limited to the celebration of agreements where consent by the European Parliament is required. However, the European Parliament must be included and listened to in the negotiation of the agreements whose conclusion depends on the Parliament's consent. Consequently, the European Parliament is not only called to give its consent or not. The involvement of the European Parliament in the process of the conclusion of international agreements is much more developed than in the Member States' constitutional systems. Monar stresses that 'unlike in the case of national governments, neither Council nor Commission is normally able to take the backing of the European Parliament for granted since the clear link between executive governmental power and a stable parliamentary majority typical for democratic parliamentary systems

[25] See former Arts. 24 and 38 of the TEU.

[26] There are only two exceptions to the application of the ordinary legislative procedure in the area of police and judicial cooperation on criminal matters. Art. 87(3) TFEU deals with operational cooperation between police authorities, and Art. 89 lays down the conditions and limitations under which the competent authorities of the Member States may operate in the territory of another Member. In both cases the Council shall act unanimously after consulting the European Parliament. Consequently, the celebration of international agreements in this area will not depend on the consent of the European Parliament.

[27] See P. Eeckhout, *EU External Relations Law* (Oxford University Press, 2011); S. Peers, *EU Justice and Home Affairs* (Oxford University Press, 2011).

does not exist in the EU'. Consequently, he argues that 'the Commission and Council will therefore have to invest more into majority building within the Parliament'.[28]

The obligation to fully inform the Parliament at all stages of the negotiation and conclusion of international agreements, including the definition of negotiating directives, is further developed in the Framework Agreement on Relations between the European Parliament and the European Commission from 2010. The Framework Agreement states that:

> in the case of international agreements the conclusion of which requires Parliament's consent, the Commission shall provide to Parliament during the negotiation process all relevant information that it also provides to the Council ... This shall include draft amendments to adopted negotiating directives, draft negotiating texts, agreed articles, the agreed date for initialling the agreement and the text of the agreement to be initialled.[29]

The Council has expressed its concern about the role attributed to the Parliament by the Framework Agreement, and in a Declaration published in the Official Journal the Council pointed out that several provisions of the Framework Agreement, in particular the provisions on international agreements, 'have the effect of modifying the institutional balance set out in the Treaties in force, according the European Parliament prerogatives that are not provided for in the Treaties and limiting the autonomy of the Commission and its President'.[30] The Council seems reluctant to accept the implications arising from the new powers enjoyed by the Parliament in the conclusion of international agreements for the relationship between the European Parliament and the EU executive institutions.[31]

[28] J. Monar, 'The Rejection of the EU–US SWIFT Interim Agreement by the European Parliament: A Historic Vote and Its Implications' (2010) 15 *European Foreign Affairs Review* 143–51.

[29] Framework Agreement on Relations between the European Parliament and the European Commission, OJ 2010 No. L304/47, p. 61.

[30] Council Statement on the Framework Agreement on Relations between the European Parliament and the Commission, OJ 2010 No. C287/1. On the interinstitutional tension on the new role conferred on the European Parliament, see A. Tizzian *et al.*, 'Eleven Months of the Treaty of Lisbon: Assessment and Perspectives', *XXIV International Federation for European Law (FIDE) Congress, Final Roundtable and Conclusions. Proceedings of the FIDE XXIV Congress* (Madrid 2010, Vol. IV), pp. 20–3.

[31] On the separation of powers in the EU, see G. Conway, 'Recovering a Separation of Powers in the European Union' (2011) 17 *European Law Journal* 304–22. The role attributed to

2 The role of the European Parliament in the negotiation of the SWIFT Agreements

2.1 *The SWIFT Agreement 2009*

The Society for Worldwide Interbank Financial Telecommunication (SWIFT) is a member-owned cooperative that offers the transfer of financial messaging data to bank entities. More than 9,000 banking organizations, securities institutions and corporate customers in 209 countries use SWIFT every day to exchange millions of standardized financial messages. SWIFT is based in Belgium and has offices in the world's major financial centres, including in the USA. SWIFT is organized into three regions: Americas, Asia Pacific, and Europe, Middle East and Africa.[32] In order to analyze the role played by the European Parliament in the negotiation of the SWIFT Agreements, it is necessary to recall the origins of the TFTP. After 11 September 2001, the US Government initiated the Terrorist Finance Tracking Program (TFTP). The aim of the Program is to fight against the financing of terrorism all over the world. In the context of this Program, the US Treasury Department issued subpoenas, among others, to SWIFT's centre in the USA to obtain financial messaging data. The US centre had servers that contained the same information as the EU SWIFT centre. Consequently, the Treasury Department had full access to the financial transfers made by many Europeans. The SWIFT company itself played an important role in shaping EU–US relations in this area, since data are selected by SWIFT and made accessible to American authorities.

In 2006 the press revealed the existence of the TFTP. It was also known that the US authorities had been widely accessing European data. The lack of compatibility with the obligations under the Data Protection Directive 95/46 as well as Member States' laws implementing that Directive caused a significant controversy in Europe.[33] At the end of 2006 the Article 29 Working Group released an opinion on the processing of personal data by

the Parliament in the negotiation process of international agreements also has major implications for access to classified information in international negotiations. A detailed analysis of this issue goes beyond the purpose of this chapter. See Curtin, 'Official Secrets and the Negotiation of International Agreements'.

[32] For more details visit www.swift.com/about_swift/company_information/swift_offices.page, accessed 24 October 2013.

[33] Directive 95/46/EC of the European Parliament and of the Council, on the protection of individuals with regard to the processing of personal data and on the free movement of such data, OJ 1995 No. L281, 23/31.

SWIFT. It was stated that the massive transfer of personal data to the USA clearly infringed European data protection rules. From the first moment, the European Parliament also expressed its concern about the violation of European and national data protection norms.[34] In a Resolution adopted in 2007, the Parliament contended that 'businesses with operations on both sides of the Atlantic increasingly find themselves caught between the conflicting legal requirements of the US and EC jurisdictions'.[35] For this reason, the Parliament called for the conclusion of an international agreement with the USA to end the legal uncertainty with regard to data-sharing and transfer between the EU and the USA.

On 28 June 2007 the US authorities made a series of unilateral commitments (the so-called TFTP Representations) to the EU regarding the controls and safeguards governing the handling, use and dissemination of data under the TFTP.[36] The US Treasury contended that the Program has been designed and implemented to meet applicable US legal requirements, in order to contribute meaningfully to combating global terrorism.[37] It was pointed out that the information obtained was used exclusively for investigating and prosecuting terrorism or its financing. The USA also accepted the appointment of 'an eminent person' to confirm that the Program is implemented consistently with these Representations for the purpose of verifying the protection of personal data originating in the EU.[38] In March 2008 the Commission appointed the French Judge J.-L. Bruguière as 'eminent European person'; he issued his first report in January 2009. Judge J.-L. Bruguière considered that the TFTP has

[34] European Parliament Resolution of 6 July 2006, on the interception of bank transfer data from the SWIFT system by the US secret services, OJ 2006 No. C303E/843.

[35] European Parliament Resolution of 14 February 2007, on SWIFT, the PNR Agreement and the transatlantic dialogue on these issues, OJ 2007 No. C287E/349.

[36] Terrorist Finance Tracking Program – Representations of the United States Department of the Treasury, OJ 2007 No. C166/18.

[37] Terrorist Finance Tracking Program – Representations of the United States Department of the Treasury, OJ 2007 No. C166/18. See also Council of the European Union, 'Processing and Protection of Personal Data Subpoenaed by the Treasury Department from the US-Based Operation Centre of the Society for Worldwide Interbank Financial Telecommunication (SWIFT)', 11291/2/07 REV 2 (Presse 157), 28 June 2007, available at: www.consilium.europa.eu/uedocs/cms_data/docs/pressdata/en/misc/95017.pdf, accessed 24 October 2013.

[38] It is stated in the document sent by the US authorities that 'the eminent person will monitor that processes for deletion of non-extracted data have been carried out' and 'shall act in complete independence in the performance of his or her duties. The eminent person shall, in the performance of his or her duties, neither seek nor take instructions from anybody.'

generated significant value for the fight against terrorism in the USA, in Europe and beyond. He stated that the TFTP is implemented in accordance with the US Representations.[39]

In order to understand the need to conclude the SWIFT Agreement, a reference should be made to the restructuring of the SWIFT servers launched in 2007 and completed in late 2009. Before the relocation of the SWIFT servers, SWIFT stored messages on two identical ('mirror') servers in order to enhance data resilience. These servers were located in Europe and the USA. According to its new messaging architecture, as of 1 January 2010 intra-EU message data will now be processed and stored exclusively within Europe. The result is that a significant part of the data that have formed the basis of TFTP subpoenas will no longer be stored in the USA.

On 27 July 2009 the Council decided to authorize the Presidency, assisted by the Commission, to open negotiations for an agreement between the EU and the USA on the processing and transfer of financial messaging data from the EU to the USA for the purposes of the TFTP on the basis of former Articles 24 and 38 TEU. The changes introduced by SWIFT made it necessary to conclude an agreement between the EU and the USA on the processing and transfer of financial messaging data. The agreement was aimed at preventing and combating terrorism and its financing, subject to strict compliance with safeguards on privacy and the protection of personal data. The agreement would allow the USA to request that designated providers, including SWIFT, make available to the US Treasury financial payment messaging data stored in the EU.

As Monar has stated, the majority of the EU Member States supported the negotiation of such an agreement, 'not only because of its contribution to transatlantic counterterrorism cooperation but also because some TFTP-provided intelligence would continue to be available for counterterrorism investigations within the EU'.[40] The SWIFT affair shows how internal data protection objectives constrain and shape EU external action, and demonstrates the difficulty in drawing a distinction between internal and external security objectives.[41] The SWIFT affair also demonstrates

[39] IP/09/264, 17 February 2009. J.-L. Bruguière 'Second Report on the Processing of EU-Originating Personal Data by the United States Treasury Department for Counter Terrorism Purposes: Terrorist Finance Tracking Programme' (2010), available at: www.statewatch.org/news/2010/aug/eu-usa-swift-2nd-bruguiere-report.pdf, accessed 24 October 2013.

[40] Monar, 'The Rejection of the EU–US SWIFT Interim Agreement', 146.

[41] Cremona, 'Justice and Home Affairs in a Globalised World', 26.

that there is no willingness to overcome the problems of accountability and governance that are present in the transatlantic transfer of personal data.[42] As will be demonstrated in the following subsection, the transfer of financial data to the USA clearly shows that the need to fight against terrorism currently prevails over the protection of fundamental rights in the external dimension of the AFSJ even more intensively that at the EU internal level.

2.2 *The implications of the Lisbon Treaty for the 2009 SWIFT Agreement*

The future of the 2009 SWIFT Agreement was indisputably linked to the entry into force of the Lisbon Treaty and the significant changes brought to the decision-making procedure in the AFSJ.[43] As was the case with the PNR Agreement after the judgment of the Court of Justice of 2006,[44] the SWIFT Agreement had to be renegotiated. In the third pillar, a marginal role was attributed to the European Parliament in the conclusion of international treaties.[45] However, now that the Lisbon Treaty has come into force, the consent of the European Parliament is required for the conclusion of the SWIFT Agreement.[46]

During the negotiations of the SWIFT Agreement the European Parliament started to affirm its new role on the conclusion of international treaties, even though at that time it was still uncertain when the Treaty of Lisbon would enter into force. On 17 September 2009 the European Parliament adopted a Resolution on the proposed SWIFT Agreement.[47] Even though the Parliament admitted the relevance of the Agreement in the fight against terrorism, it also pointed to 'the need to strike the right

[42] See Fahey, 'Law and Governance as Checks and Balances'.

[43] Cremona, 'Justice and Home Affairs in a Globalised World', 17.

[44] Joined Cases C-317/04 and C-318/04, *Parliament* v. *Council* [2006] ECR I-4721. See L. González Vaqué, 'El Tribunal de Justicia de las Comunidades Europeas anula el Acuerdo entre la Comunidad Europea y los EEUU para la transmisión de los datos sobre los pasajeros por las compañías aéreas' (2006) 20 *Revista Española de Derecho Europeo* 557–77; G. Gilmore and J. Rijma, 'Joined Cases C-317/04 and C-318/04, *European Parliament* v. *Council and Commission*, judgment of the Grand Chamber of 30 May 2006, [2006] ECR I-4721' (2007) 44 *Common Market Law Review* 1,081–99.

[45] See Santos Vara, 'The External Dimension of the Area of Freedom, Security and Justice in the Lisbon Treaty', 592.

[46] See Art. 218(6)(a).

[47] European Parliament Resolution of 17 September 2009, on the envisaged international agreement to make available to the United States Treasury Department financial payment messaging data to prevent and combat terrorism and terrorist financing, P7_TA(2009)0016.

balance between security measures and the protection of civil liberties and fundamental rights, while ensuring the utmost respect for privacy and data protection'. Since the conclusion of the Agreement was absolutely necessary, the Parliament sought to ensure the following minimum requirements:

- data were transferred and processed only for the purposes of fighting terrorism, as defined in Article 1 of Council Framework Decision 2002/475/JHA of 13 June 2002 on combating terrorism;[48]
- the processing of data was not disproportionate to the objective for which those data had been transferred;
- EU citizens and enterprises were granted defence rights and the right of access to justice;
- a reciprocity mechanism was included in the Agreement, requiring US authorities to transfer relevant financial messaging data to the competent EU authorities;
- the inclusion of a sunset clause in the Interim Agreement not exceeding twelve months; and
- the conclusion of a new agreement in accordance to the Lisbon Treaty that fully involves the European Parliament.

However, disregarding the Parliament's concerns, on 30 November 2009, one day before the entry into force of the Treaty of Lisbon, the Council authorized the Presidency to sign the Interim Agreement on the transfer of Financial Messaging Data from the EU to the USA for Purposes of the Terrorist Finance Tracking Programme.[49] The Agreement was applied on a provisional basis from 1 February 2010, pending its entry into force, and would last for a maximum duration of nine months. It was to be replaced by a long-term agreement to be concluded in accordance with the Treaty of Lisbon. Also on 17 December 2009, the Commission adopted a formal proposal to conclude the SWIFT Agreement.[50]

The need to seek the Parliament's approval to conclude the SWIFT Agreement was used by Parliament to put into effect the new powers granted by the Treaty of Lisbon.[51] On 10 February 2010 the European

[48] Council Framework Decision of 13 June 2002, on combating terrorism, OJ 2002 No. L164/3.

[49] See 2010 SWIFT Agreement, 9.

[50] COM (2009) 0703 final. The decision was based on Arts. 82(1)(d), 87(2)(a) in relation to Art. 218(6)(a) TFEU.

[51] Recommendation of February 2010 on the Proposal for a Council Decision on the Conclusion of the Agreement between the European Union and the United States of

Parliament adopted the report of the Committee on Civil Liberties, Justice and Home Affairs (LIBE Committee), recommending the rejection of the Agreement.[52] Even though the Parliament admitted the importance of transatlantic cooperation for counterterrorism purposes, it stressed that the TFTP 'must be considered as a departure from European law and practice in how law enforcement agencies would acquire individuals' financial records for law enforcement activities, namely individual court-approved warrants or subpoenas to examine specific transactions instead of relying on broad administrative subpoenas for millions of records'.[53] In addition, the Parliament complained about the unwillingness to give the Parliament full information at all stages of the negotiation process, including the opinion of the Council Legal Service and the two reports made by Judge J.-L. Bruguière.[54] Moreover, the Parliament stressed that the duty of parliamentary information was a reflection of the more general duty on the institutions to practise mutual sincere cooperation. In order to avoid the rejection of the Agreement, the Council issued a Declaration on 9 February 2010, one day before the vote in the Parliament.[55] The Council pointed out that the Agreement should have a transitional nature, having a maximum duration of nine months, and that it contained an important number of the guarantees that were called for by the Parliament's Resolution of 17 September 2009. The Council also accepted the negotiation of a longer-term EU–US TFTP Agreement and called on the Commission to adopt draft negotiation guidelines that fully took into account the concerns expressed by the Parliament. It was admitted that the Parliament must have been fully informed at all stages of the negotiation procedure when its consent was required before the formal conclusion of the Agreement.[56]

America on the Processing and Transfer of Financial Messaging Data from the European Union to the United States for Purposes of the Terrorist Finance Tracking Programme, A7-0013/2010.

[52] European Parliament Legislative Resolution of 11 February 2010, on the proposal for a Council decision on the conclusion of the Agreement between the European Union and the United States of America on the processing and transfer of financial messaging data from the European Union to the United States for purposes of the Terrorist Finance Tracking Programme (05305/1/2010 REV 1 – C7-0004/2010 – 2009/0190(NLE)).

[53] *Ibid.*

[54] IP/09/264, 17 February 2009. Bruguière, 'Second Report on the Processing of EU-Originating Personal Data'.

[55] Council of the European Union, EU–US Agreement on the Transfer of Financial Messaging Data for Purposes of the Terrorist Finance Tracking Programme, Council Document No. 6265/10, 9 February 2010, available at: www.consilium.europa.eu/uedocs/cms_data/docs/pressdata/en/jha/112850.pdf, accessed 24 October 2013.

[56] *Ibid.*

Alarmed by the possible rejection of the Interim SWIFT Agreement, the US Administration made an unprecedented lobbying effort towards the European Parliament.[57] For instance, on 5 February 2010 H. Clinton, the US Secretary of State, made a phone call to Parliament President J. Buzek and sent him a joint letter with T. Geithner, Treasury Secretary, warning the Parliament about the negative consequences arising from the rejection of the Agreement. In addition, the Spanish Presidency of the Council tried to persuade the Parliament to back the SWIFT Agreement, offering the Parliament full access to classified information during the negotiation of the permanent Agreement.[58] Even though Member States did not have exactly the same view on the Agreement, they shared a preference for healthy transatlantic relations. On 11 February 2010, despite all these guarantees, the European Parliament voted against the Agreement.[59] Consequently, the provisional application of the Agreement was no longer possible, and the Council Presidency had to send a communication to the USA, stating that the EU could not become a party to the SWIFT Agreement.

In conclusion, in the period of transition to the Lisbon Treaty, faced with the urgent need to reach an agreement on the transfer of financial messaging data to the USA, the Council and the Commission presented the Agreement as a fait accompli, an agreement that would start to apply provisionally on 1 February 2010 and could not be renegotiated.[60] The strategy failed completely. The rejection of the SWIFT Agreement by the European Parliament has shown how significantly the Lisbon Treaty has strengthened the role of the Parliament in the conclusion of international agreements, in particular in the AFSJ. As Monar has said, 'the SWIFT case mean[s] that the Council and the Commission will have to reckon much more with the Parliament's interests and position in the case of nearly all international agreements, and this is not only at the conclusion stage but already at the negotiation stage'.[61]

[57] Monar, 'The Rejection of the EU–US SWIFT Interim Agreement', 145.

[58] C. Brand, 'New Offer to Save EU–US Data Deal', *European Voice*, 9 February 2010.

[59] Member States severely criticized the European Parliament. See A. Illmer, 'European Parliament Rejects SWIFT Deal for Sharing Bank Data with US', *Deutsche Welle*, 11 February 2010, available at: www.dw.de/european-parliament-rejects-swift-deal-for-sharing-bank-data-with-us/a-5238246, accessed 24 October 2013; A. Ripoll Servent and A. MacKenzie, 'The European Parliament as a "Norm Taker"? EU–US Relations after the SWIFT Agreement' (2012) 17 *European Foreign Affairs Review* 71–86.

[60] Cremona, 'Justice and Home Affairs in a Globalised World', 17.

[61] Monar, 'The Rejection of the EU–US SWIFT Interim Agreement', 147. See also Cremona, 'Justice and Home Affairs in a Globalised World'; Curtin, 'Official Secrets and the

Another instance, namely the rejection of the Anti-Counterfeiting Trade Agreement (ACTA) by the European Parliament in July 2012, is a good example for illustrating the Parliament's enhanced role in conclusion of international agreements. The detailed analysis of ACTA goes beyond the purpose of this chapter; nevertheless, this case again affirms that the Parliament must be involved at early stages of the negotiation process in the case of agreements the conclusion of which requires Parliament's consent.[62]

2.3 *The 2010 SWIFT Agreement*

Faced with the difficult situation arising from the rejection of the SWIFT Agreement, the Commission and the Council reacted with much haste. On 24 March 2010 the Commission proposed a draft mandate of negotiations that was adopted by the Council on 11 May 2010, showing their willingness to fully consult the Parliament during the negotiations. On 5 May 2010 the European Parliament adopted a Resolution on the new draft negotiations mandate.[63] The Parliament 'welcome[d] the new spirit of cooperation demonstrated by the Commission and the Council and their willingness to engage with Parliament, taking into account their Treaty obligation to keep Parliament immediately and fully informed at all stages of the procedure'.[64] The Parliament also emphasized that bulk data transfers mark a departure from the principles underpinning EU legislation and practice. It proposed the designation in the EU of a judicial public authority with the responsibility to receive requests

Negotiation of International Agreements'; Fahey, 'Law and Governance as Checks and Balances'.

[62] European Parliament Legislative Resolution of 4 July 2012, on the draft Council decision on the conclusion of the Anti-Counterfeiting Trade Agreement between the European Union and its Member States, Australia, Canada, Japan, the Republic of Korea, the United Mexican States, the Kingdom of Morocco, New Zealand, the Republic of Singapore, the Swiss Confederation and the United States of America (12195/2011 – C7-0027/2012 – 2011/0167(NLE)). On the role of the European Parliament in ACTA, see D. Matthews and P. Žikovská, 'The Rise and Fall of the Anti-Counterfeiting Trade Agreement (ACTA): Lessons for the European Union' (2013) 44 *International Review of Industrial Property and Competition* 625–55.

[63] European Parliament Resolution of 5 May 2010, on the Recommendation from the Commission to the Council to authorize the opening of negotiations for an agreement between the European Union and the United States of America to make available to the United States Treasury Department financial messaging data to prevent and combat terrorism and terrorist financing, P7_TA (2010)0143.

[64] *Ibid.*

from the US Treasury Department. However, if the above arrangements were not feasible in the short term, the Parliament was willing to reach a compromise, differentiating between the inclusion of strict safeguards in the envisaged Agreement, on the one hand, and 'the fundamental longer-term policy decisions that the EU must address', on the other hand. In this respect, it pointed out that the extraction of data should take place in the EU by an EU judicial authority or joint EU–US investigation teams.

The negotiations were successfully concluded on 11 June 2011, and the revised Agreement was signed on 28 June 2011.[65] The European Parliament gave its consent to a new Agreement on 8 July 2010,[66] and a few days later the Council adopted the Decision concluding the Agreement between the EU and the USA on the processing and transfer of financial messaging data from the EU to the USA for the purposes of the Terrorist Finance Tracking Programme.[67] The 2010 SWIFT Agreement came into force on 1 August 2010. There is no doubt that the European Parliament was led to give its consent to the conclusion of the Agreement not only by the improvements in data protection standards, but also by the fact that on this occasion it was fully informed and involved at all stages of the negotiation process.[68]

Sophie in' t Veld, Vice Chairperson of the Committee on Civil Liberties, Justice and Home Affairs, did not get access to the Council Legal Service's report on the competence of the EU to negotiate the SWIFT Agreement because the document was classified as restricted. She brought an action seeking the annulment of the Council's Decision of 29 October 2009

[65] See 2010 SWIFT Agreement.

[66] European Parliament Legislative Resolution of 8 July 2010, on the draft Council decision on the conclusion of the Agreement between the European Union and the United States of America on the processing and transfer of financial messaging data from the European Union to the United States for the purposes of the Terrorist Finance Tracking Program (11222/1/2010/REV 1 and COR 1 – C7-0158/2010 – 2010/0178(NLE)). Some MEPs were reluctant to give their consent. The Dutch MEP S. in't Veld held that 'the United States is looking for a needle and we're sending them the entire haystack' (European Parliament, 'SWIFT: MEPs Want to Limit Data Transfers to USA', Press Release, 8 April 2010, available at: www.europarl.europa.eu/sides/getDoc.do?type=IM-PRESS&reference=20100406IPR72166&language=EN, accessed 24 October 2013).

[67] See 2010 SWIFT Agreement. In accordance with Protocol No. 21 on the position of the United Kingdom and Ireland in respect of the area of freedom, security and justice, the United Kingdom has notified its wish to take part in the adoption and application of this Decision, but Ireland is not taking part in the Decision.

[68] See J. Santos Vara, 'El acuerdo SWIFT con Estados Unidos: génesis, alcance y consecuencias' in J. Martín y Pérez de Nanclares (ed.), *La dimensión exterior del Espacio de Libertad, Seguridad y Justicia* (Madrid: Iustel, 2012), pp. 355–80, at p. 366.

refusing full access to the Council Legal Service Opinion.[69] The General Court accepted that disclosure of the strategic objectives pursued by the European Union in the negotiations that were ongoing at the time when the contested decision was adopted would undermine the negotiations. However, the General Court annulled Council's Decision insofar as it refused access to the undisclosed parts of document 11897/09 other than those that concerned the specific content of the envisaged Agreement or the negotiating directives.[70] The Court held that the Council should have taken into account that the Agreement affected the protection of personal data and established the widest possible access to the requested documents. It remains to be seen whether or not the Court of Justice confirms the legal reasoning followed by the General Court.[71]

The aim of the Agreement is to ensure that financial payment messages referring to financial transfers and related data stored in the territory of the EU by providers of international financial payment messaging services that are designated in the Agreement are provided to the US Treasury Department for the exclusive purpose of the prevention, investigation, detection or prosecution of terrorism or terrorist financing; the relevant information obtained through the TFTP is also provided to law enforcement, public security or counterterrorism authorities of Member States, or Europol or Eurojust.[72] The US Treasury Department committed itself to communicate to law enforcement, public security or counterterrorism authorities of concerned Member States, and, as appropriate, to Europol and Eurojust, information obtained through the TFTP that may contribute to the investigation, prevention, detection or prosecution by the EU of terrorism or its financing.[73] It is also stated that the EU authorities may send requests for TFTP searches when 'there is reason to believe that a person or entity has a nexus to terrorism or its financing'.[74]

The Agreement does not only relate to the exchange of personal data, but also to the protection of these data. However, it does not include Article 16 TFEU as a legal basis, despite the fact that Article 1 of the Agreement underlines a high level of data protection as one of its main purposes. Article 16 TFEU is therefore not less relevant as a legal basis than Articles 82 and 87 TFEU relating to law enforcement cooperation. According to Article 16 TFEU, the European Parliament and the Council:

[69] Case T-529/09, *Sophie in' t Veld* v. *Council*, not yet published.

[70] *Ibid.* para. 60.

[71] Case C-350/12 P *Council* v. *in' t Veld*, lodged on 24 July 2013.

[72] Art. 1(1), 2010 SWIFT Agreement. The provider of international financial payment messaging services designated in the Agreement is only SWIFT.

[73] Art. 9, 2010 SWIFT Agreement.

[74] Art. 10, 2010 SWIFT Agreement.

> shall lay down the rules relating to the protection of individuals with regard to the processing of personal data by Union institutions, bodies, offices and agencies, and by the Member States when carrying out activities which fall within the scope of Union law, and the rules relating to the free movement of such data. Compliance with these rules shall be subject to the control of independent authorities.

The right to the protection of personal data is also enshrined in Article 8 of the Charter of Fundamental Rights.

The 2010 SWIFT Agreement has met some of the concerns raised by the European Parliament: the Agreement includes a clearer definition of terrorism as defined by the Council Framework Decision 2002/475/JHA; Europol shall verify whether the requests comply with the requirements of the Agreement (Article 4); onward transfer of information to third countries is regulated in the Agreement (Article 7); a detailed regulation of the rights to rectification, erasure or blocking is included (Articles 14–18); and an independent person is appointed by the EU to monitor the use of the data (Article 12). However, the Agreement is not fully satisfactory with respect to the protection of personal data, and the main causes of concern raised by the European Parliament have not been removed. First, the system is still based on the bulk transfer of data, because SWIFT does not technically allow targeted searches. The European Data Protection Supervisor (EDPS) held that 'the fact that the current SWIFT system does not allow a targeted search cannot be considered as a sufficient justification to make bulk data transfers lawful according to EU data protection law'.[75] The transmission of bulk data does not meet the proportionality and necessity requirements. Second, it is not acceptable that the Agreement allows keeping non-extracted data for five years. Third, as regards judicial review, the Agreement explicitly states that the Agreement 'shall not create or confer any right or benefit on any person or entity, private or public' (Article 18). The EDPS pointed out that 'this provision seems to annul or at least question the binding effect of those provisions of the agreement providing for data subjects' rights which are currently neither recognised nor enforceable under US law, in particular when data subjects are non US citizens or permanent residents'.[76] In consequence, the provisions for the protection of the rights of EU citizens would not give access to any kind of judicial review in the USA.

[75] Opinion of the European Data Protection Supervisor on the Proposal for a Council Decision on the Conclusion of the Agreement between the European Union and the United States of America on the Processing and Transfer of Financial Messaging Data from the European Union to the United States for Purposes of the Terrorist Finance Tracking Programme, OJ 2010 No. C355/12.

[76] *Ibid.*

Even though some of the concerns raised by the European Parliament found a satisfactory solution in the 2010 SWIFT Agreement, data protection provisions are not satisfactory.[77] In this respect there are no remarkable differences between the first and second SWIFT Agreements. Since the European Parliament was involved in the negotiation process for the second Agreement, it was more willing to make this compromise. The Parliament was fully informed at all stages of the negotiations and its views were taken into account by the actors involved in the process.

3 The influence of the European Parliament in the 2011 PNR Agreement with the United States

3.1 *The 2004 PNR Agreement and 2006 Interim Agreement*

After 9/11, the USA adopted the US Aviation and Transportation Security Act of 2001, which imposed the obligation on air carriers to submit electronically to the US Department of Homeland Security (DHS) passenger data contained in the PNR. The PNR data can include the passenger's full name, date of birth, home and work addresses, telephone number, email address, passport details, credit card details and method of payment, as well as details of any special meal requirements or seating preferences. In principle, the transfer of PNR data amounted to a violation of EU data protection.[78] Airlines not complying with the US demands might face heavy fines and even lose landing rights. In order to solve this conflict of law and overcome the legal uncertainty for the airlines, the Commission started negotiations with the USA. After the adoption of a Commission Decision on 14 May 2004 under the Data Protection Directive establishing the adequacy of the protection granted to PNR data by the US authorities,[79] the First PNR Agreement was signed on 28 May 2004 in Washington.[80]

[77] On the review of the implementation of the Agreement, see Chapter 10 of this volume by S. in't Veld.

[78] Directive 95/46/EC of the European Parliament and of the Council, on the protection of individuals with regard to the processing of personal data and on the free movement of such data, OJ 1995 No. L281, 23/31.

[79] Commission Decision (EC) 535/2004 of 14 May 2004, on the adequate protection of personal data contained in the Passenger Name Record of air passengers transferred to the United States' Bureau of Customs and Border Protection, OJ 2004 No. L235/11.

[80] See Agreements on the Use and Transfer of Passenger Name Records (PNR) to the US Department of Homeland Security (DHS) of 2004 (OJ 2004 No. L183/84), 2006 (OJ 2006 No. L298/29), 2007 (OJ 2007 No. L204/18) and 2011 (OJ 2012 No. L215/1). See also K. Archick, 'EU–US Cooperation Against Terrorism' Congressional Research Service

On 27 July 2004 the Parliament brought two actions before the European Court of Justice seeking the annulment of the Commission's adequacy decision and the Council's decision concluding the Agreement. The Parliament claimed that the adoption of the decision on adequacy was *ultra vires*, and the legal basis for the decision on the conclusion of the Agreement was not appropriate and fundamental rights had been infringed.[81] The Court of Justice held that former Article 95 of the EC Treaty (Treaty Establishing the European Community) (now Article 114 TFEU), read in conjunction with Article 25 of Directive 95/46 on the protection of individuals with regard to the processing of personal data and on the free movement of such data, cannot justify Community competence to conclude the Agreement.[82] In the Court's view, the transfer of PNR data to the USA constituted processing operations concerning public security that fell outside the EU first pillar. The Court held that:

> while the view may rightly be taken that PNR data are initially collected by airlines in the course of an activity which falls within the scope of Community law, namely sale of an aeroplane ticket which provides entitlement to a supply of services, the data processing which is taken into account in the decision on adequacy is, however, quite different in nature. [The transfer] concerns not data processing necessary for a supply of services, but data processing regarded as necessary for the safeguarding of public security and for law-enforcement purposes.[83]

The Court decided to preserve the effects of the Agreement until 30 September 2006.

Subsequently, negotiations for the conclusion of the Second PNR Agreement started in July 2006. As a consequence of the Court of Justice ruling, the Agreement has to be negotiated within the framework of the third pillar.[84] Due to the difficulties in concluding a new agreement in a short period of time, it was decided to conclude an Interim Agreement. On 11 October 2006 the Council adopted a decision authorizing the Presidency to sign an Interim Agreement with the USA on the continued

7-5700 (21 May 2012); Pawlak (ed.) *The EU–US Security and Justice Agenda in Action*; Mitsilegas, 'EU–US Co-operation in Criminal Matters Post-9/11'; V. Papakonstantinou and P. de Hert, 'The PNR Agreement and Transatlantic Anti-Terrorism Cooperation: No Firm Human Rights Framework on Either Side of the Atlantic' (2009) 46 *Common Market Law Review* 885–919.

81 Joined Cases C-317/04 and C-318/04, *Parliament* v. *Council* [2006] ECR I-4721.

82 See Directive 95/46/EC of the European Parliament and of the Council, on the protection of individuals with regard to the processing of personal data and on the free movement of such data, OJ 1995 No. L281, 23/31.

83 See Cases C-317/04 and C-318/04 *Parliament* v. *Council*, para. 57.

84 See former Art. 24 TEU.

use of PNR data.[85] The Parliament also expressed serious concerns on the lack of adequate data protection.[86] The Interim Agreement enabled PNR data to continue to be transferred to the USA in the same way as under the previous Agreement. As in the 2004 Agreement, it was noted that 'in view of the Undertakings issued on 11 May 2004 by the DHS, Bureau of Customs and Border Protection, the United Sates can be considered as ensuring an adequate level of protection for PNR data transferred from the European Union concerning passenger flights to or from the United States'.[87] Consequently, the Interim Agreement referred to the Undertakings made by the DHS within the framework of the First PNR Agreement.

The Interim Agreement provisions were similar to the 2004 Agreement.[88] The American authorities could have access to thirty-four fields, and the purpose of the data transfer was to prevent and combat terrorism and related crimes, other serious crimes, including organized crime, which are transnational in nature, and flight from warrants or custody for the crimes described above.[89] The Interim Agreement continued to be based on the pull system. The Interim Agreement expanded the number of American agencies that could have access to PNR data.[90] Even though the Interim Agreement did not substantially differ from the 2004 PNR Agreement, the Side Letter annexed to the Council's Decision on the adoption of the Interim Agreement has the effect of worsening the situation.[91] For example, the DHS was allowed to give access to PNR data

[85] See Agreements on the Use and Transfer of Passenger Name Records (PNR) to the US Department of Homeland Security (DHS) of 2004 (OJ 2004 No. L183/84), 2006 (OJ 2006 No. L298/29), 2007 (OJ 2007 No. L204/18) and 2011 (OJ 2012 No. L215/1).

[86] European Parliament, *Balancing Security and Data Protection for Air Travel And Judicial Cooperation*, 4 September 2006, available at: www.europarl.europa.eu/sides/getDoc.do?type=IM-PRESS&reference=20060901BKG10232&language=FI, accessed 24 October 2013.

[87] See Agreements on the Use and Transfer of Passenger Name Records (PNR) to the US Department of Homeland Security (DHS) of 2004 (OJ 2004 No. L183/84), 2006 (OJ 2006 No. L298/29), 2007 (OJ 2007 No. L204/18) and 2011 (OJ 2012 No. L215/1).

[88] See J. Faull and L. Soreca, 'EU–US Relations in Justice and Home Affairs' in B. Martenczuk and S. van Thiel (eds.), *Justice, Liberty, Security: New Challenges for EU External Relations* (VUBPRESS Brussels University Press, 2008), pp. 393–420.

[89] Para. (3), Undertakings of the Department of Homeland Security Bureau of Customs and Border Protection, 69 US Federal Register 2004, No. 131, 41,543–7, at 41,543, available at: www.statewatch.org/news/2004/jul/PNR-Federal-REG-undertakings.pdf, accessed 24 October 2013.

[90] Preamble, Interim PNR Agreement, see note 6.

[91] Letter from the US Department of Homeland Security (PNR interpretations); Reply by the Council Presidency and the Commission to the Letter from the USA's Department of Homeland Security.

to any US agencies with counterterrorism functions, and the DHS could broaden the number of PNR data required, which would be stored for periods longer than three-and-a-half years.[92]

3.2 *The 2007 PNR Agreement*

The negotiations for a long-term deal between the EU and the USA that started on 26 February 2006 led to the conclusion of an Agreement on 29 June 2007.[93] Although the European Parliament had a limited influence under the third-pillar framework, it expressed its concerns about the volume of data being passed to the USA and the lack of an appropriate data protection system. The Agreement has been applied provisionally since 26 July 2007, awaiting ratification by all Member States before it can enter into force. The Agreement was based on former Articles 24 and 38 TEU.

The Agreement itself is completed by two other documents. The Commissioner in charge of the negotiations stated before the EP that:

> the agreement [was to be] divided into three parts. First, an agreement signed by both parties. Second, a letter which the United States sent to the EU in which it set out assurances on the way in which it will handle European PNR data in the future. And third, a letter from the EU to the United States acknowledging the receipt of assurances and confirming that on that basis it considers the level of protection afforded by the US Department of Homeland Security to be adequate for European PNR data.[94]

This complex structure has led to intensive criticism. As a result of the fact that many of the substantial clauses of the Agreement were inserted into the letter exchange documents, data protection has been weakened.[95]

The number of PNR data areas has been reduced from 39 to 19 in the 2007 PNR Agreement. However, this reduction does not amount to an improvement of the right to privacy afforded to EU citizens. It is only the result of a process of rationalization of previous fields and not a real decrease in the number of data transferred to the US authorities.

92 Papakonstantinou and de Hert, 'The PNR Agreement and Transatlantic Anti-Terrorism Cooperation', 906.

93 See Agreements on the Use and Transfer of Passenger Name Records (PNR) to the US Department of Homeland Security (DHS) of 2004 (OJ 2004 No. L183/84), 2006 (OJ 2006 No. L298/29), 2007 (OJ 2007 No. L204/18) and 2011 (OJ 2012 No. L215/1).

94 Statement by Franco Frattini before the European Parliament, 9 July 2007, available at: www.europarl.europa.eu/sides/getDoc.do?type=CRE&reference=20070709&secondRef=ITEM-018&language=EN, accessed 3 March 2014.

95 See Papakonstantinou and de Hert, 'The PNR Agreement and Transatlantic Anti-Terrorism Cooperation', 909.

In addition, sensitive data could be accessed by the DHS in exceptional cases, 'where the life of a data subject or of others could be imperilled or seriously impaired'.[96] The 2007 PNR Agreement presented serious shortcomings as regards the amount of data disclosed to the American authorities.

As regards the purpose of PNR data processing, it was stated in the DHS letter sent to the EU that it was to use:

> EU PNR strictly for the purpose of preventing and combating: (1) terrorism and related crimes; (2) other serious crimes, including organized crime, that are transnational in nature; and (3) flight from warrants or custody for crimes described above. PNR may be used where necessary for the protection of the vital interests of the data subject or other persons or in any criminal judicial proceedings, or as otherwise required by law.[97]

The American authorities will keep the data for a period of fifteen years. For the first seven years the PNR data will be held in an active analytical database, after which the data will be retained for eight years on a dormant, non-operational status. The 2007 Agreement imposed a deadline on air carriers to switch to the push method of transfer no later than 1 January 2008, but this obligation has never been enforced. It means that the DHS has access to the PNR data by using the pull system. In the push method of transmission, PNR data are transmitted by the carrier to the national authority, instead of the pull method in which the national authority obtains access to the reservation system of the air carrier and takes the data.

Even though the 2007 Agreement substantially reduced the list of PNR transferred and imposed a deadline to switch to the push system no later than 1 January 2008, the Agreement was not in compliance with EU data protection standards. The data transfer was not supervised by an independent authority and there were no effective means of redress. On 12 July 2007 the European Parliament said that the PNR Agreement was 'substantively flawed in terms of legal certainty, data protection and legal redress for EU citizens, in particular as a result of open and vague definitions and multiple possibilities for exceptions' and regretted 'the failure of the PNR agreement to offer an adequate level of protection of PNR

[96] PNR Agreement 2007, p. 5. Sensitive information means data revealing racial or ethnic origin, political opinions, religious or philosophical beliefs, trade union membership, or concerning the health or sex life of the individual.

[97] *Ibid.*, p. 4.

data'.[98] It was not demonstrated that this intrusive system for the protection of personal data was effective and indispensable in the fight against terrorism.

3.3 The 2011 PNR Agreement

After the entry into force of the Lisbon Treaty, the 2007 PNR Agreement that had been applied provisionally could only be concluded after obtaining the consent of the European Parliament. However, as happened a few months before with the SWIFT Agreement, the Parliament used its new powers conferred by the Lisbon Treaty in respect of the conclusion of the PNR Agreements with Australia and the USA.[99] On 5 May 2010 the European Parliament decided to postpone the vote on the request for consent on the PNR Agreements with Australia and the USA.[100] The European Parliament held that the proposed agreements did not provide an adequate level of protection for the processing of personal data.[101] The Parliament demanded that new agreements should be negotiated with the USA and Australia as well as with Canada (with the latter two PNR Agreements having been in force since 2006).[102] The Parliament also asked the Commission to propose a coherent approach on the use of PNR data, based on a single set of principles to serve as a

[98] European Parliament Resolution of 12 July 2007 on the PNR Agreement with the United States of America, P6_TA (2007)0347.

[99] Proposal for a Council Decision on the Conclusion of the Agreement between the European Union and the United States of America on the Processing and Transfer of Passenger Name Record (PNR) Data by Air Carriers to the United States Department of Homeland Security (DHS) (2007 PNR Agreement) (COM(2009)0702); Proposal for a Council Decision on the Conclusion of the Agreement between the European Union and Australia on the Processing and Transfer of EU-sourced Passenger Name Record (PNR) Data by Air Carriers to the Australian Customs Service (COM(2009)0701).

[100] European Parliament Resolution of 5 May 2010, on the launch of negotiations for Passenger Name Record (PNR) agreements with the United States, Australia and Canada, P7_TA (2010)0144, OJ 2011 No. C81E/70. The EU–Australia PNR Agreement has also been applied provisionally since 2008. See Council Decision 2008/651/CFSP/JHA of 30 June 2008, on the signing, on behalf of the European Union, of an Agreement between the European Union and Australia on the processing and transfer of European Union-sourced Passenger Name Record (PNR) data by air carriers to the Australian Customs Service, OJ 2008 No. L213/47.

[101] At the Council meeting of Justice and Home Affairs of 2–3 December 2010, the Council adopted negotiating directives for agreements on the transfer and use of passenger name records (PNR) with Australia, Canada and the United States.

[102] See also European Parliament Resolution of 11 November 2010, on the global approach to transfers of passenger name record (PNR) data to third countries, and on the recommendations from the Commission to the Council to authorize the opening of

basis for agreements with third countries, bearing in mind the need to conclude PNR agreements with other countries.[103] It was also proposed that the EU should develop its own PNR system, aiming to harmonize Member States' provisions on obligations for air carriers operating flights between a third country and the territory of at least one Member State. This EU proposal constitutes a good example of internalization of US initiatives in the fight against terrorism. The European Parliament does not seem willing to adopt it.[104] If the Parliament gives its consent to the EU PNR proposal as it currently stands, this would contradict its traditional approach of demanding a high standard of protection of fundamental rights in international data transfers. The European Parliament stressed that the PNR agreements should meet the following minimum requirements:[105]

- PNR data transfer must be limited clearly and strictly to counterterrorism and the fight against serious transnational crime, on the basis of clear legal definitions laid down in Council Framework Decision 2002/475/JHA of 13 June 2002 on combating terrorism[106] and in Council Framework Decision 2002/584/JHA of 13 June 2002 on the European Arrest Warrant.[107]
- Compliance with data protection legislation at national and European levels, in particular regarding purpose limitation, proportionality, legal redress, and limitation of the amount of data to be collected and of the length of storage periods.
- PNR data shall in no circumstances be used for data mining or profiling.
- The method of transfer must be only 'push'.

negotiations between the European Union and Australia, Canada and the United States, P7_TA(2010)0387.

[103] On 21 September 2010 the Commission issued a communication on the global approach to transfers of passenger name record (PNR) data to third countries, COM (2010) 0492. In February 2011 the Commission also released a proposal for an EU PNR system aiming at protecting citizens against terrorist offences and serious crime. See Proposal for a Directive on the Use of Passenger Name Record Data for the Prevention, Detection, Investigation and Prosecution of Terrorist Offences and Serious Crime, COM (2011) 32; EU-PNR Commission Staff Working Paper Impact Assessment COM (2011) 32 final.

[104] See H. Mahony, 'MEPs Vote Down Air Passenger Data Scheme', *EU Observer*, 24 April 2013, available at: http://euobserver.com/justice/119926, accessed 24 October 2013.

[105] European Parliament Resolution of 5 May 2010, on the launch of negotiations for Passenger Name Record (PNR) agreements with the United States, Australia and Canada, P7_TA(2010)0144, OJ 2011 No. C81E/70.

[106] OJ 2002 No. L/3.

[107] OJ 2002 No. L190/1.

- The onward transfer of data by the recipient country to third countries shall be in line with EU standards on data protection, to be established by a specific adequacy finding.
- The results of the data processing will immediately be shared with the relevant authorities of the EU and of the Member States.
- Appropriate mechanisms for independent review and democratic control must be established. There are many review mechanisms in the PNR and SWIFT Agreements concluded with the United States.

The operation of the reviews of these two Agreements shows the weaknesses of governance in transatlantic security.[108] In January 2011 the Commission started new negotiations with the USA, Australia and Canada on the PNR Agreements. The Agreement with Australia was signed by the Council on 29 September 2011 and the European Parliament gave its consent on 27 October 2011.[109] The draft PNR Agreement between the EU and the USA was discussed with the Parliament and the Council in May 2011 and thereafter the Parliament's Rapporteur held that the draft Agreement did not meet the conditions laid down by the Parliament in its resolutions. Also, the Commission Legal Service warned that there were grave doubts as to the compatibility of the proposed Agreement with the fundamental right to data protection.[110]

Following new negotiations between the parties, on 23 November 2011 the Commission proposed that the Council adopt a decision approving the conclusion of the new PNR Agreement between the EU and the USA.[111] On 13 December 2011 the Council decided to sign the EU–US PNR Agreement and sent it to the Parliament with a view to obtaining

[108] Fahey, 'Law and Governance as Checks and Balances'.

[109] Agreement between the European Union and Australia on the Processing and Transfer of Passenger Name Record (PNR) Data by Air Carriers to the Australian Customs and Border Protection Service, signed on 29 September 2011. The negotiations with Canada succeeded in May 2013. At the time of writing the Civil Liberties, Justice and Home Affairs Committee (LIBE) had not yet delivered its report on the PNR Agreement with Canada. See Proposal for a Council Decision on the Conclusion of the Agreement between Canada and the European Union on the Transfer and Processing of Passenger Name Record Data, COM (2013) 528 final, 18 July 2013.

[110] European Commission Legal Service, 'Subject: Draft Agreement on the Use of Passenger Name Records (PNR) between the EU and the United States', SJ.f (2011) 603245, 18 May 2011.

[111] Proposal for a Council Decision on the Conclusion of the Agreement between the United States of America and the European Union on the Use and Transfer of Passenger Name Records to the United States Department of Homeland Security, COM(2011) 807 final.

its consent.[112] The European Parliament's Rapporteur in't Veld recommended the Parliament to withhold its consent to the Agreement.[113] The Rapporteur acknowledged the efforts made by the European Commission to reach a better agreement, but considered that the conditions required by the European Parliament to provide its consent had not been met.[114] However, the Civil Liberties, Justice and Home Affairs Committee (LIBE) disregarded the Rapporteur's opinion and approved the new Agreement on the transfer of EU air passengers' personal data to the USA.[115] The PNR Agreement was approved with 31 votes in favour, 23 against and 1 abstention. Many MEPs considered that it was better to have an agreement, even though not entirely satisfactory, than to have no agreement at all. Finally, on 19 April 2012 the European Parliament gave its consent to the conclusion of the new Agreement on the transfer of passengers' personal data to the US authorities.[116] The Agreement was approved by the Council on 19 April 2012 and entered into force on 1 July 2012, in accordance with Article 27 of the Agreement.[117] The new Agreement replaced the 2007 PNR Agreement that had been applied provisionally in recent years. Similarly to the 2010 SWIFT Agreement, Article 16 TFEU is not included in the legal basis of the Agreement. Since the purpose of the Agreement is to ensure that the transfer of PNR data to the USA respects

[112] Council of European Union, 'Council Gives Green Light for the New EU-US Agreement on Passenger Name Records (PNR)', Press Release, 13 December 2011, available at: http://europa.eu/rapid/press-release_PRES-11-490_en.htm, accessed 24 October 2013.

[113] Justice and Home Affairs, Draft Recommendation on the Draft Council Decision on the Conclusion of the Agreement between the United States of America and the European Union on the Use and Transfer of Passenger Name Records to the United States Department of Homeland Security (17433/2011–C7-0511/2011–2011/0382(NLE)), 30 January 2012.

[114] See also the Opinion of the European Data Protection Supervisor on the Proposal for a Council Decision on the Conclusion of the Agreement between the United States of America and the European Union on the Use and Transfer of Passenger Name Records to the United States Department of Homeland Security, 9 December 2011; and the Report by Art. 29 Data Protection Working Party, Ref. Ares (2012)15841, 6 January 2012.

[115] European Parliament, 'Civil Liberties Committee Green Light for Air Passenger Data Deal with the US', Press Release, 27 March 2012, available at: www.europarl.europa.eu/news/en/pressroom/content/20120326IPR41838/html/Civil-Liberties-Committee-green-light-for-air-passenger-data-deal-with-the-US, accessed 24 October 2013.

[116] See L. Abellán, 'La Eurocámara acepta seguir entregando los datos de los viajeros a EE UU', *El País*, 19 April 2012, available at: http://sociedad.elpais.com/sociedad/2012/04/19/actualidad/1334836877_242927.html, accessed 24 October 2013.

[117] Information concerning the date of entry into force of the Agreement between the United States of America and the European Union on the use and transfer of passenger name records to the United States Department of Homeland Security, OJ 2012 No. L174/1.

data protection standards, the Agreement should not only be based on Articles 82(1)(d) and 87(2)(a), in conjunction with Article 218(6)(a) TFEU, but also on Article 16 TFEU.

The EU–US deal on the transfer of PNR data was adopted with 409 votes in favour, 226 against and 33 abstentions. It seems that the MEPs were divided on whether the Agreement provides satisfactory protection of fundamental rights.[118] As some MEPs said, the Agreement may set a negative precedent on the future negotiation of PNR agreements with other partners. It was noted that, despite certain improvements, the most serious concerns were not removed. First, the processing of PNR data is allowed not just for the purpose of preventing and prosecuting terrorism and serious transnational crimes. The data may also be used to investigate and prosecute 'other crimes that are punishable by a sentence of imprisonment of three years or more and that are transnational in nature'.[119] Second, Article 4(2) allows for the use of PNR 'if ordered by a court'.[120] This clause would allow the use of PNR for any purpose, provided that it is ordered by a court. Third, the 2011 PNR Agreement retains data almost indefinitely. The data shall be retained for an initial period of five years and then in a dormant database for a period of up to ten years. Following the dormant period, data retained must be rendered fully anonymized. Fourth, even though the Agreement recognizes that any individual may seek administrative and judicial redress in accordance with US law,[121] this does not amount to admit a judicial redress

[118] See G. Hornung and F. Boehm, 'Comparative Study on the 2011 Draft Agreement between the US and the EU on the Use and Transfer of Passenger Name Records to the US Department of Homeland Security', 14 March 2012; T. Vogel, 'MEPs Back Data-Transfer Deal with US', *European Voice*, 19 April 2012, available at: www.europeanvoice.com/article/2012/april/meps-back-data-transfer-deal-with-us/74181.aspx, accessed 24 October 2013; European Parliament, 'Parliament Gives Green Light to Air Passenger Data Deal with the US', *European Parliament News*, 19 April 2012, available at: www.europarl.europa.eu/news/en/pressroom/content/20120419IPR43404/html/Parliament-gives-green-light-to-air-passenger-data-deal-with-the-US, accessed 24 October 2013.

[119] Justice and Home Affairs, Draft Recommendation on the Draft Council Decision on the Conclusion of the Agreement between the United States of America and the European Union on the Use and Transfer of Passenger Name Records to the United States Department of Homeland Security (17433/2011–C7-0511/2011–2011/0382(NLE)), 30 January 2012.

[120] PNR may be used and processed on a case-by-case basis where necessary in view of a serious threat and for the protection of vital interests of any individual or if ordered by a court.

[121] Art. 13, PNR Agreement 2011.

equivalent to the right to effective judicial redress in the EU.[122] Article 21 explicitly states that the Agreement 'shall not create or confer, under US law, any right or benefit on any person or entity, private or public'. Finally, it is not acceptable that data may also be used to ensure border security. According to Article 4(3), 'PNR may be used and processed by DHS to identify persons who would be subject to closer questioning or examination upon arrival to or departure from the United States or who may require further examination.'

Similarly to the 2010 SWIFT Agreement, the new PNR Agreement provides stronger protection of EU citizens' right to privacy than the 2007 EU–US PNR Agreement. EU citizens will have the right to access their own PNR data and seek corrections, including the possibility of erasure or blocking of their PNR data. However, the new PNR Agreement is not satisfactory from the perspective of EU protection of fundamental rights. The Parliament decided not to contest US preferences on the transfer of EU air passengers' personal data. It must be recognized that it was easier to oppose resistance to US demands when the Parliament was not a relevant actor in the conclusion of agreements in the AFSJ than after the Lisbon Treaty. In the author's view, it is disappointing that the Parliament decided not to continue its previous behaviour of demanding a high standard in the protection of fundamental rights in the transatlantic relationship. The new powers vested in the European Parliament by the Treaty of Lisbon raised many expectations for the strengthening of democratic accountability in transatlantic relations. The analysis of parliamentary scrutiny in the 2007 PNR Agreement demonstrates that the shortcomings of accountability and governance in the transatlantic transfer of personal data are not yet overcome.

4 Conclusions

The application of the ordinary legislative procedure to the adoption of Acts in the area of police and judicial cooperation in criminal matters has led to enhancing the role of the European Parliament in the conclusion of international agreements. The analysis of the SWIFT precedent shows clearly that the Parliament will not hesitate to use its power to veto the

[122] See also the Opinion of the European Data Protection Supervisor on the Proposal for a Council Decision on the Conclusion of the Agreement between the United States of America and the European Union on the Use and Transfer of Passenger Name Records to the United States Department of Homeland Security, 9 December 2011.

conclusion of international agreements. The Council and the Commission will have to involve the Parliament when defining negotiation mandates and keep it fully informed during the negotiation process. However, the Parliament was not included in the bargaining process that led to the 2009 SWIFT and 2007 PNR Agreements. As a consequence of the rejection of both Agreements, the Parliament was included and listened to in the negotiations of the 2010 SWIFT and 2011 PNR Agreements.

Analyzing the Parliament's role in the negotiations of the SWIFT Agreements and the 2011 PNR Agreement with the USA clearly shows that the new powers vested in the European Parliament by the Lisbon Treaty have enabled it to influence the negotiation of agreements in the area of police and judicial cooperation in criminal matters, in particular in the field of data processing. Even though the 2010 SWIFT Agreement and the EU–US 2011 PNR Agreement did not fully meet the criteria laid down by the European Parliament, more safeguards were introduced than in the past in respect of the right to the protection of personal data enshrined in Article 16 TFEU and Article 8 of the Charter of Fundamental Rights.

Moreover, bulk transfer of data is not excluded in the 2010 SWIFT Agreement. Solutions should be found to ensure that financial transaction data are filtered in the EU, ensuring that only relevant and necessary data are sent to US authorities. The Council seems willing to develop an equivalent EU system that would allow for the extraction of data on EU territory.[123] Once the EU SWIFT system is developed, data transfers to the USA would take place according to EU standards. The improvement in data protection has not led to the introduction of judicial scrutiny. Since there are no remarkable differences between the two Agreements, it seems that the European Parliament was more willing to accept the second SWIFT compromise because it was involved in the negotiation process. The Parliament was fully informed at all stages of the negotiations and its views were taken into account by the actors involved in the process.

The same conclusions apply to the influence of the European Parliament in the 2011 PNR Agreement with the USA. The Agreement provides stronger protection of EU citizens' right to privacy than the 2007 EU–US PNR Agreement. EU citizens will have the right to access their own PNR data and seek corrections, including the possibility of erasure or blocking of their PNR data. However, EU citizens will not have full access to US

[123] See Commission Communication, A European Terrorist Finance Tracking System: Available Options, COM (2011) 429 final, 13 July 2011, available at: www.csm.it/Eurojust/CD/19.pdf, accessed 24 October 2013.

courts to seek judicial redress. In addition, the purpose limitation is too broad and the number of data to be transferred to the US authorities is disproportionate and contains too many open fields.

The NSA scandal poses the need for genuine parliamentary oversight of the illegal surveillance activities developed by the American authorities, which could amount to an infringement of the SWIFT and PNR Agreements. Since the inquiry into American surveillance activities constitutes an unprecedented test for democratic accountability in the EU, the Parliament has an excellent opportunity to enhance its role in transatlantic security relations. It is too early to reach a final conclusion. At the time of writing, the LIBE Committee Inquiry on Electronic Mass Surveillance of EU Citizens is holding its hearings, and it is due to present its report by the end of 2013.

Analysis of the negotiation saga of the SWIFT and PNR Agreements reveals that the EP decided not to resist US demands on data transfers. Even though many MEPs expressed strong reservations about these Agreements, the Parliament decided to accept most of the US requirements. It is true that the USA threatened the EU by suspending visa-free travel to the USA in case of a negative vote for the PNR Agreement. However, in the author's opinion, the change of the Parliament's position is due to fact that it felt included in the negotiation process and listened to by the actors involved. In conclusion, the European Parliament is using its new powers conferred by the Lisbon Treaty more to assert its new role in the negotiation and conclusion process of international treaties in the area of police and judicial cooperation in criminal matters than to influence the substantial content of the transatlantic agreements.

13

Transatlantic counterterrorism cooperation and European values

The elusive quest for coherence

VALSAMIS MITSILEGAS

1 Introduction

9/11 has acted as a catalyst for the adoption of a plethora of security measures in the United States and beyond. For the European Union, one of the key challenges has been to adapt to the new security landscape and to respond to US security demands. Securitisation post-9/11 accelerated and facilitated the adoption of internal EU law in the field of criminal justice, with landmark third-pillar legislation including the Framework Decision on the European Arrest Warrant and the Decision establishing Eurojust (but also the first-pillar second money laundering Directive) being adopted months after 9/11, repackaged as counterterrorism measures.[1] A similar boost was given to EU external action in the field, with the need for enhanced transatlantic counterterrorism cooperation justifying the emergence of the European Union as a global security actor. At the heart of EU external action has been the conclusion of a series of international agreements with the United States, addressing a number of different components of a new transatlantic counterterrorism consensus. The legal framework on transatlantic counterterrorism cooperation has been evolving over time, with a number of agreements being repealed and replaced by new texts to address internal EU constitutional developments and concerns.

Central to the discussions on the evolution of transatlantic counterterrorism cooperation has been the issue of the impact of EU external action in the field on the preservation of European values, and in particular the protection of fundamental rights and the rule of law. The need

[1] For an analysis see V. Mitsilegas, *EU Criminal Law* (Oxford: Hart, 2009).

for the European Union to uphold these values in its external action is emphasised in the Lisbon Treaty. A key feature of the Treaty is its emphasis on the values upon which the Union is deemed to be founded. References to European values and their constituent elements can be found throughout the general part of the Treaty on European Union (TEU), as well as in parts of the Treaty on the Functioning of the European Union (TFEU). These values are central not only in defining European identity internally, but also in guiding the external action of the Union. Not surprisingly, respect for fundamental rights, democracy and the rule of law are expressly included in the list of EU values found in Article 2 TEU. This enumeration of the values upon which the Union is founded is not merely declaratory. According to Article 3(1) TEU, the promotion of these values is a key aim of the Union. The role of the Union in promoting its values is further highlighted with regard to EU external action, with Article 3(5) TEU stating that 'in its relations with the wider world, the Union shall uphold and promote its values and interests and contribute to the protection of its citizens'. The centrality of the values of the Union when it acts at the global level is further confirmed by the specific Treaty provisions on external action. According to Article 21(1) TEU, 'the Union's action on the international scene shall be guided by the principles which have inspired its own creation, development and enlargement, and which it seeks to advance in the wider world', which include: democracy, the rule of law, the universality and indivisibility of human rights and fundamental freedoms, and respect for human dignity. According to Article 21(2) TEU, the Union will define and pursue common policies and actions, and will work for a high degree of cooperation in all fields of international relations, in order to, inter alia, safeguard its values and consolidate and support democracy, the rule of law, human rights and the principles of international law. Article 205 TFEU reiterates that these provisions will guide the Union's action on the international scene. It is thus clear that the respect of fundamental rights and the rule of law constitute key values that the European Union must uphold and promote in its external action.

After offering a typology of the transatlantic counterterrorism cooperation agreements and casting light on their impact on European values in Section 2, Section 3 of this chapter will categorise and evaluate the various mechanisms put forward to ensure coherence between EU internal and external action in the field. Academic literature thus far has focused largely on the institutional/competence aspects of coherence, putting forward categorisations based on the distinction between vertical coherence (coherence between the action of EU institutions and Member States) and horizontal coherence (coherence between various substantive EU policies, inter-pillar coherence[2] or interinstitutional coherence[3]), or distinctions between negative and positive coherence.[4] For the purposes of this chapter, coherence should be understood as a concept transcending these traditional categorisations. The analysis here will rather focus on coherence between EU external action in the field of counterterrorism and European values as a constitutional foundation of the Union. The positive and proactive obligation to promote European values globally – which is reminiscent of conceptions of the European Union as a normative power[5] – leads to a holistic understanding of coherence extending beyond a narrow concept of consistency between EU internal and external action in the field of security.[6] It perceives coherence as a broader obligation to safeguard and promote European values in EU external action on counterterrorism.

2 Transatlantic counterterrorism cooperation: a typology of EU–US agreements and their impact on European values

Transatlantic counterterrorism cooperation has evolved through the conclusion of a series of agreements between the European Union and the United States covering a wide range of issues and triggered primarily by the events of 9/11. The conclusion of these agreements has created a multi-layered and extensive framework of transatlantic legal relationships in the field of security, which poses significant challenges to the EU legal order. The transatlantic counterterrorism agreements fall into three main categories. The first category consists of 'traditional' agreements between the

[2] See M. Cremona, 'Coherence through Law: What Difference Will the Treaty of Lisbon Make?' (June 2008) 3(1) *Hamburg Review of Social Sciences* 11–36, at 16ff.; C. Gebhard, 'Coherence' in Ch. Hill and M. Smith (eds.), *International Relations and the European Union*, 2nd edn (Oxford University Press, 2011), pp. 101–27, at pp. 107–8.

[3] M. Cremona, 'Coherence in European Union Foreign Relations Law' in P. Koutrakos (ed.), *European Foreign Policy: Legal and Political Perspectives* (Cheltenham: Edward Elgar, 2011), pp. 55–94, at p. 61.

[4] C. Hillion, '*Tous pour un, un pour tous!* Coherence in the External Relations of the European Union' in M. Cremona (ed.), *Developments in EU External Relations Law* (Oxford University Press, 2008), pp. 10–36.

[5] I. Manners, 'Normative Power Europe: A Contradiction in Terms?' (2002) 40 *Journal of Common Market Studies* 235–58.

[6] On the distinction between coherence and consistency see inter alia C. N. K. Franklin, 'The Burgeoning Principle of Consistency in EU Law' (2011) 30 *Yearbook of European Law* 42–85; P. Gauttier, 'Horizontal Coherence and the External Competences of the European Union' (2004) 10 *European Law Journal* 23–41; Gebhard, 'Coherence'.

EU and the USA in criminal justice matters, creating obligations for the two parties and for EU Member States. Such instruments are the EU–US Agreements on Extradition and Mutual Legal Assistance.[7] Their signature formed an important constitutional precedent for the European Union, with the Agreements being the first major international agreements concluded under the third pillar.[8] The second category includes agreements concluded between the US and EU criminal justice bodies with legal personality. The USA has signed international agreements with Europol[9] and Eurojust[10] on the exchange of personal data. The third category of agreements can be characterised as 'executive' or 'operational' agreements. These are agreements that have been concluded as a response to US unilateral emergency security measures adopted post-9/11. Two sets of agreements have been evolving over time in this context: EU–US Agreements on the Transfer of Passenger Name Record (PNR) Data, and EU–US Agreements on the Terrorist Finance Tracking Programme (TFTP). Rather than imposing obligations solely on the parties, these Agreements serve to impose obligations on private-sector entities to cooperate with the United States on counterterrorism, thus entailing a privatisation of security governance. Executive transatlantic cooperation agreements have had quite a turbulent history. As regards PNR, following the acceptance by the Commission of the adequacy of US data protection standards, transatlantic cooperation in this context began as a first-pillar international agreement (between the Community and the USA) in 2004.[11] Following a European Court of

[7] Agreement on Extradition between the European Union and the United States of America, OJ L181, 19 July 2003, p. 27; Agreement on Mutual Legal Assistance between the European Union and the United States of America, OJ L181, 19 July 2003, p. 34. See also the Council Decision, on the basis of Articles 24 and 38 TEU, concerning the signature of these agreements: OJ L181, 19 July 2003, p. 25.

[8] See V. Mitsilegas, 'The New EU–US Co-operation on Extradition, Mutual Legal Assistance and the Exchange of Police Data' (2003) 8 *European Foreign Affairs Review*, 515–36.

[9] Doc. 13689/02 Europol 82, 4 November 2002. See Mitsilegas, 'The New EU–US Co-operation on Extradition'.

[10] See V. Mitsilegas, 'Judicial Co-operation in Criminal Matters between the EU and Third States: International Agreements' in M. Leaf (ed.), *Cross-Border Crime* (London: JUSTICE, 2006), pp. 79–92.

[11] Commission Decision on the Adequate Protection of Personal Data Contained in the Passenger Name Record, of Air Passengers Transferred to the United States Bureau of Customs and Border Protection, OJ L235, 6 July 2004, p. 11 (including an Annex with the relevant US Undertakings); and Council Decision on the Conclusion of an Agreement between the European Community and the United States of America on the Processing and Transfer of PNR Data by Air Carriers to the US Department of Homeland Security, Bureau of Customs and Border Protection, OJ L183, 20 May 2004, p. 83 (the Agreement is annexed to the Decision).

Justice (ECJ) ruling against the legality of the first-pillar legal basis used,[12] the EC–US Agreement was replaced by third-pillar agreements between the EU and the USA.[13] Following the refusal of the European Parliament to grant consent to the 2007 EU–US PNR Agreement, a new EU–US PNR Agreement has now been concluded after the entry into force of the Lisbon Treaty.[14] As regards TFTP, the revelation by the press of the secret US programme of access to European SWIFT data[15] led as a first step to the issuance of Representations to the European Union, explaining the legal basis for the collection of SWIFT data under US law.[16] Pressure by the European Parliament and a change in the SWIFT system architecture resulted in the conclusion of an EU–US TFTP Agreement, signed one day before the entry into force of the Lisbon Treaty.[17] Notwithstanding the exercise of considerable political pressure by the US administration, the European Parliament

[12] Joined Cases C-317/04 and C-318/04 *European Parliament* v. *Council* [2006] ECR I-4721.

[13] An Interim Agreement to address the legal vacuum resulting from the Court's ruling in 2006 was followed by another agreement in 2007: Council Decision 2006/729/CFSP/JHA, on the signing, on behalf of the European Union, of an Agreement between the European Union and the USA on the processing and transfer of PNR data by air carriers to the US Department of Homeland Security (L298, 27 October 2006, p. 27 (the text of the Agreement is annexed to this Decision)); and Agreement between the European Union and the United States of America on the Processing and Ttransfer of Passenger Name Record (PNR) Data by Air Carriers to the United States Department of Homeland Security (DHS) (2007 PNR Agreement), OJ L 204, 4 August 2007, p. 18. See also Council Decision approving the signing of the Agreement on the basis of Articles 24 and 38 TEU, at p. 16.

[14] Council Decision of 13 December 2011, on the signing, on behalf of the European Union, of the Agreement between the United States of America and the European Union on the use and transfer of Passenger Name Records to the United States Department of Homeland Security, OJ L215/1, 13 August 2012; Council Decision of 26 April 2012 on the conclusion of the Agreement between the United States of America and the European Union on the use and transfer of Passenger Name Records to the United States Department of Homeland Security, OJ L215/4, 13 August 2012.

[15] Eric Lichtblau and James Risen, 'Bank Data is Sifted by US in Secret to Block Terror', *New York Times*, 23 June 2006, available at: www.nytimes.com/2006/06/23/washington/23intel.html?pagewanted=all&_r=0, accessed 18 February 2014.

[16] Terrorist Finance Tracking Program, Representations of the United States Department of the Treasury OJ C 166/18, 20 July 2007.

[17] Council Decision 2010/16/CFSP/JHA of 30 November 2009, on the signing, on behalf of the European Union, of the Agreement between the European Union and the United States of America on the processing and transfer of financial messaging data from the European Union to the United States for purposes of the Terrorist Finance Tracking Programme, OJ L8, 13 January 2010, p. 9 (and p. 11 for the text of the Agreement). For the background see A. Amicelle, *The EU's Paradoxical Efforts at Tracking the Financing of Terrorism: From Criticism to Imitation of Dataveillance*, CEPS Paper in Liberty and Security in Europe, No. 56, August 2013.

rejected the Agreement.[18] This rejection led to a new round of transatlantic negotiations, this time fully post-Lisbon, resulting in the conclusion in the summer of 2012 of the second EU–US TFTP Agreement, which is currently in force.[19]

The conclusion of these agreements by the European Union has been met by strong objections and concerns on political, democratic and human rights/rule of law grounds. Concerns with regard to the uncritical adoption of US standards by the EU have been compounded by the marked lack of democratic scrutiny and transparency in the negotiation and conclusion of the agreements. From a constitutional point of view, the fact that the agreements were ultimately negotiated under the third pillar meant that negotiations were led formally by the Presidency of the European Union and that the European Parliament did not have any role in the process of negotiation and signature. These constitutional constraints were combined by the negotiating practice of Member States (and at times the Commission) that effectively shielded the agreements from any kind of meaningful debate and scrutiny. The EU–US Agreements on Extradition and Mutual Legal Assistance remained classified until the very last weeks before signature, notwithstanding repeated requests for their publication for the purposes of scrutiny.[20] The Europol–US and Eurojust–US Agreements have not even been published in the Official Journal. The first version of the PNR Agreement (between the Community and the USA) was transmitted to the European Parliament for examination under deadlines that, according to Parliament, did not enable it to conduct meaningful scrutiny – with the handling of scrutiny leading to Parliament challenging the Agreement in the ECJ.[21] Similar scrutiny concerns have arisen with regard to the choice of dealing with the

[18] For further details see J. Monar, 'Editorial Comment. The Rejection of the EU–US SWIFT Interim Agreement by the European Parliament: A Historic Vote and Its Implications' (2010) 15 *European Foreign Affairs Review* 143–51.

[19] Council Decision on the Conclusion of the Agreement between the European Union and the United States of America on the Processing and Transfer of Financial Messaging Data from the European Union to the United States for the Purposes of the Terrorist Finance Tracking Programme OJ L195/3, 27 July 2010.

[20] See House of Lords European Union Committee, *EU–US Agreements on Extradition and Mutual Legal Assistance*, 38th Report, session 2002–3, HL Paper 135.

[21] V. Mitsilegas 'Border Security in the European Union. Towards Centralised Controls and Maximum Surveillance' in E. Guild, H. Toner and A. Baldaccini (eds.), *Whose Freedom, Security and Justice? EU Immigration and Asylum Law and Policy* (Oxford: Hart Publishing, 2007), pp. 359–94. The Court's ruling resulted in the agreements being negotiated under the third pillar with the Parliament having a much more limited scrutiny role.

Decision confirming the adequacy of the US data protection framework for the purposes of the PNR Agreement via comitology.[22] The first TFTP Agreement, on the other hand was, as seen above, signed a day before the entry into force of the Lisbon Treaty – in an attempt to conclude it under the intergovernmental process of the 'old' third pillar and thus pre-empt the Community elements brought about by Lisbon, and effectively sideline the European Parliament. Moreover, significant limits have been placed by the Council on the transparency and scrutiny of documents related to the negotiations by Members of the European Parliament.[23] The conclusion of these agreements, negotiated with minimal transparency in the face of sustained and growing fundamental rights concerns expressed by parliaments, EU expert bodies and civil society,[24] was presented as a fait accompli, with signature dates set out in advance and leaving limited time for debate and scrutiny.[25] As will be seen in the section on coherence below, secrecy remains a feature as regards the implementation of some of these agreements and their scrutiny.

The democratic and rule of law challenges posed by transatlantic counterterrorism cooperation are combined with serious challenges to the protection of fundamental rights. These fundamental rights challenges are the result of two separate but interrelated factors: of the highly invasive content of the EU–US Agreements, which substantially increase the power of the executive (in particular as regards the USA) at the expense of individual rights; and of the significant differences in the legal systems of EU Member States and the EU on the one hand, and the United States on the other as regards the protection of fundamental rights. The key area of concern is the impact of these agreements on the

[22] V. Mitsilegas, 'Contrôle des étrangers, des passagers, des citoyens: Surveillance et anti-terrorisme' (2005) 58 *Cultures et Conflits* 155–82.

[23] D. Curtin, 'Official Secrets and the Negotiation of International Agreements: Is the EU Executive Unbound?' (2013) 50 *Common Market Law Review* 423–58.

[24] On the extradition/Mutual Legal Assistance Agreements and the Europol–US Agreement, see Mitsilegas, 'The New EU–US Co-operation on Extradition'. On the PNR Agreements, see V. Mitsilegas, 'The External Dimension of EU Action in Criminal Matters' (2007) 12 *European Foreign Affairs Review* 457–97. On SWIFT, see the Opinion of the European Data Protection Supervisor of 25 January 2010 and the Opinion of the Article 29 Working Party of 22 January 2010.

[25] A number of the agreements envisaged an *ex post* scrutiny at the national level, with their conclusion being subject to Member States' internal constitutional procedures. While the EU–US Agreements on Extradition and Mutual Legal Assistance were signed in 2003, their conclusion on behalf of the EU took place only in 2009. See Council Decision 2009/820/CFSP, OJ L291, 7 November 2009, p. 40.

rights to the protection of private life and personal data.[26] The EU–US Mutual Legal Assistance Agreement and the Agreements between the USA and Europol and Eurojust respectively allow for the transfer of a wide range of personal data to the USA. In addition to this largely reactive model of data transfer, the executive transatlantic agreements have introduced significant quantitative and qualitative changes to the collection and transfer of personal data. As with the pre-existing anti-money-laundering legal framework, the PNR and TFTP Agreements signify the privatisation of financial surveillance and are yet another example of the 'responsibilisation strategy' whereby the private sector is co-opted by the state in the fight against crime.[27] However, while in the anti-money-laundering framework the private sector is called on to transfer proactively private financial data to the state on the basis of specific suspicions,[28] under the PNR and TFTP systems private entities are obliged to transfer private financial data to the US authorities *en masse* and in bulk, without any prior internal risk assessment. Massive quantities of everyday personal data are thus collected by the US government for the primary purpose of risk assessment of future threats – constituting what de Goede has termed speculative security practices.[29] This move towards speculative security, under a system of pre-emptive surveillance, poses fundamental challenges to the rights to private life and data protection (in particular as regards the questionable legality of the very collection of such personal data in bulk by the executive), but also more broadly to the presumption of innocence and concepts of citizenship and trust within the framework of the relationship between the individual and the state.[30]

[26] The EU–US Agreements on Extradition and Mutual Legal Assistance also raise concerns in relation to the right to life related to the possibility of the imposition of the death penalty following extradition or the provision of information under mutual legal assistance. For an analysis see Mitsilegas, 'The New EU–US Co-operation on Extradition'.

[27] On the responsibilisation strategy, see D. Garland, 'The Limits of the Sovereign State: Strategies of Crime Control in Contemporary Society' (1996) 36 *British Journal of Criminology* 445–71.

[28] V. Mitsilegas, *Money Laundering Countermeasures in the EU* (The Hague: Kluwer Law International, 2003).

[29] M. de Goede, *Speculative Security* (Minneapolis: University of Minnesota Press, 2012).

[30] V. Mitsilegas, 'The Value of Privacy in an Era of Security', *International Political Sociology*, forthcoming.

3 The elusive quest for coherence

In addition to the inclusion of specific safeguards – in particular on data protection – in the text of the various EU–US agreements, transatlantic negotiations have resulted in attempts to ensure coherence between EU external security action and European values, most notably relating to the protection of the rights to private life and the protection of personal data. These mechanisms of achieving coherence are particularly visible in the two executive transatlantic agreements (on TFTP and PNR), as these agreements have evolved over time in the face of sustained and considerable criticism by the European Parliament (which has an enhanced scrutiny role on international agreements after the entry into force of the Lisbon Treaty), expert EU data protection bodies and civil society. These mechanisms of ensuring coherence will be categorised and analysed below, by focusing primarily on the provisions in the EU–US TFTP Agreement and complementing this analysis with provisions from other agreements where relevant. As will be demonstrated from the analysis, efforts to achieve coherence have had mixed, if not limited success, with fundamental concerns as to the challenges that the agreements pose to European values still remaining.

3.1 Coherence via operational oversight

To address concerns regarding the extensive scope of transfer of financial data to US authorities, a key innovation in the EU–US TFTP Agreement has been to embed a series of mechanisms of oversight into the operational aspects of the transfer of SWIFT data to the USA. Going beyond the EU–US PNR Agreement, which focused on US oversight,[31] the EU–US TFTP Agreement establishes mechanisms of oversight by the European Union. Calls to establish EU operational oversight mechanisms were central to the negotiating position of the European Parliament as regards the second TFTP Agreement, with the Parliament insisting on the need for judicial oversight, in particular as regards the extraction of personal data under the Agreement.[32] The Agreement does provide for operational

[31] See Article 14 of the EU–US PNR Agreement.

[32] European Parliament, Motion for a Resolution on the Recommendation from the Commission to the Council to Authorise the Opening of Negotiations for an Agreement between the European Union and the United States of America to Make Available to the United States Treasury Department Financial Messaging Data to Prevent and Combat Terrorism and Terrorist Financing, 19 April 2010, Doc. B7/0243/2010, in particular point 10.

oversight, however, not by a judicial authority, but by Europol. According to Article 4(1) of the Agreement, upon receipt of a request for data transfer, Europol will verify as a matter of urgency whether the request complies with the requirements of Article 4(2), which require in particular requests by US authorities to identify as clearly as possible the data that are necessary for counterterrorism purposes, to substantiate clearly the necessity of the data and to be tailored as narrowly as possible in order to minimise the amount of data requested. According to Article 4(5), once Europol has confirmed that the request complies with the requirements of Article 4(2), the request will have binding legal effect as provided under US law, within the EU as well as in the USA, and the Designated Provider (SWIFT as indicated in the annex to the Agreement) is thereby authorised and required to provide the data to the US Treasury Department. Europol thus acts as a gatekeeper, whose approval is essential in order to authorise the transfer of SWIFT data to the USA. This represents a significant move from private oversight of the transfer of private personal data to the state to public oversight by a European body.[33]

Conferring these oversight powers upon Europol constitutes a change to its traditional role and represents an extension of Europol's powers, which is not envisaged in the 2009 Europol Decision[34] and is not provided for in the recent draft Regulation on Europol.[35] It thus appears that Europol's powers have been extended via an international agreement. In addition to these legal basis concerns, there are a number of effectiveness and human rights concerns associated with the scrutiny role of Europol under the Agreement. These concerns stem from the nature and powers of Europol and its position in the European security landscape. Europol is a law enforcement body with a clear security mandate. The TFTP Agreement has thus entrusted the scrutiny of US security services to another piece of the security apparatus, this time in Europe. Rather than legislating for judicial or privacy/data protection scrutiny of the operation of the TFTP Agreement, the European legislator has thus entrusted the scrutiny of the activities of parts of the US security services to their EU security/law enforcement counterparts. This choice casts doubts on the effectiveness of Europol's oversight role and has led to allegations that Europol is

[33] A. Amicelle, 'The Great (Data) Bank Robbery: Terrorist Finance Tracking Program and the "SWIFT Affair"', Research Questions No. 36, May 2011, Centre d'études et de recherches internationales SciencesPo, p. 20.

[34] Council Decision Establishing the European Police Office (Europol), OJ L121/37, 15 May 2009, Article 5.

[35] COM (2013) 173 final.

unduly uncritical as regards requests from the US authorities, and that this has led to inadequate and ineffective oversight. It should be noted in this context that Europol is in the position under the Agreement of both scrutinising US requests for data transfers under Article 4 and having the option of requesting a search for relevant information obtained through the TFTP under Article 10. As the European Data Protection Supervisor has eloquently noted, it is hard to reconcile this power of Europol, which may be important for the fulfilment of Europol's task and which requires good relations with the US Treasury, with the task of Europol to ensure independent oversight.[36] These concerns seem to be confirmed by the recent Joint Review of the controls set out in the Agreement, according to which in no cases did the verification by Europol lead to a rejection of a US request.[37]

These concerns become exacerbated when one reads Europol's report to the European Parliament on its role under Article 4.[38] In its report, Europol appears to adopt a rather flexible approach with regard to the purpose limitation and specificity requirements of the Agreement: according to Europol, surprisingly, identifying a nexus to terrorism in specific cases is a requirement under other provisions in the Agreement '*and forms no part of the request as submitted by the US Department of the Treasury to the Designated provider under Article 4*'.[39] Moreover, it is noted that:

> Due to the specific construction of the TFTP Agreement the US authorities must demonstrate a concrete nexus to terrorism in individual cases only in the context of the individual searches under Article 5(5) of the TFTP Agreement, once the received data are used for concrete search and/or analysis activities etc. Consequently Article 4(2) of the TFTP Agreement does not prohibit that the requests received by Europol exhibit a certain level of abstraction.[40]

These assertions by Europol are contrary to the very architecture of the Agreement, to the purpose of the safeguards inserted therein and to the very wording of Article 4(2), compliance with which Europol is entrusted to scrutinise. In particular, Article 4(2) requires US requests to identify as clearly as possible the data that are necessary for the purpose of the prevention, investigation, detection, or prosecution of terrorism or terrorist

[36] European Data Protection Supervisor (EDPS), para. 25.
[37] Second Joint Review, p. 6.
[38] File No. 2566-566, 8 April 2011.
[39] *Ibid.*, p. 4 (emphasis added). [40] *Ibid.*, p. 7.

financing.[41] Requests must also be tailored as narrowly as possible in order to minimise the amount of data requested.[42] The willingness of Europol to accommodate relatively uncritically the requests from US security services confirms Bigo's theory of the socialisation of transnational security professionals. According to Bigo, the transnationalisation of bureaucracies has created a socialisation and a set of differentiated professional interests that take priority over national solidarities.[43] This reasoning can apply by analogy to EU solidarities: Europol demonstrates greater solidarity with its US security counterparts rather than with the interests of EU citizens, parliamentarians and data protection/privacy professionals. The limits of privacy oversight by a security agency are thus vividly demonstrated.

In addition to the operational oversight entrusted to Europol in Europe when US requests are received, the EU–US TFTP Agreement provides for a second level of post-transfer operational oversight in the USA. Following the model established by the appointment of an Eminent Person located in the USA, the Agreement provides in Article 12, entitled 'Monitoring of Safeguards and Controls', for oversight of the data protection and purpose limitation safeguards set out in the Agreement by independent overseers, including by a person appointed by the European Union, with the agreement of and subject to appropriate security clearances by the USA.[44] According to Article 12(1), such oversight will include the authority to review in real time and retrospectively all searches made of the data provided, the authority to query such searches and, as appropriate, to request additional justification of the terrorism nexus. In particular, independent overseers shall have the authority to block any or all searches that appear to be in breach of Article 5 of the Agreement (which establishes a series of safeguards for the processing of data). Article 12(2) of the Agreement further provides for the monitoring of the independence of oversight in the framework of the review of the Agreement established under Article 13, and states that the Inspector General of the US Treasury will ensure that the independent oversight described in Article 12(1) is undertaken 'pursuant to applicable audit standards'. This provision can be seen as an

[41] Article 4(2)(a). [42] Article 4(2)(c).

[43] D. Bigo, 'Globalized (In)Security: The Field and the Ban-opticon' in D. Bigo and A. Tsoukala (eds.), *Terror, Insecurity and Liberty: Illiberal Practices of Liberal Regimes after 9/11* (London: Routledge, 2008).

[44] Article 12(1). According to the Commission's Report on the second Joint Review of the Agreement, the parties have agreed on the appointment of a deputy EU overseer (p. 8). The legal basis for this appointment is unclear.

attempt to address EU calls for the establishment of a system of independent data protection supervision in the USA that would reflect the system established under EU law.[45] It is questionable whether the Treasury audit mentioned in Article 12 is equivalent to independent data protection supervision. However, it constitutes an attempt – together with the innovative mechanism of locating an EU-appointed official with specific powers of operational oversight in the USA – to enhance oversight and meet EU requirements to some extent.

3.2 *Coherence via regular monitoring and review*

In a similar fashion to the safeguards established in the EU–US PNR Agreement,[46] another mechanism to ensure coherence and that the safeguards set out in the TFTP Agreement are met is the joint review of the Agreement on a regular basis. This mechanism is established by Article 13 of the Agreement and it involves both parties, the EU and the USA, in monitoring the effectiveness of the safeguards, controls and reciprocity provisions set out in the Agreement. Article 13(2) sets out in greater detail areas to be covered by the review, which include the number of financial payment messages accessed, the number of occasions in which leads have been shared with Member States, third countries, and Europol and Eurojust, the implementation and effectiveness of the Agreement, including the suitability of the mechanism for the transfer of information, cases in which the information has been used for the prevention, investigation, detection or prosecution of terrorism and its financing, and compliance with the data protection obligations specified in the Agreement. The review will include a representative and random sample of searches and a proportionality assessment. For the purposes of the review, the European Union will be represented by the Commission and the USA by the Treasury, and each party may include in its delegation security, data protection and judicial experts – however, only the EU delegation is obliged to include in the delegation representatives of two data protection authorities, at least one of which must be from a Member State where a Designated Provider (thus far SWIFT) is based.[47] Following the review,

[45] See EDPS, para. 36.

[46] Article 23 of the EU–US PNR Agreement. The mechanism of joint review of the transatlantic PNR Agreements by the USA and the EU has been well established and present in all agreements since the conclusion of the first one in 2004. See Preamble, recital 17.

[47] Article 13(3).

the Commission will present a Report to the European Parliament and the Council on the functioning of the TFTP Agreement.[48]

The joint review envisaged by the TFTP Agreement is an important transparency tool and brings into the public domain a variety of information on the detailed functioning of the Agreement. The Commission Report on the first Joint Review made a number of recommendations for improvement, including the need to further substantiate the added value of the TFTP programme – in particular via the collection and analysis of more feedback in order to provide more verifiable insights into the actual added value of the TFTP, the collection of more statistical information that should be made public and the provision of as much information as possible substantiating the requests provided to Europol in a written format in order to support it in its tasks under Article 4, to allow for more effective independent review.[49]

The second Joint Review proved to be more controversial, in particular as regards the intensification of the scrutiny of the Agreement beyond the strict confines set out by the Review itself. In its Report on the second Joint Review of the EU–US TFTP Agreement,[50] the Commission felt obliged to report on parallel scrutiny efforts conducted by the Europol's Joint Supervisory Body on data protection (JSB). The JSB has produced a number of critical reports, highlighting gaps in data protection and Europol's scrutiny role (i.e. that the written requests Europol received were not specific enough to allow it to decide whether to approve or deny them, but despite this, Europol approved each request it received) as well as gaps in transparency and scrutiny resulting from the persistent informality in the practices of Europol (noting that Europol advised that orally provided information plays a role in its verification of each request, information which is provided to certain Europol officials with the stipulation that no record is made).[51] The JSB has highlighted further the secrecy

[48] Article 13(2) final indent.

[49] Commission Report on the Joint Review of the Implementation of the Agreement between the European Union and the United States of America on the Processing and Transfer of Financial Messaging Data from the European Union to the United States for the purposes of the Terrorist Finance Tracking Programme 17–18 February 2011, Brussels, 16 March 2011.

[50] Commission Staff Working Document, Report on the Second Joint Review of the Implementation of the Agreement between the European Union and the United States of America on the Processing and Transfer of Financial Messaging Data from the European Union to the United States for the Purposes of the Terrorist Finance Tracking Programme. October 2012, SWD (2012) 454 final, Brussels, 14 December 2012.

[51] First Report, 2 March 2011.

surrounding aspects of the scrutiny of the TFTP Agreement, noting that due to Europol's classification of most TFTP-related information as EU SECRET, the JSB's Final Report is classified as EU SECRET, a fact which has led the JSB to prepare a public statement in lieu of a second Inspection Report, in which it reiterated the limits inherent in Europol's oversight and that the current classification level applied to much of the information related to the Agreement prevents the release of a large proportion of relevant information.[52]

In its third Report, the JSB noted that, with a view to ensuring transparency, the assessment of the outcome of that year's inspection had been drafted in such a way as to allow full publication and, therefore, the widest possible audience. It welcomed progress made after its two prior inspections but sustained its focus on the practices of Europol and highlighted the continuation of the transfer of personal data in bulk.[53]

The Commission Report on the second Joint Review criticised, instead of applauding, the additional layer of data protection scrutiny provided by the Europol JSB, noting that 'parallel or uncoordinated initiatives or inquiries should be avoided because they undermine the Article 13 review process and have caused considerable workload of the Treasury in particular'.[54] This comment can be seen as a response to the US government's concerns over the perceived interference and increased transparency that scrutiny by the Europol JSB may entail.[55] Highlighting data protection and secrecy concerns to the European Parliament is viewed as a breach of mutual trust, but raises the question of mutual trust between whom as important from an EU constitutional perspective. The text of the Commission's Report on the Joint Review reveals an alignment of the Commission's interests not with other EU bodies and actors, but with the US government, in a striking example of security socialisation.

The Commission's willingness to uphold security interests and to justify the securitised function of Europol as an overseer of the Agreement under Article 4 can also be found in the second Joint Review. According to the Review, Europol has established an intensive dialogue with its Treasury counterparts, which has turned out to be a very important monitoring element, in addition to the formal regular reviews under Article 13.[56] It is

[52] Second Inspection, November 2011.
[53] Third JSB Report, November 2012.
[54] COM second Joint Review, pp. 15–16.
[55] *Ibid.* [56] *Ibid.*, p. 16.

striking that Europol's perceived data protection role is here applauded, at the same time as the work of the data protection scrutineer *par excellence*, the Europol JSB, is being criticised.

The security focus of the Commission as regards the Review of the EU–US TFTP Agreement is also visible vis-à-vis the evaluation of the performance of Europol under Article 4. While the Review accepts that in no cases did verification by Europol lead to a rejection of a US request,[57] the Commission's report has gone at great length to stress and justify the operational considerations underpinning Europol's role under the Agreement. According to the Commission:

> Europol explained that it carries out its verification task under Article 4 based on an *operational* assessment of the validity of the US request … The fact that the verification task under Article 4 has been given to Europol, i.e. to a law enforcement and not to a data protection body, shows that, ultimately, the verification criteria set out in Article 4 have to be assessed in the light of operational considerations and security needs. This is particularly true for the difficult question whether the US requests are 'as narrowly tailored as possible' (Article 4 (2) (c)).[58]

The above comments by the Commission cause concern with regard to the extent to which scrutiny by Europol under Article 4 can operate as an effective safeguard and meaningful control of US requests for financial data under the TFTP Agreement. The second Joint Review remains essentially uncritical as regards the oversight approach adopted by Europol. According to the Commission, the review teams felt that 'it is not for them (not for any other monitoring body) to replace Europol's final decision by their own less informed judgement'.[59] Here the emphasis is placed again on security, with the reviewers exhibiting undue deference to Europol's operational considerations placed within a securitised framework and demonstrating a confluence between EU and US law enforcement interests. Securitisation is here linked with depoliticisation, with the review team in essence negating the Review task entrusted to it by the TFTP Agreement. This depoliticisation is accepted explicitly in the Commission's Report, noting that the second Review was based on the understanding that *it was not its task to provide a political judgment of the Agreement*, this being considered outside the scope and mandate under Article 13.[60] At the same time, the Review of the Agreement was accompanied by great efforts to accommodate US

57 *Ibid.*, p. 6.
58 *Ibid.*, p. 7 (emphasis added).
59 *Ibid.*, p. 7.
60 *Ibid.*, p. 4.

concerns with regard to maintaining secrecy,[61] limiting the amount of information provided during the Review,[62] but also with producing a version of the Report that would be acceptable to the Treasury.[63]

3.3 *Coherence via the presumption of adequacy*

A key and tested technique in attempting to address concerns over the limitations of the US data protection framework has been for the EU to declare that US standards on privacy and data protection are adequate. Declarations of adequacy have been central to the conclusion of transatlantic PNR Agreements.[64] Following a similar pattern, Article 8 of the EU–US TFTP Agreement states that subject to ongoing compliance with the commitments on privacy and protection of personal data set out in the Agreement, the US Treasury Department is deemed to ensure an adequate level of data protection for the purposes of this Agreement. This declaration is a demonstration of trust towards US authorities and must be read together with the Preambular provision stressing the parties' 'common values governing privacy'.[65] It serves to legitimise the transfer of personal data to the USA, but the question of whether the US system provides an adequate level of data protection and privacy standards compared with EU standards remains open. The assessment of adequacy is a positive declaration of trust in the US system of data protection and constitutes a step forward from the negative framing of trust formulated in the EU–US Mutual Legal Assistance Agreement.[66] However, EU data protection and privacy standards form part of fundamental rights whose

[61] The second Commission Report on the Joint Review of the Agreement highlighted persistent limitations on the provision of some documents during the Review (*ibid.*, p. 3).

[62] *Ibid.*, pp. 5–6.

[63] *Ibid.*

[64] For the background, see Mitsilegas, 'Border Security in the European Union'. See Article 19 of the latest EU–US PNR Agreement.

[65] Preamble, recitals 8 and 10.

[66] According to Article 9(2)(b) of the Agreement, generic restrictions with respect to the legal standards of the requesting state for processing personal data may not be imposed by the requested state as a condition to providing evidence or information. The Explanatory Note to the Agreement states that Article 9(2)(b) is meant to ensure that refusal of assistance on data protection grounds may be invoked only in exceptional cases: 'A broad, categorical, or systematic application of data protection principles by the requested State to refuse cooperation is therefore precluded. Thus, the fact the requesting and requested States have different systems of protecting the privacy of data (such as that the requesting State does not have the equivalent of a specialised data protection authority) or have different means of protecting personal data (such as that the requesting State uses means other than the process of deletion to protect the privacy or the accuracy of the personal

protection is a key value that the Union must safeguard and promote in its external action.[67]

To back up the assertion of adequacy, the EU–US TFTP Agreement includes a number of data protection safeguards. In addition to the safeguards included in relation to US requests, the Agreement provides safeguards applicable to the processing of provided data, which include purpose limitation, the prohibition of data mining, the prohibition of interconnection of provided data with other databases, the requirement to respect necessity and proportionality in data processing, and the requirement for all searches of provided data to be based upon pre-existing information or evidence that demonstrates a reason to believe that the subject of the search has a nexus to terrorism or its financing.[68] The Agreement also includes specific provisions on data retention and deletion,[69] with Article 6(4) stating that all non-extracted data received on or after 20 July 2007 shall be deleted not later than five years from receipt. However, as has been noted in the Commission's Report on the second Joint Review of the Agreement, the Treasury informed the EU review team that the deletion of data cannot be implemented as an ongoing process on a rolling basis but that their intention would be to carry out this exercise only after longer intervals.[70] The Agreement also includes a series of provisions on specific data protection rights, including transparency,[71] the right of access,[72] the right to rectification, erasure or blocking,[73] the maintenance of the accuracy of the information,[74] and a provision of redress.[75] However, these safeguards do not negate the fact that the EU–US TFTP Agreement has legitimised and allows for what the Europol Joint Supervisory Body has called a 'massive, regular, data transfer from the EU to the US'.[76]

3.4 *Coherence via reciprocity*

As with the EU–US PNR Agreement, another key element in the EU-US TFTP Agreement is the emphasis on reciprocity. Reciprocity operates at two levels: the first level involves the operational gain that the transfer of personal data under the Agreements may entail for EU law enforcement;

data received by law enforcement authorities), may as such not be imposed as additional conditions.'

67 Preamble, recital 4. 68 Article 5.

69 Article 6. 70 COM second Joint Review, p. 10.

71 Article 14. 72 Article 15.

73 Article 16. 74 Article 17.

75 Article 18. 76 Third JSB Report.

the second level of reciprocity relates to the future reconfiguration of the Agreements in the event that the European Union establishes its own PNR and TFTP systems. As regards the TFTP Agreement, the first level of reciprocity is reflected in Articles 9 and 10 of the Agreement, which call respectively for the proactive (spontaneous) and reactive provision of information obtained through the TFTP system by the US authorities to law enforcement, public security or counterterrorism authorities of EU Member States as well as Europol and Eurojust. This is an effort to demonstrate an added value of this Agreement for the EU by attempting to ensure security benefits for the EU and Member States.[77]

The second level of reciprocity involves the potential future establishment of an EU TFTP system. The establishment of a European TFTP system has been proposed by the European Parliament as a step to ensure a move from personal data being transferred in bulk to the USA to the extraction of the relevant personal data in the EU under a European system.[78] It may also be seen as an effort to minimise European reliance on US intelligence.[79] Article 11 of the Agreement states that during its course the Commission will carry out a study into the possible introduction of an equivalent EU system allowing for a more targeted transfer of data,[80] adding that if the EU decides to establish an EU system, the USA will cooperate and provide assistance and advice to contribute to the effective establishment of such a system.[81] If the EU decides to establish such a system, the parties should consult to determine whether this Agreement would need to be adjusted accordingly.[82] According to the Decision on the Conclusion of the Agreement, if, five years after the entry into force of the Agreement, the equivalent EU system has not been set up, the Union shall consider whether to renew the Agreement in accordance with Article 21(2) thereof.[83] The Commission's Report on the second Joint Review of the Agreement indicates that there will continue to be close cooperation and consultation with the USA on this issue[84] and states explicitly that the functioning of reciprocity under the Agreement is an essential factor in assessing the necessity of a possible

[77] COM second Joint Review, pp. 12–13: 'Reciprocity – The EU Benefiting from TFTP Data'.

[78] European Parliament Resolution of 5 May 2010 P7_TA-PROV(2010)0143.

[79] A. Ripoll Servent and A. MacKenzie, 'The European Parliament as a "Norm Taker"? EU–US Relations after the SWIFT Agreement' (2012) 17 *European Foreign Affairs Review* 71–86, at 83.

[80] Article 11(1). [81] Article 11(2).

[82] Article 11(3). [83] Article 2 third indent.

[84] See also Article 11(3) of the Agreement.

establishment of an equivalent EU system.[85] In this manner, the two levels of reciprocity are linked together by the Commission essentially presenting an EU TFTP system as an alternative if the US authorities do not cooperate sufficiently with the EU under the EU–US TFTP Agreement. This is a departure from the European Parliament rationale for the establishment of an EU system, the security focus of which is confirmed by the view of the Commission that the further information provided by the Treasury and Europol in the course of the second Joint Review constitutes useful and important input for the completion of the Commission's Impact Assessment and the subsequent decision on the possible establishment of an EU system. The Commission published a Communication setting out options for a European TFTP system.[86] The aims of such a system would be to contribute to the fight against terrorism and its financing, and to limit the amount of personal data transferred to third countries. The system should provide for the processing of the data required to run it on EU territory, subject to EU data protection principles and legislation.[87]

While the establishment of an EU TFTP system along these lines may be seen as an attempt to establish coherence by addressing data protection concerns ensuing from the transfer of financial data in bulk to the USA, in reality, as is the case with similar proposals in the field of the transfer of PNR data, the effect of establishing an EU TFTP system will be to import within the EU and legitimise internally a highly invasive programme of executive action and to thus normalise an emergency security response without questioning the necessity of the mass transfer of everyday financial data to the state authorities in the first place.

As with the TFTP Agreement, the EU–US PNR Agreement focuses on reciprocity at two levels: at the level of seeking the provision of intelligence data from US authorities (the Department of Homeland Security) to Member States' law enforcement authorities and EU criminal justice bodies; and at the level of seeking to develop a European PNR system. Article 18 of the Agreement places the DHS under the duty to provide information obtained by PNR to Member States' law enforcement authorities, Europol and Eurojust.[88] This represents a stronger commitment than the text of the US letter to the EU within the framework of the 2007

[85] COM second Joint Review, p. 14.

[86] Commission Communication, A European Terrorist Finance Tracking System: Available Options, COM (2011) 429 final, Brussels, 13 July 2011.

[87] *Ibid.*, p. 2. [88] Article 18(1).

Agreement, whereby the DHS would merely 'encourage' the transfer of such data.[89] Such transfer of information must be consistent with existing agreements between the USA and EU Member States, Europol and Eurojust.[90] European authorities may also request access to PNR data or relevant analytical information obtained from PNR, and the DHS must, subject to existing agreements, provide such information.[91] In this manner, EU and Member State authorities are allowed to obtain information following transfers of personal data that pose challenges on EU privacy and data protection law. At the same time, the Agreement envisages the establishment of an EU PNR system and states that, if and when an EU PNR system is adopted, the parties will consult to determine whether this Agreement would need to be adjusted accordingly to ensure full reciprocity. Such consultations will in particular examine whether any future EU PNR system would apply less stringent data protection safeguards than those provided for in this Agreement and whether, therefore, this Agreement should be amended.[92] This is a striking provision,[93] which seems to disregard the current challenges that the Agreement poses on EU fundamental rights standards and the requirement that any internal EU legislation in the field must comply fully with fundamental rights, and in particular privacy and data protection as enshrined in the ECHR and the Charter. The necessity and compatibility of an EU PNR system with EU law remain questionable.

The European Commission tabled a proposal for a Framework Decision on an EU PNR system as early as 2007.[94] The Commission explained that the proposal was a result of the 'policy learning' from inter alia the existing EU PNR Agreements with the United States and Canada.[95] Agreement on the proposal was not reached before the entry into force of the Lisbon Treaty, a fact which led the Commission to table new legislation

[89] Point IX, second paragraph. [90] *Ibid.*

[91] Article 18(2). See also the Commission Report on the 2010 Joint Review in which the EU urged the DHS to respect its commitment to proactively share analytical information flowing from PNR data with EU Member States, p. 12.

[92] Article 20(2).

[93] See also the wording of the US letter to the EU within the framework of the 2007 Agreement, according to which the DHS expected not to be asked to undertake data protection measures in its PNR system that are more stringent than those applied by the US for its PNR system – point IX, paragraph 1. See also Preamble of the Agreement, recital 5.

[94] Commission Proposal for a Council Framework Decision on the Use of Passenger Name Records (PNR) for Law Enforcement Purposes, COM (2007) 654 final (6 November 2007).

[95] *Ibid.* at 2.

post-Lisbon, this time in the form of a Directive.[96] The Commission justified the establishment of a European system of PNR transfer as necessary for law enforcement purposes due to its potential for risk assessment of passengers, and proposed a system that is very similar to the US PNR system, at least as regards the categories of transferred data[97] and the emphasis on risk assessment.[98] As with the US system, the potential for the proposed PNR system to lead to the profiling of individuals is considerable.[99] Moreover, the necessity of an internal EU PNR system for law enforcement purposes is questionable, in particular in the light of the major data protection and privacy challenges posed by its establishment. The adoption of the PNR Directive is facing a rocky road, having been rejected by the Civil Liberties Committee of the European Parliament in spring 2013.[100] However, the draft Directive (as with its predecessor draft Framework Decision) constitutes a prime example of the internalisation of the US security model by the European Union, leading to the lowering of internal EU privacy and data protection standards.[101] While this internalisation may be seen as justified by the need to ensure coherence between internal and external action on security – by establishing internal EU standards from scratch that can act as benchmarks for EU external action – in reality the necessity of the adoption of such internal measures has not been justified, and their adoption would in fact undermine coherence between EU external security action and EU values, by challenging significantly the fundamental rights to privacy and data protection.

[96] Commission Proposal for a Directive of the European Parliament and of the Council on the Use of Passenger Name Record Data for the Prevention, Detection, Investigation and Prosecution of Terrorist Offences and Serious Crime, COM (2011) 32 final (2 February 2011).

[97] Requested data includes all forms of payment information, including billing address, travel status of passenger (including confirmations), check-in status, no show or go show information, seat number and other seat information, number and names of other travellers on PNR, and 'general remarks'.

[98] V. Mitsilegas, 'Immigration Control in an Era of Globalisation: Deflecting Foreigners, Weakening Citizens, Strengthening the State', 2012 19(1) *Indiana Journal of Global Legal Studies* 3–60.

[99] See Opinion of the European Data Protection Supervisor on the Proposal for a Directive of the European Parliament and of the Council on the Use of Passenger Name Record Data for the Prevention, Detection, Investigation and Prosecution of Terrorist Offences and Serious Crime (25 March 2011), pp. 4–5.

[100] 'Civil Liberties Committee Rejects EU Passenger Name Record Proposal', 24 April 2013. European Parliament Press Release, available at: www.europarl.europa.eu.

[101] On the internalisation point, see further J. Argomaniz, 'When the EU is the "Norm-Taker": The Passenger Name Records Agreement and the EU's Internalisation of US Border Security Norms' (2009) 31 *Journal of European Integration* 119–36.

3.5 *Coherence via the development of global security standards*

Another way of attempting to ensure coherence is the externalisation of transatlantic counterterrorism cooperation via the promotion of global standards. This approach has been central as regards the transfer of PNR data. Calls for approaching PNR negotiations from a global perspective have been made by the European Parliament following the adoption of the 2007 EU–US PNR Agreement. The rationale for these calls has been the perceived need for the European Union to adopt common principles underpinning the negotiating position of the EU, not only with the United States but also with other third countries, bearing in mind that the EU has also negotiated PNR Agreements with Australia and Canada. The European Commission responded by issuing a Communication on a Global Approach to Transfers of PNR Data to Third Countries.[102] In its Communication, the Commission went a step further and argued for the adoption of global standards in the field. The Commission called upon the European Union to consider initiating discussions with international partners that use PNR data and those that are considering using such data in order to explore whether there is common ground between them for dealing with PNR transfers on a multilateral level. The move towards multilateralism is justified as follows:

> As more and more countries in the world use PNR data, the issues arising from such use affect the international community. Even though the bilateral approach which has been adopted by the EU was the most appropriate one under the circumstances and seems to be the most appropriate one for the near future, it risks ceasing to be appropriate if many more countries become involved with PNR. The EU should therefore examine the possibility of setting standards for the transmission and use of PNR data on an international level. The Guidelines on PNR access that have been developed by ICAO in 2004 offer a solid basis for the harmonisation of the modalities of transmissions of PNR data. However, these guidelines are not binding and they deal insufficiently with data protection issues. They are therefore not sufficient in themselves, but should rather be used for guidance, especially on matters affecting the carriers.[103]

In this manner, the specific issues arising in the negotiations of EU agreements with third countries, including the USA, are exported at the global level. The European Union is emerging as a global actor that is aiming to shape global, multilateral standards on PNR transfers. However, in doing

[102] COM (2010) 492 final, 21 September 2010.
[103] *Ibid.*

so, it legitimises and accepts the far from globally accepted US approach, focusing on the generalised surveillance of mobility that forms a central part of the US security response post-9/11. This signifies a move from US unilateral emergency action to the normalisation and generalisation of such action first via its internalisation in EU law (a European PNR Directive) and then via the development of global standards regulating the transfer of PNR data. Global standards in this context have the potential to result in an obligation for members of the international community to adopt systems of PNR data transfers, although currently these systems are used by only a minority of states. The very logic and purpose of PNR systems is thus not questioned, and the model of the generalised surveillance of mobility they entail becomes globalised.

3.6 *Coherence via the development of a transatlantic privacy framework*

Another way to ensure coherence between EU–US counterterrorism cooperation and European values has been to attempt to bridge the parties' differences with regard to data protection and privacy by developing a framework enabling a level playing field on privacy. The first step towards the establishment of such a level playing field has been the parties' agreement on a series of common data protection principles reached in 2009.[104] Along with reference to a series of specific data protection standards, the parties aimed at reaching a broad understanding of equivalence of data protection taken 'as a whole', and not an understanding that is based upon the scrutiny of specific (singular) examples.[105] This approach is reminiscent of the equivalence provisions in the EU–US Mutual Legal Assistance Agreement[106] and in the Europol–US Agreement,[107] where it is stated that

[104] US Mission to the European Union, 'US–EU Reach Agreement on Common Data Protection Principles', joint statement adopted at the 28 October 2009 US–EU JHA Ministerial, available at: http://useu.usmission.gov/useu_dataagreement_102809.html, accessed 25 February 2014.

[105] 'On equivalent and reciprocal application of data privacy law, the European Union and the United States should use best efforts to ensure respect for the requirements, taken as a whole as opposed to singular examples, that each asks the other to observe.'

[106] Article 9(2)(a) of the EU–US Agreement on Mutual Legal Assistance.

[107] Article 5(4) of the Europol–US Agreement states that the grounds for refusing or postponing assistance should be limited to the greatest extent possible. In the Exchange of Letters accompanying the Agreement (Doc. 13996/02 Europol 95, 11 November 2002) it is stated that Article 5(4) is to be understood not to permit the imposition of generic restrictions with respect to the sharing of personal data.

generic differences in data protection should not constitute an obstacle to the exchange of personal data. It is, however, questionable whether such a broad approach to equivalence will suffice in all cases to ensure compliance with EU data protection and privacy standards. What is key to this approach, however, is the focus essentially on mutual recognition of the data protection systems of the EU and the USA taken as a whole, based upon the presumption that the systems do in fact in principle offer an acceptable level of protection.

The emphasis on mutual recognition based on the development of common data protection standards is evident in the next step in the transatlantic privacy dialogue, which consists of efforts to conclude a transatlantic agreement on privacy. In 2009 the European Commission adopted a mandate for the negotiation of an EU–US Agreement on privacy, which would aim to provide for a number of data protection safeguards that would be applicable in transatlantic agreements authorising the transfer of personal data.[108] Negotiations towards a transatlantic privacy agreement in the field started in 2010 and are ongoing.[109] According to a Joint Statement on the negotiation of the Agreement by European Commission Vice-President Viviane Reding and US Attorney General Eric Holder, such an agreement will allow for even closer transatlantic cooperation in the fight against crime and terrorism, through the mutual recognition of a high level of protection afforded equally to citizens of both the United States and the European Union, and will thus facilitate any subsequent agreements concerning the sharing of a specific set of personal data.[110]

Achieving mutual recognition in the light of the deep differences in privacy and data protection law between the two parties may be easier said than done. The experience with the application of the principle of mutual recognition internally in the European Union in the area of freedom, security and justice has demonstrated that even in a Union whose members are all signatories to the European Convention on Human Rights (ECHR), there are in practice limits to mutual recognition caused

[108] IP/10/609, Brussels, 26 May 2010, 'European Commission Seeks High Privacy Standards in EU–US Data Protection Agreement'.

[109] K. Archick, 'US–EU Cooperation Against Terrorism', Congressional Research Service Report for Congress 7-5700, RS22030, 4 September 2013, provides an overview of the contested issues in negotiations.

[110] Joint Statement on the Negotiation of an EU–US Data Privacy and Protection Agreement, Brussels, 21 June 2012, MEMO/12/474.

by differing implementation of human rights provisions.[111] On the basis of the internal EU lessons on mutual recognition, negotiations towards a transatlantic privacy agreement seem to go in the right direction in focusing on the establishment of common standards on privacy and data protection, but it is the implementation of these standards on the ground, and the *de jure* and de facto compliance of state action with fundamental rights as enshrined in the ECHR and the Charter of Fundamental Rights, that will be key for the success of the Agreement from a European perspective. Having said that, the inclusion of high-level standards, compliant with EU fundamental rights, in a transatlantic privacy agreement has the potential to make a positive contribution to the evolution of transatlantic security relations[112] in the future and to introduce additional safeguards to the implementation of the existing transatlantic security agreements.[113]

4 Conclusion

The negotiation and conclusion of the EU–US counterterrorism agreements presented the European Union institutions with the significant challenge of responding to perceived global security needs, but also unilateral emergency security requirements imposed by the US executive in a manner that would be compliant with fundamental rights and the rule of law and would not undermine European values. The result has been a series of complex agreements, which include – in particular in the case of the executive transatlantic Agreements on the transfer of PNR and SWIFT data – a number of innovative provisions on transatlantic security governance. The evaluation of the impact of these provisions on the content of the transatlantic Agreements depends on the perspective adopted. From the perspective of furthering trust in transatlantic relations, the PNR and TFTP Agreements can be seen as accepting and legitimising US executive choices and their logic, but also insert a number of layers of scrutiny and transparency with regard to US practices. From the

[111] See V. Mitsilegas, 'The Limits of Mutual Trust in Europe's Area of Freedom, Security and Justice. From Automatic Inter-state Cooperation to the Slow Emergence of the Individual' (2012) 31 *Yearbook of European Law* 319–72.

[112] The European Parliament has called for the resumption of negotiations on the Agreement following the PRISM scandal. See Resolution P7_TA(2013)_03222, 4 July 2013, para. 6.

[113] The retroactive application of the Agreement to agreements (such as PNR and TFTP) that have already been concluded is a bone of contention and resisted by the USA. See Archick, 'US–EU Cooperation Against Terrorism', p. 16.

perspective of safeguarding and promoting European values, however, the result is less satisfactory. Notwithstanding the safeguards included in the Agreements, both their text and implementation confirm their focus on security. Despite the existence of multiple avenues of scrutiny, efforts to maintain secrecy remain. The recent debate on the NSA surveillance scandal demonstrates that the existence of trust in the US system of privacy and data protection should by no means be taken for granted.[114] Calls to address this lack of trust via the conclusion of a transatlantic privacy agreement may not be sufficient to counter effectively the paradigm of surveillance that transatlantic counterterrorism cooperation entails. Following on from the already broad provisions of data transfer included in the EU–US Mutual Legal Assistance Agreement and in the Europol–US and Eurojust–US Agreements, the PNR and TFTP Agreements not only legitimise the bulk transfer to the US government of everyday personal data, but also open the door to the internalisation of this paradigm of surveillance in the European Union, via the potential establishment of European PNR and TFTP systems.

This example of mimesis serves to highlight a third, and perhaps not as visible, institutional/competence perspective. By attempting to provide safeguards to address the challenges posed by US demands, the PNR and TFTP Agreements have developed a number of institutional innovations, including an increase in the powers of Europol, the appointment of an EU scrutiny authority in the territory of a third country, and the potential development of specific EU legislation on surveillance. The institutional aspect also becomes prevalent in the light of the calls to globalise transatlantic security standards with respect to the transfer of PNR data, which would have the effect of both externalising the issue and normalising what was started as unilateral emergency action at a global level. While such externalisation and globalisation may represent a step forward for the emergence of the EU as a global security actor, its negative impact on the protection of fundamental rights at the global level may be considerable.

[114] The Home Affairs Commissioner Cecilia Malmström has called for the opening of consultations under Article 19 of the EU–US TFTP Agreement (on dispute resolution) to investigate allegations about the possible access of the US National Security Agency to the data exchanged through the Agreement: Intervention by Cecilia Malmström on the EU–US TFTP Agreement in the European Parliament, LIBE Committee Hearing, 24 September 2013, SPEECH/13/742.

INDEX

9/11 attacks, 50, 147

accountability
 European Parliament's enhanced role, 258–64, 286–8
 European values, impact of EU–US agreements on, 294–6
 personal data, transfer of, 256–61
 PNR Agreements, 276–86
 promotion of, 57–8
 SWIFT Agreements, 265–76
 TTIP, democratic risks of, 226–8
 TTIP democratic accountability, 212–14, 229–34
 weakness in oversight of transatlantic relationship, 238–45
adjudication techniques
 alternative techniques, 69–72, 100–1
 Commerce Clause, application of, 72–81, 92–3
 internal market harmonisation clause, 81–92
 political process, 93–6
 proportionality, principle of, 96–7
 SCOTUS and ECJ approaches compared, 92–3
 subsidiarity, principle of, 98–9
Affordable Care Act (ACA), 70, 78–81
Afghanistan, 246, 252
African Union, 45
Agreement on Technical Barriers to Trade (TBT Agreement) (WTO, 1995), 172
Agreement on the Application of Sanitary and Phytosanitary Measures (SPS Agreement), 138, 163, 204–6
Ahearn, R.J., 195
Alien Tort Statute, 142, 146
amicus curiae, 22–3, 141–2, 144, 146
Angelo, H., 131
Anti-Counterfeiting Trade Agreement (ACTA)
 European Parliament, role of, 212–13, 272
 non-disclosure agreement, 244–5
 transparency and democratic accountability, 38, 229–31, 242
arbitration, 199
area of freedom, security and justice (AFSJ)
 European Parliament's enhanced role, 258–64, 286–8
 mutual recognition, 313–14
 PNR Agreements, 276–86
 SWIFT Agreements, 265–76
Argentina, 224
assemblies, 45
Assembly of European Regions (AER), 112, 113–14
Association of Southeast Asian Nations (ASEAN), 155n. 101
Atlantic community of law, *see* transatlantic community of law
Australia, 281, 283
Australia–New Zealand Trans-Tasman Model, 194
Austria, 111–12, 151
Aviation and Transportation Security Act, USA, 276

Barroso Initiative, 66
Bartl, Marija, 5–6
Belgium, 111–12, 119–20, 151

Bermann, G., 95
Besselink, L., 67
Bickerton, C.J., 39–40
Bigo, D., 300
bilateral exchanges between courts, 19–20
bilateral rule-making, 147–53
biotechnology, 170, *see also* genetically modified organisms (GMOs)
black sites (CIA prisons), 242, 250–1
Boeing–Airbus dispute, 138
Bomberg, E., 113
Bradford, Anu, 120n. 113, 143
Brenncke, M., 92
Breyer, Stephen, 17, 19–20, 21, 22, 29–30
Britain, *see* United Kingdom (UK)
Bruguière, J.-L., 266–7, 270
Brussels effect (transfer of regulatory standards), 143–5, 153
'Building Bridges between the EU and US Standards Systems' (TEC), 172
Burghardt, Gunter, 117
Bush, George H.W., Sr, 94
business participation in HLWG report preparation, 216–18
Buzek, Jerzy, 56, 271

Cassis de Dijon (*Rewe-Zentrale* v. *Bundesmonopolverwaltung fur Branntwein*), 189–90
Centre for Economic Policy Research (CEPR) Report, 218–22
Chang, W.-C., 25n. 70
Cheney, Richard, 250
Chevron, 224n. 49
CIA (Central Intelligence Agency), 242, 250–1
civil society engagement in international relations, 122–7
Claes, Monica, 25–6
Clarke, Kenneth, 251
Clinton, Hillary, 271
coherence between EU counterterrorism action and values
  challenge of, 289–91, 314–15
  European values, impact of EU–US agreements on, 291–6
  global standards, development of, 311–12
  mechanisms for achieving coherence, 297–314
  monitoring of EU–US agreements, 301–5
  operational oversight, 297–301
  reciprocity in agreements, 306–10
  transatlantic privacy framework, 312–14
  US privacy standards, adequacy of, 305–6
Cohesion Policy, EU, 106, 109–11
Commerce Clause
  application of, 72–81, 92–3
  interpretation of, 70, 85
  political process, 93–6
  proportionality, absence of, 96–7
  subsidiarity, absence of, 96, 98–9
Committee of the Regions (CoR), 112–13
Committee on Foreign Affairs (AFET), European Parliament, 40
Common Foreign and Security Policy (CFSP), 36–7, 39, 65–6
Common Security and Defence Policy (CSDP), 36–7, 65–6
Common Understanding on Regulatory Principles and Best Practices (High-Level Regulatory Cooperation Forum, 2010), 172
communication, *see* transatlantic judicial communication
community of law, *see* transatlantic community of law
comparative law, use of, 27–33
Compassionated Use Act (CUA), California, 76–7
conferences, 18–21, 136
conferral, *see* enumerated powers
confidentiality, 198–9
Congress, USA, 37–8, 72–81
Controlled Substance Act (CSA), USA, 76–7
Convention on Biodiversity, 152
Convention on Cybercrime, 151

Corporate Europe Observatory, 215
COSAC (Conférence des Organes Spécialisés dans les Affaires Communautaires), 65, 66
Council, the (Council of Ministers)
  European Parliament powers, 232, 263
  information withheld from European Parliament, 38
  PNR Agreements, 277, 283–4
  sub-national authorities' access to, 111–12
  SWIFT Agreements, 239–40, 269–70, 272–3
Council of Europe, 45
counterterrorism
  coherence between EU counterterrorism action and values, 289–91, 314–15
  coherence mechanisms, 297–314
  EU weakness in oversight of transatlantic relationship, 237–45
  European Parliament's enhanced role, 258–64, 286–8
  European values, impact of EU–US agreements on, 291–6
  global standards, development of, 311–12
  monitoring of EU–US agreements, 301–5
  operational oversight by EU, 297–301
  personal data, transfer of, 256–61
  reciprocity in agreements, 306–10
  rule-transfer, 144–5, 306–10
  transatlantic privacy framework, 312–14
  US policy and transatlantic cooperation, 246–55
  US privacy standards, adequacy of, 305–6, *see also* Passenger Name Records (PNR) Agreements; surveillance by USA; SWIFT Agreements
Court of Justice of the European Union (ECJ)
  comparative law, use of, 27–33
  foreign legal materials, use of, 24–5
  internationalisation of law, 15–18
  jurisdiction, 13–14
  litigation relating to bilateral disputes, 139–41
  national and supranational courts, relations between, 12–15
  transatlantic judicial communication, 9–12, 33–4
  visits between the USA and EU, 18–21, 136
Cowles, Maria Green, 217
Cremona, M., 41, 60
Curtin, Deirdre, 37, 38, 67, 230
cybercrime, 150–3
cybersecurity, 150–3
Czech Republic, 224

Dann, P., 36
Dassonville (*Procureur du Roi* v. *Dassonville*), 189–90
data protection
  agreements between criminal justice bodies, 292
  EU weakness in oversight of transatlantic relationship, 239–45
  European Parliament's enhanced role, 258–64, 286–8
  EU–US Data Protection Agreement, 143, 244
  mechanisms for achieving coherence between counterterrorism actions and values, 297–314
  right to protection, 295–6
  transatlantic counterterrorism cooperation, 256–61
  transatlantic privacy framework, 312–14
  US approach to counterterrorism, 253–5
  US lobbying of European Parliament, 245, 271, *see also* Passenger Name Records (PNR) Agreements; SWIFT Agreements
Davids, Willibrord, 21
De Gucht, Karel, 50–1, 223
De Ville, F., 221–2
De Visser, Maartje, 25–6
death penalty, 141–2, 144, 145

Dekker, I., 37
democratic accountability
  European Parliament's enhanced role, 258–64, 286–8
  European values, impact of EU–US agreements on, 294–6
  personal data, transfer of, 256–61
  PNR Agreements, 276–86
  promotion of, 57–8
  SWIFT Agreements, 265–76
  TTIP, democratic risks of, 226–8
  TTIP accountability, 212–14, 229–34
  weakness in oversight of transatlantic relationship, 238–45
Department of Homeland Security (DHS)
  PNR Agreements, 276, 278–9, 280
  reciprocity relating to PNR Agreements, 308–10
dialogue
  effectiveness of, 180–2
  Transatlantic Economic Council (TEC), 180–2
  transatlantic judicial communication, 25–7, 136–7, *see also* Transatlantic Legislators' Dialogue
dispute resolution
  bilateral mechanism, need for, 184
  European Commission's view, 161–2
  EU–US dispute resolution, 137–9
  WTO dispute settlement mechanism, 159, 161–2, 166
drones, 251–2

Early Warning System (EWS), EU, 66
EEA (European Economic Area) Agreement, 190n. 15
Eeckhout, P., 36–7, 39, 232
Eminent European Person, TFTP/SWIFT oversight, 266–7, 270, 300–1
Emissions Trading Scheme, EU, 61–2, 142–3, 144
enemy combatants, 248–9
enhanced interrogation, 249–50
enumerated powers
  alternative adjudication techniques, 69–72, 100–1
  Commerce Clause, application of, 72–81
  internal market harmonisation clause, 81–92
  political process, 93–6
  proportionality, principle of, 96–7
  SCOTUS and ECJ approaches compared, 92–3
  subsidiarity, principle of, 98–9
equivalency
  in EU and US trade agreements, 191–3, 197
  features of, 196–9
  harmonisation, 189–91
  initiation of, 194–6
  legal test, equivalency as, 196–9
  liberalisation, approaches to, 186–9
  multilateral benefits, potential of, 208
  prevalence of equivalency, 193–4
  transatlantic privacy framework, 312–14
  US privacy standards, adequacy of, 305–6
  WTO considerations, 200–8
Eurojust, 294, 296
EuroLat (Euro-Latin American Parliamentary Assembly), 45
'Europe of the Regions', 106–16
European Commission
  Framework Agreement on Relations with European Parliament, 264
  free trade, 161–2
  global standards, development of, 311
  HLWG membership, 214–16, 231
  HLWG stakeholder participation, 216–18
  information withheld from European Parliament, 38
  knowledge and parliamentary accountability, 38, 231–4
  monitoring of EU–US agreements, 301–5
  PNR Agreements, 277, 282n. 103, 283–4
  PNR, EU system proposal, 309–10

European Commission (*cont.*)
regulatory cooperation negotiations, 180–1
SWIFT Agreements, 241, 272–3
TFTP, EU system proposal, 307–8
transparency, 229–31
TTIP horizontal provisions, 225–9
TTIP impact assessment, 218–19
TTIP institutions, 222–5
European Convention on Human Rights, 155n. 101
European Court of Justice (ECJ)
adjudication approach compared to SCOTUS, 92–3
alternative adjudication techniques, 71–2, 100–1
enumerated powers, principle of, 70–2
internal market harmonisation clause, 81–92
PNR Agreements, 277
political process, 93–6
proportionality, principle of, 96–7
subsidiarity, principle of, 98–9
European Data Protection Supervisor (EDPS), 275, 299
European Economic Area (EEA) Agreement, 190n. 15
European Investment Bank, 107–8
European Parliament
ACTA role, 212–13, 272
constitutionalisation of powers, 67–8
cybersecurity, 152
delegations, 47
democratic scrutiny of agreements, 294–6
enhanced role of, 258–64, 268–72, 286–8
foreign affairs powers, 35–9
foreign affairs role, 39–42, 140–1
formal transatlantic relations, 48–51
Framework Agreement on Relations with European Commission, 264
free trade, 161–2
informal transatlantic relations, 51–6
information withheld from, 38
international agreements, 37, 39
knowledge and parliamentary accountability, 38, 231–4
Liaison Office, 56–7
lobbying by USA, 245, 271
national parliaments, role of, 64–6
parliamentary diplomacy, 41–2
parliamentary diplomacy benefits, 57–64
parliamentary diplomacy, legal basis of, 46–8
parliamentary diplomacy, origins of, 43–6
PNR Agreements role, 40–1, 59–60, 241–2, 254, 286–8, 292–3, 294–5, 310
PNR Agreements, threat to suspend, 51, 260
SWIFT Agreements role, 38–9, 40–1, 59–60, 63, 265–76, 286–8, 293–4, 295
SWIFT Agreements, threat to suspend, 51, 260
TFTP operational oversight, 297
Treaty of Lisbon effects, 262–4, 268–72
Treaty on European Union (TEU) role, 261–2
Treaty on the Functioning of the EU (TFEU), 263
TTIP scrutiny, 50–1, 55, 212–14, 229–34
US surveillance programme investigation, 3, 51, 213, 238, 259–60, 288
weakness in oversight of transatlantic relationship, 238–45
European Regional Development Fund (ERDF), 109
European Union (EU)
amicus curiae briefs to US Supreme Court, 22–3, 141–2, 144, 146
Association Agreements, 190n. 15
bilateral rule-making, 147–53
Cohesion Policy, 106, 109–11
'common interest' discourse in trade policy, 220–1

data protection, joint EU–US regulation, 143, 244
Emissions Trading Scheme, 61–2, 142–3, 144
enumerated powers, principle of, 69, 70–2
equivalency provisions in EU trade agreements, 191–3, 197
European Parliament Liaison Office, 56–7
formal transatlantic relations, 48–51
harmonisation of regulations, 189–91
informal transatlantic relations, 51–6
internal market harmonisation clause, 81–93
internalisation of US security policy, 257–8, 282, 306–8, 315
Korea, equivalency provisions in trade agreement with, 191–3, 197
laws, transatlantic impact of, 60–2
national parliaments, role of, 64–6
non-bilateral interactions with the USA, 141–6
parliamentary diplomacy, benefits of, 57–64
personal data, transfer of, 256–61
PNR, EU system proposal, 155, 308–10
quasi-institutionalised relations with the USA, 133–41
risk assessment approach, 166
rule-transfer, 143–5, 153–7, 306–10
sub-national authorities engagement, risks of, 122–7
sub-national authorities and EU–US relations, 102–5, 116–22
sub-national authorities influence on EU policy, 105–16
surveillance by USA, 3, 51, 213, 238, 239, 259–60, 288
TFTP, EU system proposal, 155, 306–8
thematic agendas, 120–1
transatlantic community of law, 1–3
US counterterrorism policy and transatlantic cooperation, 246–55
US law applied extraterritorially, 242–4
US preference for an integrated EU, ix
weakness in oversight of transatlantic relationship, 238–45, *see also* Court of Justice of the European Union (ECJ); European Parliament; Passenger Name Records (PNR) Agreements; SWIFT Agreements; transatlantic community of law; transatlantic counterterrorism cooperation; transatlantic judicial communication; transatlantic regulatory cooperation; Transatlantic Trade and Investment Partnership (TTIP)
European values
coherence between EU counterterrorism action and values, 289–91, 314–15
coherence mechanisms, 297–314
global standards, development of, 311–12
impact of EU–US agreements, 291–6
monitoring of EU–US agreements, 301–5
operational oversight, 297–301
reciprocity in agreements, 306–10
transatlantic privacy framework, 312–14
US privacy standards, adequacy of, 305–6
Europol
data protection, 312–13
European values, impact of EU–US agreements on, 294, 296
information withheld from European Parliament, 38
Joint Supervisory Board (JSB), 302–4
operational oversight of TFTP Agreement, 297–301
scrutiny of TFTP, 302–5
SWIFT data, 240
EU–US Development Dialogue, 53–4

EU–US Education Policy Forum, 53–4
EU–US Energy Council, 53–4
EU–US Financial Markets Regulatory Dialogue, 53–4
EU–US Guidelines for Regulatory Cooperation and Transparency (2002), 170, 171, 176
EU–US Insurance Regulatory Dialogue, 53–4
EU–US Regulatory Cooperation Best Cooperative Practices, 171
EU–US Task Force on Biotechnology Research, 53–4
exports, *see* trade
extradition, 291–2
extraordinary rendition, 239, 242, 250–1

Fahey, Elaine, 5–6, 41
Farrah, J.E., 197n. 34
federal systems, 103n. 7
Foreign Account Tax Compliance Act (FATCA), US, 244
Foreign Intelligence and Surveillance Act (FISA), US, 242–3
Foreign Intelligence and Surveillance Court, 243
foreign policy, 39–42, 143–4, 248–53
Framework Agreement on Relations between the European Parliament and the European Commission (2010), 264
Framework for Advancing Transatlantic Economic Integration (2007), 171
France, 18, 25, 120–1, 139–40
France v. *Commission*, 139–40
free trade
  liberalisation approaches, 183–4, 186–9
  ongoing trade agreement negotiations, 161–5, 184–5, 186–8, *see also* trade; Transatlantic Trade and Investment Partnership (TTIP)
Freedom of Information Act (FOIA), US, 244
fundamental rights, 295–6

Garcia v. *San Antonio Metropolitan Transit Authority*, 94
Gaza, 145
Geithner, Tim, 271
General Agreement on Tariffs and Trade (GATT)
  equivalency recognition, 200–4, 206–7, 208
  influence of EU–US trade position, 158
General Agreement on Trade in Services (GATS), 204–6, 207–8
genetically modified organisms (GMOs), 170, 182, 227–8, 234n. 83
Geneva Convention, 155n. 101
Germany
  Council representation, 111–12
  EU law, integration of, 114–15
  national courts and the ECJ, 15–16
  regional offices, 114
  sub-national authorities, influence of, 118
  Tobacco Advertising II, 86–9
ghost prisons, 250–1
Gibbons v. *Ogden*, 96
Ginsburg J, 19–20, 21, 79, 80
Glenn, Patrick, 9n. 1
Goede, M. de, 296
Gonzales v. *Raich*, 76–8
Gordon, Philip, 124
Greece, 224
Guantánamo Bay detention centre, 239, 248–9
Gun-Free School Zone Act (GFSZA), US, 73–5, 94
Gutierrez-Fons, José A., 4

Halberstam, D., 98–9
Hammarskjöld, Dag, 43
Harbour, Malcolm, 55
hard law, xiv
harmonisation of regulations, 189–91
health insurance, 70, 78–81
Helms–Burton Act, 137–8
High-Level Working Group on Jobs and Growth (HLWG)
  knowledge and parliamentary accountability, 232

membership of, 214–16, 231
recommendations, 163–5, 187–8, 214
stakeholder participation in report preparation, 216–18
third countries, 221
TTIP proposal, 211, *see also* Transatlantic Trade and Investment Partnership (TTIP)
High-Level Regulatory Cooperation Forum, 177, 180, 184–5
Holder, Eric, 313
Howse, R., 227

imports, *see* trade
industry participation in HLWG Report preparation, 216–18
information-sharing
information withheld from European Parliament, 38
in transatlantic relations, 239–45
US approach to counterterrorism, 253–5, *see also* Passenger Name Records (PNR) Agreements; SWIFT Agreements
Initiative to Enhance Transatlantic Economic Integration and Growth (EU–US Declaration), 171
institutionalisation
quasi-institutionalised relations, 133–41
transatlantic regulatory cooperation, 175–82
and transatlantic relations, 3–4, 135–7
TTIP institutions, xiii, 211–12, 222–5
institution-light, xii, 135–7
in't Veld, Sophie
ACTA Agreement, 229–30
EU role, 237
PNR Agreements, 284
SWIFT Agreements, 38–9, 273n. 66, 273–4
transatlantic relations and security, reflections on, 6, 237–45
intellectual property, 190–1
internal market harmonisation clause (Article 114 TFEU)
application of, 81–93
interpretation of, 71
political process, 93–6
proportionality, principle of, 96–7
subsidiarity, principle of, 98–9
international agreements
coherence between EU counterterrorism action and values, 289–91, 314–15
coherence mechanisms, 297–314
European Parliament, role of, 37, 39
European Parliament's enhanced role, 258–64, 286–8
European values, impact of EU–US agreements on, 291–6
global standards, development of, 311–12
monitoring of EU–US agreements, 301–5
operational oversight by EU, 297–301
parliamentary diplomacy, benefits of, 59–60
personal data, transfer of, 256–61
reciprocity in agreements, 306–10
rule-transfer, 144–5, 306–10
transatlantic privacy framework, 312–14
US privacy standards, adequacy of, 305–6, *see also* Passenger Name Records (PNR) Agreements; SWIFT Agreements; transatlantic counterterrorism cooperation
international assemblies, 45
internationalisation of law, 15–18
Internet Corporation for Assigned Names and Numbers (ICANN), 151
Investor–state dispute settlement (ISDS) mechanism, 223–5
Iraq, 246
Italy, 111–12

Jančić, Davor, 4
Joint Supervisory Board (JSB) of Europol, 302–4
Joint US–EU Statement on Early Warning and Problem Prevention Mechanism (1999), 169–70

judicial communication,
see transatlantic judicial communication

Katzenbach v. *McClung*, 72–3
Kennedy, John F., ix
knowledge and parliamentary accountability, 231–4
Korea, 191–3, 197

Laeken Declaration on the Future of the European Union, 124
Lamy, Pascal, 159
language, 32–3
law, *see* transatlantic community of law
Law, D.S., 25n. 70
law-light, 133–5
law making, privatisation of, 227–8
legal materials, 21–5, 27
legalisation of transatlantic relations, xiii
legitimacy, 198–9
Lenaerts, K., 92
Lisbon Treaty, *see* Treaty of Lisbon
Lopez (*United States* v. *Lopez*), 73–5, 85, 93, 94, 98–9, 100

Mak, Elaine, 4
Malmström, Cecilia, 315n. 114
Malta, 151
Mandelson, Peter, 160, 162
Marshall CJ, 96
Mathis, James, 5
mediation, 192–3, 199
Medicaid, 70, 78–81
Mediterranean Union (MU), 120–1
Mercosur, 45
Mitsilegas, Valsamis, 6
Mohamed, Binyam, 251
Mohammed, Khalid Sheikh, 250
Monar, J., 60, 263–4, 267, 271–2
Monsanto, 234n. 83
Moreira, Vital, 55
Morgenthau, Hans, 102–3n. 5
Morpho (security company), 243
Morrall, J.F., 174
Morrison (*United States* v. *Morrison*), 75–6
most-favoured nation (MFN) obligations
country-based recognition, 200–1
equivalency recognition, 200–2
origin-based recognition, 200–1
multilateral exchanges, 21
Mutual Legal Assistance Agreement, 291–2, 296, 305, 312–13
mutual recognition agreements (MRAs)
assessment of, 173–4
implementation of, 168–9
marine equipment, 170
organic trade, 173
trusted traders, 173

national courts, 12–15
National Federation of Independent Business (*'NFIB'*) v. *Sebelius*, 70, 78–81, 93
national parliaments, 64–6, 95–6
Netherlands, the 18, 25
Network of the Presidents of the Supreme Judicial Courts of the EU (NPSJC), 21
New Transatlantic Agenda (NTA), 49, 51, 168, 210
non-papers on the TTIP
horizontal provisions, 225–9
institutions of the TTIP, 222–5
stakeholder participation in HLWG Report preparation, 217
non-tariff barriers (NTBs)
benefits of elimination, 159–60
equivalency instruments, features of, 196–9
equivalency instruments, initiation of, 194–6
equivalency instruments, WTO considerations, 200–8
equivalency provisions in EU and US agreements, 191–3
equivalency of regulation, prevalence of, 193–4
harmonisation, 189–91
liberalisation, approaches to, 183–4, 186–9
multilateral benefits, potential of, 208
regulatory cooperation, approaches to, 167–75

regulatory cooperation, institutional framework for, 175–82

Obama, Barack, 249, 250, 253
ObamaCare (Patient Protection and Affordable Care Act), 70, 78–81
Occupy movement, 126n. 151
O'Connor J, 19–20
operational oversight of EU–US agreements, 297–301
Organic Trade Equivalence Arrangement, 173
outsourcing impact assessment, 218–19

Pakistan, 252
Pan-African Parliament of the African Union, 45
Panama, 190n. 15
Panetta, Leon, 251
Parlasur, 45
Parlatino (Latin American Parliament), 45
parliamentary diplomacy by the European Parliament
  benefits of, 57–64
  constitutionalisation of EP powers, 67–8
  delegations, 47
  as enhancement to foreign affairs profile, 41–2
  European Parliament Liaison Office, 56–7
  formal transatlantic relations, 48–51
  informal transatlantic relations, 51–6
  legal basis, 46–8
  national parliaments, role of, 64–6
  origins of, 43–6, *see also* European Parliament
Passenger Name Records (PNR) Agreements
  2004 Agreement, 276–7
  2006 Interim Agreement, 277–9
  2007 Agreement, 279–81
  2011 Agreement, 281–6
  bilateral rule-making, difficulties of, 148–50
  EU internalisation of US policy, 257–8, 282, 308–10, 311–12, 315
  EU system proposal, 155, 308–10
  European Parliament, role of, 40–1, 59–60, 241–2, 254, 286–8, 292–3, 294–5, 310
  European Parliament's threat to terminate, 51, 260
  European values, impact on, 292, 294–5, 296, 314–15
  global standards, development of, 311–12
  Lisbon Treaty implications, 281–6
  reciprocity relating to, 308–10
  US privacy standards, adequacy of, 305
Patient Protection and Affordable Care Act (PPACA), 70, 78–81
Patriot Act, USA, 242–3, 253
personal contacts, 18–21
personal data
  agreements between criminal justice bodies, 292
  EU weakness in oversight of transatlantic relationship, 239–45
  European Parliament's enhanced role, 258–64, 286–8
  EU–US Data Protection Agreement, 143, 244
  mechanisms for achieving coherence between counterterrorism actions and values, 297–314
  right to protection of, 295–6
  transatlantic counterterrorism cooperation, 256–61
  transatlantic privacy framework, 312–14
  US approach to counterterrorism, 253–5
  US lobbying of European Parliament, 245, 271, *see also* Passenger Name Records (PNR) Agreements; SWIFT Agreements

Petersmann, E.U., 162
Peterson, J., 113
pharmaceutical industry, 217
Phillips, Lord, 21
police and judicial cooperation in criminal matters (PJC)
  European Parliament's enhanced role, 258–64, 286–8
  personal data, transfer of, 256–61, *see also* Passenger Name Records (PNR) Agreements; SWIFT Agreements
Pollack, M.A., 63, 104, 121, 122
poultry dispute, 138, 180–1
PRISM surveillance programme, 3, 51, 239
private life
  coherence between counterterrorism actions and values, 297–314
  right to, 295–6
  transatlantic privacy framework, 312–14
proportionality
  in EU and US systems, 32
  principle of, 96–7
  Tobacco Advertising I, 86
  Tobacco Advertising II, 88
  Vodafone, 90–1, 92

racial discrimination, 72–3
Raich (*Gonzales* v. *Raich*), 76–8, 93, 97, 100
REACH Directive, 182
Reding, Viviane, 313
Rees, Wyn, 6
regional trade agreement (RTA) exceptions, 206–8
regions
  Cohesion Policy, EU, 106, 109–11
  meaning of, 103–4n. 8
  sub-national authorities engagement, risks of, 122–7
  sub-national authorities and EU policy, 105–16
  sub-national authorities and EU–US relations, 102–5, 116–22
regulation, 143–5, 153, *see also* transatlantic regulatory cooperation
regulatory capture, 217–18
regulatory cooperation
  approaches to, 167–75
  benefits of barrier removal, 159–60
  dialogue, effectiveness of, 180–2
  equivalency instruments, features of, 196–9
  equivalency instruments, initiation of, 194–6
  equivalency provisions in EU and US agreements, 191–3
  equivalency of regulation, prevalence of, 193–4
  harmonisation, 189–91
  importance of EU–US trade, 158–9
  institutional framework, 175–82
  liberalisation, approaches to, 183–4, 186–9
  multilateral benefits, potential of, 208
  ongoing trade agreement negotiations, 161–5, 184–5, 186–8
  rationale for, 166–7
  regulatory barriers, 159–61
  risk assessment approaches, contrast in, 166
  WTO considerations, 200–8
Regulatory Cooperation Council, 211
Rehnquist CJ, 70, 73–8
responsibilisation strategy, 296
Roadmap for EU–US Regulatory Cooperation (2005), 170–1, 174, 176
Roberts CJ, 21, 70, 78–81
rule-transfer, 143–5, 153–7, 306–10
Rumsfeld, Donald, 250
Rusk, Dean, 43

Safe Harbour Framework, 243–4
Santos Vara, Juan, 6
Sapir, A., 181
Sarbanes–Oxley Act, 182
Scalia, Antonin, 30
Schulz, Martin, 56

Schütze, R., 232
Scotland, 118–19
sector-specific regulatory dialogues, 176
security surveillance by USA, *see* surveillance by USA
Shaffer, G.C., 104, 121, 122
Shortell, C., 78
Skouris, Vassilios, 20
small and medium enterprises (SMEs), 197–8
Snowden, Edward, 3, 51, 240–1, *see also* surveillance by USA
social networks, 126n. 152
soft law, xiv
space, peaceful use of, 137n. 29
Spain, 111–12
speculative security, 296
SPS Agreement (Agreement on the Application of Sanitary and Phytosanitary Measures), 138, 163, 204–6
stakeholder participation in regulatory dialogue, 179–80, 216–18
state autonomy
  adjudication techniques, 69–72, 100–1
  Commerce Clause, application of, 72–81
  internal market harmonisation clause, 81–92
  political process, 93–6
  proportionality, principle of, 96–7
  SCOTUS and ECJ approaches compared, 92–3
  subsidiarity, principle of, 98–9
Stavridis, S., 44
Stevens J, 77, 97
'Stronger EU–US Partnership and a More Open Market for the 21st Century, A' (EU Commission, 2005), 171
sub-national authorities (SNAs)
  EU policy, influence on, 105–16
  and EU–US relations, 102–5, 116–22
  meaning of, 103–4n. 8
  risks of SNA engagement in international relations, 122–7
subsidiarity
  in EU and US systems, 32
  principle of, 96, 98–9
  regional policy, 109, 111
  Treaty of Lisbon, 95–6
  Vodafone, 92
Supreme Court of the United States (SCOTUS)
  adjudication approach compared to ECJ, 92–3
  alternative adjudication techniques, 71–2, 100–1
  Commerce Clause, application of, 72–81, 92–3
  Commerce Clause interpretation, 70, 85
  comparative law, use of, 27–33
  EU submissions to, 22–3, 141–2, 144, 146
  foreign legal materials, use of, 22–4
  internationalisation of law, 15–18
  jurisdiction, 13
  national and supranational courts, relations between, 12–15
  political process, 93–6
  proportionality, principle of, 96–7
  subsidiarity, principle of, 98–9
  transatlantic judicial communication, 9–12, 33–4
  visits between the USA and EU, 18–21, 136
surveillance by USA
  coherence between EU counterterrorism action and values, 315
  EU complicity, 239
  European Parliament's response, 3, 51, 213, 259–60, 288
  weakness in oversight of transatlantic relationship, 238
SWIFT Agreements
  2009 Agreement, 265–8
  2010 Agreement, 272–6
  civil liberties approaches of EU and USA, 254

SWIFT Agreements (*cont.*)
European Parliament, role of, 38–9, 40–1, 59–60, 63, 265–76, 286–8, 293–4, 295
European Parliament's enhanced role, 286–8
European Parliament's threat to terminate, 51, 260
European values, impact on, 293–4, 295, 296
European values, mechanisms for achieving coherence with, 297–314
in't Veld's involvement, 38–9, 239–41, 273n. 66, 273–4
Lisbon Treaty implications, 268–72
origins of, 265–8, *see also* Terrorist Finance Tracking Programme (TFTP)

Takács, Tamara, 5, 186
Task Force on Critical Infrastructure Protection, 150
technical barriers to trade (TBT)
Agreement on Technical Barriers to Trade, 172
equivalency recognition, 204–6
ongoing trade agreement negotiations, 163, 164–5
terrorist attacks, 50, 147, 246–55, *see also* counterterrorism
Terrorist Finance Tracking Programme (TFTP)
bilateral rule-making, difficulties of, 148–9
EU internalisation of US policy, 257–8, 306–8, 315
EU system proposal, 155, 306–8
European values, impact on, 292, 295, 296, 314–15
European values, mechanisms for achieving coherence with, 297–308
monitoring of EU–US agreements, 301–5
operational oversight, 297–301
reciprocity relating to, 306–8
SWIFT Agreements, origins of, 265–8
US privacy standards, adequacy of, 305–6, *see also* SWIFT Agreements
Thym, D., 37–8, 44–5
Titanium Dioxide (*Commission* v. *Council* (*Titanium Dioxide*)), 82
Tobacco Advertising I, 70–1, 83–6, 93, 98–9, 100
Tobacco Advertising II, 71, 86–9, 93, 100
torture, 249–50
trade
benefits of barrier removal, 159–60
dialogue, effectiveness in regulatory cooperation, 180–2
influence of EU–US trade, 158–9
liberalisation, approaches to, 183–4, 186–9
ongoing trade agreement negotiations, 161–5, 184–5, 186–8
regulatory barriers, 159–61
regulatory cooperation, approaches to, 167–75
regulatory cooperation, institutional framework for, 175–82
regulatory cooperation rationale, 166–7
risk assessment approaches, contrast in, 166
WTO dispute settlement mechanism, 159, 161–2, 166, *see also* equivalency; non-tariff barriers (NTBs); Transatlantic Trade and Investment Partnership (TTIP)
transatlantic adjudication techniques
alternative techniques, 69–72, 100–1
Commerce Clause, application of, 72–81, 92–3
internal market harmonisation clause, 81–92
political process, 93–6
proportionality, principle of, 96–7
SCOTUS and ECJ approaches compared, 92–3
subsidiarity, principle of, 98–9
Transatlantic Business Council (TABC), 53–4, 55
Transatlantic Business Dialogue (TABD), 54–5, 136–7, 179–80

transatlantic community of law
  alternative interpretations, 131–3, 157
  bilateral relations, 137–9
  bilateral rule-making, 147–53
  dispute forums, 137–9
  institutionalisation, 3–4, 135–7
  integration through law, 133–5
  legalisation of transatlantic relations, xiii
  litigation in the EU legal order, 139–41
  non-bilateral interactions, 141–6
  purpose of this volume, 1–3
  quasi-institutionalised relations, 133–41
  rule-transfer, 143–5, 153–7, 306–10
  US dominance in security policy, 237–45
Transatlantic Consumer Dialogue (TCD)
  equivalency instruments, 199
  rule-making role, 136–7
  Transatlantic Economic Council (TEC), 54–5
  transatlantic regulatory cooperation, 53–4, 179–80
transatlantic counterterrorism cooperation
  coherence between EU counterterrorism action and values, 289–91, 314–15
  coherence mechanisms, 297–314
  EU weakness in oversight of transatlantic relationship, 237–45
  European Parliament's enhanced role, 258–64, 286–8
  European values, impact of EU–US agreements on, 291–6
  global standards, development of, 311–12
  monitoring of EU–US agreements, 301–5
  operational oversight by EU, 297–301
  personal data, transfer of, 256–61
  reciprocity in agreements, 306–10
  rule-transfer, 144–5, 306–10
  transatlantic privacy framework, 312–14
  US counterterrorism policies, 246–55
  US privacy standards, adequacy of, 305–6, *see also* Passenger Name Records (PNR) Agreements; surveillance by USA; SWIFT Agreements
Transatlantic Declaration on EC–US Relations (1990), 48–9, 51, 167–8
Transatlantic Dialogue on Climate Change and Security, 53–4
Transatlantic Dialogue on Sustainable Development, 53–4
Transatlantic Donors Dialogue, 53–4
Transatlantic Economic Council (TEC)
  dialogue, 180–2
  role of, 53–5, 171–2, 177–9
  standards recognition, 172
  strategic leadership, 184–5
Transatlantic Economic Partnership (TEP), 50, 62, 139–40, 168, 180
Transatlantic Environment Dialogue, 136–7
Transatlantic Innovation Action Partnership, 173, 178–9
transatlantic judicial communication
  comparative law, use of, 27–33
  dialogue between judges, 25–7, 136–7
  emergence of, 15–18
  foreign legal materials, use of, 21–5, 27
  future of, 33–4
  methodology, development of, 31–3
  national and supranational courts, relations between, 12–15
  socio-legal research approach, 9–12
  visits between the USA and EU, 18–21, 136, *see also* police and judicial cooperation in criminal matters (PJC)
Transatlantic Labour Dialogue, 53–4, 136–7
Transatlantic Legislators' Dialogue
  equivalency instruments, 199
  European Parliament use of, 64
  oversight of transatlantic relationship, 63, 68, 238
  quasi-institutional relations, 135–6
  transatlantic regulatory cooperation, 180
  work of, 51–5

Transatlantic Partnership Agreement, 161–2
Transatlantic Policy Network, 53–4
transatlantic privacy framework, 312–14
transatlantic regulatory cooperation
approaches to, 167–75
benefits of barrier removal, 159–60
dialogue, effectiveness of, 180–2
equivalency instruments, features of, 196–9
equivalency instruments, initiation of, 194–6
equivalency provisions in EU and US agreements, 191–3
equivalency of regulation, prevalence of, 193–4
harmonisation, 189–91
importance of EU–US trade, 158–9
institutional framework, 175–82
liberalisation, approaches to, 183–4, 186–9
multilateral benefits, potential of, 208
ongoing trade agreement negotiations, 161–5, 184–5, 186–8
rationale for, 166–7
regulatory barriers, 159–61
risk assessment approaches, contrast in, 166
WTO considerations, 200–8
Transatlantic Trade and Investment Partnership (TTIP)
benefits of, 219–22
democratic accountability, 212–14, 229–34
democratic risks of, 225–9
European Parliament, role of, 50–1, 55, 212–14, 229–34
HLWG, membership of, 214–16
horizontal provisions, 225–9
impact assessment, 218–19
institutionalisation of EU–US relations, xiii, 211–12, 222–5
institutions of, 222–5
legal cooperation, 133–4, 139
negotiations, 3, 210–11
regulatory cooperation, 185
Regulatory Cooperation Council, 211
stakeholder participation in HLWG Report preparation, 216–18
transnational parliamentary bodies, 45
transparency
equivalency instruments, 198–9
restrictions on, 244–5
TTIP scrutiny, 229–31
Treaty of Lisbon
Committee of the Regions (CoR), 113n. 71
European Parliament role, 35–6, 262–4, 268–72
European Parliament's influence on counterterrorism agreements, 258–61, 286–8
European Parliament's influence on regulatory cooperation, 181, 212–13
European values, 289–90
national parliaments, role of, 64–6
PNR Agreements, effect upon, 281–6
subsidiarity, 95–6
SWIFT Agreements, effect upon, 268–72
Treaty of Maastricht, 64, 109
Treaty of Rome, 107–8
Treaty on European Union (TEU)
enumerated powers, principle of, 69
European Parliament, role of, 261–2
European values, 290
parliamentary diplomacy, legal basis, 46–7
Treaty on the Functioning of the EU (TFEU)
Article 16, 274–5, 284–5
Article 114, application of, 81–92
Article 114, interpretation of, 71
European Parliament role, 263
internal market harmonisation clause, 71, 81–92
personal data, 274–5, 284–5
PNR Agreements, 284–5
SWIFT Agreements, 274–5
trusted traders, 173
Tushnet, Mark, 9n. 1, 77

UN Convention Against Torture and Other Cruel, Inhuman or Degrading Treatment, 250
Union for the Mediterranean, 120–1
United Kingdom (UK), 18, 111–12, 118–19, 251
United Nations (UN), 43, 250
United States (US)
  Agreement Regarding Certain Sanitary and Phytosanitary Measures and Technical Standards Affecting Trade in Agriculture Products, 190n. 15
  bilateral rule-making, 147–53
  data protection, joint EU–US regulation, 143, 244
  enumerated powers, 69–70
  equivalency provisions in US trade agreements, 191–3
  European Parliament Liaison Office, 56–7
  European Union Emissions Trading Scheme, 61–2, 142–3, 144
  extraterritorial application of US law, 242–4
  foreign policy, 248–53
  formal transatlantic relations, 48–51
  harmonisation of regulations, 189–91
  homeland security, 253–5, 276, 278–9, 280, 308–10
  informal transatlantic relations, 51–6
  integrated EU, benefits of, ix
  Korea, equivalency provisions in trade agreement with, 191–3
  lobbying of EU on data protection regulation, 245, 271
  monitoring of EU–US agreements, 301–5
  non-bilateral interactions with the EU, 141–6
  obstacles to cooperation, 246–55
  parliamentary diplomacy, benefits of, 59–64
  privacy standards, 305–6
  quasi-institutionalised relations with the EU, 133–41
  risk assessment approach, 166
  rule-transfer, 143–5, 153–7
  security policy, dominance in relation to, 238–45
  sub-national authorities and EU–US relations, 102–5, 116–22
  sub-national authorities engagement, risks of, 122–7
  thematic agendas, 120–1
  transatlantic community of law, 1–3, *see also* Passenger Name Records (PNR) Agreements; Supreme Court of the United States (SCOTUS); surveillance by USA; SWIFT Agreements; transatlantic community of law; transatlantic counterterrorism cooperation; transatlantic judicial communication; transatlantic regulatory cooperation; Transatlantic Trade and Investment Partnership (TTIP)
United States (US) Congress, 37–8, 72–81
United States (US) Supreme Court, *see* Supreme Court of the United States (SCOTUS)
Universal Declaration of Human Rights, 250
Unmanned Aerial Vehicles (UAVs), 251–2
Uzbekistan, 252

Violence Against Woman Act (VAWA), 75–6
visits between US and EU judges, 18–21, 136
Vodafone, 71, 89–92, 100

'War on Terror', 246–55
Wechsler, H., 93–4
Weisglas, Frans, 45–6
Wickard v. *Filburn*, 72
Working Group on Cybercrime and Cybersecurity (WGCC), 150–3
World Trade Organization (WTO)
  country-based recognition, 200–1

World Trade Organization (*cont.*)
dispute settlement mechanism, 159, 161–2, 166
equivalency recognition considerations, 200–8
equivalency test, 196–7
EU–US dispute resolution, 137–9
EU–US trade, 158–9
GMO dispute, 170
harmonisation, 191n. 16
origin-based recognition, 200–1
poultry dispute, 138, 180–1

Yemen, 252
Young, E., 94, 95
Yousaf, Humza, 119n. 104

Zeben, Josephine A.W. van, 4–5